The Complete Antique Collector

Edited by David Coombs

Ebury Press
London

Published by Ebury Press
Division of The National Magazine Company Ltd
Colquhoun House
27-37 Broadwick Street
London W1V 1FR

First impression 1988

The material in this book originally appeared in *The Antique Collector*.

ISBN 0 85223 673 5

Typeset in Great Britain by H Garnett & Co Ltd
Printed and bound in Italy by New Interlitho S.p.a., Milan

CONTENTS

INTRODUCTION

THERE ARE AS MANY WAYS of collecting as there are people who collect or who aspire to be collectors. Furthermore, no collection is ever truly complete: there is always another item to add or one better or more interesting to substitute for something already possessed. This may be a dining room table (p. 173), a pair of cuff links (p.126) or even a Bugatti (p.164)!

You will already see that this is an unusual book. The chapters have been selected from articles published in *The Antique Collector* magazine in the last few years. They show, individually but particularly collectively, just how the notion of collecting or being a collector has developed in modern times. Nowadays, the opportunity for enjoying the pursuit of collecting, is open to anyone who has the inclination. Knowledge is the key to the whole thing not money. For example, a bargain is nothing less than something you have recognized that is being offered at a price less than it might have obtained in more glamorous or more specialized circumstances. At the other extreme, some of the best and most interesting of collections can be made entirely in one's head: fine, beautiful or scarce items that are unobtainable for one reason or another, yet haunt one's memory and affect one's judgement of everything else seen or possessed.

Another key to success therefore is the need to learn to look. That may seem rather an obvious point but is more profound than it appears. Just as you learn to judge a person on much more than their appearance, or the way they dress, so you must learn to judge an item on more than its general impression. To look at the details, at the methods of making or construction, to understand all these and then to relate them to the whole, is all part of the process of learning to be a collector. While the very best may be out of the reach of most of us (but there is always the chance of a bargain never forget) it is most important to have knowledge of the best. It is only that way that we can gradually acquire a set of standards by which to compare everything else. Hence the importance of museums and historic houses and the reason for the chapters in this book concerned with, for example, the English furniture collected by Noel G Terry (on show in Fairfax House, York, see p.200) and another on the fans in the Messel collection (now in the Fitzwilliam Museum, see p.12). Both collections are relatively unknown to the public.

One of the many changes that have occurred in the so-called art market in recent years is the way that ease of travel has affected the opportunities now open to collectors. Those moving about the world on business or for pleasure can so easily call into local dealers or auction houses and be attracted by items little known outside their country of origin. Examples here include pre-Columbian textiles (p.24) and American art nouveau stained glass (p.6). It is a mistake to think that the traffic in works of art is always one way. Nonetheless it is fascinating to learn of the important collection of English silver in Los Angeles (p.102) especially in view of the fact that it was formed by an immigrant English couple, Mr and Mrs Gilbert. Then, in the 19th century the superb quality of modern English ceramics was recognized by the newly formed Musée des Art Décoratifs in Paris (p.156) and by private collectors in the United States who donated their items to the Cincinnati Museum of Fine Arts (p.148).

Once having understood the real reason for learning about grand things, the fact still remains that we all need to learn how to start collecting. The first thing to be clear about is that everyone makes mistakes, however much they may know or think they know. It follows from this, that there is no dishonour in admitting to only having a little knowledge or in accepting that you have made a mistake. In both instances you are more likely to receive help and advice.

At the end of the day price can be the crucial factor. Once again this book will help you. The articles on French carriage clocks (p.114) and decorative chandeliers (p.33) for example, will guide you through the processes of learning about, of judging and then acquiring examples for yourself. All this information, including the prices, has been directly related to actual examples seen on the market when the chapter was being written.

Another factor that is a continuous process is the discovery or rediscovery of information about items or people that may have lain forgotten for years, sometimes centuries. At the one extreme you will find a new biography of the sporting and genre artist Heywood Hardy (p.62) and at the other new information about the lives and works of some 18th century goldsmiths (p.91).

Another process is the opening up of new areas of opportunity for collectors due simply to the passing of time and changes in the ways in which things are seen. Examples here include 20th century plastics (p.238) and fountain pens (p.229). Even the photographs of A W Cutler (p.220) although recent, had lain forgotten.

It is traditional, because based on the way we all live, to divide collecting subjects into various basic categories. This is the method chosen to help you find your way through the pages of this book. Thus under furniture you will find a chapter on the 19th century cabinet makers Holland and Sons (p.192); under textiles, lace collars (p.18); under English pictures, William Westall's paintings of early Australia (p.55); under prints, the mezzotints of John Constable (p.226); and 19th century decanters, under glass (p.37). Other categories include watercolours, Judaica and medical.

There are other ways too of dividing the subject of collecting. One might be the way in which women have always played a crucial role: was it Hepplewhite or his wife that was responsible for the famous 18th century design book? For the answer see p.208. The work of Louie Burrell reminds us of the importance of women artists (p.84). Many fine items would not have been made without women as patrons or recipients; paste jewellery is one example (p.124). Men too have their particular interests: enamelled cigarette cases (p.132) and wrist-watches (p.234) might be two examples.

In general however the home is the place that we all have in mind when we go looking to add to our collection today. There is nothing wrong in setting out to buy a brand new carpet, or in receiving a brand new silver canteen as a present. Nonetheless you might prefer, after due consideration, to buy yourself an old oriental rug. In which case the information on p.136 will guide you. If you would like to gather together your own collection of old silver flatware, then another piece (p.98) will also be of considerable help.

The whole field of collecting is so diverse that it knows no boundaries. You will already have appreciated that neither size, nor age, need be a consideration. Nor indeed is price, for expensive is not always necessarily equivalent to good.

There is very little reference to "investment" in this book. It was a brief, dubious and harmful influence on the whole market a few years ago. Suffice it to say that buying the best quality you can at the best possible price has generally proved to be wise in the long term.

Within the two covers of this book you will find an amazing diversity of items. If you just want to browse then the many illustrations will delight and intrigue you.

If you are beginning to think about collecting then the many chapters of practical information will help you. If you are experienced and knowledgeable already you will also find much here that is new and perhaps surprising.

Whilst on the subject of surprises some readers may be taken aback by the piece on the American abstract painter Mark Rothko (p.42). It will repay reading carefully; not only does it set a modern master in the context of the old masters but it illustrates the writer's own struggle in coming to terms with a new and difficult subject.

Lastly, nowhere in this book, will you find advice on "good taste". What matters is your taste, your opinion, your decision. It is helpful to be guided by knowledgeable and experienced people and foolish to disregard their views and opinions. However, whatever you buy, you have to live with. Have confidence therefore and enjoy what you acquire. It's your collection: whether you have only one object or a houseful.

STAINED GLASS IN AMERICA

Alix Gudefin

Prior to the latter half of the 19th century, most stained glass was imported from Europe and inferior in quality. Weak and dull in impact, its colour was no longer an integral part of the glass but was produced by paint instead. The birth of the stained glass craft in America was stimulated by a multitude of optimal, social and economic circumstances, including the influx of immigrants, the westward territorial expansion, a sweeping religious fervour, and a vigorous climate of wealth in all economic sectors favouring unprecedented ecclesiastical and secular construction. Opalescent glass windows were an accurate reflection of the growth and opulence of the United States. Until recently, this quintessential American decorative form was branded as an aesthetic outcast; it is still only in the infancy of discovery.

Contrary to popular belief, John La Farge (1835-1910), and not Louis Comfort Tiffany (1848-1933), was the true inventor of opalescent glass. Discouraged by the lamentable state of the art in America, the artist – a painter born of French parents – accidentally discovered the limitless possibilities of this glass form when glancing at a cheaply made toothpowder jar which appeared variegated, streaked and fissured in the streaming sunlight. Although opaque opal glass had long been available, it was La Farge who modified and perfected its composition so that its transparency could be controlled and its body multicoloured. With

Figure 1. Song of Spring, *about 1896, by Rudy Brothers, a highly reputable studio from Pittsburgh, Pennsylvania. Based on a painting by William Adolph Bouguereau. 152 × 94 cm (60 × 37 in)*

Figure 2 (opposite) *Landscape panel executed by Tiffany Studios, about 1895, for the Krueger mansion, Newark, New Jersey. Perhaps an idyllic translation of the neighbouring countryside, the window characteristically features a stretch of rippled blue water set in a hilly landscape dotted with dogwood and irises. 99 × 88 cm (39 × 35 in)*

this discovery, patented on 24 February 1880, began the opalescent age where colour and texture would be achieved within the glass itself, thereby eliminating the necessity of paint.

Characterised by a semi-translucent iridescence, opalescent glass displayed an unprecedented degree of colour saturation and an infinity of texture and hue. Inspired by numerous influences, including Impressionism, Art Nouveau, and Japanese art, La Farge's opalescent glass windows featured a diversity of materials such as old fashioned pot metal glass, chipped glass, broken bottles, moulded glass, roundels, alabaster slices, and semi-precious stones. When creating his innovative masterpieces, the artist also used all the traditional stained glass techniques, among them silver stain, enamel, and paint, the latter of which became an integral part of the design. Most innovative was the plating technique whereby the glass was layered up to half a dozen times, thus allowing for the creation and control of subtle colour nuances within different design areas. Moreover, La Farge revolutionised the traditional concept of lead lines as a cumbersome and restrictive necessity by making them a vital and integral part of the window's design *(Figure 5)*.

While Tiffany produced tens of thousands of windows, La Farge only created some 2500 secular and ecclesiastical examples, all personally supervised and displaying the ultimate in artistic sophistication.

Figure 3. Daffodils *by Tiffany Studios, signed, about 1895, featuring a characteristic profusion of flowers and a brilliant array of hues. 68.5 × 84 cm (27 × 33 in)*

Following the success of his first opalescent window, executed in 1879 for Dr Richard H. Derby's Long Island residence, the artist won the patronage of America's wealthiest families and the most exclusive architectural firms. Most notable was his work executed in the 1880s for the New York Fifth Avenue mansions of Cornelius and William K. Vanderbilt, particularly *Peonies Blown in the Wind,* a lancet window in the former's residence, exhibiting deeply moulded soft white panels set against a pale blue background. More monumental were the panels designed for William Vanderbilt's home which included a triptych 12 feet wide depicting the goddess of commerce, an allegory of the Vanderbilts' rise to wealth.

Regrettably, La Farge's success was rapidly overshadowed by that of his arch-rival, Louis Comfort Tiffany, also a painter by training. Commercially naive, the former was plagued by misfortune, particularly by the bankruptcy of his stained glass firm. Tiffany however was backed by the family fortune amassed by his father, Charles Lewis Tiffany, the founder of New York's prestigious silver and jewellery firm, and was thus better able to conduct and publicise his experiments. Equally importantly, he delegated responsibilities to his craftsmen, thereby producing lower quality work which was, however, less expensive and more quickly executed than that by La Farge.

Tiffany's reputation was solidly established at the 1893 Chicago World's Columbian Exposition where he displayed a chapel decorated with stained glass windows, lamps, and other accoutrements. Moreover, his opalescent glass became known in Europe as 'Tiffany glass' or 'verre americain' thanks to the backing of Samuel Bing, the reputed French critic and dealer who commissioned Tiffany to produce panels by French painters including Bonnard and Vuillard. Displayed at the annual Salon-de-Mars and at Bing's Salon de l'Art Nouveau in 1895, the windows brought Tiffany's fame to a peak.

From the 1870s through to the early 20th century, he experimented tirelessly in New York glasshouses, mainly at his Corona, Long Island factory, working on variations on La Farge's techniques, and constantly striving to attain the ideal glass form. Among the more characteristic varieties were mottled glass, drapery glass (created to simulate vestment folds) and fractured glass, today known as confetti glass, in which pieces of coloured glass were embedded into sheets of clear glass. Tiffany also further explored the possibilities of plating to better provide perspective and to diffuse light. Brilliant gem-like effects were produced by the insertion of glass jewels, available in a limitless range of colours, sizes, and shapes including ovals and faceted prisms. The workmanship was such that Tiffany Studios boasted the use of over 5000 different colours and varieties of glass. Moreover, the firm pursued the integration of lead lines into the panels' framework, using them for artistic details such as twigs and drapery folds, which until then had been painted. Although Tiffany Studios claimed that its windows featured no paint, it was later often used for flesh tones and details such as flower centres.

While most of Tiffany's stained glass production was ecclesiastical, the firm was also responsible for an impressive range of secular windows designed for the nation's most distinguished private citizens. Because of his favourable financial circumstances, he was the darling of the wealthy and his interiors were the height of fashion. Among his better known clients were President Chester Arthur (under whom he decorated the White House), the steel magnate Andrew Carnegie, and the railroad baron Richard Beattie Mellon. For Joseph Raphael Delamar, the owner of a gold mine fortune, he produced a number of exquisite windows including *The Bathers*. His windows were also featured in eminent American universities such as Yale, Dartmouth, and Columbia, as well as libraries, schools, hospitals, hotels, theatres, museums (including the Smithsonian Institution), and even the

Figure 4. *An exquisite turn-of-the-century figural window attributed to Lamb Studios, New York, a reputable firm still in existence. 129 × 134 cm (51 × 53 in)*

Hoboken Line ferry boats. Of particular note was the extravagant Laurelton Hall, Tiffany's 84-room estate in Oyster Bay, Long Island, completed in 1906 and burned down in 1957. The surviving panels, including the famous *Four Seasons* composition, are now on display at the M. Morse Gallery of Art, Winter Park, Florida, the world's finest Tiffany collection.

Among Tiffany Studios' secular window themes are figure windows depicting portraits and historical and mythological subjects. Notable are four rose windows symbolising *Knowledge, Fame, Genius* and *Study* at Princeton University's Alexander Commencement Hall, and a portrait window of Delamar's wife Nellie Virginia Sands. Most characteristic are his landscape panels, idyllic evocations of the neighbouring countryside and its various moods *(Figure 2)*. Among these panels favourite themes are dow-like boats sailing on rippled blue water, a Greek temple's pediment placed against a setting sun, and peacocks perched on balustrades. Also prolific are floral windows illustrating a profusion of flowers such as trumpet vines, magnolias, dogwood and peonies *(Figures 3 and 6)*.

Tiffany's aggressive promotion inspired a number of craftsmen, including Tiffany Studios' associates such as Henry Keck, to independently produce windows in a similar style. These were characterised by brilliantly coloured, highly realistic and artistic designs with almost fruity colours. Attributing prove-

Figure 5. Hollyhocks *window, executed in 1881 for the New York residence of financier J. P. Morgan; an exquisite example of John La Farge's floral windows, showing Japanese influence and a rare sense of colour, texture and elegance in composition. 89 × 134 cm (35 × 53 in)*

nance to Tiffany is further complicated by the overwhelming lack of signatures, by the craftsmen's ability to duplicate the artists' techniques, by their frequent wanderings from one studio to another and, perhaps most important, by a resounding lack of information.

The literature is equally scant on other opalescent stained glass artists of the time, including, in New York, Lamb Studios *(Figure 4)* whose work is typically Victorian and traditional, D. Maitland Armstrong, Mary Tillinghast, Joseph Lauber and Thomas Wright. Meanwhile Chicago and the Midwest boasted of such firms as George Healy & Louis J. Millet, Thomas Augustin O'Slaughnessy, Linden Glass Company, Rudy Brothers *(Figure 1)* and Flanagan & Biedenweg.

By World War I the mood had swung against opalescent stained glass as a result of the Gothic revival, the decline in religious fervour, and 'poor man's Tiffany windows' – inferior-quality goods produced by thousands of smaller studios which only further damaged the reputation of opalescent glass. The war ended production of the materials needed, as well as fine workmanship. Most critical was the disappearance of jealously guarded trade secrets, such as using gold to produce the colour red, with the death of master craftsmen. Tiffany glass became ridiculously 'passé' and was consigned to the trash heap. It is interesting to note that the artist has subsequently been better remembered for his iridescent Favrile glass objects, notably lamps and vases, produced from excess window glass.

Since the revival of Tiffany lamps in the 1950s, opalescent stained glass windows have slowly awakened interest among collectors and are only now beginning to inspire serious research. Even today many of the panels sold on the market are incorrectly attributed, including those produced by La Farge. According to Sean McNally, one of the

Figure 6. *One of a pair of* Wisteria *landscapes by Tiffany Studios, about 1905, designed to bring a permanent summer freshness and bucolic calm into the room. Wisteria was one of Tiffany's favourite floral themes. 127 × 83 cm (50 × 33 in)*

Illustrations by courtesy of Window Shopping

few dealers and experts in this medium, the finest windows sell privately and not at auction, with prices now reaching thousands of dollars. Indeed, while fifteen years ago an extraordinary Tiffany panel would scarcely have reached $500 (£450), today it would command about $60 000 (£55 000). Nonetheless, although high, prices still do not reflect the cost of current production and should continue to rise.

Particularly difficult to come by are La Farge windows, such as figural and animal panels, which are generally more expensive than Tiffany's. Thus La Farge's floral windows command $75 000 to $80 000 (£64 000-£72 000), depending on their quality, while Tiffany panels will sell for about $40 000 to $60 000 (£36 000-£55 000). Tiffany landscape windows are particularly desirable, and range from $20 000 to $150 000 (£18 000-£137 000) with figural works fetching about $30 000 to $80 000. More plentiful are geometric compositions with those created by La Farge and Tiffany reaching $2000 to $20 000 (£1800-£18 000) and abstract windows, the work of all studios, ranging from $2000 to $10 000 (£1800-£9000). The purely decorative panels created by minor studios whose prices start from under $500 to $5000 (£450-£4500), are far more accessible.

Buyers should entrust themselves to a noteworthy dealer and be wary of signatures, which can be indicative of forgery since few La Farge and Tiffany panels were signed. Most importantly, a collector should buy the very best, and restore only if major sections are missing. Unwarranted and poor restoration could permanently alter the window's composition and thus harm its value.

May 1985

THE ART OF THE FAN

Nancy Armstrong

A collection of about 600 fans has recently been acquired by the Fitzwilliam Museum at Cambridge. Leonard Messel (1872–1953) made the collection in a quiet and private manner: his daughter Anne, Countess of Rosse, has conserved and cared for it since his death (neither adding nor subtracting from it on impulse), and now has seen it correctly housed. Indeed, once before it nearly went to a similar establishment but, on learning that there would only be space to show one fan at a time, Leonard Messel withdrew. Now the Fitzwilliam Trustees intend building a Gallery to show the majority on a permanent basis – when they have raised the money.

The importance of the collection is its variety of types (roughly 400 occidental and 200 oriental), together with its scholarly content. The seven fans selected for this article have been chosen for especial Englishness; all are featured in the exhibition, but have not been written about before.

Probably the rarest fan in the collection is the 'Feather Fan' *(Figure 2)*. English merchant adventurers founded the East India Company in 1600; this was followed by the Dutch Vereenigde OstIndische Compagnie in 1602 and the French Compagnie des Indes in 1664. All brought spices and exotic trade goods, which must have included some of the feathers from rare birds which decorate this fan. Its long handle is a reminder of Tudor times and the beating of errant girls with the handles of fans, and is reminiscent of the interest in the turning of wood for furniture in the early 17th century.

Figure 1 *The English cockade quizzing fan, about 1790–1810. Horn, inlaid with cut steels.*

Figure 2 (opposite) *The post-Jacobean 'Messel Feather Fan'. English or Dutch. Probably the rarest fan in the collection.*

The fan has a curiously unique shape, being composed of five separate sections of drawn-thread work on concealed frames, covered with gorgeous feathers (differently coloured on each side); these feathers seem as bright in their flashing colour as the day they were applied. Feathers are so apt to invite mites, or fade in light, that it is a minor miracle that this small fixed fan remains with us today after about 350 stormy years of history: we must also thank the change of fashion from fixed to folding fans.

A most intriguing fan is the printed historical fan: made of paper, and painted in watercolours, it is dated on the lefthand guard 'Oct 26 to ye late Act 1740' *(Figure 3)*. The scene shows one of the many versions of the murder of 'Fair Rosamond'. There are several legends about this dramatic mistress, and some of them are pictured here. Right in the centre of the stage is the (unproven) murderess, Queen Eleanor of Aquitaine (about 1122–1204), wearing a crown and carrying a dagger and a cup of poison. On the right, seated in her bower, is 'Fair Rosamond', the daughter of Walter de Clifford, and the mistress of King Henry II of England (1133–1189). It was erroneously claimed that she was the mother of two of the King's sons – William Longsword, Earl of Salisbury, and Geoffrey, Archbishop of York. Born about 1140 (died 1176), Rosamond was 18 years younger than the Queen, who had to suffer the King's many infidelities.

Figure 3 *The 'Fair Rosamond Fan'. English, about 1740. Printed on paper and painted in watercolours.*

Written evidence in the 14th century *French Chronicle of London* referred to an earlier document of 1263, which stated that Rosamond was made to bleed to death in a bath of boiling water. Then in a ballad of 1611, later collected by Bishop Percy, further legends appeared, mentioning a dagger, a cup or bowl of poison, and a maze. On this fan we can all see the different stories put together.

But what of the building to the left? That is Woodstock Palace, seen in the 17th century. During Saxon times it had been a royal hunting lodge, and eventually it was granted to John Churchill, first duke of Marlborough, in the 18th century. He levelled it to build Blenheim Palace.

'Fair Rosamond' is said to have been buried at Godstow Nunnery, near Oxford. There was a report in 1191 that Hugh, Bishop of Lincoln, visited Godstow and was so offended at the sight of Rosamond's richly decorated tomb (right in the centre of the Quire, before the altar) that he ordered it to be removed – probably to the Chapter House. It has been suggested that the tiny scene at the top of the fan is Godstow.

Like the 'Fair Rosamond' fan, the silk fan of about 1780–5 is a folding fan *(Figure 5)*. The leaf is double and painted in gouache, then embroidered with gold beads and gilt sequins. The scene shows typical 'English restraint', and is beautifully balanced in its composition: there appear to be three cartouches, with no firm baroque outlining, but having sequined and painted feathers limpidly floating past them, lightly encompassing each scene, together with sprigs of English flowers.

The central scene could have come straight out of an Arthur Devis painting, with the typically stiff little seated ladies, an elegantly languid gentleman, a romping child and the usual small 'society' dog . . . it all epitomises England at its most assured. The 18th century started with a dilemma (political, philosophical and artistic) and ended in revolution, spinning at a furious pace in a series of cartwheels, with here and there a pool of wealthy contentment and tranquillity in England, as epitomised by our great artists: this is one of those isolated moments. And nothing could be more quietly elegant than the pierced and silvered ivory sticks and guards, backed by strawberry-coloured foil, set with a dazzling paste rivet.

Why are the English so obsessed with secrets? They seem to adore the apparatus of secrecy, the excitement of the unmasking and, above all, the fascination of people who appear to lead secret lives. One thing about 'Four Scenes' fans is that (unless you care to divulge it) they conceal a secret *(Figure 6)*. It seems generally agreed that the English were the inventors of the intricate ribboning of fans so that (contrary to normal usage) they can open not only from left to right, but also from right to left. Should the fan have a painting on both back and front it means that a total of *four* scenes emerge when opened all ways.

This unique brise fan is made of small overlapping leaves of paper 'ribboned', or attached, by two rows of invisibly placed chickenskin sections, inside, just below the painted 'ribbon' border. It is so professionally carried out that one whole side of the fan appears all blue, another pink; opened the other way, the third scene is lavender and the last is grey; on each surface is painted either a lady or a gentleman of fashion. The clustered straight sticks are of bone, the guards having some silver sequins inlaid. It was made fractionally early for Jane Austen (1775-1817), that high-priestess of gossip and quintessentially English woman, whose 'Come now, let us have no secrets among friends' is the gossip's credo. That fan would have been a star amongst her teacups.

Captain Cook (1728-1779), accompanied by Joseph Banks (1744-1820), discovered Botany Bay in 1770 (having originally christened it 'Stingray Har-

Figure 4 (above) *The 'Mrs Fitzherbert Fan', about 1785. Ivory, with piercing, fretting and painted details.*

Figure 5 (below) *English folding silk fan, about 1780-5. Painted in gouache, then embroidered with gold beads and gilt sequins.*

Figure 6 (above) *English 'Four Scenes' fan, about 1785. By opening the fan in different ways, three other scenes are revealed.*

bour') and the world afterwards gloried in the variety of new plant species found there. Back in England the fashion in many of the decorative arts soon creamed in showing botanical specimens – notably on porcelain. But here we see a 'Botanical Fan' published by Sarah Ashton, printed and hand-coloured on paper *(Figure 7)*. Sarah Ashton, of 28, Little Britain, London, was admitted a member of the Worshipful Company of Fan Makers on 1 February 1770: a good many of her printed fans may be seen in the Schreiber Collection at the British Museum, and there is a selection in the Messel-Rosse collection. On the obverse there are flowers, seeds etc, with a border of leaves – all numbered; on the reverse are details of all the numbered items. It seems so right that this fan was collected by such a great horticulturist as Leonard Messel.

The 'Mrs Fitzherbert Fan' *(Figure 4)* was made when the Worshipful Company of Fan Makers were at their artistic height in England, and is a marvellous amalgam of both art and craft. Of course it is also a great draw, for the English (on the whole) love any tales of the monarchy and they adore a juicy scandal! This ivory brisé fan was painted by the School of Cosway (*how* we would have treasured a signature!) and shows three vignettes painted on three ivory palettes amongst the myriad of piercing, fretting and painted details.

The central scene shows the Prince of Wales and Mrs Fitzherbert, with a woman ('Religion') and a putto ('Hymen'). In the other two scenes they appear again, Mrs Fitzherbert as 'Fidelity' and the Prince as 'Constancy'. The Prince (1762–1830) became Prince Regent in 1810, and succeeded his father as King George IV in 1820; he made a secret marriage with Mrs Fitzherbert (*née* Maria Anne Smythe, 1756–1837), a Roman

Figure 7 *The 'Botanical Fan' by Sarah Ashton, about 1792. Printed and hand-coloured on paper.*

Catholic widow, in 1785. As the marriage was contracted without the King's permission it was considered invalid under the Royal Marriage Act of 1772 – and the Prince afterwards even denied that there had been any marriage at all! This enchanting fan may have been made to commemorate the wedding in 1785. Fortunately here they both look incredibly happy (and slim).

The final, typically English fan makes many people gasp with delight at its miniature sparkle. It has several purposes: to be eminently fashionable, to show you through the mirrors who is standing behind you, and to provide the central pivotal quizzing glass *(Figure 1)*. The normal practical use for a fan has to be abandoned, for nothing so small (and perforated to boot) could ever remotely keep you cool!

By the time this fan was made (about 1790–1810) fashions had altered to Republican colours (white, gold and purple) and cheaper fabrics (muslins, cottons and batistes) which clung to the slimmer figure. Fans reflected this philosophy, being made from less-expensive materials (horn and wood) and becoming tiny. These 'imperceptible' fans were fashioned into every shape imaginable: 'Love's Arrows'; 'Catherine Wheels'; fretted and painted with tiny garden or field flowers or even, *en camaieu*, with La Fontaine's fables.

Here the gold-coloured horn fan has been lavishly inlaid with cut steels, to reflect candlelight, and create as much eyecatching attention as the owner dared. Life was now beginning to be eminently practical, and the fan followed suit with its quizzing glass, its mirrors, and its method of construction which meant you could instantly twitch it around and stuff all six inches of it into your new silk reticule. Practical, frivolous and fun!

Virtually every fan in the collection has a story to tell, like the seven English fans above. Lady Rosse learned them all at her father's knee years ago, and wants us all to share them with her at the Fitzwilliam Museum in the future. Fan lovers will be immensely pleased when the Fan Gallery is finished, together with the two catalogues (on European and Oriental fans), and the whole glorious collection is on permanent display.

December 1985

FASHIONABLE LACE COLLARS

Deborah Rogers

Lace collars formed an essential part of the wardrobe of the fashion conscious lady of the 19th century. Although designed to harmonise with the style of dress worn at the time, collars were purchased separately from the dress and were not permanently stitched to the neckline, allowing for their removal and separate careful washing and starching.

The 19th century saw the gradual demise of the hand-made lace industry and the introduction of machine-made lace, the consequent drop in price bringing lace dress accessories within the budget of a greater part of the feminine population. Much of this lace has survived, often in extremely good condition, and building up a collection of collars from the 19th and early 20th centuries can provide a fascinating insight into both the different techniques used in making hand and machine lace and also the changes in the style of women's dress and trimmings.

It was during the late 1820s that the separate lace collar became fashionable. Day dresses were high waisted with a full skirt and gathered sleeves worn with the cape-like collar known as the pelerine which was fashionable throughout the 1830s. The simplest were only approximately 5 mm wide at the back and were cut away from the throat to the shoulders in front to reveal the bodice of the dress. More elaborate pelerines would extend over the shoulders and upper arm with scarf-like extensions descending below the waist. Pelerines would often take the form of a double collar, i.e. a small collar on top of a larger with perhaps an additional stand-up frill at the neck. The edges of the collar were either trimmed with a narrow border of lace or were scalloped or vandyked (pointed scallops).

Figure 1 *Honiton lace collar. 19th century. Round neck 40 cm (15¾ in), depth at back 10 cm (4 in). £10 (c US$11.50).*

Most pelerines were made of fine white muslin, hand embroidered in white cotton, the main features of the design being worked in padded satin stitch with cut out sections filled in with needlepoint lace stitches *(Figure 2)*. The designs used during this period are particularly dainty, consisting of small sprigs of flowers and leaves entwined with garlands, the pattern tending to be concentrated around the edge of the collar. This type of embroidery is known as 'Ayrshire work' and was a cottage industry in Scotland.

In the 1840s and 1850s a change in the cut of the bodice to a longer-waisted, more elaborate style meant that large, all-enveloping collars became unnecessary. The introduction of the crinoline in the late 1850s focused attention on the lower part of the dress, the bodice being very simple with a plain round neck and buttons down the front. Small flat 'Peter Pan' collars suited this style, often topped by a band of ribbon encircling the neck and secured with a brooch.

Collars of bobbin lace were popular at this time, particularly Honiton lace *(Figure 1)*. The various components of the design, the flower heads, leaves etc, were made individually and then joined together either by bobbin or needle made 'brides' or by appliqué on to machine-made net. This method is ideally suited to

Figure 2 and detail (above) *Embroidered muslin pelerine.*
About 1830. Round neck 45 cm ($17\frac{3}{4}$ in), depth at back 18 cm (7 in). £30-40 (c US$34-46).

Figure 3 (below) *Bedfordshire lace collar and cuffs set. Late 19th century. Round neck 40 cm ($15\frac{3}{4}$ in), depth at back 6 cm ($2\frac{1}{3}$ in). £10-12 (c US$11-14).*

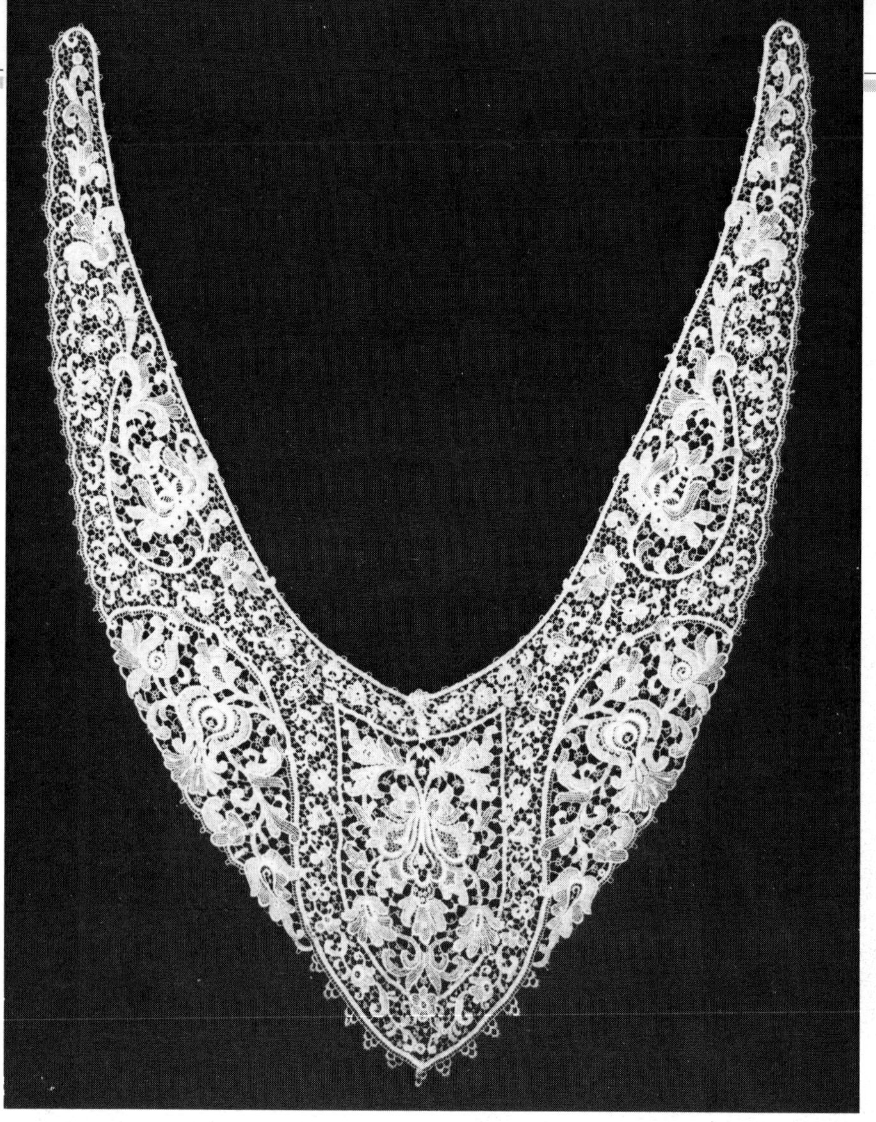

Figure 4 *Collar of chemical lace. Late 19th century. Round neck 114 cm (44¾ in), depth at back 28 cm (11 in). £20 (c US$23).*

irregularly shaped articles such as collars because the design could be attractively arranged to fit around the circular neck and the finished pieces of lace then joined together. The designs were characteristic with clusters of naturalistic roses, thistles and leaves.

Collars of finest quality Honiton lace were, and indeed still are, highly sought after. Unfortunately the industry was in decline during the 19th century and much of the lace produced was of an inferior quality, the poor designs being known locally as 'slugs and snails'.

The other main centre for bobbin lace making in England was in the East Midlands where workers produced a type of lace known as Bedfordshire Maltese because it was copied from Maltese lace exhibited at the 'Great Exhibition' of 1851. The background and the solid parts of the design were worked together, the threads travelling diagonally across the lace from one part of the design to the other, using a strong cotton thread. The designs were simple and bold, consisting of circular or curved shapes filled in with open flower heads and geometric patterns. Bedfordshire Maltese lace was first used for the narrow collars of the 1850s but became particularly popular later when coarser lace became fashionable *(Figure 3)*.

The crinoline went out of fashion in the late 1860s and the new style of dress favoured a tall slender outline, the main decorative feature being the bustle. As we have seen before, when the eye is drawn to the skirt, collars tend to be rather insignificant in comparison. Small stand collars were worn, trimmed with a narrow frill of lace which was either stitched to the dress itself or mounted on a circular wire and worn around the neck under the dress.

Machine-made lace became popular in the latter part of the 19th century, particularly the type known as 'chemical lace' which was developed in 1883. An embroidery machine worked the design on to a backing of silk which was then dipped in an acid bath to dissolve the silk, leaving the lace intact. Chemical lace was very versatile and was not only ideally suited to making shaped articles such as collars but also had the capacity to create the most complicated of designs cheaply and easily *(Figure 4)*.

In the late 19th century lace making became a popular pastime for ladies following patterns published in magazines. Lengths of narrow machine made tape were stitched to a stiff backing material, folding or gathering the tape to follow the design and then working fancy buttonhole and needlepoint lace stitches to fill the spaces. The designs varied from the simple to the very complex and were usually of the Art Nouveau style with flowing curves and stylised flowers *(Figure 6)*.

The period 1890–1910 has left us with a greater variety of collars than at any other time during the 19th century and it is from this period that the majority of collars found in antique shops today date. By now, the stand collar had crept up to cover the entire throat leaving no room for the narrow frill of lace that had topped collars of the previous decade. The collar was usually an integral part of the garment but detachable lace collars were also worn, the high neck often strengthened by bone or wire and attached to a bib or circular yoke of lace.

Wide frills of lace were worn around the yoke on blouses and tea gowns and these were occasionally formed as a separate collar *(Figure 7)*. Tailored costumes were popular for everyday wear, worn over a tucked shirt with a separate starched linen collar, like a man's. Large lace collars displaying stylised Art Nouveau flowers were also worn over boleros or jackets, the fronts of the collar descending to a point at the waist *(Figure*

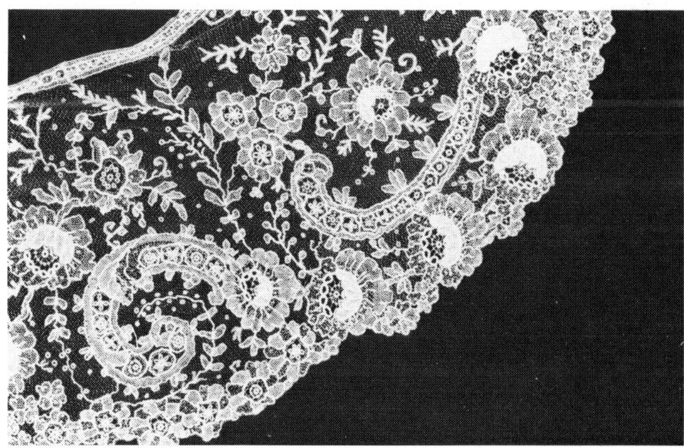

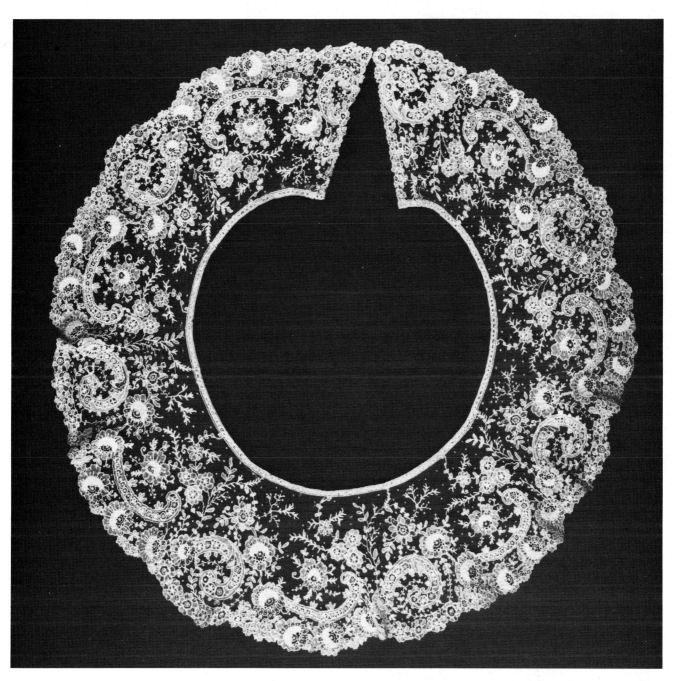

Figure 5 and detail *Bertha collar of Brussels point de gaz* (some repair to background mesh). *Early 20th century. Round neck 100 cm (39½ in), depth at back 16 cm (6¼ in). £20-30 (c US$23-34.50).*

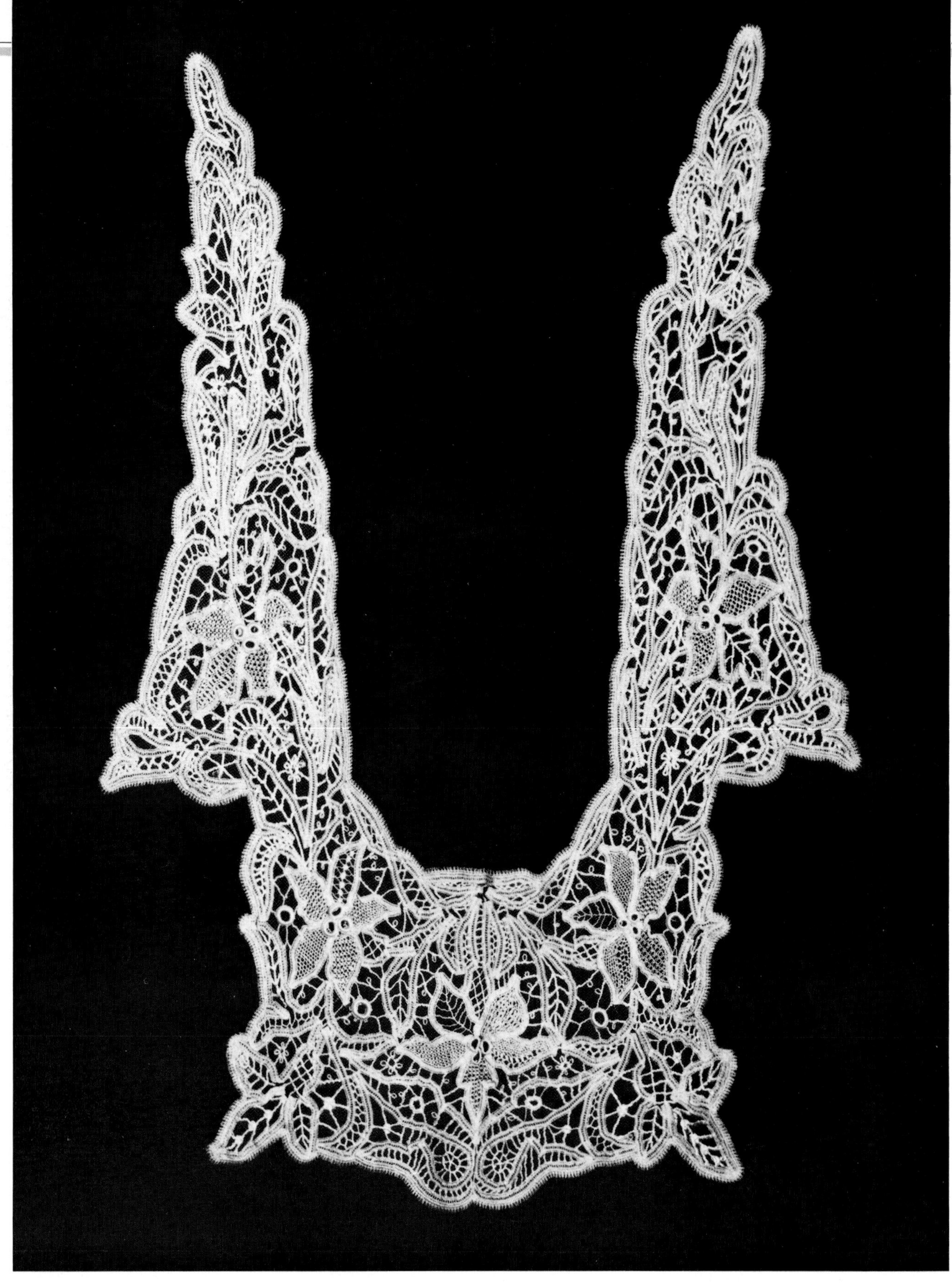

Figure 6 Collar of tape lace in particularly good condition. Late 19th century. Round neck 106 cm (41¾ in), depth at back 20 cm (7¾ in). £20-25 (c US$23-28)

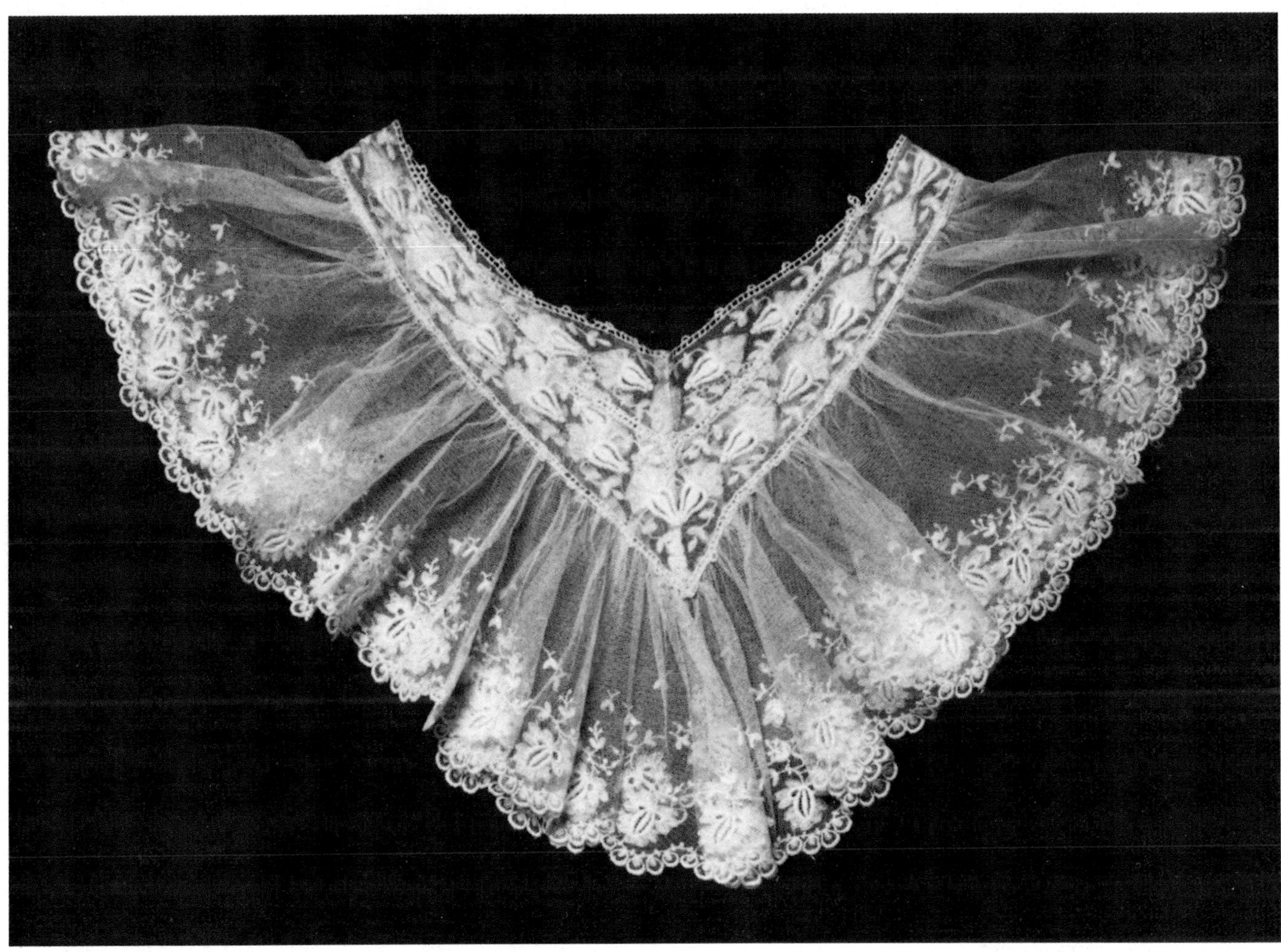

Figure 7 *Collar of machine embroidered net gathered onto a yoke. Late 19th/early 20th century. Round neck 76 cm (30 in), depth at back 18 cm (7 in). £20 (c US$23).*

4) and the back of the collar often being cut square like a sailor collar *(Figure 6)*. Collars of the late 19th century tend to be cream or buff rather than white.

One type of collar not yet mentioned is known as a bertha, which was a long circular collar worn round an off the shoulder evening gown, the lace falling in graceful folds over the upper arm. It was popular from the 1830s through to the late 1870s and again during the Edwardian era. Bertha collars could be made of Honiton applique, Bedfordshire Maltese and a particularly fine type of needlepoint lace known as Brussels *point de gaz* which was made from the 1850s right through into the 20th century. The mesh background of this lace was very light, made of single buttonhole stitches looped through each other, the floral pattern being composed of sprays and garlands of flowers, the roses in particular often having layered petals giving a three dimensional effect. This was one of the best quality laces of the period as may be expected of the lacemakers of Brussels which had been the main European centre for lacemaking in the 18th century *(Figure 5)*.

The Edwardian period was the last time that fine lace was worn in any quantity and indeed after this date the wearing of lace at all became distinctly *démodé*. We should be grateful to those ladies who appreciated the quality of their lace and preserved it for the delight of collectors today.

Collecting

Lace collars can be readily obtained from most of the larger antiques markets in London and the provinces and many antiques fairs, and indeed some general antiques shops have lace collars. There are a few shops specialising in textiles where high quality lace can be obtained.

The main criteria for determining the price of a collar are the condition and quality of the lace. Small collars of average quality can be obtained for under £10. Larger collars may cost £20 or so, depending on 'wearability', i.e. whether the style of the collar will fit in with current fashion. Highest quality workmanship with no tears or iron mould stains will command a higher price, possibly £50 or more, but such specimens are rare.

PRE-COLUMBIAN TEXTILES

Alix Gudefin

Pre-Columbian textiles, one of the greatest artistic legacies of the American hemisphere, have only recently stimulated serious interest among archaeologists and collectors. Their sumptuous colours, superior dyes, striking designs, and exquisite workmanship dazzled the Spanish Conquistadores who brought back the finest examples to the motherland. None of these is known to have survived, but little effort has yet been invested toward their recovery.

Thanks to the endeavours of 19th century antiquarians and collectors, many textiles found their way into private and public European and North American collections, namely the Museum of Völkerkunde in West Berlin. Today, pre-Columbian textiles are only beginning to be considered as genuine works of art, a reputation well overdue for weavings featuring some of the most complex and intricate designs known to man.

Counting only a few exceptions, the vast majority of these fabrics originate from ancient Peru – encompassing modern-day Peru and Bolivia – in the Western coastal and highland regions whose exceedingly dry climate preserved them for centuries in almost flawless condition. Although important textile traditions are known to have existed in other pre-Columbian regions, such as Mexico under the Aztecs, virtually no examples exist today having been destroyed by humidity.

In ancient Peru, textiles and their production processes were attributed a unique importance – equalling that of agriculture – in the economic, political, social, religious, and military spheres. Under the Incas, for instance, no event was ever complete without textiles being volunteered, bestowed, exchanged, or burned in sacrifice. Basically square or rectangular in shape, they were put to many uses including daily clothing and ceremonial and funerary garb. Among the most frequently encountered items are ponchos, mantles, belts, headgear, camping cloths and sacks, temple wallhangings, and mummy wrapping cloths.

Clothing often denoted a particular social status, professional activity, and perhaps military rank. Thus, for instance, decorated poncho shirts of the Tiahuanaco and the Incas may have been used as officials' uniforms. Meanwhile, the average person wore simple cotton or wool clothing sometimes merely adorned with decorative borders, stripes, or plaid.

The majority of existing fabrics were found in tombs, including items specifically pertaining to the burial rite, including mantles and mummy wrappings, and personal clothing and belongings, such as gold, ceramic, and wood objects. These gifts were all designed to ensure the departed's tranquility in the outer world. The fabrics were among the most sumptuous having been destined for the elite's funerary ritual, the greatest of all possible honours.

As shown by the great number of discovered tombs, including that of the Paracas find at Cerro Colorado by Julius C. Tello in 1929, fabrics played a paramount role in pre-Columbian cultures' concept of life and death. Mummies were wrapped in a series of textiles of many types, the last one of which, usually the finest, was placed over the funerary bundle. Under the Paracas, spectacular garments were used to wrap the dead, perhaps symbolizing the transformation of the impure body into an otherworldly spiritual state. So important was the function of textiles that weavers' graves have revealed looms complete with unfinished textile samples and accessories. Under the Incas, certain animal designs – including gods and demons – were attributed a talismanic importance signifying some type of protection for the weaver, both in life and death.

Moreover, for the Incas at least, textiles rivalled llamas as primary sacrificial objects as they were buried, burned, or thrown into rivers as offerings. They were also an important form of taxation which the ruler distributed to the people on special festive or ceremonial occasions. Bestowed with an amulet-like quality, Inca textiles were a jealously guarded and defended possession with which the Spaniards had to contend.

The advent of the Conquista destroyed the religious, social, and political structure whereby this textile art flourished, untouched by any outside influence for

Figure 1 *Tiahuanaco woven textile panel, South Coast, about 700-900 AD, featuring one half of a skirt with bands of rectangles, each containing a running warrior wearing a headdress and carrying long staffs with streamers. Note the ubiquitous black-and-white 'divided eye' motif. 211.5 × 51.5 cm (83½ × 20½ in). Sold for US$16 500 (c £11 000) on 10/6/80 at Sotheby Parke Bernet.*

centuries. Some form of traditional weaving has nonetheless persisted until today, particularly in the Peruvian and Bolivian highlands, featuring similar methods, dyes, and materials. Yet, with the Indians' loss of pride, integrity, and power, have departed their inspiration and incentive and hence their weavings' exquisite quality.

Of the some hundred identifiable pre-Columbian periods, less than a dozen have left today's collectors with a significant number of identifiable fabrics. Among the earliest and most remarkable are those woven by the Paracas of the South Coast (about 900-100 BC) whose best-known examples are executed in the so-called Necropolis style *(Figure 2),* chiefly featuring elaborately embroidered garments in rich shades of yellow, red, dark green, and blue. Meanwhile, the coastal Tiahuanaco culture (about 700-1100AD) produced a number of fascinating textiles, most interestingly fabrics, such as poncho shirts exhibiting highly abstract, almost Picassoesque designs. Displayed on a varying number of vertical bands, the designs, mainly in yellows, oranges, and light browns, often illustrate the progression from a particular design to an unrecognizable abstraction. Generally depicted were animals, birds, human beings, and anthropomorphic creatures often featuring the characteristic 'divided eye' where the eye is divided into black and white halves *(Figure 1).*

Best known today are textiles from the later periods (ie. about 1100-1400AD), namely the Chimu on the North Coast *(Figure 4)* and the Chancay on the Central Coast. Common subjects include birds, especially pelicans, cats, human beings, as well as genre scenes, executed in a combination of reds, yellows, browns, and whites. Painstakingly documented by the Spaniards, albeit less plentiful, are Inca fabrics (about 1438-1532AD) characterized by technical excellence and formal arrangements of mainly geometric motifs. The Incas, whose powerful empire controlled the coast and highlands from Ecuador to northern Chile and Argentina, produced increasingly regimented and standardized fabrics. Especially characteristic are the poncho shirts with a V-shaped neck area

Figure 2 *Detail of a Paracas Necropolis-style embroidered mantle, 400-100 BC displaying a border characterized with a repeating, alternately inverted motif, including in its outer line a feline with a monkey at the end of its tail, its curling body enclosing smaller monkeys, the tongue and head streamer ending in trophy-heads with flowing streamers, and grasping a trophy-head in its forefeet. 249 × 132.1 cm (98 × 52 in). Sold for US$25 300 (c £16 800) on 27-28/11/84 at Sotheby Parke Bernet.*

Figure 3 (right) *South Coast feather panel, about 1000-1300 AD, originally a wallhanging composed of alternating quadrants of brilliant blue and yellow macaw feathers, each feather wrapped around a cotton string and attached in overlapping rows to a plain weave thick cotton backing. 219.8 × 80 cm (86½ × 31½ in). Sold for US$37 400 (c £25 000) on 27-28/11/84 at Sotheby Parke Bernet.*

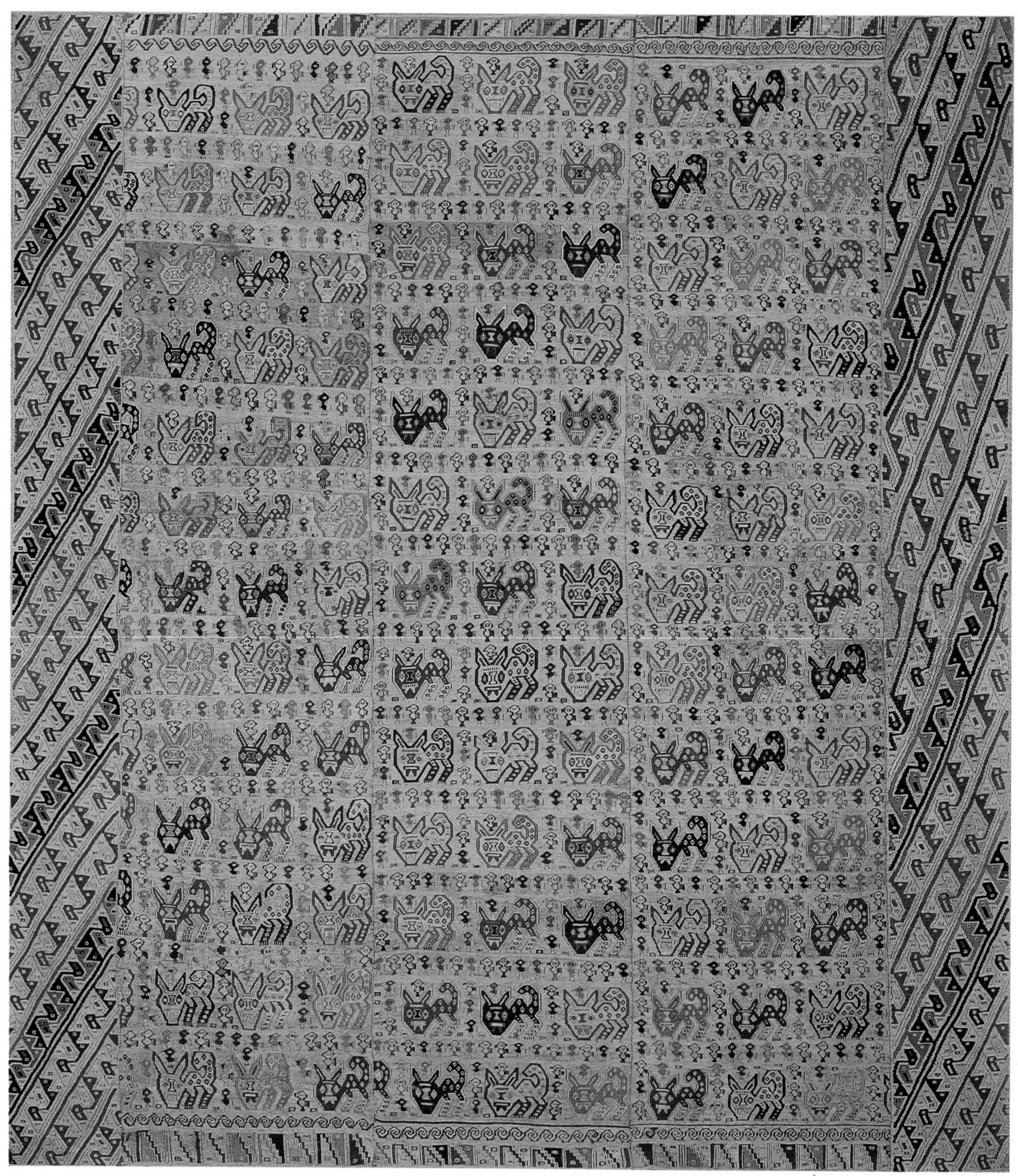

Figure 4 (above) *Chimu tapestry-woven mantle, about 1100-1400 AD exhibiting stylized repeats of cats and birds with the top and bottom borders depicting the characteristic step motif and the lateral borders featuring more stylized birds. 156.2 × 177.8 cm (62½ × 70 in). Price: US$25 000-$30 000 (c £16 000-£20 000). Martin & Ullman Artweave Textile Gallery.*

Figure 5 (opposite) *A complete Chancay mantle, about 1100-1400 AD exhibiting the supplementary weft technique and double-serpent repeats with cat heads. Stylized cats decorate the top and bottom borders. 129.5 × 188 cm (51 × 74 in). Price: US $10 000-$15 000 (c UK £6600-£10 000). Martin & Ullman Art-Weave Textile Gallery.*

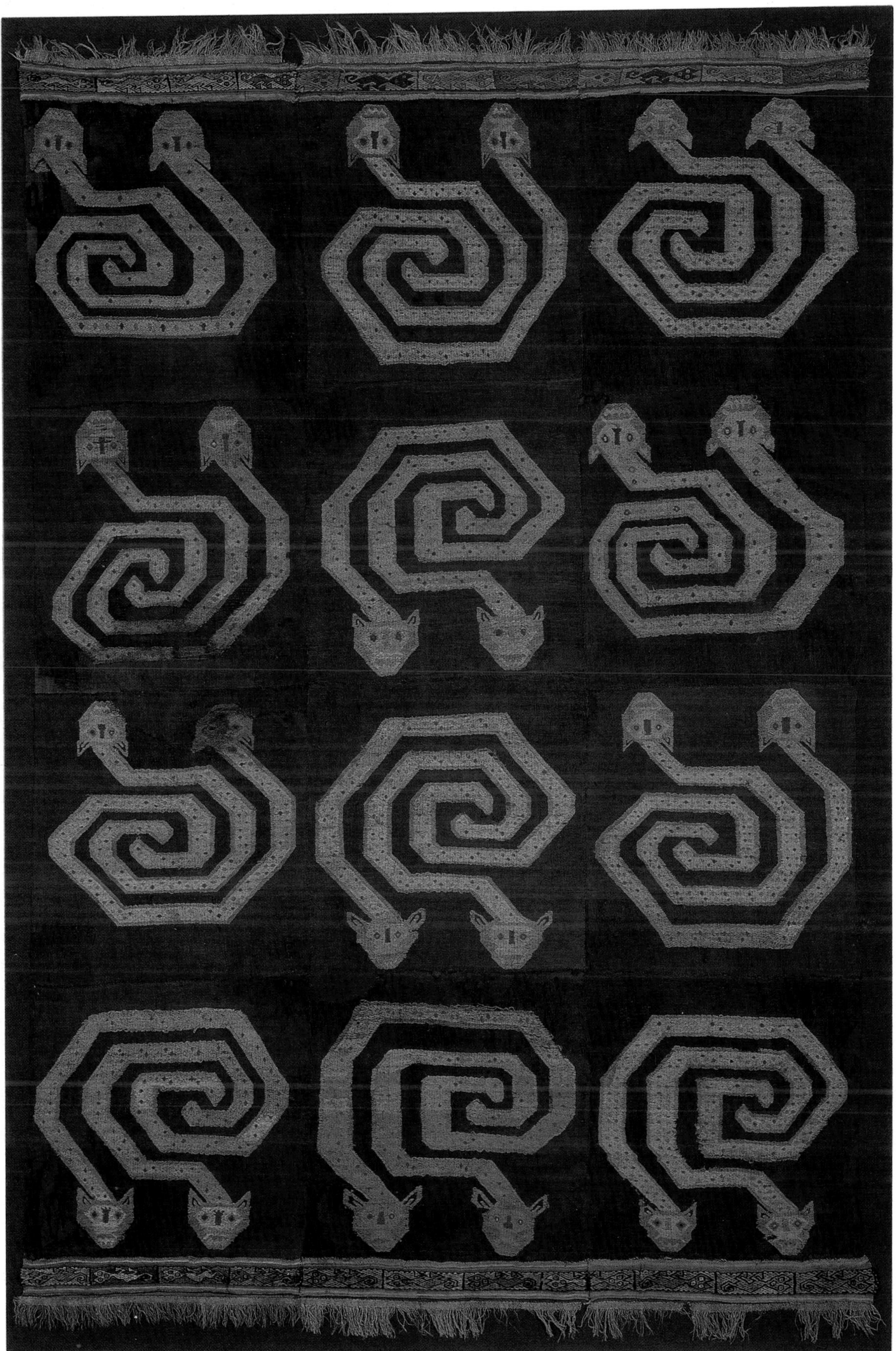

featuring a different sort of pattern from the rest of the piece *(Figure 7)*.

From the technical standpoint, ancient Peruvian textiles have been eulogized as the most exquisite in the world. Prior to the invention of the loom, the earliest textiles, dating as far back as around 2000BC, were produced with techniques such as twining and looping. Later, the Conquistadores were amazed to discover the Peruvians' ability to produce superb work with three simple types of looms: a backstrap or belt loom, a horizontal ground loom, or a vertical frame loom. Most commonly used were cotton of various natural shades and wool from the cameloids, including vicuña, alpaca, and llama, the latter of which was the most popular. Also found, primarily in cordage, braiding, and knotted netting are hard fibres, bast, and even human hair.

Anonymous women weavers usually produced the textiles which were rarely cut but instead woven to the size and shape required. Generally woven or embroidered, some fabrics also featured feathers *(Figure 3)*, gold and silver threads, and even square gold plaques. Particularly spectacular were the iridescent featherworks pertaining to ceremonial garments and accessories and probably bestowed with magical powers. Still yet other textiles displayed boldly painted patterns, brushed or stamped onto a cotton ground, while gauzes were decorated with generally white-coloured filigree or lace-like designs.

Remarkably, there is virtually no known technique that has not been used in pre-Columbian textiles and many practices cannot be duplicated today. Among the countless complex techniques known – often combined in a single fabric – were plain, warp and weft interlocking, tapestry, brocading, embroidery, appliqué, and wrapping. Also admirable was the wide range of hues achieved, combined and juxtaposed with unparalleled good taste. In addition to the rich colours obtained from vegetable dyes, such as red from madder, other shades – whites, greys, blacks, and ochres – were derived from vicuña and llama wool. Tie-dyeing was also practiced as far back as the Paracas and *ikat*, resist-dyeing of warp or weft before weaving, also existed.

Collecting

Although collected since the 19th century with older pre-Columbian art, specific interest in these textiles as a collectable entity is recent. According to Fatma Turkkan-Wille at Sotheby Parke Bernet, the collecting trend began in the 1930s and 1940s when they were purchased by wealthy collectors including the Rockefellers. Pre-Columbian textiles, together with their Coptic counterparts, are among the earliest historic fabrics collected. In the last two decades, their appreciation has increased with the resurgent interest in textiles and with their strong appeal among modern art collectors. Indeed, these mainly abstract masterpieces foreshadow many 20th century artists' conventions. Also attractive to today's collector, according to Ocsi Ullman of the Martin & Ullman Artweave Textile Gallery, New York, are their enormous price ranges.

Given the necessary time and funds, today's enterprising collector can find examples from nearly all the principal cultures. More important in assessing a piece's value, however, are its age, design and iconography, rarity, and condition. By far, Chimu and Chancay pieces are most available with fragments ranging from about \$400 to \$1000 and complete items, such as mantles, sashes, and belts starting from about \$1000 to \$30 000. Rare and more priceless are textiles from other cultures, especially Paracas, where, for instance, a complete embroidered mantle could command up to \$250 000 and a single embroidered fragment \$5000 to \$10 000. Also sought-after are Tiahuanaco pieces for their sophisticated 'Cubist' look. While fragments can be had for about \$800 and up, a complete poncho in superb condition can fetch anywhere from \$30 000 to \$70 000. Surprisingly, Inca textiles are relatively hard to find, probably because they were worn and not buried, and complete ponchos can range from \$5000 to \$50 000.

Also collected are particular types of textiles, such as feathered and painted, from various cultures. While feather panels – mainly Inca, Chimu, Chancay, and Huari – go from about \$30 000 to \$50 000, feather headdresses can command up to \$20 000. Recently popular are painted textiles – Chavin, Nasca, Huari, Chancay, and Chimu – fetching anywhere from \$1000 to \$30 000.

As with any art form, experts advise potential collectors to buy what they like and the very best possible in terms of condition, degree of completeness, and quality. Moreover, the rarer the piece the sounder the investment. Thus, for instance, a Paracas mantle section that sold for \$15 000 in 1977 would now easily command about \$100 000. Professional counsel, including that of textile conservators, is a must prior to considering a purchase.

Despite problems concerning the legality of obtaining pre-Columbian artifacts directly from Peru, most experts are optimistic about the market's future. According to Edward Merrin of the Edward H. Merrin Gallery, NY,

Figure 6 (opposite top) *Late Huari-early Chimu painted cotton panel, about 700-1000 AD, perhaps part of a mantle, depicting spotted felines. 108 × 110 cm (44 × 68 in). Price: US \$18 000 (c £12 000). Photograph © Justin Kerr 1985. Photo courtesy of Edward H. Merrin Gallery, Inc.*

Figure 7 (opposite below) *One half of an Inca poncho about 1438-1532 AD, characteristically displaying a V-shaped neck area featuring a distinctive pattern from the rest of the garment. The plain striped design is merely adorned with a few scorpions, another traditional motif. 63.5 × 67.3 cm (25 × 26½ in). Price: US \$6200 (c £4100). Photograph © Justin Kerr 1985. Photo courtesy of Edward H. Merrin Gallery, Inc.*

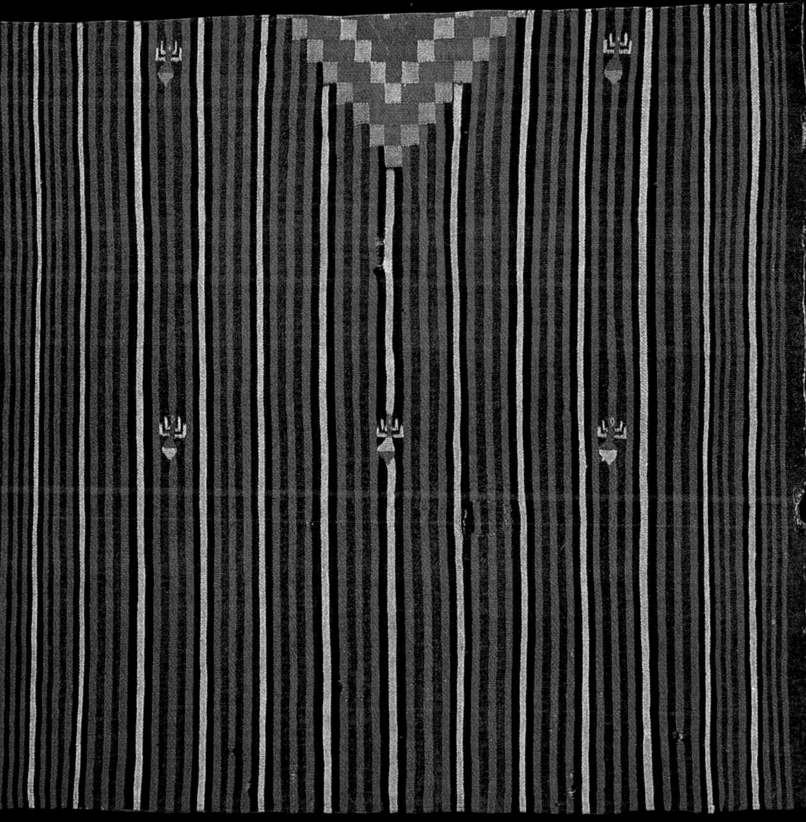

Peruvian fabrics can only appreciate, as they are still an undiscovered art form and are reasonably priced given their extraordinary quality. At first based in New York, the market has now become international and will continue to strengthen with the increasing rarity of materials. Potential collectors would do well to explore purchasing possibilities now when the opportunity still lies.

Collections

The following is a list of the best-known pre-Columbian textile museum collections in the world. Please note that the textiles are not necessarily on permanent view.

American Museum of Natural History New York, USA
Brooklyn Museum New York, USA
Bruning Museum Lambayeque, Peru
Dallas Museum of Fine Arts Dallas, Texas, USA
Dumbarton Oaks Washington DC, USA
Metropolitan Museum of Art New York, USA
Musée de l'Homme Paris, France
National Museum of Anthropology and Archaeology Lima, Peru
Museum of Völkerkunde West Berlin, West Germany
Reitberg Museum Zurich, Switzerland

Figure 8 *Proto-Nasca panel, possibly a poncho, about 100 BC-100 AD, displaying the characteristic step motif. 66 × 124 cm (26 × 49 in). Price: US $28 000 (c £18 600). Photograph © Justin Kerr 1985. Photo courtesy of Edward H. Merrin Gallery, Inc.*

DECORATIVE CHANDELIERS

Felice Mehlman

One of the most difficult choices to make when furnishing a room is what to place over the bare bulb suspended on a plastic cord from the ceiling. So perplexing is this problem that not only have sales of paper lanterns soared (due to an otherwise poor selection of inexpensive shades) but many superbly finished interiors have discarded overhead illumination altogether, in favour of table lamps and discreetly placed spotlights. Modern light fittings undoubtedly enhance high-tech environments, and tracks of roving 'eye' spots are useful for highlighting kitchen work areas, but for rooms furnished with antiques they appear to clash with the carefully preserved details of a 'period' atmosphere. One solution is to persevere with the concept of a single overhead light (perhaps supplemented by table lamps to soften the effect) for which purpose a decorative chandelier is required.

Many splendid antique light fittings are to be found – such as those of Irish manufacture of finely cut silvery-grey lead glass, or fanciful Venetian pieces adorned with coloured glass flowers and baubles – but the majority are well beyond the reach of the modest collector. Modern reproductions of antique styles can also be surprisingly expensive, and their often monotonous designs and poor quality materials (using thin sheets of yellow brass, or displaying bright 'white' glass reflecting a garish rainbow iridescence) continue to disappoint many potential customers. On a limited budget of, say, less than £500, however, a good and varied selection of 19th and early 20th century chandeliers can be found, and are well worth considering when furnishing a room with antiques. These may be grouped broadly into two categories: reproductions, in imitation of earlier styles; and those created in the spirit of their own time, for example, in the Art Nouveau taste.

With the revivalist trends and historicism which marked the course of the

Figure 1 *Elegant six-branch brass chandelier in the Dutch 17th century style. This turn-of-the-century reproduction departs from antique prototypes by the addition of an unusually large globular base, reflecting the surrounding interior below. The surface has not been polished or treated, and retains an attractive golden colour seldom found on modern pieces. H 107 cm (42 in).* PAMELA HODGES. *Price £250 (c. US$156).*

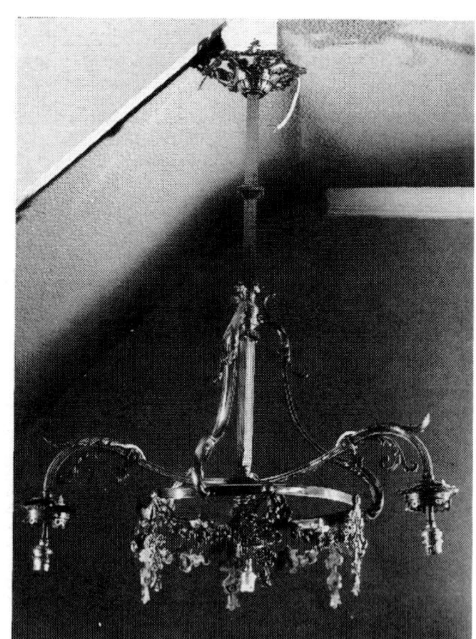

Figure 2 *Regency-style chandelier adorned with cascading glass drops of octagonal form, accented by pear- and spire-shaped pendants suspended at intervals from the gilt-metal frame. Although the pieces have been moulded and faceted by machine, the central ball at the base has been hand-cut for added brilliance. About 1900–20; H 76 cm (30 in). PAMELA HODGES. Price £95 (c. US$59).*

Figure 3 *Three-branch brass chandelier of flowing form, inspired by the Art Nouveau style and adorned with swags of flowers and applied leaves which echo the curvilinear structure. This model is hung from the ceiling by a fixed brass bracket, decorated in a similar fashion. Probably French, about 1900; H 61 cm (24 in). THE GOODAY SHOP AND STUDIO. Price £360 (c. US$225).*

Figure 4 *Unusual ormolu chandelier having ten branches, fashioned in the French Empire taste with classical ornaments such as the pineapple finial at the base. The boldly curved arms and swirls of applied acanthus leaves are reflective of late 19th century interpretations. Of continental manufacture; H 61 cm (24 in). MOLLIE EVANS. Price £425 (c. US$265).*

Victorian and Edwardian eras (and which later returned to vogue in England during the 1920s and '30s), many chandeliers were modelled on the classical robust lines of their 17th and 18th century predecessors. These reproductions, invariably mass-produced, were not intended as true and faithful copies, and far from being correct in every detail they represented in best Victorian fashion an eclectic jumble of 'period' details imbued with elements of fantasy and novelty. The brass chandelier illustrated here *(Figure 1)*, of about 1880–1910, exemplifies this incongruous admixture of stylistic features. Based roughly on classical Dutch designs of the period about 1550–1700, the pattern is intruded upon by the addition of an enormous globular base of somewhat bizarre proportions. It remains, nevertheless, an attractive piece, combining an 'Old Master' effect with Victorian frivolity. It is solidly constructed (weighing some 40–50 lbs) and

Figure 5 *Fine lead glass crystal chandelier in the 18th century style, hand-cut throughout and hung with variously shaped pendant drops. The glass surface possesses a silvery-grey tone, a subtle effect rarely achieved by modern reproductions. English, about 1900. H 46 cm (18 in). THE GOODAY SHOP AND STUDIO. Price £380. (c. US$237).*

Figure 6 *Eight-light chandelier of whimsical medieval inspiration, combining gilt-metal with cut glass drops, suspended by thick cord. The tassle decoration was probably added at a later date. About 1900; H 46 cm (18 in). THE GOODAY SHOP AND STUDIO. Price £180 (c. US$112).*

Figure 7 *Six-branch lead glass crystal chandelier of traditional design, the ribbed arms hung decoratively with elegantly shaped drops, fixed to the surface by moulded 'flower' bolts. English, about 1900; H 38 cm (15 in). THE GOODAY SHOP AND STUDIO. Price £300 (c. US$187).*

over the years the brass exterior has mellowed to a pleasing golden shade. Modern reproductions in brass seldom achieve this character and warmth of tone.

The 'Regency' chandelier with its cascading glass drops, illustrated here *(Figure 2)*, is another example of later manufacture, of the period about 1900-1920. This style was one of many to be revived and mass-produced during the early 20th century. As here, they were adorned typically with variously shaped drops of machine-moulded glass, faceted to imitate the brilliance of hand-cutting. Sometimes both methods were combined in a single composition. The star-shaped, spire and hexagonal pieces were strung onto wires to form gracefully tiered constructions. Small examples, such as the one illustrated *(Figure 8)*, are suitable for hanging in halls, staircases and bedrooms – and are especially effective in dark rooms since the faceted pieces reflect and spread the light brilliantly. The muted silvery-grey tinge of the glass creates a subtle effect, sadly lacking in modern reproductions (with the exception of the costlier lead glass chandeliers produced by factories such as Waterford).

Apart from turn-of-the-century reproductions, chandeliers in styles ranging from high Victorian to Art Deco may also be found for purchase for under £500. Indeed, it is interesting to note that original examples are often more modestly priced than their modern, mass-produced equivalents sold through department stores and specialist shops. Victorian brass and copper lanterns make attractive light fittings for entrance halls and porches, and are sometimes found with etched glass sides adorned with flowers and other motifs. Metals such as brass and bronze were favoured for decorative chandeliers, as employed on the piece illustrated in *Figure 3* with its moulded leaf decorations and swags of flowers. Art Nouveau designs of the period c.1890-1905 are among the most graceful, although signed pieces of wrought iron, glass and bronze can exceed the price limit set for this article. The ormolu chandelier *(Figure 4)* combines the flowing lines of this turn-of-the-century style with French 'Empire' designs, featuring urn and pineapple motifs and wreath finials. This unusual example represents remarkably good value.

Decorative light fittings of the 1920s and '30s conformed largely to the Art Deco styles fashionable at the time. Chandeliers in chrome and glass, featuring bold angular branches and arms with applied motifs of floral or abstract content, are most typical of the period. Clear and frosted glass shades, with painted and etched decorations of ziggurats and other geometric configurations, were also popular, suspended from the ceiling on brass chains. Traditional designs continued to be produced contemporaneously, in keeping with the vogue for mock-Elizabethan and Tudor-style interiors. This is evidenced, for example, by the appearance of wooden chandeliers of sombre medieval design.

When purchasing a chandelier, it is essential to consider the dimensions and decorations of the room in which the piece is to be displayed. Many antique examples are large and heavy (such as the brass chandelier illustrated) and were intended originally to hang in expansive interiors with high ceilings. Having ensured that the proportions and style are in keeping with the design of the interior, the next step is to check the piece for wiring. Many antique chandeliers have been adapted for modern electricity; others have not, and therefore will need to be re-wired and hung by a competent electrician. Often, the shop where the piece is purchased will be able to carry out the wiring and other necessary restoration for an additional charge.

Figure 8 *Glass chandelier having a fluted top, pierced for hanging strings of moulded glass drops. Light fittings in this style were mass-produced during the early 20th century – intended, by virtue of their small size, for bedrooms and staircase landings. English, about 1910; H 38 cm (15 in). PAMELA HODGES. Price £35 (c.US$22).*

Some pieces, such as the ormolu example, are fixed directly onto the ceiling, while others hang below, attached to a brass hook by a length of chain. The original is often missing or too short, and careful thought should be given to matching the chandelier to a new length. The links must be neither too large nor too small, and it is essential not to hang a bright brass chain which clashes with the light fitting. Modern brass can be 'aged' quite easily – most simply by sponging the surface with black boot polish.

Branched chandeliers with pendant arms require candle-style bulbs, which are available widely in both clear and frosted glass. Some, particularly those of downlight construction, might also benefit from shades. Glass chandeliers always look best with clear (as opposed to 'pearl') bulbs, to maximise the effects of clarity and brilliance.

Glass pendant drop chandeliers, invariably comprised of dozens of moulded or hand-cut pieces, are rarely found for purchase in perfect condition. Small chips may be evident on close examination, and in complicated constructions a few of the lustres may be missing. The latter can sometimes be replaced (or a close match found) at a specialist glass shop. Minute areas of damage are generally considered 'acceptable' if they do not detract from the attractiveness of the overall design.

The glass pendant drops can be removed easily from their wired frames for cleaning. They may be washed in warm soapy water, rinsed and dried with a soft linen cloth. Since the lustres are prone to chipping, they should be handled with great care – particularly at their sharp pointed ends.

Brass chandeliers, especially those of pleasing colour and patina, are often best left in their original state. If polishing is required, a proprietary paste or wadding may be applied, taking care not to dislodge any of the branched arms or finials. Areas of corroded or pitted brass may be improved by using a strong alkali solution sponged over the surface, or the piece may be cleaned professionally.

Sources

Inexpensive light fittings of the period c.1850-1935 may also be found at antique shops which feature a range of decorative accessories and furnishings – these are well worth visiting on a regular basis, for their frequently changing stock of pieces brought in from country house sales and auctions. Specialist shops offer an extensive range of examples dating from the 17th century onwards – but with prices largely in excess of £500, the collector on a limited budget must look elsewhere.

19TH CENTURY GLASS DECANTERS

Nicholas Rootes

During the 18th century, the binning of wine in sealed bottles became possible owing to the development of close-fitting corks and also necessary due to the increasing popularity of port, a drink that needs to acquire bottle age. Before binning became common practice, wine was drawn straight from the cask and poured into serving bottles. But wine left in casks that were in constant use soon soured through contact with the air, while in sealed bottles it could develop to maturity. Since wine with considerable bottle age throws a deposit, it began to be 'canted' from the bottle in which it was stored into a decanter. The object of decanting is not only to leave the sediment in the bottle, but also to allow wine to become sufficiently aerated to release its bouquet.

By the 19th century, the habit of decanting had become such an essential element in the rules of social etiquette, that even champagne and white wine were sometimes decanted. In 1840, Lord Cardigan placed one of his officers on a charge for bringing a bottle of hock to the mess table, instead of transferring the wine into a decanter. Decanters for champagne and white wine were fitted with internal pockets in which ice could be placed without diluting the contents.

The beginning of the 19th century was characterised by a change in style. The restrained Hellenic motifs of the Adam period were replaced by a heavier classical style, typical of the Regency period. The tapering shape of decanters was superseded by the more ponderous Prussian-shaped decanter *(Figure 2, left)*.

The tentative experiments with cutting glass in the 18th century came to fruition during the Regency period and such decoration became deeper and less restrained. Diamond cutting, that is deep mitre-cut channels, criss-crossed to form a diamond pattern in relief, became popular *(Figure 2, centre)*. More intricate variations of this were developed by elaborating the surface of each diamond shape. Other typical motifs were radial cuts on the base of a decanter, known as star-cutting, and a series of parallel cuts rising from the base, part of the way up the body, called comb-fluting.

In the first quarter of the 19th century cut glass decoration became more pervasive, until the whole surface area of a

Figure 1 *One of a pair of claret jugs finely engraved and wheel carved with sprays of thistles. The ormulu mounts are cast with flowerheads and leafy tendrils, a style typical of the Art Nouveau preoccupation with curvilinear shapes and naturalistic form. H 32.1 cm (12½ in)* CHRISTIE'S *Pair sold for £864 (c US$1235)*

Figure 2 *Three decanters showing changes in style of cut decoration during the first three decades of the 19th century. L to r: Prussian-shaped decanter with restrained fluting on the body, typical of the first decade. About 1810. H 25 cm (9¾ in). £120 (c US$171). A similarly shaped decanter with horizontal bands of cut decoration over the entire body and a step-cut neck, about 1820. £120 (c US$171). A cylindrical decanter with vertical pillar fluting on the body and step-cut shoulders, about 1830. Vertical decoration suited the cylindrical shape that became popular in the 1830s.* PRYCE & BRYSE ANTIQUES *£95 (c US$136)*

decanter was often covered with horizontal bands of decoration. This horizontal emphasis was further accentuated by step-cutting. Horizontal mitre-cut channels were cut parallel to each other, initially from shoulder to neck *(Figure 2, right)* but by around 1830, these extended over the entire body.

Not all decanters were elaborately cut, because this technique was wasteful of glass and consequently expensive. The crystal had to be thick enough to withstand the depth of cutting and the glass, which was heavily taxed by the Glass Excise Act of 1745, was sold by weight. Ireland was free of this tax and once restrictions on the export of Irish glass were lifted in 1780, the industry flourished there. Factories were established at Belfast, Waterford, Cork and Dublin, and their wares were exported to America and England. Since the Irish followed contemporary English styles and imported English expertise, it is often not possible to distinguish between an Irish and an English decanter, unless there is a manufacturer's mark on the base. Decanters with these marks are certainly not common, but the least rare mark is for the Cork Glass Company. Within this category is found the occasional forgery, which can usually be detected by an expert quite easily, though a small number are hard to distinguish. In 1825, excise duty was also imposed on Irish glass and the output of the factories consequently declined.

During the 1830s, cylindrical decanters with angular shoulders became popular *(Figure 2, right)*. The development of this shape is now attributed to the popularity at the time of the international Empire style. This change in shape was simultaneous with a change in surface decoration. Less use was made of mitre-cut diamond motifs, instead shallower cutting techniques became the fashion. Fluting was used in a way that imparted a vertical decorative emphasis to decanters.

The Victorians were plagiarists of past styles and so it is not surprising that in the late 1830s, a shape of decanter reminiscent of the first glass wine bottles of the 17th century appeared. These decanters had globular bodies and long narrow necks and were skilfully cut around the body with a series of arches containing decorative features, such as diamond patterns or plant motifs *(Figure 4)*.

The removal of excise duty on glass in 1845, allowed glass-makers to indulge themselves in an excess of cut decoration, which reached an apogee at the Great Exhibition of 1851. In reaction to such excess, cut decoration became less popular in the following decade. But there were more innovative techniques on display at the Exhibition. Sulphides, a term used for vessels containing cameos, were in evidence. Originally developed by Apsley Pellat in 1819 as a method of enclosing cameo portraits within clear glass, this technique was revived by John Ford and Company of Edinburgh in the mid-19th century. These portraits embellished decanters, but are now very rarely found.

Another form of decoration that began to be assimilated in the 1840s from the stylistic influences of Central Europe, was coloured glass. This was produced in clear and opaque colours, and also in layers which when cut revealed further colours beneath the surface. Such methods produced opulent decorative effects, but also unfortunately concealed the colour of the wine decanted. The most skilful manifestation of coloured glass was cameo glass, which made use of a technique first developed by the

Figure 3 *A cameo glass claret jug by Webb of Stourbridge, dated 1886. The silver mount is American, for the vessel was exported to America unmounted to avoid import duty on silver. Such pieces sell for high prices owing to the painstaking and skilful techniques required for the production of cameo glass. H 24 cm (9½ in)* ASPREY *£4000 (c US$5720)*

Figure 4 *Rare Victorian cut glass decanter with an unusual flanged stopper. The globular body and long neck are reminiscent of early 17th century 'shaft and globe' wine bottles. About 1840. H34 cm (13½ in)* JEANETTE HAYHURST *£225 (c US$321)*

Figure 5 *One of a pair of ship's decanters with a star-cut base, fluted body and bull's eye stopper. The shape provides a low centre of gravity for maximum stability on board ship. About 1810. H 23 cm (9 in).* DELOMOSNE *£850 (pair) (c US$1215)*

Romans. This involved carving away an outer layer of opaque-white glass in order to leave a pattern in relief. The tone of the pattern varied according to the thickness of the outer layer remaining and this could be used to simulate the transparency of robes or to give a sense of perspective *(Figure 3)*.

Engraved decoration filled the vacuum created by the temporary decline in popularity of cut glass. In addition to wheel engraving, other methods were employed. In the 1830s experiments were made with acid etching which was patented by Benjamin Richardson in 1857. Also, a technique known as rock crystal engraving emerged in the 1880s. Glassmakers were able to achieve the effect of sculpted glass by fully integrating the engraved surfaces into the shape of the vessels, through polishing out the sharpness of the engraving. A further development was the use of a deeper method of engraving, using cutting wheels larger than those normally required for the purpose. Known as intaglio engraving, this was often used in conjunction with cut decoration *(Figure 7)*.

The shapes of decanters were not simply dictated by the prevailing fashion of each period, though such influences were always in some way apparent. Decanters were to some extent shaped according to use, as already mentioned with ice decanters used for champagne and white wine. Accordingly, ship's decanters were designed with broad-based conical bodies that provided a low centre of gravity and hence the stability required on board ship. They were popularly known as Rodney's in memory of Admiral Rodney, who defeated the French in 1782 in a naval battle off Cape St. Vincent *(Figure 5)*.

Claret jugs, as their name implies, also had a specific use, though why claret should be served in a jug remains something of a mystery. Possibly such an association came about from the immense popularity of claret in the late 17th century, when George Ravenscroft was manufacturing the very earliest 'decanter bottles', one style of which was jug-shaped.

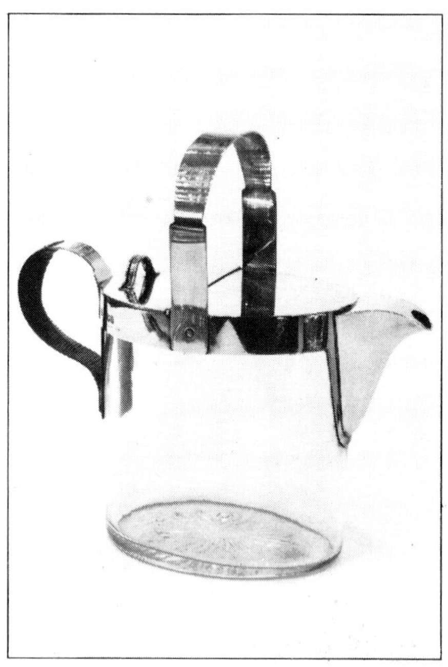

Figure 6 *A functional claret jug made by Heath and Middleton in 1896. With its silver mounts and wicker-covered handle, it reflects the intellectual revolt against heavily cut glass. H 21.5 cm (8½ in)* SUE & ALAN THOMPSON *£820 (c US$1172)*

Spirit decanters too, were made to a convenient shape, suited to a particular need. A tantalus for instance, is a case or stand in which spirits may be locked away. In order to fit into a tantalus, a square-section decanter had to be designed *(Figure 8)*.

Two years after the Great Exhibition of 1851, the art critic and arbiter of taste John Ruskin declared that cut glass was 'barbaric'. Ultimately, he could not stem the tide of popular taste, for cut glass once again became popular in the last two decades of the century, but there were those who believed that cut decoration hid the ductile nature of glass.

Rejecting the excesses of Victorian ornamentation and searching for more functional forms, designers towards the end of the 19th century, who imposed an intellectual philosophy on their work, tended to avoid excessive cut decoration. Christopher Dresser designed decanters with silver or plated mounts that must have been shocking in their simplicity to the contemporary eye. The exponents of

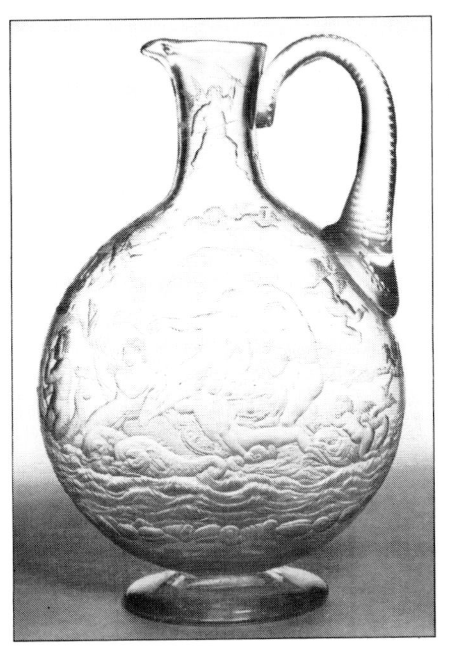

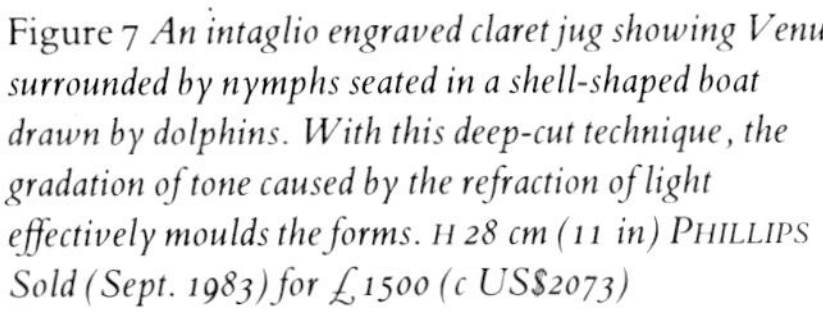

Figure 7 *An intaglio engraved claret jug showing Venus surrounded by nymphs seated in a shell-shaped boat drawn by dolphins. With this deep-cut technique, the gradation of tone caused by the refraction of light effectively moulds the forms.* H *28 cm (11 in)* PHILLIPS *Sold (Sept. 1983) for £1500 (c US$2073)*

Figure 8 *A tantalus, made in oak with silver-plate e mounts, containing three heavily cut spirit decanters, spirit glasses, silver-plate ashtrays, a humidor for cigars in the base and a mirror in the lid. A plaque on the lid reveals that it was presented to Dr A. J. E. Parker by the grateful patients of Easington Lane, Hetton Le Hole, in 1899.* H *(case) 38 cm (15 in)* ASPREY *£1850 (c US$2645)*

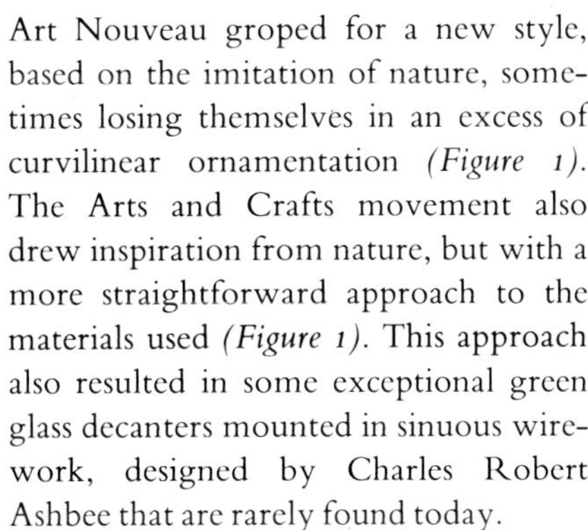

Art Nouveau groped for a new style, based on the imitation of nature, sometimes losing themselves in an excess of curvilinear ornamentation *(Figure 1)*. The Arts and Crafts movement also drew inspiration from nature, but with a more straightforward approach to the materials used *(Figure 1)*. This approach also resulted in some exceptional green glass decanters mounted in sinuous wirework, designed by Charles Robert Ashbee that are rarely found today.

Styles of 19th century decanters are enormously diverse, from the heavy pomp of Regency classicism, through the eclectic designs and indulgence of Victorian glass, to the simple functionalism of Dr Dresser's designs. Fortunately for buyers of 19th century glass, this means that almost all tastes can be accommodated, and a collection can be built around whichever particular style each individual finds most appealing.

Sources

19th century decanters may be found in many antique shops though they may frequently lack their original stoppers. Some of the most enduring styles are still reproduced, but there is plenty of choice amongst antique decanters from under £100, to several hundred pounds for an exceptional example or a good pair. A unique decanter may cost thousands. Chipped glass tends to reduce the value of a vessel substantially.

MARK ROTHKO IN RETROSPECT

Alistair Smith

I count myself especially fortunate to have seen, in 1962, the first one-man exhibition of Rothko's work to be shown outside the United States. Two circumstances made that experience particularly fruitful. First, I had scarcely heard of the subject of art-history, let alone of Mark Rothko, and consequently I viewed his work fresh. I saw the paintings as physical objects uninformed by any chronology of Abstract Expressionism or by any development of abstraction in the 20th century. Second, it was around Christmas and bitterly cold, which kept people at home. As a temporary *emigré* in Paris, devoid of seasonal responsibilities, I found myself virtually alone in the exhibition, one person among forty-four strange objects in the Musée d'Art Moderne.

Figure 1. The Rothko Room. *Left.* Black on Maroon, 1958. *266.7 × 365.8 cm (105 × 144 in). Right.* Black on Maroon, 1959. *266.7 × 457.2 cm (105 × 180 in). Tate Gallery, Gift of the Artist. Rothko refused to deliver the series of murals which he had painted for the Seagram Building and returned his fee. He donated one series to the Tate Gallery where it is displayed in what might be described as a 'Rothko Chapel' with the light slightly lowered. The series was influenced by Michelangelo's entrance to the Medici Library in Florence.*

Figure 2, Number 15, 1948. *Oil on canvas, 132 × 73.7 cm. (52 × 29 in). National Gallery of Art, Washington D.C. Gift of the Mark Rothko Foundation. In 1947, Rothko abandoned his earlier Surrealism-based style and began to develop paintings composed of colourful if indistinct rectangles. The use of line is abandoned and relationships are created by colour, shape and position within the painting.*

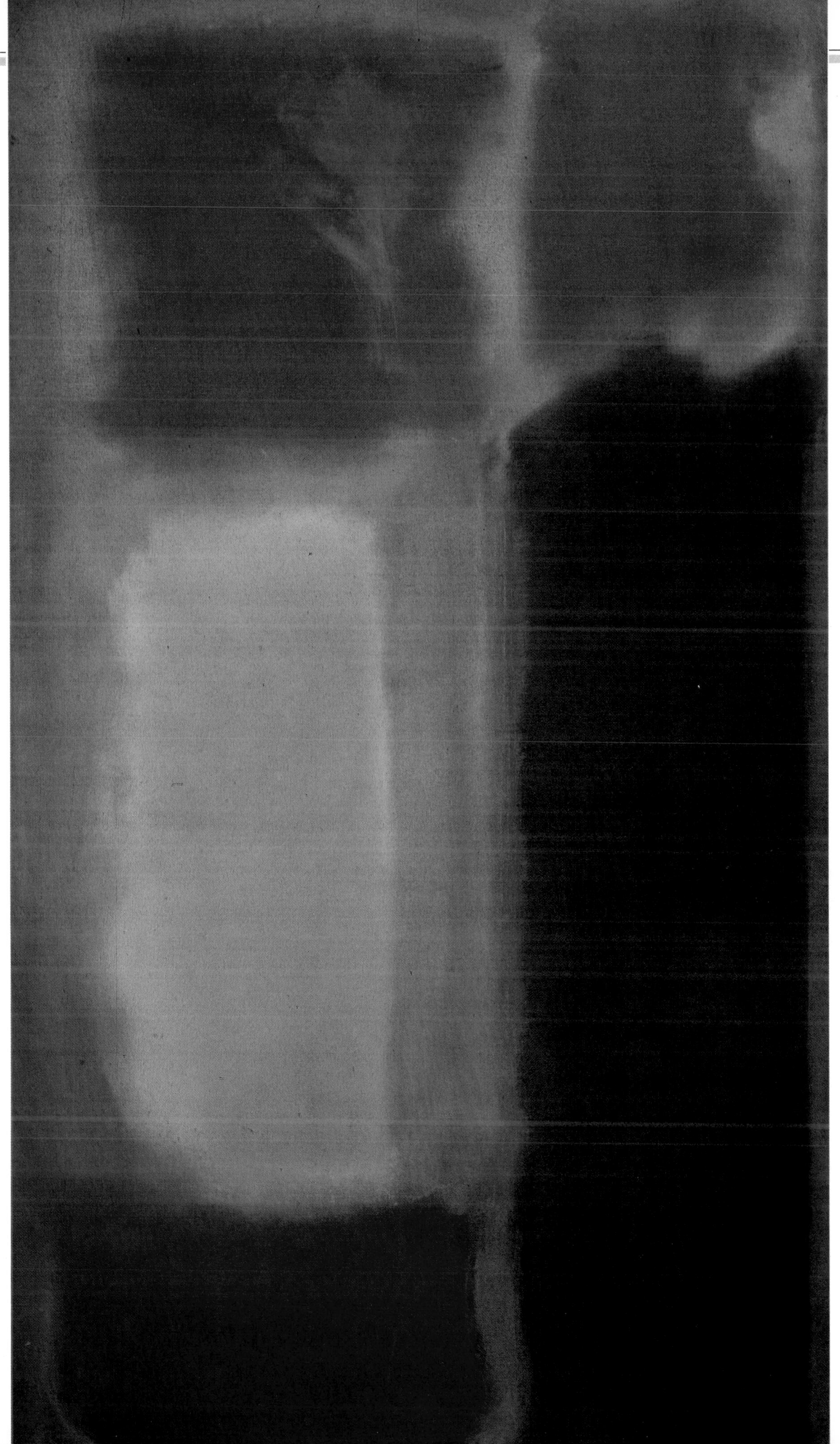

On both counts the physical qualities of the paintings were emphasised, which was right. Rectangles larger than oneself seemed to float near the wall, rather than hang on it. They were like those indistinct images which become imprinted on the retina after staring at a bright window. Only these were enormous and unfading and imprinted on the whole body.

Large can be bombastic or even just aggressive, but the scale of Rothko's paintings belies their subtlety, for the effects of colour are anything but obvious. Trying to describe a painting in words resulted in incoherence: 'Upper horizontal rectangle deep red; centre squarish one is brown but showing maroon through it; lower horizontal rectangle vivid blue and floats on the brown-maroon base. The edges are fluffy and the colour shines through'. My notes to the 1962 catalogue are totally banal. One might say more revealingly that Rothko's paintings combine the monumentality of great ancient architecture with the kind of painstakingly detailed craftsmanship that one looks for in lace-making or filigree.

The paintings operate on more than one level. Their size – eight foot is commonplace – and their large shapes have a direct physical effect on the spectator. The more general colour works its own emotions within this effect. Then as the eye becomes attuned to the image, it perceives that certain sections have underpainting shining through, and that this underpaint might relate to one of the other rectangles, or to the background field. Relations and correspondences, contrasts, rhythms, harmonies; the technique is close to being musical, but also akin to types of symbolism. In art and in life, a rose can be a flower and also an expression of love. Similarly, Rothko's works are, first objects and then, something else.

What is that something else? What are the paintings meant to be? One indication might lie in the titles given them by their creator. Of the selection illustrated, one maintains perfect inscrutability being *Untitled (Figure 6)*. Other titles like *Orange Red and Red (Figure 7)* or *Green and Maroon (Figure 4)* are of no greater assistance, indeed they serve only to generalise the complexities of the colour rendered in the painting. *Number 15, 1948 (Figure 2)* at least tells that it was the fifteenth painting made in that year, but it offers no more. This habit of numbering his paintings was begun by Rothko only in 1947, the year in which he began to establish the style by which he is now recognised, the year of his forty-fourth birthday. Described as *Ancestral Imprint* or *Primeval Landscape*, those pictures were much more derivative, clearly influenced by Surrealism (resembling Max Ernst in particular) and parallel to the work of Arshile Gorky.

When Rothko's mature art began to emerge, these evocative titles disappeared but the aspiration towards the sense of magic or mysticism, which they suggested, intensified. His *Number 15, 1948 (Figure 2)* is one of the first group of works in which line has been totally eliminated and in which the composition is principally made up of inchoate rectangles. It was in 1949, that the paintings took the form which is now seen as one of the milestones of twentieth-century art. His *Green and Maroon* of 1953 is typical *(Figure 4)*. Ninety inches high, the coloured shapes hang against a light blue background which is in some places (for example, when close to the red) strong enough to appear, paradoxically, close to the spectator. The blue, green and red describe nothing but themselves; yet, at this time they still have primitive associations – sky, grass, energy.

The more linear passages between the rectangles in Rothko's pictures have often been said to resemble a horizon line in a landscape painting, and consequently the paintings have been compared to certain types of

Figure 3, The Evening Star *by J. M. W. Turner, about 1830. Oil on canvas, 92.1 × 122.6 cm (36¼ × 48¼ in). The National Gallery, London. On temporary loan to the Clore Gallery at the Tate Gallery. Turner like Rothko was an artist in the Romantic tradition using landscape subjects as a springboard for meditations on man and nature. With a composition divided by the horizon line into two clear rectangles, a tiny human figure emphasises the immensity of the universe. The sheer size of Rothko's paintings obtains the same effect.*

Figure 4, Green and Maroon, 1953. *Oil on canvas, 231 × 139 cm (91¼ × 54¾ in). The Phillips Collection, Washington D.C. A 'typical' painting from the period in which Rothko forged his mature style. The colour can still be thought to have descriptive associations – sky, grass, energy – and the linear divisions have been compared to horizon lines in conventional landscape painting. Paintings like this have been described as 'landscapes of the spirit'.*

traditional landscape painting. In this context both J. M. W. Turner and Caspar David Friedrich have been cited. Both of these artists use at times a pronounced horizon line, dividing their compositions into two clear rectangles – a superficially Rothko-like arrangement *(Figure 3)*. More significant than this however is the fact that both were Romantics, who instilled their art with definite moods, be they of lyricism or melancholy, awe or comfort. If Rothko's art needed historical justification, this could be easily provided by demonstrating his place within the tradition of transcendental Romanticism.

The similarities are manifest, for the landscape subject-matter of both Friedrich and Turner eventually becomes no more than a springboard for their meditations on man and nature. Both made paintings in which tiny figures act as scaling devices to calibrate the immensity of the universe. The sheer size of Rothko's paintings obtains the same effect. One feels before them like one of Friedrich or Turner's little men set before a vast empty seascape. The experience is intense, the detail of it undefined, its moral still to be sought. One returns to life more questioning.

Rothko certainly knew Turner's work, and the late, quasi-abstract watercolours of the British Romantic artist certainly resemble Rothko's paintings. Yet while they *look* similar – lack of defined shape, colour released from line, emphasis on light – and cast moods which are similar, the differences should be recognised. Although Turner often ended by creating images which are not immediately interpretable as landscape, he always started from a landscape experience – a sky, a condition of the weather, an effect of the sun. After achieving his mature manner, Rothko's work always began from the *opposite* premise. He wished to avoid any vestige of imitation, eventually even the kind of colour associations mentioned above; he started from abstraction rather than from representation. Nevertheless, there are distinct resemblances in the way that the two artists' work acts on the spectator. In each, there results a mood of contemplation – in Rothko, very often a sense of harmony and tranquillity. Both artists are transcendentalists, although they start from different premises – Turner from this world, Rothko from the abstract world. Rothko was inventing a way of painting abstract concepts, or even thought itself.

Rothko's own words describe his development and his ambitions:

> 'The progression of a painter's work as it travels in time from point to point, will be towards clarity: toward the elimination of all obstacles between the painter and the idea and between the idea and the observer. As examples of such obstacles, I give (among others) memory, history or geometry, which are swamps of generalisation from which one might pull out parodies of ideas (which are ghosts) but never an idea itself.'

The aim is to translate the *idea* to the observer, and to translate a certain *kind* of idea *(Figure 6)*.

> 'I paint very large pictures. I realize that historically the function of painting large pictures is painting something very grandiose and pompous. The reason I paint them, however – I think this applies to other painters I know – is precisely because I want to be very intimate and human.'

Figure 5 (previous page), Black on Maroon, 1958. *Oil on canvas, 266.7 × 365.8 cm (105 × 144 in). Tate Gallery. Gift of the Artist. One of the series of canvases which Rothko was commissioned to paint for the restaurant of the Seagram Building in New York. Rothko gradually revolted against the idea of his paintings acting as a backdrop to rich people over-eating and painted images which might disturb them. For the first time, he turns from lyricism to brooding tragedy.*

Figure 6 (above), Untitled, 1969. *Acrylic on paper 128 × 107.2 cm (50⅜ × 42¼ in). National Gallery of Art, Washington D.C. Gift of the Mark Rothko Foundation. Physically weakened during the two years before his death in 1970, Rothko reduced the size of his pictures and began to use acrylic which dries much quicker than oil. He was thus able to complete works more quickly. His final series display more of the hand of the artist, who used the brush more, rather than staining the canvas. They achieve great directness of effect. 'The progression of a painter's work will be towards clarity'.*

Rothko's statements, taken together with his life, consolidate the view that his abstraction, his *idea*, carries with it a certain morality. Abstract painting exists within a sociological context, exactly as abstract thought (philosophy) does. However void of content it may seem, it is simply that the content is ordered in a different way. It is surprising, for example, how the great mural paintings in the Tate Gallery can carry so much pictorial meaning and can simultaneously illuminate Rothko's *idea* so fully *(Figures 1 and 5)*.

The series originated in 1958 as a commission for the restaurant of the Seagram Building in New York. The work went on for months and resulted in not one, but three, series each with deep maroon backgrounds – the paintings becoming darker in tone and in mood as the execution progressed. They are paintings in the minor key. For the first time Rothko's art turned from lyricism to brooding tragedy. Undoubtedly they reflect the artist's state of mind at the time and, in retrospect, seem to prefigure his eventual tragic suicide. Rothko talked of them later,

> 'I realized that I was much influenced subconsciously by Michelangelo's walls in the staircase room of the Medicean Library in Florence . . . he makes the viewers feel trapped in a room where all the doors and windows are bricked up, so that all they can do is butt their heads forever against the wall.'

After accepting the commission, Rothko said, he became revolted by the idea of his paintings acting as a back-drop to rich people over-eating, and found himself painting something which might well disturb their appetites and digestion. In the end, he refused to deliver the pictures and returned the fee. One of the three series he donated to the Tate Gallery, where the installation is one of the most profoundly moving to be seen in any museum in the world. Displayed in rather lower light than normal, the paintings glow with a deep inner light *(Figure 1)*.

Rothko's negative response to the Seagram commission is only one of a number of examples of his feeling that he was at odds with established society. Disagreements with patrons and with museum administrations were frequent. They mirror perhaps the attitudes that led him to join politically active trade unions in the 1930s which he felt to be a step against injustice. Despite this he did not wish his art to be politically motivated. While his art is a-political, it partially results from and expresses an essentially idealistic view of things which eventually evidenced itself in more overtly religious references. In 1962, he adopted the traditionally religious form of the triptych. Later he accepted a commission to create a mural series for a Roman Catholic chapel. This was eventually realised as the interdenominational 'Rothko Chapel' affiliated with the Institute of Religion and Human Development in Houston.

These examples of a fundamentally religious temperament are the less surprising when one remembers that Rothko's favourite painter was Fra Angelico. His method of creation too, is related, his paintings being made in conditions close to meditation. Rothko would sit for hours in front of his canvases considering his next action. The paintings similarly become more rewarding when the spectator contemplates them for a certain length of time, as if they were images of conventional religious subject-matter *(Figure 7)*. They can be viewed in fact as heirs to a tradition of spiritual art that reaches back beyond the dawn of Christianity. They are twentieth-century developments of both landscape *and* religious art . . . 'landscapes of the spirit'.

July 1987

Figure 7, Orange, Red and Red, 1962. *Oil on canvas, 236.2 × 203.2 cm (93 × 80 in). Dallas Museum of Art. Gift of Mr and Mrs Algur H. Meadows and the Meadows Foundation. Painted during the year of Rothko's 59th birthday, this picture almost sums up his achievement to that date. Eight feet high, its physical presence is overpowering and the colour is able to imprint itself on the wholy body. The effect is, eventually, more spiritual than physical, Rothko being heir to a tradition of spiritual art which stretches back beyond Christianity.*

THE ART OF YACHTING

Deborah Scott

Figure 1 *Sir Thomas Sopwith's 'Endeavour', one of the finest of the J class, that came near to winning the America's cup in 1934. Drypoint etching by Rowland Langmaid, about 1934. Signed artists proof. 16.5 × 35 cm (6½ × 14 in).* THE WYLLIE GALLERY *£350 (c US$500)*

As the excitement and publicity of the challenge for the America's Cup focuses unaccustomed attention on the sport of yachting, it kindles an annual interest among collectors in the yacht in art. The history of yachting, or boating for pleasure rather than trade, extends back to the time of Charles II, who developed a taste for it while in exile in the Netherlands. Its popularity increased throughout the 18th century, and the first yacht clubs were formed, amongst them the Cumberland Fleet which engaged in racing on the Thames. The Regency period saw the formation of the Royal Yacht Club (later Squadron) at Cowes, though this was initially devoted less to racing than to social activities. However, the accession of the young Queen Victoria with her interest in yachting and her love for Cowes firmly established the supremacy of the Royal Yacht Squadron there. During her reign innumerable yacht clubs sprang up for 'Gentlemen interested in the sport of Yachting' and racing became increasingly popular. Meanwhile, on the other side of the Atlantic, the New York Yacht Club was formed in 1844, reflecting the rise of interest in yachting, and inspiring great developments in design.

In 1851, spoiling for a challenge, the New York Yacht Club dispatched its new schooner, the America, across the Atlantic. The Royal Yacht Squadron offered a silver ewer worth 100 guineas to the winner of a race around the Isle of Wight which was open to all nations. The story of that race is legend, and the outcome only too well known, as the schooner America became the most famous yacht in history. Accustomed to ruling the waves, this defeat awoke British yachtsmen from their complacency and stimulated many advances in yacht design. Indeed the quest for this trophy has affected the development of racing yachts more than anything else since that first contest over a century ago. *Figure 5* shows this vessel cracking along in a stiff breeze off the Lizard. On her way across the Atlantic she set a record, making the crossing in 20 days and 5 hours.

The clipper bow of the America and her schooner rig were emulated, and her influence was seen amongst many racing yachts of the next 20 years (see *Figure 4*, Egeria). The second half of the 19th century saw great changes in yacht design, not all for the best. The rating rules, by which a yacht was assessed for competitive purposes, encouraged some extraordinary and unstable designs to take to the water. But by the 1890s, a more sensible rule based on water line length and sail area had been adopted and fine large yachts were built.

The enthusiasm of the Prince of Wales, later Edward VII, for yachting was expressed in his famous cutter Britannia, which was a familiar, elegant sight in the Solent around the turn of the century *(Figure 7)*. This was the period of enormous yachts. Britannia was herself 121 ft long, and the largest ever to race for the America's Cup was the Reliance in 1903, the overall length of which was over 143 ft. With a sail area of some 16 000 ft she was a giant amongst yachts, and she and her racing companions of the period inspired many an artist.

Figure 3, Sailing off the Needles, *by R. H. Neville Cumming, gouache, signed and dated 1907. The work of this artist has not been widely renowned, which allows some scope for those who perceive its quality. 42.5 × 63 cm (16¾ × 23¾ in)* OLIVER SWANN *£1800 (c US$2574)*

Figure 2 (above) A Yawl off the Coast, *watercolour by F. Sanderson, signed and dated 1877. This modest example of a 19th century yachting painting is by an unknown artist, and is comparatively inexpensive. 25 × 35 cm (10 × 13¾ in)* THE PARKER GALLERY *£175 (c US$250)*

Racing continued in the interwar years, with the most remarkable yachts being those of the J class. These vessels, with their Bermuda rig (compare to gaff rig, *Figure 3*), and overall length of 120 ft were a splendid and awesome sight *(Figure 1)*. The three 1930s challenges for the America's Cup were sailed in vessels of this class.

Collecting

Unfortunately, the spectacular visual appeal of these splendid yachts from the past is widely appreciated, and this is, therefore, an expensive area for collecting. The works of well known 19th century marine artists – Nicholas Matthew Condy, James Buttersworth, Arthur Fowles and Richard Beechey for example – can command many thousands of pounds. Collectors who

Figure 4 (above) *Watercolour by Charles Taylor the Younger (fl. 1841-83) of racing yachts in Southampton Water in 1870. They are John Mulholland's schooner Egeria, one of the most famous of the schooners that became popular in the 1860s, and Thomas Chamberlaine's cutter Arrow, which dates from much earlier in the century. 56 × 106 cm (22 × 42 in)*
THE PARKER GALLERY
Price in excess of £5000 (c US$7150)

Figure 5 (left) The Old Trail. *The schooner yacht America off the Lizard. Oil on canvas by John Fraser, signed and dated 1913. Although the America continued to exist well after this date, it seems likely that this is a retrospective portrayal. 96 × 170 cm (38 × 67 in)*
N. R. OMELL *£3500 (c US$5005)*

cannot stretch to these prices would do better to concentrate on good quality work by less known artists. Look for signs of quality – the ability to paint water and a yacht's relationship to it, and to portray speed and excitement while maintaining realism.

John Fraser's work *(Figure 5)* has been underestimated, although this is now changing. An artist whose work is good although little is known of him is J. Edmunds who painted at the end of the last century *(Figure 7)*. There are also artists of the 1930s, such as R. Craig Wallace *(Figure 6)*, who are hardly known.

However unsung these artists, one will be lucky to find a good oil painting of a yachting scene for less than £1500, most of the examples mentioned being nearer £3000. To put this in perspective, one should realise that the work of fine modern artists in this field such as Stephen Dews and Tim Thompson can command sums of between £5000 and £10 000.

Watercolours can be acquired for rather less, though again the work of recognised artists *(Figure 4)* can command a premium. If the yachts can be identified, this adds substantially to the price, even of a work by a little known artist. Another factor affecting price is the weather. Surprising as it may seem, storm tossed scenes sell less easily than calm seas and blue skies, all other factors

Figure 6, Yachts Racing on the Clyde, *by Robert Craig Wallace. A Scot based in Glasgow, this artist exhibited between 1929 and 1940, but otherwise little is known of him, though his bold vigorous style of painting is attractive. This painting shows a gaff rigged yawl racing three Bermudan sloops. Oil on canvas. 51 × 76 cm (20 × 30 in). N. R. OMELL About £2500 (c US$3575)*

being equal.

In the more realistic price range, there are simple Victorian watercolours by unknowns, like *Figure 2,* which offer an inexpensive way of starting a collection. Other options are offered by prints, including aquatints, lithographs and etchings. Lithographs by the renowned Victorian artist Thomas Dutton and others from the mid-19th century may be purchased for £500 to over £2000 depending on subject matter. Etchings of yachting scenes by William Lionel Wyllie from the early years of this century now command around £400-£600, (his watercolours and oils very much more, of course). His friend and student Rowland Langmaid did etchings in similar style, though less accomplished, including several of the J class *(Figure 1).* These command £100-£350 depending on subject and source. Chromolithographs are less expensive; for example those by Henry Shields of Clyde Yachts of 1888 may be purchased for under £100. Also under £100 are small engravings, but anything of any size will command higher prices. Spurred on by demand, there is a healthy market for prints reproduced by various photographic methods. These range from sepia copies of early yachting photographs by the famous company of Beken of Cowes (from £10), to photogravures of John Fraser paintings of late 19th century for up to £300. The collector must decide himself whether this latter is money well spent, though the availability of original works, however scarce, for less suggests that it is not.

Modern marine painting deserves attention, since not all commands the sums mentioned above. The Royal Society of Marine Artists holds an exhibition every autumn, of which details may be obtained from the Secretary of the Society in London.

Further Information

Yachting – A History by Peter Heaton, Batsford, 1955.

The Paintings of the America's Cup 1851-1987 by Tim Thompson, text by Ranulf Rayner, David & Charles 1986.

February 1987

Figure 7 (top right) *The Prince of Wales's Yacht Britannia and the American Challenger 'Navahoe' racing for the Brenton Reef Cup. Oil on canvas, by J. Edmunds, signed and dated 1893. 33 × 48 cm (13 × 19 in). N. R. OMELL. About £3500 (c US$5005)*

Figure 8, The International Yacht Race, Cambria passing Sappho off the Isle of Wight, *by William Broome, a Ramsgate painter of the late 19th century. This painting records the 1868 race in which the English yacht Cambria beat the American Sappho, thus encouraging Cambria to make the first challenge for the America's cup in 1870. 61 × 107 cm (24 × 42 in) BONHAMS Sold (1985) for £3800 (c US$5434)*

WILLIAM WESTALL WITH FLINDERS IN AUSTRALIA

Stephen Deuchar

Figure 1, Part of King George III Sound, on the south coast of New Holland, December 1801. *61 × 86.4 cm (24 × 34 in). The drawing on which this was based (National Library, Canberra) shows barren scrubland on the hills near the sea, modified here to suggest verdant vegetation. The two natives and the Eucalpytus tree are derived from sketches taken elsewhere.*

The Admiralty House Picture Collection is perhaps best known for its remarkable group of paintings by William Hodges (1744-97), an individualistic visual interpretation of his voyages with Captain Cook which has been on long-term loan to the National Maritime Museum since the special exhibition of 1979-80. While Hodges' works will justly continue to be on public view at Greenwich, much of the Collection must remain at its original home, Old Admiralty House, a fine late 18th century building in the heart of Whitehall. There, the Maritime Museum has implemented a new picture hanging scheme giving particular prominence to another unusual series of Australasian views – the paintings of William Westall (1781-1850) based on the voyage of investigation led by Matthew Flinders in 1801-3.

While the respective accomplishments of Flinders and Westall are never likely to receive the acclaim enjoyed by their predecessors Cook and Hodges, their story – a curious and in many ways sad one – certainly deserves some notice. It began in 1801, when the explorer and the artist were aged 27 and 20. By then Flinders was a man of some experience: at 16, as he later recalled, he had been 'induced to go to sea . . . from reading *Robinson Crusoe*' and over the following decade his emerging skills as a navigator and hydrographer were put to use in the South Seas by better-known contemporaries such as Captain William Bligh and George Bass. Aboard the *Reliance* off the coast of New South Wales in 1798, his work with Bass led to the discovery and naming of the Bass Strait – an achievement which both nurtured his personal ambitions as an explorer and brought him to the attention of the Admiralty, itself keen to encourage investigative voyages to new tracts of potential empire. In 1801, with Britain and France at war in Europe and vying for commercial and territorial gain elsewhere, Flinders' proposal to lead an expedition to survey and chart the north, south and east coasts of 'New Holland' (Australia) was willingly received by the Admiralty and was even offered financial assistance by the British East India Company.

Whatever its political and economic overtones, the liberally funded expedition was conceived by Flinders himself essentially as a scientific one. Having secured from the navy the *Xenaphon,* a 334-ton sloop which was re-fitted and re-named the *Investigator*, he gathered together a group of 'scientific gentlemen' recommended by Sir Joseph Banks. Among them were two artists. One, Ferdinand Bauer, was a natural history painter whose role would be to record any botanical discoveries made; the other, Westall, was hired to act firstly as a topographer of coastal scenery and secondly as a kind of visual publicist of the expected achievements of the expedition. The job had come to Westall, an inexperienced and apparently temperamental student at the Royal Academy, purely by default. William Daniell, already a respected topographer of Indian scenery, had been the first choice – but having initially accepted he then withdrew after becoming engaged to Mary Westall. It was evidently he, with the influential support of Benjamin West PRA, who suggested his future brother-in-law as a replacement. Flinders, himself about to marry, seems to have been both surprised by Daniell's decision and disappointed with his proposed substitute; Westall was a youth, he reflected, whose 'foolish days are not yet passed', and only in the absence of an alternative did he agree to include him in the expedition. Westall, excited by the prospect of finding and recording the kind of exotic scenery which had brought fame to Hodges and Daniell, duly signed a contract with the Admiralty, undertaking nonetheless to defer to Flinders' opinion as to which subjects were 'most fitting to be delineated'.

The *Investigator* sailed from Spithead on 18 July 1801, and after an eventful voyage via Madeira (where Westall fell overboard, an incident which allegedly 'affected . . . his Head') arrived off the south-west coast of Australia at King George's Sound (*Figure 1*) on 8 December. The following six months were devoted to surveying in minute detail the whole of the south and south-east coasts – and their islands – up to Port Jackson (Sydney), an undertaking never before attempted. The drawings taken by Westall on this part of the journey provided the basis for the later paintings illustrated here in *Figures 2, 3, 8 & 9*. The *Investigator* was re-fitted in Port Jackson during June and July 1802 whilst the crew recovered from the rigours of their work: it may have been some relief to Westall and his companions to escape from the rigid discipline exercised by Flinders (amongst his eccentricities was an unswerving insistence on twice-weekly shaving on Thursdays and Sundays) and the dietary restrictions of life on board (pease soup was the staple for four meals out of seven). Part two of the voyage, beginning in late July 1802, was devoted to surveying the east, north-east, and north coasts (*Figures 5-7*), a still more arduous project which ended with the *Investigator* limping back to Port Jackson in June 1803, where, leaking badly, she was deemed unfit for further service. The zealous Flinders nevertheless determined to return to England to raise funds to renew the expedition, and, in company with Westall and other crew members, set out as a passenger on the *Porpoise,* bound for home in convoy with the *Bridgewater* and the *Cato*.

After only seven days at sea, disaster struck. The *Cato* and the *Porpoise* were wrecked on a reef in the Coral Sea, and the *Bridgewater,* inexplicably and controversially, sailed on without searching for survivors. All but a few of the passengers and crew had in fact reached safety, swimming to a low sandy island, retrieving much of the stores and equipment from the *Porpoise,* and establishing a makeshift camp (*Figure 4*). Flinders took charge, and set off for help in a small cutter, leaving Westall (whose

Figure 2, Entrance to Port Lincoln from behind Memory Cove, February 1802. *61.6 × 87 cm ($24\frac{1}{4} \times 34\frac{1}{4}$ in). Exhibited at the RA in 1812, this is an interpretation of a drawing dated 23 February.*

Figure 3, View on the north side of Kanguroo Island, March 1802. *62 × 86.4 cm ($24\frac{1}{2} \times 34$ in). The kangaroos discovered on this island near Cape Spencer were viewed by the crew of the* Investigator *not so much as objects of scientific or artistic interest but as food for slaughter. 'In gratitude for so reasonable a supply', wrote Flinders, 'I named this southern land KANGUROO ISLAND'. Westall seems to have painted the animals from memory; the composition relates closely to a sketch of seals in the same setting.*

sketches were 'wetted and partly destroyed') and his marooned companions, 'much oppressed with fatigue', to await rescue some weeks later. Though help did arrive, Westall's patience with Flinders was exhausted, and once back on dry land he wrote to Banks to express his deep dissatisfaction with this 'hazardous voyage'. Not only had his life been endangered but he claimed to have been profoundly unimpressed with the artistic possibilities of 'the barren coast of New Holland'. He had found in it none of the fashionably 'picturesque' qualities through which he had hoped to make his name, and he begged to go now to India, Ceylon and China, which he believed would be more fertile. Though he was subsequently given permission to do this (on the condition that he sent the Australian drawings directly to the Admiralty) Banks was keen that he should eventually produce some publicly exhibitable oil paintings based on Flinders' enterprise. On Westall's return to England Banks managed to persuade the Admiralty – now less than enamoured with the difficult artist and faintly embarrassed by Flinders, who had been arrested and imprisoned in Mauritius on suspicion of spying – to commission a set of Australian views. Westall began in 1809 and, using his sketches for reference, finally produced the series illustrated here.

A comparison between the topographical drawings (most are now in the care of the National Library, Canberra) and the Admiralty paintings reveals that in the latter Westall aimed to make up for the supposed deficiencies in the landscape itself by 'improving' in oil what he had recorded in pencil. He selected, modified, and repeated motifs which pleased him and rejected those which did not, much as Hodges had done before him. Unlike Hodges, however, he did not attempt to interpret his subject matter through any scholarly (and now outdated) infusion of classicism. Instead, in keeping with the nascent tradition of romanticism in landscape painting (fostered not least by his erstwhile fellow Royal Academy student, John Constable) he wished to persuade the spectator of the bleak, exhilarating, and emotive potential of this unfamiliar land, tempered carefully with a close observation of botanical and atmospheric phenomena. In some instances the result of this conscious formula is both visually unsatisfactory and strangely alluring (e.g. *Figure 9*); in others, notably in *Wreck Reef Bank* (*Figure 4*) he has created truly romantic images of extraordinary poignancy. Certainly, some of the set appealed enough to contemporary taste both to bring him election to associate

Figure 4, Wreck Reef Bank, taken at low water, August 1803. *59.7 × 86.4 cm (23½ × 34 in). 'Mr Westall has represented the corals above water . . . but in reality the tide never leaves any considerable part of them uncovered', wrote the serious Flinders of this most evocative description of the* Porpoise's *and* Cato's *survival camp.*

Figure 5 (top), View of Murray's Islands with the natives offering to barter, October 1802. *61 × 86.4 cm (24 × 34 in). Murray's Islands lie near the north end of the Great Barrier Reef. Flinders' expedition found the natives friendly and commercially-minded. The view was derived from two pencil sketches and a watercolour, the latter reportedly damaged by sheep when drying out after the Wreck Reef catastrophe.*

Figure 6 (below left), View of Sir Edward Pellew's Group, Gulf of Carpentaria, December 1802. *88.9 × 106 cm (35 × 42 in). The bark shelter shown in this view on the north coast contains two decorated stones used by the Aborigines in a totemic ritual which intrigued the crew of the* Investigator.

Figure 7 (below right), View of Malay Bay from Pobassoos Island, February 1803. *61 × 86.4 cm (24 × 34 in). One of Westall's more dramatic evocations of scenery which he claimed to find thoroughly uninspiring.*

Figure 8 (left), Bay on the south coast of New Holland, January 1802. *61.6 × 87.6 cm (24¼ × 34½ in). The* Investigator *is shown in Lucky bay, so named by Flinders after his lengthy search on 9 January for a safe sheltering place in which to anchor. The painting is based on a drawing dated 10 January.*

Figure 9 (below), View of Cape Townshend and the Islands in Shoal Water Bay, taken from Mount Westall, March 1802. *134 × 157 cm (53 × 62 in). The Cape was named by Captain Cook after Charles Townshend, a lord of the Admiralty, 1765-1770. 'The view was . . . most extensive from this hill', recorded Flinders, 'and in compliment to the landscape painter I named it* Mount Westall.'

membership of the Royal Academy in 1812 and to be engraved as illustrative plates to Flinders' official account of the expedition, the rather turgid *A Voyage to Terra Australis,* published in 1814.

Flinders himself, released from detention as late as 1810, died shortly before his book was published, having earnestly hoped – not entirely in vain – that his account would establish his place in the annals of maritime history. Westall's long-term reputation was less secure. Some critics thought that his romanticised Australian views were visually dishonest and casually painted – a predictable charge in view of his open disenchantment with the raw material he had worked from – and, perhaps in response, he subsequently painted an uninspiring series of English landscapes in a more strictly topographical vein. His later career was always overshadowed by that of his rather more successful elder half-brother Richard, and also by bouts of mental illness; Richard lamented William's occasional brain fevers (allegedly the consequence of 'inattention to diet' on the Australian voyage) during which 'he acts like an insane man giving his money away and doing many irregular things'. But whatever the trauma – artistic and emotional – occasioned by Flinders' expedition, later in life Westall was to return repeatedly to Australian subject matter, dying, it is said, whilst working on a new interpretation of his most haunting composition of all, *Wreck Reef Bank.*

Bibliography

The principal source for the journey and paintings is Matthew Flinders, *A Voyage to Terra Australis,* 1814. There is a wealth of useful information in T. M. Perry and D. H. Simpson, *Drawings by William Westall,* 1962, and an exhaustive biography of the artist in R. J. Westall, 'The Westall Brothers', *Turner Studies,* vol. 4, no. 1, pp 23-38.

Note

The reception rooms at Old Admiralty House, used frequently for Government functions, are not normally available to public view. Scholars or researchers with a specialist interest may, however, arrange to see specified pictures from the Admiralty House Collection by contacting the National Maritime Museum, London.

THE PAINTINGS OF HEYWOOD HARDY

Brian Stewart and Mervyn Cutten

Heywood Hardy, the distinguished portrait, animal and sporting artist, is largely remembered for his colourful genre paintings, which are now so sought after that they can command five figure sums in commercial galleries and at auction. Despite the undoubted popularity of his work little was known about the life and personality of the artist. Recent research has, however, uncovered fresh information.

Heywood Hardy was born in Chichester, West Sussex on the 25 November 1842. He was the youngest of six children of the artist James Hardy senior and Elizabeth (née Vinson). Heywood's elder brothers James Hardy junior and David Hardy were also painters, while his cousin, Frederick Daniel Hardy, was a leading member of the Cranbrook Colony of artists.

When Heywood was a small boy the Hardy family left their residence at 55 Westgate, Chichester and moved to Bath. All their possessions were piled onto a farm cart and they set off at walking pace across country. The journey took four days and they camped, much to Heywood's delight, by the roadside at night.

At Bath Heywood's father earned a living by painting portraits and landscapes. James was, however, a difficult man, as his granddaughter Madeleine testified: 'Originally his taste was towards music and he became chief trumpeter to George IV. Failing to obtain his way in some little adventure in his profession, one day in a fit of temper, of which he had an abundance, he threw the trumpet to the ground, stamped on it and made a vow to earn his living by portrait painting. For his new venture in life he was lucky to obtain an extensive and wealthy patronage, chiefly in Bath and for a number of years was in great respect. In his later years however, he gradually lost the patronage he obtained, by developing a religious mania, obtruding his views in an irritating manner upon his patrons in private,

Figure 1, Heywood Hardy. *Photograph courtesy of C. Ivens.*

Figure 2 (opposite top), The Refreshment. *One of a pair. 50.8 × 6.2 cm (20 × 30 in). Richard Green Galleries.*

Figure 3 (opposite below), A Meeting by the Stile. *61 × 86.4 cm (24 × 34 in). Richard Green Galleries.*

and upon the public in general by preaching at street corners whenever the opportunity occurred.'

It was his father's quarrelsome nature that led Heywood to leave home at 17. After a furious argument the young artist moved to Keynsham, where he attempted to earn a living by painting animal pictures. This he was unable to do and after a short time in the 7th Somerset Volunteers, he borrowed some money from his older brother James, and in 1864 travelled to Paris where he entered the Beaux Arts to study under the battle artist, Pielse.

At this stage of his career, life was extremely difficult. He lived a fairly impoverished existence and most of his spare time was spent copying pictures in the Louvre, and eating in cheap soup restaurants called 'bouillons'. Eventually he left the Beaux Arts and joined a private atelier run by an artist called Coreine. At this time he shared a studio/apartment with two friends and their lives were brightened from time to time by dabbling in the occult with the help of a visiting medium. However, the political situation in France became more difficult, and before the outbreak of war with Prussia, Heywood left Paris for Antwerp where he continued to copy pictures in the art galleries.

He returned to England some time before 1868, where

Figure 4 (above), An American Coaching Scene. *44.4 × 82.4 cm (17½ × 13½ in). Christie's.*

Figure 5 (below), An Anxious Moment, *1872. 54.6 × 105.4 cm (21½ × 41½ in). Christie's.*

Figure 6 (opposite top), The Night Coach. *50.8 × 76.2 cm (20 × 30 in). Richard Green Galleries.*

Figure 7 (opposite below), The Cast Shoe, *1917. 50.8 × 6.2 cm (20 × 30 in). Richard Green Galleries.*

he was often invited to country estates to paint portraits, sporting pictures and animal studies. Among his distinguished patrons were Colonel Wyndham Murray, the Marquis of Zetland and the Sitwells of Renishaw. As a young man he was a keen sportsman and while carrying out such commissions he would often accept an invitation to go shooting on the estate. On one such occasion in Ireland he wounded a hare. As he went to pick up the animal he had the impression that it looked at him with imploring eyes, tears trickling down its face. He was so moved by this that he never shot again. He sold his gun and instead purchased field glasses.

Heywood continued to enjoy commissions for portraits, animal studies and hunting scenes. However he gradually concentrated on painting genre works which he exhibited at most of the major galleries including the Royal Academy, The British Institution, The Royal Society of British Artists and the Old Watercolour Society. He also provided illustrations for magazines such as *The Illustrated London News* and *The Graphic,* as well as producing etchings of his work published by the leading print sellers of his day.

On the 30 June 1868 Heywood married Mary, youngest daughter of Admiral F. W. Beechey. She was the grand-daughter of the artist Sir William Beechey, court painter to Queen Charlotte and friend of Nelson. Heywood and Mary set up home in the High Street of Goring, Oxfordshire, in the house that later became the pub called 'The Miller of Mansfield'. They had four daughters. Their third daughter, Mabel, married the brother of author Somerset Maugham.

In 1870 Heywood and his family moved to St. John's Wood, London – an area noted for its artists. For a short time he shared a studio with Briton Riviere, and among his close neighbours were the artists William Frederick Yeames RA, George Dunlop Leslie RA, Philip Hermogenes Calderon and James Tissot. He was also a friend of such eminent artists as John Singer Sargeant, Lawrence Alma Tadema, J. E. Millais and James McNeil Whistler. During this period his career flourished and he was elected a member of a number of societies including The Royal Society of Painters and Etchers, The Royal Institute of Oil Painters and The Royal Society of Portrait Painters.

He became successful enough to afford a nurse and three domestic servants. However, his marriage to Mary was not a success. She was considered a very strong minded person and difficult to live with. After 36 years of marriage the couple decided to live separate lives. She moved to Elgin Avenue, Maida Vale, while he kept his studio at St. John's Wood.

Heywood's grand-daughter Clarisse Farrell remembers looking forward to her visits to his studio in St. John's Wood, where she and the other children would play in the garden:

'He was such a lovely person and used to keep us all amused by drawing pictures of animals and dragons. He had a good sense of humour, was kind, intelligent, thoughtful and understanding. He was always good with children, was very fond of animals, and enjoyed reading, writing and music. Indeed he was a wonderful man and charming in every way – we all adored him. My mother and her sisters were devoted to him.'

Mr Carl Ivens also remembers his grand-father with fondness:

'You might think it would have been rather dull for a small boy like myself to spend summer holidays in an old gentleman's house, but in fact he was great fun and always

Figure 8, In the Lap of Luxury, *1880. 34 × 24 cm (13½ × 9½ in).*
Roy Miles Fine Paintings.

ready for a walk or an adventure. He loved cowboy films. He used to say to me "If we set off early we shall just have time to have a cup of tea and see another film before the bus returns home." He said he visited the cinema to study the movements of the horses, but we all knew he loved the shooting in cowboy films as much as we did. He was fascinated by the Wild West, and used to buy large quantities of Cowboy magazines, which he piled up on a small table by the fireside chair. He was also a good musician and played the Austrian zither and the guitar. He encouraged us with his enthusiasm to take up the guitar and the mandolin, and evenings at his house often rang with the sound of the family orchestra playing old music hall songs and popular French tunes.'

In 1909 Heywood moved to West Sussex, where he lived at the Rosery in East Preston (now The Forge Restaurant). At the age of 83 he painted the first of a series of eight panels depicting biblical scenes for the chancel of Clymping Church, to mark its 700th anniversary in 1925. He painted the pictures as a free gift for the church, partly for his old friend Canon E. F. Leach who was incumbent at the time, and partly as a memorial to himself. At the time these panels caused considerable controversy as they depicted Christ walking in the Downs and farmlands of Sussex, amidst modern figures, said to be portraits of residents from the village. The panels represent apathy, poverty, power, innocence and gaiety, and can still be seen in the church.

On the 20 January 1933, at the age of 90, Heywood passed away while staying with his daughter Mrs Ruth Curtis at South Lodge, Woodcote Road, Epsom. He was cremated and his ashes were buried at Clymping Church.

Figure 9, Lost on the Sands. *37 × 27 cm (94 × 68.6 in). Christie's.*

Collecting

In this uncertain economic climate many businessmen are becoming reluctant to place much capital in the city. Turning to art as a form of investment, there is little doubt that the consistent popularity of Hardy's paintings will appeal to investors, for it seems reasonably certain that his paintings will continue to rise steadily in price in the foreseeable future.

Small studies, and less significant works can be purchased for as little as £500. Examples of his genre paintings frequently appear at auction and in galleries and range in price from £7000 to £25 000 according to quality and composition. Those works painted in his characteristic bright, clear colouring seem to be the most popular. However, the collector should avoid works where the paint surface has worn thin, and only purchase paintings in good condition.

In recent years few examples of his more ambitious sporting pictures have appeared on the open market, but the price of such works have undoubtedly increased along with the current rise in prices of most British Sporting Art. Indeed, one of Heywood Hardy's sporting paintings recently fetched at Christie's an impressive £62 640.

August 1986

PORTRAITS OF PEDIGREE LIVESTOCK

Amanda Kavanagh

Historic portraits of prize pedigree livestock are now almost as extinct as the breeds they portray. Prompted by the agrarian revolution and the first scientific breeding of improved livestock during the late 18th century and early 19th century, these rare portraits record the remarkable shapes, sizes and colours of these new breeds. The same disproportionate dimensions which thrilled the original owners of these animals as a sign of agricultural advance, now delight the aesthete for their decorative effects.

A tradition for animal portraiture, particularly horses and hounds, had been well established by a school of professional sporting artists, such as Ben Marshall, George Stubbs, Thomas Bewick and James Ward, already *au-fait* with the pride and joy that owners invested in their animals. It is perhaps of no surprise to learn that a greater profit was reaped by the average sporting painter than human portraitist, a fact realised by Ben Marshall, who discovered 'many a man who will pay me 50 guineas for painting his horse, who thinks 2 guineas too much for painting his wife'.

Although the first artists to be consulted were those connected with sporting art, livestock portraiture was to

Figure 1. The Old Fashioned Breed of Chinese Pig *by James Clark (active 1858-1909), about 1890. 35.6 × 45.1 cm (14 × 17¾ in).*

become the almost exclusive domain of the itinerant, amateur artist. The strikingly naive and humorous qualities of these works, for which they are now sought, deprived them of any scholarly significance. No attempts were therefore made to salvage such art from the attic and devoid of an academic pedigree, these portraits were allowed to perish.

It was the practical demands of livestock breeders that gave rise to this genre of painting, as the only means of illustrating their innovations in this field. These breeders soon realised that their new ventures required publicity, and portraits of these improved livestock proved the most effective way of advertising their work. Such portraits, immediate in their visual impact, appealed not only to the educated, but to the illiterate, who were unable to glean from words alone the new appearance and distinguishing qualities of these beasts. Unlike all other aspects of amateur art, these are the only naive works to have been painted for a particular purpose.

One of the objects of improved breeding was to increase the amount of fat in an animal, and artists were required to record these new pedigree livestock, prized for their grotesque proportions. Gillray's engraving, depicting *The Duke of Bedford Admiring Another Triumph of Selective Breeding* caricatures this craze for indiscriminate fattening *(Figure 4)*. As first president of the Smithfield Club, and a member of the Original Board of Agriculture, the Duke of Bedford was renowned for his agricultural accomplishments, and his ability to breed fat cattle and sheep on his model farm at Woburn.

Such prints suggest the political significance of this farming phenomenon, a fact that the great brewer and politician Samuel Whitbread II noted: 'the great agriculturalists are almost without exception, real friends of Liberty and Reform.' (In a letter from Whitbread to Thomas Creevey, quoted by Roger Fulford in *Samuel Whitbread: A Study in Opposition*, 1967, p. 223.) Closely akin to agricultural advance was national prosperity and political reform, and parliamentarians such as Whitbread began publicly to liken progressive farming to the Whig's campaign for parliamentary reform. 'Sold' as a 'democratic' concept, it was a means of 'contributing to the increase of human sustenance . . . endeavouring to improve the cultivation of the earth . . . to raise food sufficient for the support of the people.' (See *Samuel Whitbread II 1764-1815 and British Art* by Stephen Deuchar, Museum of London, 1984, p. 223.) Fully aware that agricultural improvement was considered an act of social benevolence and philanthropy, statesmen and landowners such as the Duke of Bedford and the MP Thomas Coke of Norfolk, chose to be portrayed amidst farmyard scenes, as part of their political propaganda.

The degree of artistic verisimilitude in these images of livestock is often disputed. Usually these portraits were genuine pictorial proof of the dimensions of the beast, but it was not beyond the client to commission a

Figure 2 (opposite top). The Craven Heiffer, about 1811-12, bred by the Rev William Carr of Bolton for William Spencer Duke of Devonshire *by an unknown artist.*
55.9 × 66 cm (22 × 26 in).

Figure 3 (opposite below), The White Shorthorn Heiffer bred and fed by Mr Robert Colling *after Thomas Weaver (1774-1843), about 1840.*
50.8 × 66 cm (20 × 26 in).

Figure 4 (above). The Duke of Bedford Admiring Another Triumph of Selective Breeding *by James Gillray (1756-1815). Engraving, published 16 January 1802 by H. Humphrey, 27 St James's Street. 34.3 × 24 cm (13⅝ × 9⅞ in). Photograph by Douglas Smith, by courtesy of the British Museum, Department of Prints and Drawings.*

certain exaggeration of features to conform with the current fashion for fat! Thomas Bewick in his *Memoirs*, 1862 (pp. 183-4), recalls such a request made by a breeder at Barmpton, whose sheep and cattle he had been asked to draw '. . . I objected to put lumps of fat here and there where I could not see it, at least, not in so exaggerated a way . . . but the animals were to be figured monstrously fat before the owners of them could be pleased.'

Particularly outstanding livestock were not merely painted but publicly exhibited, and spent much of their life touring the country and providing a profitable spectacle in market towns. Such was the case with the Yorkshire Hog, which weighed 1344 pounds 'and would feed to a much greater weight were he not raised up so often to exhibit his stature.' (Quoted from a print in the Rothamsted collection. See *A Record of the Rothamsted Collection* by D. H. Boalch, 1958, p. XVII, print no. 163, illus. XXVIII.) Most admired of such animals was the *White Shorthorn Heiffer*, painted by Thomas Weaver and bred by Robert Colling *(Figure 3)*, *The Durham Ox*, painted by John Boultbee and bred by Charles Colling, and *The Lincolnshire Ox* painted by George Stubbs and bred and owned by John Gibbons *(Figure 8)*. The latter was brought to London in 1790 and exhibited by permission of HRH The Duke of Gloucester at his riding house in Hyde Park, and then at the Lyceum in the Strand. Due to the popularity of such pedigree, engravings were made after the paintings, effecting a still more widespread publicity campaign.

Professional painters such as George Stubbs seldom worked entirely in this field, and it was artists of a more amateur nature, who were exclusively employed by the pioneers of husbandry. The self-taught Thomas Weaver of Shropshire was such a man, whose career was spent travelling from farm to farm painting livestock. By attracting the patronage of such eminent figures as the MP Thomas Coke of Norfolk, famed for his Southdown Sheep, and the Earl of Leicester, he established his reputation and was able to secure his livelihood by painting animals and proud owners of a less distinguished nature, as seen in *Mr Freestone and his Sheep (Figure 7)*.

Varieties of local livestock differed in their capacity for improvement, and portraits often served as a simple pictorial progress report and a yardstick for future ideals. Shorthorns were perhaps most frequently depicted, for they proved particularly satisfactory in terms of experimentation and evolution. According to the great breeder George Culley, Shorthorns were to be found 'from the southern extremity of Lincolnshire to the borders of Scotland' (see *Animals on the Farm, Their History From Earliest Times to the Present Day* by Judy Urquhart, Macdonald, 1983, p. 96.) and were known by such different names as the Yorkshire, Durham, Teeswater and Craven *(Figure 2)*.

Foreign livestock was also popular with the pioneers of selective eugenics who believed that by blending new specimens with original British breeds, they could raise superior stock. With pig breeding this method was most successful and with the arrival of the *Chinese Pig*, immediate improvements occurred *(Figure 1)*. It is generally accepted that the Chinese pig arrived in Britain around 1770-80. Various varieties of the Oriental pig, closely related to the Chinese pig originally hailed from the Far East and first began to make their way to Europe during the late 17th century. Rotund with prick ears and a black coat suited to the oriental clime, the Chinese Pig was prized as a domestic animal for its ability to live in confined space and produce large quantities of meat. It was this particular cross of the New Chinese with the Old English, that began the systematic breeding of smaller, fatter pigs. Colour prejudice was a cause of concern however, especially amongst those with a fastidious palette. They objected to black pigs because they blued their meat, and preferred more traditional white pigs *(Figure 5)*, which left the meat untainted!

Specialisation in poultry breeding was slightly slower in taking off, but aided by Bonnington Moubray's *Practical Treatise on Breeding, Rearing and Fattening all Kinds of Domestic Poultry*, 1815, the new methods of farming were likewise applied to fowl. The practice of poultry breeding was further enlivened by a demand for 'fancy' birds, and those favoured for their more exotic points and patterned plumage had to be found and imported from abroad. Such was the case with the *Black Spanish Hen (Figure 6)*, an ancient black feathered, red combed breed, which, scanty and dry in flesh, was redeemed by its prolific laying of large and white shelled eggs. Gradually, a cult for chickens gripped the country, and poultry shows became one of the more fashionable events which filled the social calendar, 'honoured by the patronage of Lords and Ladies . . . Earls, Marquises and Dukes, all of whom shared in the glory of the exhibition and on the day of the sale, competed for the possession of the meritorious bird.' (See Judy Urquhart's book, mentioned earlier, p. 10.)

The political and social significance of such events was typified by the annual sheep shearing festival founded in 1797 by the Duke of Bedford. In an atmosphere ostensibly devoid of class distinction, peers and peasants, scientists and statesmen, were likewise united by their interest in farming. Indeed the agrarian revolution enlisted the interest of all sectors of society and for many laymen,

Figure 5, A Middle White Pig *by R. Whitford (active 1854-about 1887), 1882. 35.6 × 114 cm (14 × 18 in).*

Figure 6, Black Spanish Hen *by George B. Newmarch (active 1828-about 1873), 1857. 50.8 × 61 cm (20 × 24 in).*

2 Shear
4 Shear
6 Shear
bred by Mr. Freestone

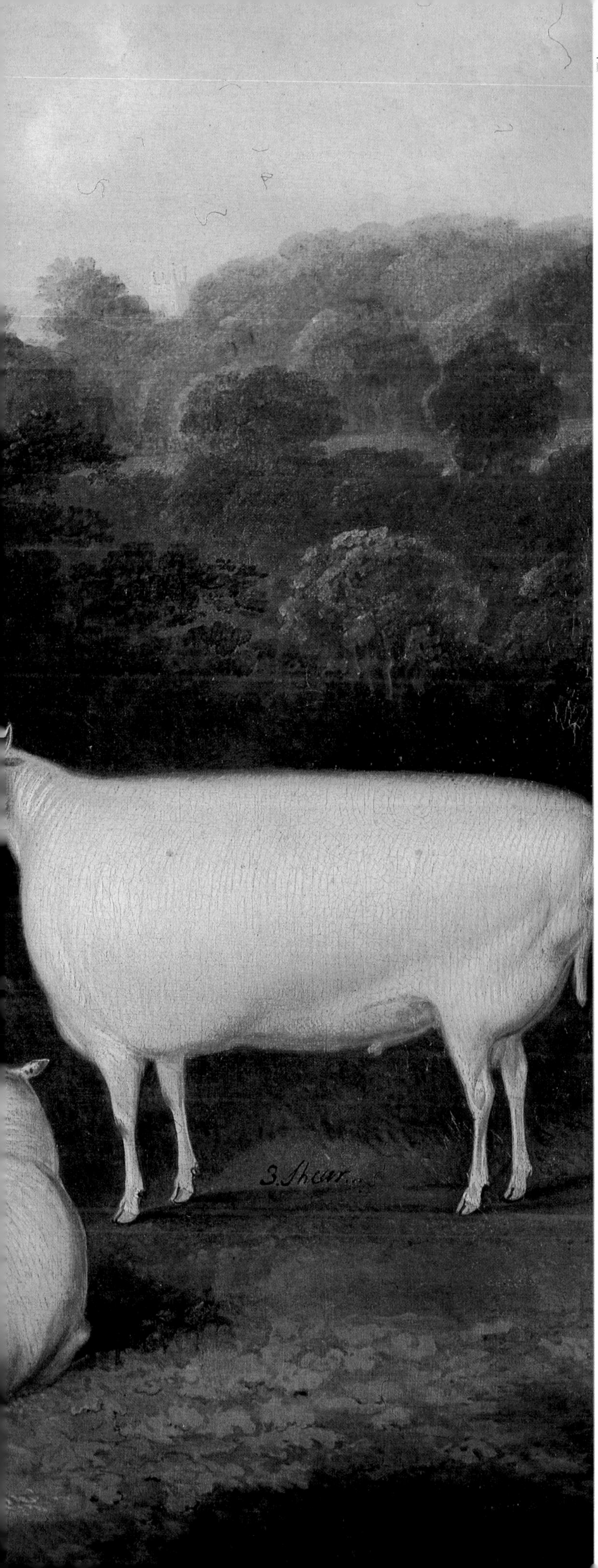

Figure 7, Mr Freestone and his Sheep *by Thomas Weaver 1824. 71.1 × 92.1 cm (28 × 36¼ in).*
Figure 8, The Lincolnshire Ox bred and owned by John Gibbons *by George Stubbs (1724-1806), 1790. 66 × 96.5 cm (26 × 38 in). Walker Art Gallery, Liverpool.*
Unless otherwise indicated the paintings are in a private collection.

farming assumed the importance of an industry rather than the relief of an idle pastime. As Young remarked 'the farming tribe is now made up of all ranks, from a duke to an apprentice.' (Walker's Quarterly, *British Farm Animals in Prints and Paintings,* by Walter Shaw Sparrow, 1932, p. 10.)

Such was the new found enthusiasm for agricultural progress and in particular, for the scientific breeding of improved livestock, which fostered this new genre of animal painting. Commissioned by the pioneers of agricultural progress, these works were painted specifically to secure a market for their new stock. Subject rather than style was the issue most at stake, and consequently these portraits were painted primarily by provincial, itinerant artists, immediately at hand. Dictated by topical relevance rather than artistic merit, these images were abandoned after their immediate appeal. The recent revival of interest in this subject and the new admiration for these works, resides in a realisation of their artistic importance; these valuable and precious portraits of livestock are an aesthetic tribute to their time, and epitomise the essence of English animal art.

Collecting

Portraits of prize pedigree livestock have become extremely scarce and prices vary considerably depending upon quality, size and rarity. They range approximately from £1000-£15 000. Portraits of prize pedigree pigs are particularly rare and therefore tend to be the most expensive.

ISLE OF WIGHT SCENERY

Robin McInnes

Figure 1 (above), Osborne House *by Alfred Brannon (1849). (24.5 × 17 cm) (9¾ × 6¾ in). This view of the newly completed Osborne House, Queen Victoria's Summer Palace, was dedicated to the Prince Consort and shows the remarkable quality of steel engraving achieved by the Brannon family in later years.*

Figure 2. The Old Undercliff Road near Chad's Rock *by George James Knox, 1866, 47 × 16.5 cm (18½ × 6½ in). The rock originally projected from the cliffs above overhanging the road. The Authorities decided it was a potential danger and blew it up whereupon it fell into the centre of the road and a new section of carriageway was constructed around it. In 1928 a great landslide swept this picturesque road away. The Author.*

Figure 3, Wheeler's Bay *between Ventnor and Bonchurch by George James Knox, Circa 1850 50 × 23 cm (20 × 9 in). Modern sea defences have completely changed the character of this area. The Author.*

Figure 4, Ventnor from Flowers Brook *by William Wells Quartremain, 1900 45 × 28 cm (17¾ × 11¼ in). This view and Figure 8 show contrasting impressions of Ventnor through the eyes of two late Victorian illustrators. The Author.*

The Isle of Wight has been a popular venue for artists since the late 18th century when early travellers such as Tomkins, Hassall, Rowlandson and Nixon came on riding tours in search of the picturesque scenery. However, it was the decision of the young Queen Victoria to build her summer palace at Osborne near East Cowes on the north-east coast of the Isle of Wight that was a major factor in the development of the Island as a fashionable holiday resort and spa; this in turn encouraged increased interest in the Island by Victorian artists. One hundred and fifty years ago Queen Victoria came to the throne and this anniversary is an appropriate occasion to consider the variety and quality of paintings executed during her reign.

The great variety of scenery within the small area of the Isle of Wight has always been its attraction and every part of the Island was painted. In the early 19th century artists found suitably picturesque subjects in the ruined ramparts of Carisbrooke Castle, the high cliffs of Freshwater and The Needles and the wildness of the southern coast. The varied coastal scenery with the shoreline activities of fisherfolk were also popular subjects and a succession of eminent marine painters including R. P. Bonington, and Clarkson Stanfield took seaside cottages at Bonchurch near Ventnor to paint just such scenes. Their stay on the Island was more agreeable than that of their predecessor George Morland who was arrested in Yarmouth as a French spy, apparently the Militia had mistaken his sketch of a spaniel in a pastoral landscape for a map of the Isle of Wight! He was forcemarched to Newport where the Bench, after lengthy scrutiny of his drawing, released him with a warning against doing any more drawings whilst hostilities continued with France. Fortunately he ignored their advice and went on to complete many excellent scenes around the Island coast.

The young Princess Victoria first visited the Island with her mother in the late 1820s when she stayed at the historic Sandrock Hotel at Niton on the southern coast. It is believed that this introduction to the Isle of Wight delighted her so much that when the idea came to her of a country retreat away from the pressures of state in London then the Isle of Wight was her obvious choice. Some thirty years earlier J. M. W. Turner had also enjoyed the Island scenery particularly of the Undercliff between Niton and Ventnor – recording it in his sketchbook (Number TB XX14). A number of these sketches were intended to be worked up into full watercolours and to be sold on commission whilst others were drawn for Landseer for his book 'Views in the Isle of Wight'.

After her wedding to Albert in 1840 the couple travelled to the Isle of Wight and chose to purchase the secluded Osborne Estate near East Cowes. With its fine position overlooking The Solent always busy with shipping, the site was a delight to Albert who was a keen sailor. The existing house was demolished and the talented Albert drafted plans for the new Italianate villa in splendidly landscaped grounds; the Palace being occupied by the Royal Couple in September 1846. The Royal presence on the Island coincided with other factors which led to a rapid expansion of the area as a spa and resort. The fashion for sea bathing, the proclamation that the climate of the southern coast was beneficial for health, improved communications and the popularity of yacht racing at Cowes all led to an influx of the wealthy, the famous and the artistic. Anne Thackeray, the daughter of the famous author, was once heard to declare 'Everyone in Freshwater is either a genius, or a poet or peculiar in some other way'! This remark related to the presence of Alfred Lord Tennyson, the Poet Laureate, who lived at Farringford in Freshwater and who was surrounded by a wealth of artistic talent and an entourage of admirers. One close neighbour of Tennyson was the famous artist George Frederick Watts as was his friend Valentine Cameron Princep.

A regular visitor to Farringford and Freshwater was Helen Allingham who painted many works on the Island. In 1874 Miss Paterson (as she was then) married William Allingham the poet, who was a close friend of Carlyle. Carlyle had taken a house on the Island for several seasons and may have told Helen of the beauties of the area whilst sitting for portraits by her in watercolour. Helen had in addition also resided in Lymington for a while – the point of embarkation for passengers to the West Wight.

Helen first visited Farringford in 1890 when she painted *The Dairy* and *Cottages at Pound Green* as well as a number of other views on the Tennyson estate. These are illustrated in her book *Happy England* which was published in 1903. During the closing years of Queen Victoria's reign Mrs Allingham took regular holidays on the Island and on at least one occasion Myles Birket Foster accompanied her. He painted some exquisite watercolours in the West Wight including a charming view of children on the cliff tops above Freshwater Bay.

To many people the Isle of Wight is synonymous with Cowes Week and yachting in The Solent. Sailing was popularised at Cowes following a visit by the Duke of Gloucester in 1813 and a club was formed by Hon Charles Pelham who later became Earl of Yarborough and First Commodore of what became The Royal Yacht Squadron. These were the days of the great yachts like Earl Yarborough's *Falcon* which was often to be seen anchored off St. Lawrence on the south coast when he took visitors and Royalty ashore to his Marine Villa.

As a subject for painting both yachting and local fishermen at work against the backdrop of the Island's magnificent coastal scenery provided the source of inspiration for many celebrated artists. Apart from yacht portraits which were in great demand, artists such as J. W.

Figure 5, Shanklin Chine from the Sea *by Harriet Gouldsmith (circa 1834), 66 × 61 cm (26 × 24 in). Miss Gouldsmith exhibited 14 works at major London exhibitions between 1826-1840 and in almost every case they were of her favourite subject, Fisherfolk at work along the shores of the Island southern coast. The Author.*

Figure 6, Shipping off The Needles *by Thomas Sewell Robins, 1851 43 × 35 cm (17 × 14 in). Robins was one of a number of eminent marine painters who portrayed shipping in the choppy Solent waters. Courtesy: Campbell's Picturecraft, Bembridge.*

Geo Gregory 1903

Figure 7, (previous page), Princes Green, Cowes *by George Gregory (circa 1880), 38 × 68.5 cm (15 × 27 in). The yachting off Cowes and the elegance of the parade and Princes Green were favourate subjects for the Island artists, father and son, Charles and George Gregory. Courtesy: Priory Gallery, Bishop's Cleeve.*

Figure 8 (above), Ventnor from the West *by Henry Wimbush 1895 28 × 18 cm (11 × 7 in). Many Wimbush watercolours were destroyed when the Raphael Tuck Repository was bombed in The Blitz. The Author.*

Carmichael, painted such scenes as 'Potting off Osborne'. Edward Duncan, E. W. Cooke and Thomas Sewell Robins *(Figure 6)* also worked on shipping scenes in the often choppy waters of The Solent and Spithead.

An important local artist was Arthur Wellington Fowles who was often to be found painting racing and regatta scenes in The Solent on canvas, usually on a large scale. By contrast his watercolours of similar scenes are surprisingly delicate and detailed. Two other local artists of note were the father and son Charles and George Gregory of Newport *(Figure 7)*. Their work has become much more widely known following research by Denys Brook-Hart in his book 'Marine Painting'. he drew attention to their excellent yachting, coastal and inland scenes around the Island: George also painted a number of Continental town views.

A familiar figure in Cowes towards the end of Victoria's reign was Eduardo De Martino who achieved great popularity with the yachting fraternity. The Queen made him 'Painter in Ordinary' in 1894 and he became official painter to the Royal Yacht Squadron. De Martino was a close friend of the Prince and Princess of Wales and he always accompanied them when they went sailing. In later years his work became in such demand that he commissioned the artist John Fraser to paint for him, providing only the finishing touches and signature himself. In one case he is reported to have only added the ship's flag before signing the work.

Looking at the paintings of the Island as a whole, it is clear which subjects were most popular. Of the 400 or so works exhibited at the principal London exhibitions during the Victorian era the scenery of the Ventnor area, The Undercliff, and Shanklin was most painted accounting for over half the subjects. Of the buildings Carisbrooke Castle was by far the most popular with many famous artists including J. M. W. Turner painting the view of the gateway with the keep looming behind on its hilltop location. Of the topographic features, The Needles featured regularly as did Shanklin Chine, a narrow and deep wooded gorge cut by the passage of melt waters in Post-Glacial times. The beautiful Undercliff, a six mile long and a quarter mile wide belt of fallen ground along the southern coast also attracted many artists and engravers including Joshua Cristall, who painted several views of the striking cliff line. Of all the painters working locally two names stand out as the most prolific exhibitors of quality works – Alfred Vickers and William Shayer (Senior). Vickers was a London resident who obviously loved the coastline and countryside here because between 1830-1868 he had over thirty such works exhibited (mainly at the RA). His paintings had a distinctive colouring with pale greens prominent and were slightly impressionistic. Overall the effects he achieved were very pleasing. William Shayer, a resident of Southampton, painted over the same timespan but his subjects were usually rustic folk (often gypsies or fishermen) about their work around the coast. His oils are to be found in several art galleries around the country. The fashion for taking a villa for the summer meant that some artists returned annually for often as many as twenty seasons to paint a particular area. Julius Godet, a London painter, visited the Island nearly every year from 1853 until the late 1870's. Another prolific exhibiting artist was Harriet Gouldsmith *(Figure 5)* whose first work appeared in1826. Virtually all her paintings were of the Ventnor and Shanklin area and show lobster fishermen at work and at least sixteen of her exhibited works were of this theme.

One of the finest topographic artists was George James Knox who worked on the Isle of Wight between 1840 and 1866 *(Figures 2 and 3)*. Painting elongated panoramic watercolours of the coast he paid great attention to detail and clearly these views were some of his best works. An artist of a similar calibre was William Gray *(Figure 9)*, a resident of Ryde who moved to Ventnor in the 1850's. His fresh, bright watercolours give a clear picture of Island life in this period of Queen Victoria's reign.

It is of course true that a vast number of topographic works of the Island were produced by unrecorded artists since art and drawing was part of the upbringing of young ladies and gentlemen, thus works of high quality were painted but never exhibited. The hope of finding an album of such works is of course the dream of every collector!

Isle of Wight art cannot be discussed without mentioning George Brannon *(Figure 1)*. At about the time that Daniell was undertaking his coastal voyage, Brannon, a self taught artist and engraver moved to Wootton near Ryde. From his cottage there he produced his book *Vectis Scenary* (Vectis is the Roman name for the I.O.W.) which was published annually from 1820 to 1857 and intermittently until 1875. George Brannon and his sons Alfred and Phillip have probably done more than anyone in the promotion of the Island. Their romantic style views illustrated the changing Island scene over the period of its most rapid development. As well as producing over 160 large plate engravings for *Vectis Scenary* he also published numerous guides for visitors as well as elaborately engraved maps. The Regency architect John Nash was so impressed by Brannon's work that he commissioned six extra-large engravings of East Cowes Castle, his Island seat. Brannon's Isle of Wight Guidebooks with engraved views were the forerunner of a succession of Island books illustrated by artists including Raye, Calvert, Harwood, Westall, the Cooke Brothers and also William Leighton Leitch who was drawing master to the Queen.

Figure 9, Yarmouth, I.O.W. *by William Gray, Circa 1880 (24 × 13½ in). A typically detailed and richly coloured watercolour by this Island artist. Private collection.*

As the Victorian age drew to a close the Island tourist industry reached its zenith. Improvements in the rail and ferry service and the availability of character villa properties for rental encouraged the rich and the artistic to enjoy the benefits of the Island as a change from such familiar resorts as Brighton. Longfellow, Dickens, Carlyle, Karl Marx and the young Winston Churchill were just a few of those who holidayed or convalesced here. By the turn of the century watercolour artists were being commissioned to paint local scenes for use as illustrations for postcards and colour plate guidebooks by firms such as J & F Salmon and Raphael Tuck. Artists including Fanny Minns, A. R. Quinton, E. W. Haslehust, Henry Wimbush *(Figure 8)*, W. W. Quatremain *(Figure 4)* and Alfred Heaton Cooper were prolific in this field.

It is surprising that with this pool of artistic talent a school never developed on the Isle of Wight as at Newlyn, St Ives and Staithes. Despite this the Island artists of Queen Victoria's reign have left us a wealth of paintings and few areas of the country can have their past so delightfully and completely documented.

Photographs: Andy Butler

August 1987

LOUIE BURRELL REDISCOVERED

Daphne Foskett

One seldom has the opportunity of bringing to light the story of an artist, who although highly thought of in her own time, has long since been forgotten.

About a year ago I heard from Miss Philippa Burrell who asked me if I would be interested in seeing some of her mother's work. Since all I knew about Louie Burrell was a short entry in my *Dictionary of British Miniature Painters* I was delighted to make this contact and invited Miss Burrell to stay and bring a selection of her mother's paintings with her. It was an exciting experience as the collection she brought contained fine examples of drawings, watercolours, miniatures, and photographs of oil portraits. It was clear to me that the artist deserved to be better known; hence this article.

Louie (Louise) Burrell née Luker was born in 1873 the elder daughter of the Victorian landscape and genre painter William Luker d. 1906 and his wife Ada Margetts c. 1841–c. 1932, also an artist. Her grandfather Frank Margetts was a well-known designer of stained-glass windows. William Luker came from a Berkshire family who were small country squires, all of whom had some artistic talents. They even formed their own orchestra which flourished in the area. William's ambition, to go to London and set up as a landscape painter was soon achieved and he obtained many commissions. Whilst in London he met Ada Margetts, then only a girl of 18: William was tall and handsome with a golden beard and she fell madly in love with him. Much against her father's wishes they were married and eventually settled at No 22 Campden Hill Square where the family lived for over 50 years.

Figure 1, Miniature of an unknown model, *signed LHL. c. 1900, watercolour on ivory ($3\frac{1}{2}$ in). The Victoria & Albert Museum.*

Figure 2 (opposite), Mrs Stanley Baldwin, *later Countess Baldwin of Bewdley, signed L. BURRELL, c. 1924, watercolour on paper ($12 \times 9\frac{1}{2}$ in). Miss P. Burrell.*

William and Ada had twelve children, of whom only six survived. Ada gave up art after her marriage, but her husband continued to paint and for some time all was well and he had good reviews. Later, however, his sales diminished as the public became bored with constant repetition of paintings of Highland cattle and cows! As in the case with so many artists he found his work no longer in demand and the family became first disillusioned and eventually poverty stricken.

When Louie showed signs of wanting to paint they tried to dissuade her, but she was from an early age strong-minded and was determined to obtain an art training somehow. Her parents refused to help her, but regardless of their protests she enrolled at the South Kensington Art School. Her parents took her away and sent her to a local high school as an art mistress. She was very unhappy both in the job and living at home, and so decided to submit some of her work to Sir Hubert von Herkomer, 1849–1914, who ran a famous art school at Bushey, Hertfordshire. (His self-portrait in watercolour sold at Sotheby's for £87 250 in June 1986).

Louie was awarded a three year scholarship, but as this only covered tuition she was unable to take it up at once and had to set about earning sufficient money to pay her way. She wrote to the headmistress of a school in

L Burrell.

Cornwall, where her Aunt Amy was on the staff, asking if she could be engaged as an art mistress. She was lucky enough to obtain the position and left for Cornwall, where she found that she could supplement her salary by painting portraits and miniatures of local people. Having saved sufficient money to cover her expenses she returned to London and entered Herkomer's school in 1900 where she found the life exhilarating and exciting. Herkomer liked her work and awarded her the 'Enamel' as the most successful student of the year for every year she worked there. When she graduated with Honours in 1904 her future as an artist seemed assured. For Louie, however, this was not sufficient; she craved for something more than just a career; she was restless and hoped for marriage and children. With this in mind, and in the certainty that the right man would appear, she set off to Africa in the year of her graduation and settled in Cape Town, where she obtained the patronage of rich Boer families, and where to her great joy she met and married the man of her dreams, Philip Henry Burrell, 1867-1908, Burrell was a well-known and popular merchant in Johannesburg, and came from a well-to-do family who lived in Berkeley Square, London.

They had a baby boy who died at birth and a daughter, born in 1908. Because of the inadequate medical care in Africa Louie returned to England for the child's birth but sadly, soon after her arrival, had news that her husband had dropped dead from a heart attack in Durban whilst waiting for a ship to England.

One of her callers soon after the baby's arrival was Dr. Winnington Ingram, Bishop of London who consoled with her on the loss of her husband and offered to christen the baby at his own house in St. James's. Louie was delighted and the child was baptised Philippa Joy.

The family settled in the old home in Campden Hill Square, but once more Louie was financially unable to support herself and her child and at once returned to her painting. She soon became well known and her work was accepted at the Royal Academy, and other Galleries. She had a distinguished clientele which included Princess Marie Louise of Schleswig-Holstein, Princess Alice, and Princess

Figure 3, Mrs Martin Burrell (Aunt Sally), *c. 1913, Ottawa, watercolour on paper. Wife of the Secretary of State for Canada. The National Gallery of Canada, Ottawa.*

Louis and Prince George of Battenberg, as well as art connoisseurs and other celebrities. Inevitably the strain of so much hard work caused her health to break down, and in 1912 the year in which she was elected Associate Royal Society of Miniature Painters, she set off for Canada together with a nurse and her daughter. They settled in Ottawa where she was well received and obtained many commissions including one from the Governor General, The Duke of Connaught, who also asked her to paint his daughter H.R.H. Princess Patricia. She enjoyed the social life and was pursued by many wealthy would-be suitors who considered her 'the adorable English widow', but Louie rejected all of them and continued with her painting. One of their closest friends was Martin Burrell, who served as Minister of Agriculture, and Secretary of State under Sir Wilfred Laurier. He was not in fact a member of the Burrell family, but was distantly connected to the Lukers. Louie's painting of his wife 'Sally' is amongst her finest works.

In 1914 Martin and some very rich friends planned a round-the-world trip – the millionaires paying! In July the party which included Louie and Philippa set off and had only reached Vancouver when War broke out and all the men returned to serve their country, confident that the conflict would soon be over. As the weeks went by it became clear that things would not be resolved quickly, and Louie decided that Vancouver was not the place for her and that it would be better to go to Victoria where she had heard, English people were welcome. To return to England was impossible so they had to make the best of it. Once more short of money Louie tried in vain to obtain commissions; finally she found a job as manageress of a boarding house, the premises were large, but the project was not a success; she moved to a small wooden house, but found that she could not even pay the rent and was almost destitute. An Army camp had been set up nearby and she decided to try her luck doing sketches of the young men who were training there. She managed to get hold of an old barn close to the Camp and having cleaned it out and whitewashed the walls she put in two chairs and erected a notice which read 'Quick portraits – 25 cents'. One by one the young men came to her, and for a few months she was kept quite busy but then the time came for them to embark for the front – and with them went her livelihood. These portraits were painted in watercolour on paper which was cheaper than miniatures on ivory.

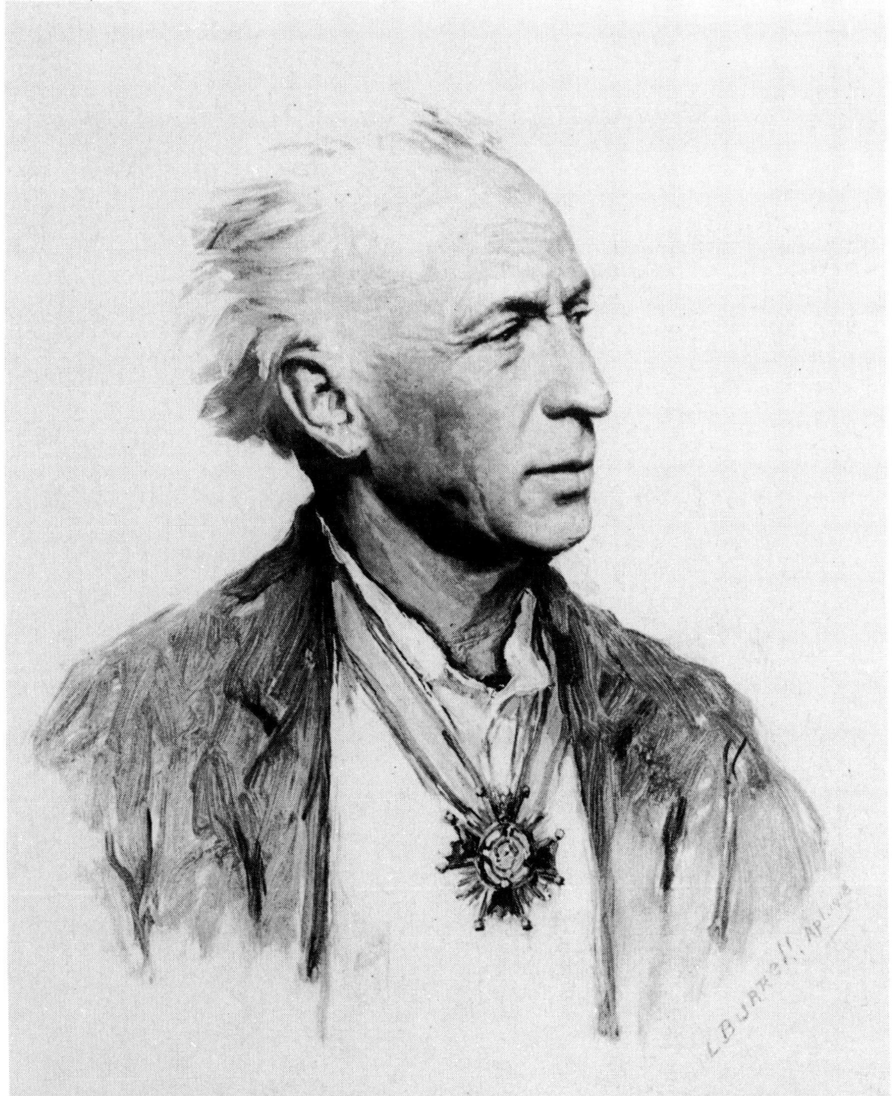

Figure 4, Charles Lummis, *signed* L. BURRELL. *Apl 1918, oil on board, (16½ × 13 in). Painted in Los Angeles. Miss P. Burrell.*

In 1916, bored with Victoria, she and Philippa took a boat to Los Angeles where they settled for the next three years. Louie soon became known, and gained the patronage of film stars and retired millionaires but in 1919 she was on the move again, returning to London which was recovering from the aftermath of war and where her art was not in demand. When things had settled down she obtained permission to sketch portraits in a shop window in Beauchamp Place and to her surprise one of her first customers was none other than Mrs Stanley Baldwin! This patronage changed her life and she was able to sell her portraits for 5 guineas a time – far more than she had ever previously earned. Encouraged by this success she began to work at home where her sitters included among others H.R.H. Princess Mary. Eventually she found that small portraits strained her eyes and she concentrated on portraits in oils, three-quarter length watercolours, and landscapes.

Although many of these (such as life size portraits of Mrs Stanley Baldwin, Princess Mary and Sir Vincent Caillard) were excellent, this transition of technique led to some sparkle going out of her work and there is no doubt that those executed prior to c. 1925 were her best and most desirable paintings.

In 1928, Philippa now aged 20, had a burning desire to travel to India and armed with an introduction from Mrs Baldwin to Lord Irwin, the Viceroy, they set off from Southampton to Bombay and from there travelled up to Simla where they spent part of the summer. Louie painted life size oil portraits of Lord Irwin and Field Marshal Sir William Birdwood, Commander in Chief in India, as well as many Indian Princes. In the July of that year they left for Kashmir where they spent the rest of the summer. They then went to New Delhi where

Figure 5, Santa Maria della Salute, Venice, *watercolour on paper, (12 × 9½ in). 1933-1938. Miss P. Burrell.*

Figure 6, Nurse and Baby (Philippa), *watercolour on paper, 1908. (7½ × 4¾ in). Miss P. Burrell.*

they lived in tents and Louie continued her portrait painting.

Throughout the whole of their time in India they had all sorts of adventures and 'ups' and 'downs' until finally Louie's health broke down again and they decided to return to England. They were so poor that they had to travel third class! Back in London they found it difficult to get cheap accommodation and struggled to survive in various lodging houses.

For Louie, this was the end of her professional life and she did not paint any more portraits. She and her daughter sold their cottage in Chelsea which had been rented out and bought an old windmill and mill cottage in Cambridgeshire, where they started a completely new life. Philippa began writing plays seriously and Louie, free from the strain of struggling for commissions, took to painting landscapes. When nearly 80 she was awarded a small annual grant from the Artists' General Benevolent Institution, and this gave her some degree of security up to her death in January 1971.

Louie Burrell was undoubtedly one of the most important miniaturists working at the turn of this century and as can be seen from these illustrations was extremely versatile, able to work in any medium, watercolours, oils, and pencil. Her early miniatures were on ivory but she later executed them on paper, on which she also painted her three quarter length portraits and landscapes of places in England, she had already painted a few in Italy and India during their travels. She painted her miniatures with a fine brush stroke which gave a soft texture to her work. Her shading is good and the position of her sitters well thought out resulting in life-like representations and depth of character. She achieved this effect with economy of draughtsmanship and an accurate knowledge of anatomy.

One of her most delightful miniatures, which her daughter has presented to the Victoria & Albert Museum, is that of a young model *(Figure 1)* her auburn hair flowing behind her. The watercolour portrait of Mrs Stanley Baldwin *(Figure 2)* is a good example of her period in Beauchamp Place, and her oil portrait of Charles Lummis, *(Figure 4)* painted in Los Angeles in 1918 shows her ability to express character. Among those oils exhibited at the Royal Academy was a life size one of Sir Vincent Caillard, a well known industrialist.

Inevitably the majority of her paintings have been dispersed throughout the world, but her daughter Philippa still possesses a representative collection from which, having examined them in some detail, I have been able to write this article. One of historic interest is that of the drawing room at No 10 Downing Street *(Figure 7)* painted in 1924 during the time that the Baldwins were electioneering and when he became Prime Minister for the second time.

Figure 7, The Drawing Room in No 10 Downing Street, *1924, signed* L. BURRELL. *Present whereabouts unknown.*

Figure 8, Study of an unknown girl, *pencil on paper, c. 1900, (9½ × 7 in). Miss P. Burrell.*

Figure 9, Miniature of a young model at Bushey, *c. 1901-02. watercolour on ivory, (3⅝ × 3⅛). Miss P. Burrell.*

As not all Louie's works are signed many may well pass unrecognised. Those signatures I have seen are either her initials, or a full signature in rather block capitals.

Philippa Burrell is an author and Playwright and has published an Autobiography of her early life and that of her mother entitled *The Golden Thread* which gives a graphic description of the 'ups' and 'downs' of their varied careers. Thanks to her daughter's persistence in helping to mount small exhibitions of Louie's work and contacting those who might be interested, it is to be hoped that she will be taken out of obscurity and gain her rightful place amongst the better known artists of the period.

June 1987

GOLDSMITHS' DISCOVERIES

John Culme

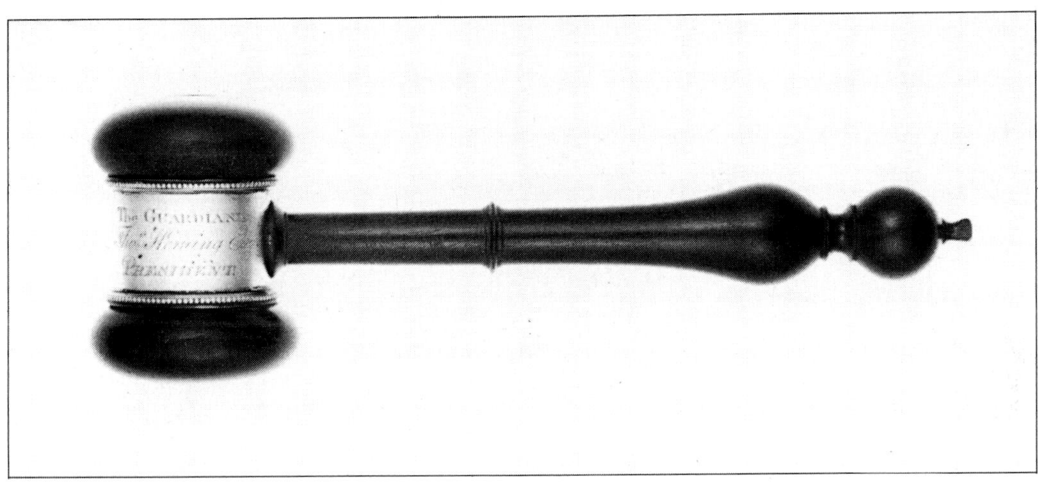

An uncle of mine was fond of saying with a snort the only thing you could believe in a newspaper was its date. Were 18th century journalists as prone to mistakes and exaggeration as he supposed their 20th century counterparts to be? 'We are informed', so ran a report in London's *The Public Advertiser* of 6 January 1768, 'that an eminent Jeweller in this City has commenc'd a Chancery Suit against an East-India Captain, relative to the Disposal of a magnificent Crown set with Diamonds, valued at 10 000l to a Nabob in the East-Indies.' Here was a cliffhanger with all the right ingredients: a looming legal battle, a mysterious Eastern potentate and fabulous riches. Only a day later, however, the publishers printed a disappointing disclaimer.

Good news, too, had its place; *The London Chronicle* shared its joy with the public upon George III's recovery, reporting on 13th March, 1789, that, 'Among the illuminations of Tuesday evening, few exceeded in brilliancy that of the London Silver Plate Manufactory in Foster-lane, the large premises of which were lighted up with solid silver three-light branches of candlesticks.'

The then proprietor of this enterprise, otherwise known as The Silver Lion, was the silversmith Thomas Daniell. No doubt doubly proud on this royal occasion, he generally boasted the establishment of the business 'upwards of 50 years'. Jabez Daniell, his father and former co-partner who had died on 4 September 1777, entered his first maker's mark at Goldsmiths' Hall in 1749. By the 1780s the firm carried a stock of 'Diamonds, Pearls, Jewellery, Watchs [*sic*], Motto Rings, Ivory Knives, and the strongest plated Goods', probably indicating that The Silver Lion was as much a retail outlet as it was a factory. This would appear to be confirmed by a pair of silver tea caddies of 1788/89 *(Figure 2)* upon which Thomas Daniell's mark is struck over that of James Mince and William Hodgkins, the actual makers. The latter seem to have owed the existence of their business to the Daniell family. Indeed, Arthur G. Grimwade in his *London Goldsmiths* surmises from other information that Mince and the Daniells may have been

Figure 1 *A Silver-mounted ebony gavel, maker's mark of Robert Hennell, London, about 1776. Inscribed: 'The* GUARDIANS, *Thos. Heming Esqr.* PRESIDENT. *Ex dono* RM, VP, *25 March 1776.' Presented by Richard Morson, first Vice President of 'The Guardians', otherwise known as the 'Society for the Protection of Trade against Swindlers and Sharpers', to their first President.* Sotheby's.

Figure 2 *A pair of silver tea caddies, makers' mark of James Mince and William Hodgkins overstruck by that of Thomas Daniell of the London Silver Plate Manufactory, London, 1788/89, with a silver-mounted ivory, hardwood and tortoiseshell case, London, 1820/21. Sotheby's.*

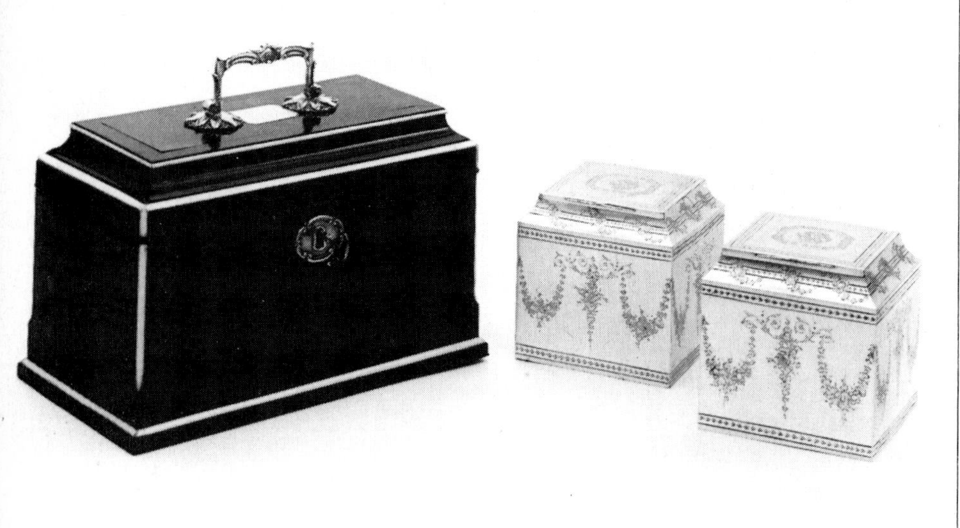

on affectionate terms. With the evidence of the elder Daniell's will, signed on 1 March 1776, and proved some eight months later, this theory is reinforced. He wrote, 'James Mince my late Servant owes me a considerable sum of money which I am persuaded he is not able to pay[.] I do therefore hereby acquit release and discharge the same and every part thereof', adding, 'I give and bequeath to the said James Mince the sum of ten pounds for Mourning.'

Sensible to the powers of advertising, Thomas Daniell stated in a handbill of about 1789 he always had on hand, 'Twenty Thousand Ounces of every species of Silver Goods. . ., finished in the highest elegance of patterns, and peculiarly excellent workmanship, and embellishments from the best and latest designs.' In 18th century newspapers advertisers were also very active, encouraging the sale of everything from the latest books to ointments for sinister afflictions of the skin. A revealing notice of this kind in *The Daily Advertiser* of 3 January 1776, began, 'To the Silversmiths', continuing, 'Wanted a Journeyman Spoon-maker, also a Journeyman that is compleat at making Punch Ladles and other Kinds of small Work; likewise a Chaser, that is compleat at Modelling and Drawing, and a Polisher, that can undertake different Kinds of small Work.' The stress on chasing and the related accomplishments of modelling and drawing is significant, for chasers were considered the aristocracy of the trade.

Next, averting our gaze from 'A young Portuguese, who picked up a Ludgate-hill Lady on Friday Night, [purchasing] her Favours with a Missal, a Rosary, and two Agnus Deis. . .', we find in *The Public Advertiser* of 21 January 1769, a notice for The Society of Tradesmen, &c. For the Protection of their Property against the Inroads of Forgers, Cheats, &c. This noble-minded body seems to have been a precursor of The Guardians or the Society for the Protection of Trade against Swindlers and Sharpers, which was founded with a flourish on 25 March 1776, and lingered on until the 1840s *(Figure 1)*. Its treasurer was Richard Morson, who until December 1774, had been in business with Benjamin Stephenson trading as goldsmiths and jewellers at the Golden Cup on Ludgate Hill. It was they who in 1772 supplied the cup presented by the Corporation of the City of London to the politician, John Wilkes. A description and engraving of the piece appeared in the October 1774, edition of *The Gentleman's Magazine (Figure 3)*, together with the unusually perceptive comment, 'Underneath, the makers names are inscribed, which, no doubt, will long preserve their memory.'

Although The Guardians by no means catered exclusively to goldsmiths and jewellers, representatives of many retail trades as disparate as ironmongery and hosiery being Members, it is interesting to find such numbers from the best houses dealing in precious goods. The first elected President was Thomas Heming, principal goldsmith to George III, who operated from premises in New Bond Street called The King's Arms. It could have been here that, according to *The London Chronicle,* a fire broke out early in the morning of 30 December 1788, in the workshop of a silversmith, 'which consumed the whole, with the working implements, and melted down a large quantity of plate, which was nearly finished.'

Fire or no, Heming's, from whence came some of the most stylish silver of the age *(Figures 4a & b)*, was also the place which offered employment during the 1760s to a youth by the name of James Neild. After a little while there, where he may have used his talent in drawing, modelling and engraving, he was able to open his own jewellery shop in 1770, an undertaking which became highly successful. This would be all we know of him were it not for a chance visit made in 1762 to a co-apprentice flung into the King's Bench for debt. Horrified at the grim conditions, Neild afterwards devoted his spare time to alleviating prisoners' discomfort *(Figure 5)* and in 1774 became Treasurer of the Society for the Relief and Discharge of Persons imprisoned for Small Debts.

Neild's artistic abilities, quite apart from his genius for making money, would have made him a useful member of a trade which relied so heavily on good workmen, especially in the finer

May every Tyrant feel
The keen deep Searchings, of a Patriot's steel. Churchill
Morson & Stephenson fec. Ludgate Hill.
R. Dighton del.
J. Jane sculp
The Cup presented to Mr. Wilkes, by the City of London in 177

Figure 3 *An engraving of the silver cup and cover presented to John Wilkes in 1772 by the Corporation of the City of London.* The Gentleman's Magazine, *October 1774.*

Figure 4a *A silver soup tureen and cover, maker's mark of Thomas Heming, London, 1761/62. Sotheby's.*
4b (below) *Detail of a soup tureen from a contemporary trade card of Thomas Heming, 'GOLDSMITH to his MAJESTY at the King's Arms in Bond Street facing Clifford Street. . .'*

branches. Even the ordinary journeymen plateworkers knew their value for in the August 1763 edition of *The Gentleman's Magazine* we learn they had 'left off work, in order to advance their wages. Their present wages is a guinea a week from 6 to 8: they insist on the same from 6 to 6.' By contrast, the activity of criminals was as important, especially when it impinged upon innocent lives, in our case private owners of silver and jewellery or shopkeepers and manufacturers whose raw materials were valuable and easily disposable. Eighteenth century newspapers, hinting at a vast underworld, are full of pleas for help from the robbed such as one from a Mr Peter Laprimaudaye which appeared in *The Public Advertiser* on Saturday, 30 October 1762. Three nights before, in weather of house-demolishing gales, his dwelling in Angel Court, Throgmorton Street, had been relieved of certain silverware including a tea kettle, a large coffee pot, a large waiter and 'Four Salts with three Feet, 23 oz. 17 dwt.' 'If any of the above things, are offered to be sold, pawned, or valued', ran Laprimaudaye's advertisement, 'you are desired to stop them and the Party, and give Notice [at the above address], or to Samuel Courtwould, Goldsmith, opposite to the Exchange, Cornhill, and you shall receive twenty Guineas Reward on conviction. . .'

Further details are to be found in the *London Sessions Papers;* reports originally published under a variety of titles for which this is a convenient substitute. These are printed accounts of trials at the Old Bailey and although not newspapers in the accepted sense, their regular appearance and verbatim reports must have been irresistible for those searching for sensation. Laprimaudaye's housebreaker turned out to be one William Autenreith, a surgeon, German by birth, in whose possession a three-legged salt-cellar was soon discovered. At the

JAMES NEILD, ESQ.
The Visitor of Prisons.
Born May 24.1744; Died Feb. 26, 1814.

Figure 5 *A silhouette of James Neild, retail jeweller of St. James's Street, and champion of imprisoned debtors.* The Gentleman's Magazine, *April 1817.*

ensuing trial in January 1763, a friend of Laprimaudaye, John Bearance, who recently had been similarly robbed of plate, swore that 'Mr Laprimaudaye [entered Autenreith's] house, and found a silver salt-seller which Mr Laprimaudaye thought to be his own, and Mr Courtwould [*sic*] said positively it was Mr Laprimaudaye's, and that he made it for him...' Samuel Courtwould, mounting the witness stand, told the court, 'I am a goldsmith.'

Poor Autenreith, found guilty, was condemned to death; Courtwould, with a salt in his hand, had delivered the fatal blow, observing, 'This is the prosecutor's property, I made it. I have made many salts, but never had an order to gild them in the inside, only this and the other three here produced.' Such information about the finish of mid-18th century silver salt-cellars is indeed a curiosity, for, although to gild their interiors was usual by the 1790s, it is unknown when the practice first became widespread. A small matter, perhaps, but so little is known about trade procedures then that each new snippet can enlighten.

We are ignorant of much else besides, the most exasperating to students of the subject being caused by the loss of two of the Goldsmiths' Company's Makers' Marks Registers. These, the Smallworkers' book in use from 1739 to 1758, and that of the Largeworkers of 1758 to 1773, were submitted to a Parliamentary Committee in 1773 and which, never returned, are presumed to have been destroyed by the fire of 1834 which engulfed the old Houses of Parliament. Although Mr Grimwade has done much to fill the gap in the 'Unregistered Marks' section of *London Goldsmiths,* owners' names of many marks remain unknown or uncertain.

Unfurling the secrets of these so-called 'unregistered' marks is a thankless task. With the disappearance of the two Registers, the only certain key, our choice of records, manuscript and printed, is dauntingly large, from insurance company files and trade directories to wills and newspapers.

So, turning to the *London Sessions Papers* again, the following case at the Old Bailey in March, 1762, is not without interest. It involved David Field, a silversmith, the prosecutor, and his journeyman, Christopher Robinson. Indicted for stealing 'two vessels of silver in the shape of a barrel, value 5s. three vessels of silver in the shape of an egg, value 6s. two vessels of silver in the shape of a jar, value 5s. and eight other vessels in the shape of an egg, value 12s.,' Robinson had worked for Field 'near 35 years.' As the trial proceeded, Field told how 'Mr [Thomas] Wintle came to me on the 26th March, and asked me, if I ever sent goods out of my shop unfinished? I said, no. Then said he, I am afraid you have got a partner...' Wintle, a retail goldsmith and jeweller at the Ring & Pearl, Poultry, when buying the things from one Samuel Yowell, recalled thinking of Field, who 'does business for me in this way. I took them to be of his work.' Wintle continued, 'I carried them to him, and he owned them directly.' Yowell, by way of confirmation, said he had bought them in turn from a pawnbroker, William Cadwallider, who, when called, stated, 'I took 15 spung [sponge] boxes in the shape of eggs, barrels, and the like, of the prisoner at the bar...'

For Robinson the result of the case was clear: found guilty, he was transported for seven years. For us it leaves an intriguing question: is the maker's mark DF noted by Mr Grimwade (No. 3514) and found on mid-18th century silver nutmeg graters and other little containers, that of David Field? *(Figures 6a, b, c.)* The modest individual values of the stolen shapes certainly points to such small objects, just as Cadwallider's description of them as 'spung boxes' might mean that he thought they were what are now termed vinaigrettes. Furthermore, the absence of Field's name from the printed Parliamentary Return of 1773, often useful in identifying some of the 'unregistered' marks, does not negate the proposition; he had already died as his will, proved in September 1770, clearly establishes. This document had not been signed, however, and in consequence of which Field's handwriting had to be identified. William Justis (the younger), 'goldsmith', having been one of Field's apprentices, was called as one of the witnesses. The other was the goldsmith Samuel Meriton (probably the elder), who had known Field well, 'having seen the said deceased[']s handwriting very often and had Bills of parcels from him in the Way of Business.' The last is of particular significance because Meriton's own maker's mark is often to be found on similar egg-shaped nutmeg graters of the same period *(Figures 6d & 7)*.

Six months after Field's appearance at the Old Bailey, John Griffice was indicted in October 1762 for and proved to have stolen eight pennyweights of silver valued at two shillings, the property of 'William Priest and Richard Pardon [*sic*].' These two gentlemen, the last called 'Richard Passiter [*sic*],' were again at the same Court the following September when, describing themselves as goldsmiths of Wood Street, they charged Abraham Basset with stealing '2 ounces of silver and wire cuttings, val. 13s.' The account of the theft in the *London Sessions Papers* runs, 'It appeared the prisoner being servant to a blacksmith, had put on a lock to a back shop belonging to a workshop of the prosecutors, on 16th August, and Mr [? Joseph] Bridges a silvercaster in Fosterlane sent to let them know the prisoner had brought the silver to him, to have cast into buckles, on 24th August. . .' Basset confessed, was found guilty and

6a

6b

Figure 6a *Maker's mark* DF *(? David Field). (Mark No. 3514 from Arthur G. Grimwade's* London Goldsmiths 1697–1837, *London, 1976, reproduced by kind permission of the author.)* 6b *Maker's mark* DF *(? David Field) from the mid 18th century plain silver nutmeg grater in 6c. Vinci Antiques.* 6c (below) *Two mid 18th century silver nutmeg graters, one plain, the other chased, both with the maker's mark* DF *(? David Field) enlarged in 6b. Vinci Antiques.* 6d (below) *A plain silver nutmeg grater, maker's mark of Samuel Meriton (? the elder) of London, about 1765. Sotheby's.*

7

8

Figure 7 *Maker's mark* SM *of Samuel Meriton (? the elder) of London, about 1765, from the nutmeg grater, Fig 6d. Sotheby's.*

Figure 8 *Maker's mark* WP JP *of William Priest and James Priest (Preist), entered at Goldsmiths' Hall, London, before 1768. (Mark No. 3271 from Arthur G. Grimwade's* London Goldsmiths 1697–1837, *reproduced by kind permission of the author.)*

6c 6d 6d 6c

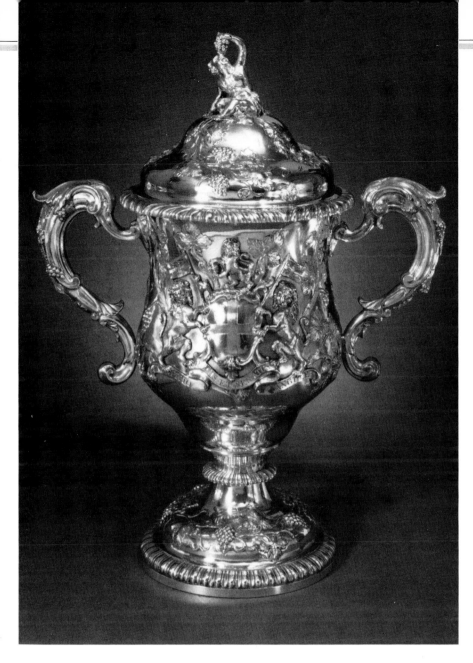

Figure 9 *A silver cup and cover, maker's mark of William Cripps, London, 1762/63, presented by the United East India Company to Captain William Webber 'for his Gallant Behaviour in the Ship Oxford in Bengall [sic] River. In the Year 1759.' Sotheby's.*

Figure 10 *Maker's mark* WP RP *(? William Priest (Preist) and Richard Pargiter [Pargeter]), attributed by Sir Charles James Jackson in* English Goldsmiths and Their Marks *(London, 1921) to W. & R. Peaston, noted on a tankard, London, 1764/65. (Mark No. 3897 from Arthur G. Grimwade's* London Goldsmiths 1697–1837, *reproduced by kind permission of the author).*

10

branded in the hand.

A look into the local Rate Books for Wood Street indicates that the prosecutors could only have been William Priest and Richard Pargiter who, in the volumes for 1762/63 and 1763/64, are noted to have shared two houses in that thoroughfare. The reference also predicates the existence of a hitherto unsuspected partnership, the knowledge of which, supposing they had entered a joint mark, has been witheld because of the lost Largeworkers' Register. Priest (otherwise Preist) is almost certainly the same individual previously in business with William Shaw, again in Wood Street, well known as makers of tankards, mugs and other holloware. Pargiter on the other hand, could be the younger Richard Pargeter mentioned by Mr Grimwade as featuring in the Parliamentary Return of 1773, listed as living near Banbury, Oxfordshire. Without further evidence other than of the similarity in design of marks between that attributed by Mr Grimwade to William Preist and James Preist (No. 3271) *(Figure 8)*, 'Entered by 1768,' and another 'unregistered' mark (No. 3897) *(Figure 10)*, stated by the same authority to be that of W. & R. Peaston, I would like to suggest that the latter is in fact that of William Priest (Preist) and Richard Pargiter (Pargeter).

Contemporary newspapers and trial reports are full of accounts which cry out for further investigation. But one of their favourite topics regarded day-to-day accidents which often made frightful reading. So, too, could notices of natural but no less spectacular passings as with that of William Cripps *(Figure 9)*, former apprentice of and successor to the younger David Willaume, and a one-time neighbour of that master of rococo plate and porcelain, Nicholas Sprimont. *The Public Advertiser* of 2nd January 1766, breathlessly revealed, 'Yesterday Evening died at his House in St. James's-Street, of a Fit of Apoplexy, Mr Crips [*sic*], a Gold and Silver-Smith of great Business. He was suddenly seized after Supper on Tuesday Night, and continued in great Agonies till he expired.' The sequel followed two days later: 'On Thursday last the Surgeons opened the Head of the late Mr Cripps, Goldsmith and Jeweller of St. James's-Street, who died on Wednesday Evening; and we hear his sudden Death was occasioned by the bursting of a Vein in his Head.'

Acknowledgement

I am most grateful to Elaine Barr for her advice and suggestions during the preparation of this article.

February 1987

BUYING A CANTEEN

Gloria Dale

In the mid-1960s, Michael Beaumont, an investment advisor in the City, impressed by the canteen of Georgian silver that a friend had made up, decided to collect antique silver flatware. What started out as a hobby became an obsession, and Mr Beaumont now has several thousand pieces of silver flatware, almost all of it in the bank, waiting to be made into canteens. In these past 20 years he has accumulated a great deal of knowledge on how to put a canteen together, the features to look for and those to avoid.

A canteen of Georgian silver can cost £950 or £4500 depending on where and how you buy it, its condition and whether it is a mixed set or one by the same maker with the same or approximately the same dates. But, as in all fields of buying antiques, there are pitfalls.

'With all the problems involved in buying antique silver, what made you decide to collect antique silver flatware rather than modern?', I asked Mr Beaumont. 'When I started to collect silver in the 1960s,' he said, 'it was obvious that Georgian flatware was too cheap. It cost little more than bullion, about £1 per troy oz, and some of it was 200 years old. New flatware was twice the price and didn't have the patina and the history of an antique. Because of the way antique flatware is made, it is much stronger than machine-made examples. For example, the bowls of handmade spoons are strengthened at the edges where they get most wear. Machine-made flatware lacks this kind of subtlety, and it has only half the lifetime of antique silver.'

He went on to say that if he was advising someone who wanted to collect a canteen of antique silver flatware, the first thing he'd do was to suggest buying *Silver Flatware, English, Irish and Scottish 1660-1980* by Ian Pickford, published by the Antique Collectors' Club in 1983.

'It is a very complete book on flatware, well illustrated, and it points out some of the difficulties as well as the positive aspects of collecting tableware. Alas, it was not available when I started so I experienced a not inexpensive learning curve. However, now that I've absorbed some basic knowledge, I collect what I like best, what best suits my pocket, allowing of course for availability.'

It is generally accepted that a flatware service consists of 12 each of the following: Table-spoons, dessert-spoons, table and dessert forks and tea or coffee spoons. Knives are not included because they are considered cutlery, not flatware. For practical reasons, matching modern knives are acceptable to go with an antique set of flatware.

The first important step to make is to decide on the pattern to be collected. It is important to ascertain that it was a popular pattern so that it won't be too difficult to find. In the past Old English and Fiddle were the most popular patterns, which makes them very collectable today *(Figure 2)*.

King's pattern, which is really a Regency design, is starting to find favour with collectors. It is wise to select a maker who was prolific and worked for a long period of time in order to be assured of having enough flatware from which to choose. Eley, Fearn and Chawner had a large production between them in various partnerships, as did Richard Crossley and the descendants of Hester Bateman. George Adams is a Victorian maker to consider as he was

Figure 1 *The Georgian dessert fork on the left, where the prongs are starting to show wear, is a Fiddle fork cut down. Compare with Victorian neighbour (engraved with initials on the wrong side) and note the even width of the lower stem, and thinning of the one time Fiddle upper stem.*

making flatware between 1840 and the 1880s.

It is possible to mix makers of the same design and still have a nice canteen *(Figure 6)*. Naturally, there will be differences in the individual pieces as to weight, shape, and length. But with hand-made flatware there is bound to be a slight difference from piece to piece even when it is made by a single craftsman working in the same year. In addition dessert-spoons and tea-spoons in particular tend to have changed shape due to use.

'How important is the date of the silver?' I asked Mr Beaumont. 'For instance, is Georgian silver more desirable than Victorian?' 'In general,' he replied, 'I'd recommend the collector to follow my example and concentrate on the years between 1784 when "top marking" started (that is hallmarking on the top of the stem instead of halfway down) and 1890 when the Queen's head disappeared. Post-1890 items are too modern. It is, of course, a matter of taste and price. Georgian silver is considered more desirable because the earlier pieces are of a more slender and graceful design. Some pieces are also more rare. Victorian silver is generally heavier by some 10-15%, and does not show the wear that Georgian silver does; but the pieces are generally heavier in appearance, the bowls of the spoons are broader *(Figures 3 and 5)*. In some cases, if you are in a hurry to finish a set, Victorian and Georgian pieces of the same pattern can be bought. When the set is together the differences will be noticeable but as flatware is spread around the table, these differences will not be noticed by your dinner guests. A canteen can always be upgraded when the opportunity avails itself.'

Figure 2 *Variations on Old English and Fiddle are Old English Thread and Fiddle and Thread. The latter, double struck, that is 'threaded', on both sides is probably the most popular pattern of all.*

Figure 3 (above right) *Compare typical Victorian (left) and George III (right) spoons of the three sizes. The bowls and stems of the latter are noticeably more slender and appealing.*

As for matching London silver with provincial Scottish or Irish pieces, it will depend on how urgent it is to complete the canteen. The more uniform the canteen as to place of origin, date and maker, the greater the value will be. When buying provincial flatware to go with a London set, take care with Fiddle as the proportions vary considerably between the London and the Scottish and Irish makers.

The provincial centres for hallmarking appointed in 1700 were Exeter, York, Bristol and Norwich. In 1702 the Newcastle Assay Office was officially established. Even though a piece of flatware may have the hallmark of a main centre, it may not have been made there as the minor silvermaking centres were required to send their finished products for assaying to the major centres.

Mr Beaumont and I discussed the problems of matching the pieces of a canteen and he stressed that matching for size and shape was a vital objective. When Mr Beaumont sets out to buy he tries to take examples of each of the five items of silver to be collected with him. When this isn't convenient, he takes a tracing of the outline of the piece he is trying to match and tests the prospective piece by placing it on the outline to see how well it matches. Matching by date is a further refinement. 'I carry a notebook showing what I already have. I'm willing to pay a premium for a fork or spoon number six of a particular year, possibly to find that the match is imperfect!'

The order of buying a set is most important. For Old English, Fiddle and most other patterns, get the dessert-forks first because these are very difficult to come by. Table-spoons are the easiest part of the set to find. If you choose Fiddle and Thread which is priced well ahead of Old English, keep in mind that the dessert and tea spoons are rare. It can be wise for collectors to go to a reputable dealer or auction house to buy these less accessible items, even if it means paying a higher price in order to get started. There were fewer dessert-forks because the emphasis was on the main courses of meals rather than the dessert courses. Also special dessert sets were manufactured. Then, too, the prongs of a fork have a shorter life than, say, the bowl of a spoon. After the dessert-forks, concentrate on table-forks, dessert-spoons and tea-spoons.

Having decided on what to buy, the next consideration is where one should go to buy. There is a wide choice of places to buy silver flatware. The salerooms are an obvious place. Christie's, Sotheby's, Phillips, and there are country auctions as well. Auction houses usually sell lots including sets of silver – six spoons of a similar date or by the same maker. This is a more expensive way of buying than buying a set piece by piece, but it is also a faster way of getting a canteen together. One must expect to pay more per item for a pair than for a single piece and much more for a straight 6 or 12 (matching pattern, date and maker). Although the principle may be to get a canteen by buying singles, a reasonably priced set should be snapped up.

If you have to buy a set of six to get one spoon remember that there is no harm in having spares. It may be a decided advantage to have them in case one goes down the waste disposal. This is one of the disadvantages of having an expensive straight set in terms of pattern, maker and year. If a single piece is lost it may be almost impossible to replace it and the value of the whole canteen will be materially decreased.

When Mr Beaumont goes to auction houses he views carefully, examining each piece for faults. He usually leaves a

Figure 4 *Both dents in the soup ladle can be hammered out, but the other items are virtually worthless. The spoon second from the left has a cracked bowl badly worn at the end, and the stem of the next has been broken and soldered together – watch out for brown solder stains! The worn bowl of the dessert spoon has been hammered to its original state but is too thin while the right hand spoon has a cracked bowl.*

Figure 5 (left) *Two pairs of table forks, Georgian on the left, Victorian on the right. Note the slimmer elegance of the earlier Bateman pair which, however, have stems which blend the 'wrong way'.*

bid with a trusted porter or with a dealer who will vet the lots, charging a percentage of the bid which is usually reasonable. There is a view that dealers 'squeeze out' private buyers in the salerooms.

In London there are street markets of which Portobello Road is the best for silver flatware; Schredds and B. Henry, while not the cheapest vendors, are reliable and very helpful. Antique shops, fairs and specialist dealers such as Mary Cooke of King Street, St. James's are worth a visit. Mr Beaumont feels that the Chancery Lane Silver Vaults are mainly for tourists.

'What mistakes have you made when buying flatware?' I asked him, 'and what must one avoid buying?' 'Most of my mistakes are a result of buying at street markets which start very early in the morning, often when it is almost dark. My vigilance tends to develop later! Damaged items are to be viewed with the gravest suspicion. When buying spoons look out for excessive wear at the end of the bowl. Avoid cracks in the bowl, generally near the stem. Dents in the bowl can be removed at a small cost but rehammering a badly worn bowl thins the metal.

'Avoid forks with worn tines unless they can be realigned with their neighbours without reducing the length materialy. Don't buy a fork with a soldered break in the tine, or one with the worn tine hammered to increase the length. Watch out for Fiddle pattern forks which have been converted to Old English *(Figure 1)*. Forks with the end of the handles turned down are uncomfortable to hold and should be avoided unless they are collected intentionally. Don't buy any pieces with broken stems that have been soldered.'

It is hardly worthwhile to collect antique knives as a part of a set of silver flatware. The handles are usually in poor condition, and even if they are satisfactory the blades are generally worn or rusted. Putting a new steel blade into an antique knife is seldom successful because the handles are too long in proportion to the new blades. Mr Beaumont suggested buying new knives with silver, bone or ivory handles.

Silver flatware is often found with initials or crests which are usually engraved on the convex side of the piece. This is advantageous because it is easier to remove the engravings from the convex rather than the concave side. Whereas crests are not considered a drawback, initials that are not one's own are less popular and affect the value of the canteen. Both can be erased but the work should be done professionally. If the decorations are deeply engraved it will weaken the metal if they are removed, and it will spoil the patina which has taken so many years to build up.

Where one is collecting for personal use, Mr Beaumont strongly advocates leaving crests and initials untouched; removal can rarely be disguised, and the silver lost can never be replaced. Sometimes crests of famous people are engraved on silver to 'improve' it. Make sure that the engraving is one of the same period as the silver by checking its sharpness with the overall condition of the piece.

As for hallmarks, as with all silver avoid buying pieces if the marks are illegible. The maker's mark is stamped separately and tends to be worn away first.

The most important feature of a canteen is its condition. Condition determines the value. Mr Beaumont always tries to get those pieces that are in the best possible condition. Pieces in poor condition have only scrap value and are not worth buying *(Figure 4)*.

William Walters, whose well-established shop in the Silver Vaults sells antique silver, doesn't recommend putting a canteen together. He feels there is too much of a risk in starting a collection that may not be able to be finished. Mr Beaumont's answer to this is that he has completed not one but a dozen or more canteens. 'If the 12th spoon of a set is missing, continue looking. Someone has it and until it is found the set can be filled in with a similar piece which can be replaced when the matching piece is found.'

In spite of the time involved and the pitfalls in buying flatware to make up a canteen, Michael Beaumont feels that it is a worth-while effort. 'As a collector I get infinite pleasure in going to the markets and looking for silver for canteens. I have made up, and can still make up, a mixed canteen of 12 place settings in a popular pattern such as Georgian Old English for about £950, and Victorian Fiddle would be easier and cheaper. You've told me that you had been quoted £3500-£4000 for an Old English canteen in good condition and dating from 1809 to 1814. I have the fun of the search and the advantage of the cost.'

August 1986

Figure 6 *A Georgian place setting (except for the modern bone-handled knives). All the silverware is of a different date and maker, but although the crests are different, note how well the items match.*

EARLY ENGLISH SILVER RARITIES

Timothy Schroder

The quantity of silver to have survived from the first half of the 16th century is minute and the pieces left too few for an adequate view of the range and styles of domestic silver to be formed. The vast majority of these are either ecclesiastical or still in the possession of the colleges or City livery companies for whom they were originally made. It is therefore remarkable that four pieces made before the reign of Queen Elizabeth should already have entered the private collection of Arthur and Rosalinde Gilbert.

Apart from a silver-gilt mounted mazer of about 1480, the earliest piece in the collection is a beaker of 1525,

Figure 1 *Casting Bottle, 1553. Maker's mark a device. H 14.8 cm ($5\frac{3}{4}$ in). An extremely rare piece, with only four other bottles of this type recorded. Photograph courtesy Sotheby's.*

which first appeared in the Dunn Gardner sale of 1902 at Christie's and was subsequently in the Pierpont Morgan collection *(Figure 3)*. Only one other hallmarked domestic beaker – a silver-gilt example of 1496 – pre-dates it, although several of Continental origin are known. The Gilbert beaker has a flat-chased design of imbricated lobes and typical stamped decoration around the foot, but its shape is quite different from that of other beakers of the period, although admittedly close to that of German glass 'Maigelein' cups. On the other hand, its proportions are also remarkably close to those of a font-shaped cup, which was a recognised form of the period, with a short, stubby stem and spreading foot. While one should be very cautious, given the tiny amount of surviving early 16th century plate, before basing an argument on comparable pieces, it is not impossible that this beaker started life as such a cup, whose stem was later removed.

Less controversial is the extremely rare casting bottle of 1553, which appeared on the market for the first time in 1984, having been sold in a West Country antique shop as brass *(Figure 1)*. Only four other bottles, or *flaçons*, of this type are recorded, of which this is undoubtedly the finest. In his *History of English Plate* Jackson states that the function of these little bottles was to sprinkle scented water over the hands after eating. Perhaps the fastidiousness of this custom helps to account for their fairly short-lived popularity, but in any event they seem from inventories of the period never to have been particularly common objects. Isolated examples are recorded on inventories from about 1520, the 1574 inventory of the Royal Jewel House lists 13 (although dozens of ewers and basins) and there were only three at Hardwick Hall in 1601. Of particular interest is the decoration of the Gilbert bottle: while the other known examples are decorated with conventional strapwork, this is embossed with the much rarer flutes and naturalistic foliage characteristic of the second quarter of the century. Similar ornament is found among the pattern books of masters such as Jacques Du Cerceau, Francesco Pelligrino and Hans Brosamer but disappears from the repertoire after about 1560.

Domestic plate of the Elizabethan period has stood the rigours of time far better than its immediate predecessors and although still extremely rare in relation to later periods, survives in sufficient numbers for a much clearer picture of its characteristics to be formed. For the obvious reason that their bullion content was less, smaller forms are represented in larger numbers than the monumental pieces that we know to have been made and which are found now only among the English 16th and early 17th century diplomatic gifts preserved in the Kremlin. For the same reason, mounted pieces, which incorporate other materials such as stoneware or pottery, survive in disproportionate numbers. The Gilbert Collection has no examples of this important category, but it does contain a fascinating jug with silver-gilt mounts of about 1545 *(Figure 2)*. The mounts are very similar to those of the Venetian glass jug of 1548 in the British Museum, but the body was presumably broken around 1680, for it was replaced at about that time with a silver body of the same

Figure 2 (opposite) *Jug with silver-gilt mounts, about 1545. H 12 cm (5 in). The body was probably broken around 1680, and replaced with a silver body of the same shape with Chinoiserie decoration, marked by Benjamin Pyne.*

Figure 3 (above) *Beaker, 1525. Maker's mark (?) a device. H 5.8 cm ($2\frac{1}{4}$ in). Of quite different shape from that of other beakers of the period.*

shape, flat-chased with Chinoiserie decoration and struck with the maker's mark of Benjamin Pyne.

Mounted pieces apart, many of the typical forms of late 16th century domestic and display plate are represented in the collection. The distinction between plate intended for use and for display is an important one. Most of the plate which survives is of a domestic nature and was made for what would today be termed an 'upper middle class' market. Very few of the important aristocratic or court commissions survive and this in part explains the relatively indifferent craftsmanship of much English silver of the period.

Two pieces in the Gilbert Collection which exhibit the finest quality workmanship, however, are a silver-gilt and rock-crystal cup and cover of 1568 and a gourd-shaped cup of 1585 *(Figures 4 and 5)*. Both were surely intended for display rather than use, a factor which helps to explain their remarkably fine condition. The early history of the rock-crystal cup is not known, but according to a tradition in the Villiers family, by whom it was sold in 1981, it was a gift from the Duke of Wellington to Lady Clementina Villiers on her christening in 1824. The cup has been subject to certain alterations, probably around that date: the gilding is certainly not original and the finial has been replaced, but in other respects the cup is of the finest quality. The maker's mark – a bird in a shaped shield – has not been positively identified, but should perhaps be attributed to Affabel Partridge, who was one of the Queen's goldsmiths and whose known dates of about 1550 to 1575 fit very well with the period over which this mark is found. When on the market in 1981 it was strongly felt in certain quarters that the cup had been altered more extensively than stated above. In fact all other aspects of the cup can be directly paralleled by identical details on other pieces by the same maker who was evidently aware of Wenzel Jamnitzer's latest designs from Nuremberg, some of which were published in printed form. Comparison with the same maker's salt cellar of 1569 (Vintners' Company) gives an indication of the likely original appearance of the cover: there the finial is very similar to the casting used on the lower part of the stem of the Gilbert cup and is surmounted by the figure of a soldier.

No such problems exist with the gourd cup *(Figure 5)*. This is pricked with the arms of Wilbraham, for Sir Thomas Wilbraham of Woodhey, Cheshire and the cup remained in the Wilbraham family until its sale at Christie's in 1930, when it was acquired by William Randolph Hearst. This and a small 'pineapple' cup of 1608 also in the collection are very much in the German taste and recall how heavily the London goldsmiths were influenced by German craftsmen at the time. Indeed, a German visitor of 1613 is quoted by Ronald Lightbown as writing that 'it is not long since that nearly all the goldsmiths in London were Germans'. But whereas the pineapple cup is quite possibly by a German, the Wilbraham cup was certainly made by an English goldsmith, since both the chasing to the foot and the engraving around the bowl and cover are entirely in the English taste. An almost identical cup of the same year and by the same maker was among the gifts of the English embassy to Moscow in 1586 and is still in the Kremlin. There can be no doubt that these two are the finest surviving examples of this type of cup.

These cups are both classic examples of the main features of the Elizabethan style. The crystal cup in particular is characterised by density and variety of ornament and a preoccupation with incorporating as many techniques as possible, including casting, chasing, engraving and die-stamping. The cover is chased with a range of strapwork, fruit and masks which was ultimately derived from the innovative plaster decoration at Fontainebleau, but which had become completely ubiquitous by the latter part of the 16th century. The gourd cup too is chased and

Figure 4 (far left) *Rock crystal and silver-gilt Cup, 1568, attr. to Affabel Partridge, one of the Queen's goldsmiths. H 38 cm (15 in). A gift from the Duke of Wellington to Lady Clementina Villiers on her christening in 1824.*

Figure 5 (near left) *Gourd Cup, 1585. Marked SB. Reveals the influence of German craftsmen on an English goldsmith.*

Figure 6 (above) *Wine Cup or Spice Plate, 1583. Maker's mark a snail. H 13.1 cm (5¼ in). The decoration on the foot is of a similar type as the salts, while the stem has a simple geometric design.*

Hollingworth
1631

engraved with strapwork, although its principle appeal lies in its strangely contrived shape.

Although made to less high standards, the tendency of domestic silver to ape the styles of more fashionable pieces is quite evident in the pieces which fall into that category. Two standing salts, of 1572 and 1581, are typical of a formula that became completely standard during the last quarter of the century and that was used both on a small scale and for some of the massive 'Great Salts'. The Mostyn Salt of 1586 in the Victoria and Albert Museum, for example, or the Reade Salt in the Norwich Castle Museum are basically of the same design, although on a much larger scale. The 1581 salt, in particular, is densely chased with typical fruit and strapwork, although less well executed than on the cover of the rock-crystal cup *(Figure 9)*.

A rarer form than the salt is the wine cup or spice plate of 1583 *(Figure 6)*. Traditionally known as 'tazzas', objects with very similar descriptions in the Royal Jewel House inventory are variously termed 'Bolles' or 'Spice plates', while a painting by Claeissens of about 1550 in the Groeningemuseum, Bruges, shows similar vessels being used for wine. The decoration to the foot is of the same type as the salts, while the stem is flat-chased with a simple geometric design. Chasing, or embossing, involves raising a relief design by hammering from behind and in front, whereas flat-chasing produces an effect much more akin to engraving, although without removing any metal. The centre of the bowl is chased with a female portrait medallion without an engraved surround, but whereas many of the finest Continental examples exploit the decorative potential of the bowl with superbly chased panels, English ones are generally much less sophisticated.

In very similar taste is the pair of silver-gilt tankards of 1602 *(Figure 8)*. Tankards have always been a special preserve of English silversmiths on account of the popularity of beer-drinking in this country, but while most 17th and 18th century examples tend to be relatively plain, 16th century tankards are treated as decoratively as most other plate of the period. The earliest recorded tankard made entirely of silver is one of bulbous form, hall-marked for 1556. But although more than two dozen Elizabethan tankards are known, only one other pair pre-dates these, namely those of 1586 formerly in the collection of the late Lord Astor of Hever.

The pair of flagons and a steeple cup of 1618 were made in the reign of James I, but both illustrate forms that evolved during the preceding century and are handled in a characteristically Elizabethan manner *(Figure 7)*. Flagons or 'livery pots', unlike tankards, were vessels intended for pouring rather than drinking from and varied in size from about six inches high to the massive forms that are still in the Kremlin. The inscription records that they were given to St. Augustine's church in the City of London by Daniel Hollingworth in 1631, presumably in order to fulfill Archbishop Whitgift's requirement that churches be equipped with 'two comely pots of silver or pewter to fetch wine to serve the Lord's table, reserved and kept clean to that purpose only'. Their very secular character, however, together with the fact that they were already 20 years old before they came into the possession of the church, proves that they were originally made as domestic plate. Indeed, as custodian of many such gifts and bequests, the church has been responsible for the preservation of a large percentage of surviving 16th century plate and it is regrettable that so many churches are now forced to consider the disposal of their treasures as a means of raising funds for repairs to their fabric.

Figure 7 (opposite top) *Pair of silver-gilt flagons, 1618. Marked M. H 28 cm (11¼ in). The inscription records that they were given to St. Augustine's Church in the City of London by Daniel Hollingworth in 1631.*

Figure 8 (opposite below) *Pair of silver-gilt tankards, 1602. Marked IB. H 21.2 cm (8¼ in). These early tankards are treated much more decoratively than most later ones.*

Figure 9 (above) *Standing Salt, 1581. Marked RM. H 27.7 cm (11 in). Densely chased with fruit and strapwork.*

DENTAL INSTRUMENTS

Elisabeth Bennion

There is a certain snobbery attached to the study of mere objects, rather as if it were the philosophy or psychology or sociology of dentistry that might be the worthier subject. A study of dental instruments, however, represents a history of the dental profession and the treatment it has afforded such as can be made no other way, for without their instruments the practitioners would have been powerless beyond the use of their hands. Their instruments were therefore an extension of their bodies, their skill and their experience. To collect these artefacts might nevertheless be considered another matter. Dental pain has been familiar to everyone at some time or another and found to be of such uncontrollable ferocity that to acquire some of the tools associated with it, albeit in its relief, might seem to savour of a singular perversity; but only a study of the past can give a necessary sense of proportion about the present.

The modern high-speed drill used with a fine jet of iced water and the fast-acting local anaesthetic we have all come to expect were not thought up overnight. An examination of the forerunners of modern dental equipment suggests a new dimension to our understanding of the past and one that brings home the fact that by gaining contemporary treatment we have lost a measure of civilised life, whereby the very apparatus of this so unpopular profession might be made ravishingly beautiful by craftsmen who were incapable of making it otherwise. One of the most important milestones of advanced surgery, the principle of antisepsis, was in itself responsible for the end of decorative detail, the end of tortoiseshell, ivory, mother-of-pearl studded with garnets and turquoises, the end of delicately turned finials; imaginatively carved handles and golden shafts giving way to the coldly efficient designs that sterilisation requires. This has to be the dividing line. In whatever other branch of collecting we can advance the antique date year by year, here it has to remain with Lister and the tardy and rather unwilling acceptance of his work from 1870 onwards.

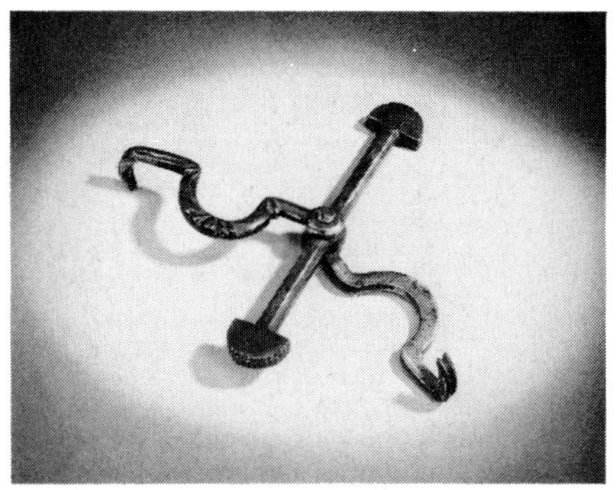

Figure 1 *A very rare early Pelican, about 1570.*

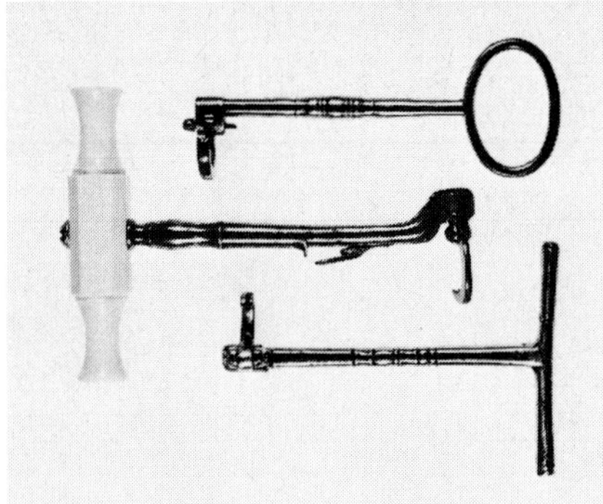

Figure 2 *Rare early ring-handled Toothkey, about 1750. 13 cm (5¼ in). Straight-shaft Toothkey with ivory handle, about 1790. 14 cm (5½ in). Early Toothkey, leather bolster. About 1750. 11.5 cm (4½ in).*

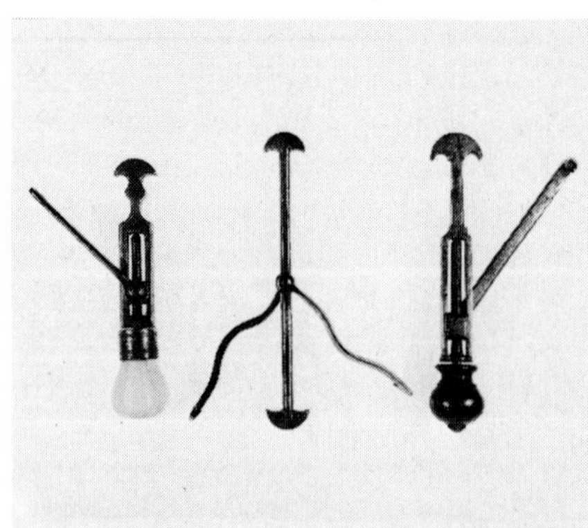

Figure 3, l to r: *Screw-operated Pelican with ivory handle, about 1770. 12 cm (4¾ in). Double-ended Pelican, about 1700. 14 cm (5½ in). Screw-operated Pelican, about 1780. 13.5 cm (5¼ in).*

There can be few countries where there are no dental collectors. Most of them but by no means all, are members of the profession. Some start their collection with the chance gift or acquisition of an instrument that so inspires their imagination they feel compelled to find some companion pieces, until the gaps in the assembly become evident and require filling; then other amplification is necessary and so on. Others have a particular interest in one branch of treatment and naturally show a curiosity about its past which is expressed in the essential instruments. Others are enthused by museum collections or illustrations in old dental treatises. Discrimination and restraint are important, together with an appreciation of quality and condition and the taste to decide whether an item is good of its own time and type.

Certainly it has never been easier to start a collection than now, with so many specialist dealers in the capital cities and

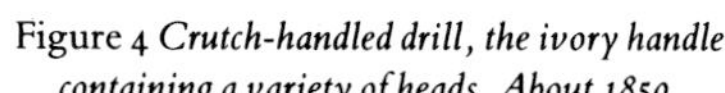

Figure 4 *Crutch-handled drill, the ivory handle containing a variety of heads. About 1850.*

other, provincial, dealers who eagerly stock what dental pieces they can find. The position over the last seven or eight years has changed dramatically. The three leading London auction houses hold regular instrument sales including dental items, their catalogues keenly awaited both there and overseas. Antique fairs, both of the bric-a-brac and more serious variety, rarely do not include dealers with dental matter to show. An awareness of the commercial value of these objects has reached even the haunts of coot and fern and gone are the days when the valuable contents of cupboards were cleared out in the direction of the interested dentist; when collections might be acquired in exchange for grateful thanks. Nevertheless, prices have still not reached their peak and are ranged for every length of pocket. The new collector can still find a tortoiseshell gum-lancet, a scaler, mirror or Victorian forceps for under £30, while the more ambitious will have to pay around £2000 for a good pelican and at least twice that for a large cased set of multiple operating instruments. Pieces with a named maker are naturally desirable as being easier to date, though even more sought after are the pre-18th century items which bear no name. Quality crosses all barriers and an appreciation of it is what one knows as taste; rarity can only be assessed with knowledge. Come what may, the intelligent and determined collector needs the services of an informed and reputable dealer, with whom it is possible to form a relationship founded on confidence and trust, if the collection is not to become a mere magpie conglomeration of unrelated objects from the past.

Many collections start that way, an indiscriminate result of where the combination of eye, taste and purse happen to rest. How much more interesting to give the collection direction from the start. One might collect extracting instruments, their use formerly seen as a radical toothache remedy when all potions,

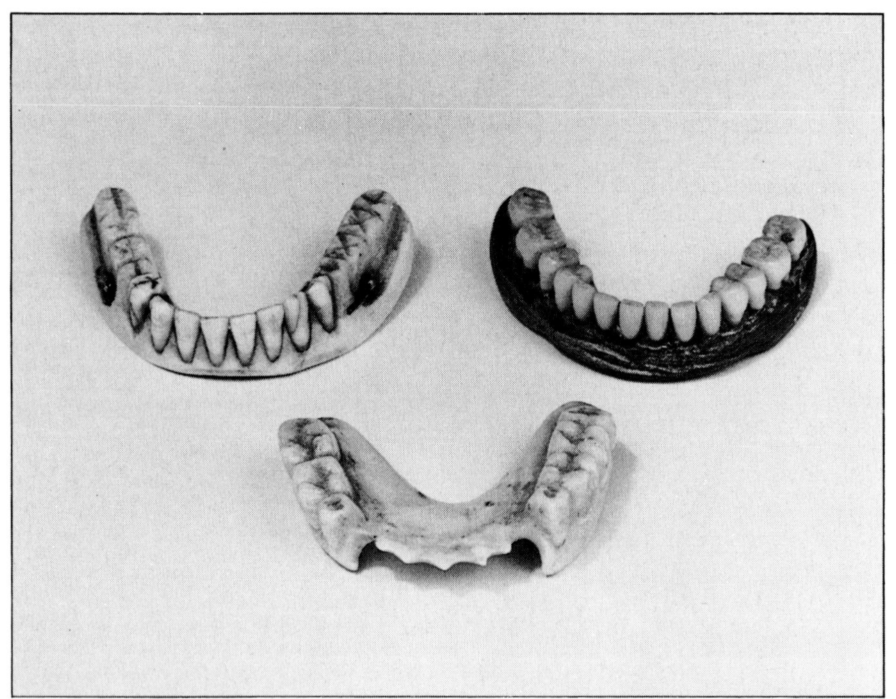

Figure 5 *Three half-sets of artificial teeth.* Top left: *Waterloo teeth set into a solid piece of carved ivory, about 1840;* top right: *Waterloo teeth set in lead, about 1810;* bottom: *solid piece of carved ivory, about 1800.*

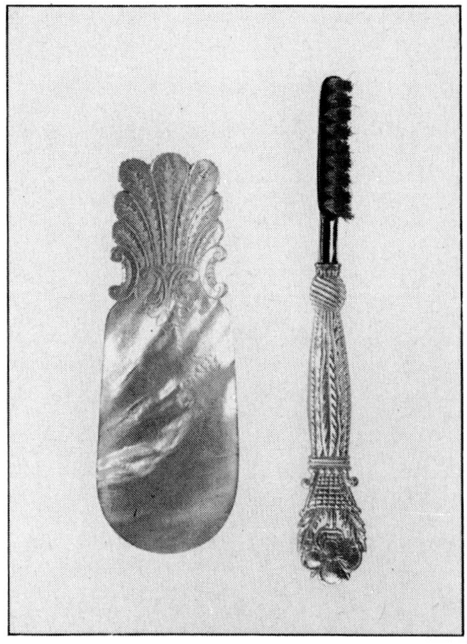

Figure 6 *French silver-gilt mounted Toothbrush, mother-of-pearl handle, about 1860. 14 cm (5½ in). Fine mother-of-pearl Tongue Depressor, about 1860. 11 cm (4½ in).*

poultices and philtres had failed. Variety would be not only in the different types of instrument: forceps, keys, pelicans, screws, elevators etc, but in the date, decoration and material of the piece. Another collection might demonstrate the history of dental fillings and include drills and other excavators, different types of filling materials and their attendant pluggers and burnishers. Some people collect dental chairs and surgery furnishing. How enviable, had one the room, to equip an entire surgery with the apparatus of a given date. Another idea might be instruments by the same maker, an attempt to acquire all the pieces of a particular catalogue. Anaesthesia equipment might be thought by the strictly dental collector too wide a subject, overlapping by too wide a margin the realms of general surgery.

For the squeamish, the least attractive subject is prosthetic dentistry. However, having overcome one's initial reaction, how absorbing is the social comment encapsulated in a carved wood or bone denture; the Waterloo teeth, gathered from the battlefield and set in an ivory base; the very slow but ceaseless endeavour to perfect the fitting and attachments that would enable the wearers to eat, enunciate and even close their mouths without force. The natural tooth, seen by primitive men as immortal and retaining magic properties was, by its loss, assumed to take with it virility and strength, anticipating death. Without teeth, over-closing of the lower jaw could cause deafness, particularly affecting the very poor who could not afford false teeth or preventive dental treatment. Without teeth, imperfect food was imperfectly masticated and caused frequent and serious digestive problems undermining general health. Without teeth, one was seen as unnecessarily old and useless. How effecting and degraded by the music hall is the history of false teeth.

Another social aspect of the subject might be displayed in a collection showing rustic dentistry, the tools of the itinerant toothdrawers. Probably made by local blacksmiths, these instruments evince a chilling crudity, undoubtedly present in the only treatment available to the majority of the populace for several centuries. Much more elegant would be the artefacts of oral hygiene: toothbrushes, tongue-scrapers, toothpicks and their cases, containers for the various cleaning agents, or perhaps dental mirrors.

In Great Britain there are some excellent museum collections to study. In London these include, principally, the museum of the British Dental Association, the Odontological Museum of the Royal College of Surgeons and the Wellcome Collection at the Science Museum. Out of town there is the Menzies-Campbell Collection in Edinburgh, the Museum of the Royal Army Dental Corps at Aldershot and the Museum of the History of Science in Oxford. Major collections abroad include those at Utrecht, Cologne and the magnificent Musée Fauchard in Paris. How very welcome is the news that at last the United States, for so long in the lead of dental treatment, is to have its first

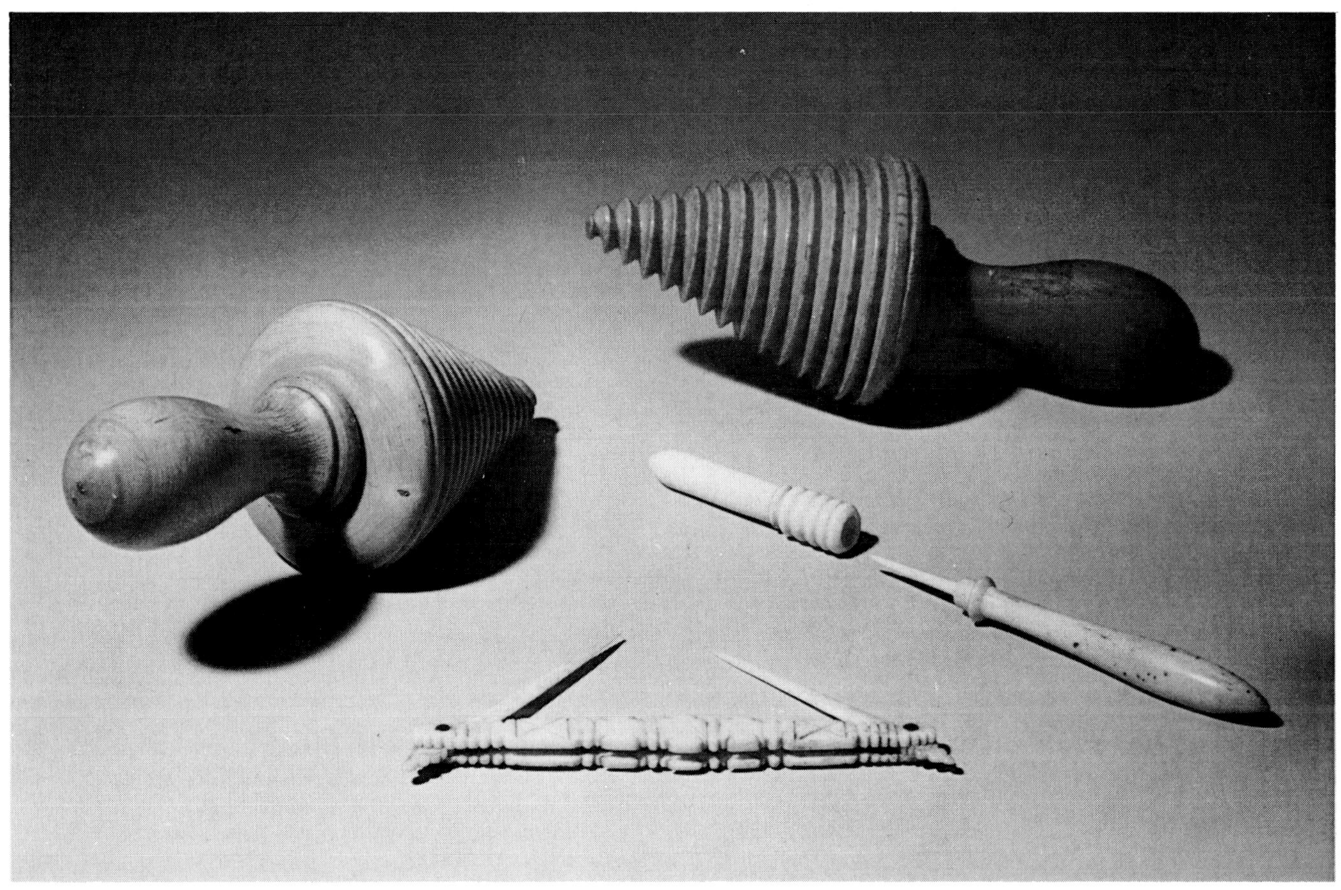

National Museum of Dental History at Baltimore. Most of the European capital cities and some of the larger American towns had their complement of instrument-makers by the turn of the 18th-19th centuries but the good museums are rarely so chauvinist as not to be international in their collections.

Alongside the collection of dental instruments is a thriving interest in the collection of ancillary objects which, in itself, affords a glimpse of an attitude not shown to other types of surgery. The dentist, his patient, his operation and his skill, or lack of it, have long been seen as a subject for humour. This must derive, presumably, from the charlatan tooth-drawers of the fairground who drew teeth as an entertainment but it has resulted in a wealth of jokey articles demonstrating not the development of treatment but our social response to it. Prints, cartoons, postcards, pottery fairings, tooth-shaped vases, carvings, 'fairy money' for shed milk teeth, dogs with toothache, angels with toothache, false teeth paper-clips; the list is endless. Collectors of this type of thing can even choose from a variety of current terms: dental ephemera, dentalia, collectibles (with a choice of spelling), collectanea, miscellanea and there has even been one regrettable sighting of dental-relatables.

Today's mania for collecting shows no sign of abating; everyone appears to want to collect something. Perhaps from dissatisfaction with the modern consumer society, to forge one's own stake in the past, from pure acquisitiveness or whatever, people will make collections of the most unlikely objects. Dental instruments, intelligently and seriously assembled, make a poignant comment on the treatment of dental disease over the years and a suitable expression of gratitude from those of us who live in the dawn of its decline.

Note

Elisabeth Bennion is author of *Antique Medical Instruments* (1979) and *Antique Dental Instruments* (1986), both Sotheby Publications.

Figure 7 *Two ivory Toothpicks and a rare pair of boxwood Mouth-openers, mid-19th century.*

Illustrations courtesy of I. Freeman & Son, Simon Kaye Ltd, London.

October 1986

Figure 1, L to r, *miniature corniche-cased timepiece signed by the notable maker Drocourt.* H *(without handle) 7cm (2¾ in). Fine quality late 19th century clock in a case which is a variation of a style called 'anglaise', with strike and repeat on a gong. Carriage clock with a cannelée case which is similar to a gorge of about 1890; it strikes and repeats, and the small dial on the front reveals that it has an alarm. A sub-miniature of a type made by the Swiss at the beginning of this century.*
DEREK ROBERTS ANTIQUES.
Prices £525, £1250, £1150, £950
(c US $771, $1837, $1690, $1396)

FRENCH CARRIAGE CLOCKS

Deborah Scott

The large number of carriage clocks that are seen on the market today are the legacy of an extraordinary industry that began in France in the 19th century. A clock-maker, Paul Garnier, combined his own type of escapement with a basic design to produce small, sturdy clocks, simple enough to be mass-produced. Characterised by a neat upright brass case and a robust spring-driven movement surmounted by a horizontal platform bearing the escapement, the carriage clock was particularly designed for travelling.

Garnier's early carriage clocks date from around the 1830s, and over the following decades a carriage clock industry developed and expanded to accommodate an ever increasing demand. Strangely this demand was not indigenous to France and the great majority of carriage clocks were exported, mostly to England. Not that this country was not producing its own carriage clocks however, but these were made to special order and were consequently of a higher quality and much more expensive.

Although many of the major French makers who followed Garnier's lead signed themselves *'à Paris'* and indeed were based there, the movements were made in one of two centres. One was a small town in Northern France near Dieppe called Saint Nicolas d'Aliermont, and the other the Jura region, near the French/Swiss border. Using escapements, mainsprings and other pieces from different specialist sources, the movements were assembled in workshops in these areas, then sent for finishing to the Parisian 'maker', who would sign the clock with his mark. To add to the confusion, a retailer, especially a foreign one, might insist on purchasing clocks unsigned by the Parisian maker so that he could then mark them himself. One thus encounters French carriage clocks with dials puzzlingly inscribed 'Dent, London', for example. Further complications arose later in the 19th century when some of the provincial workshops began to supply fully finished clocks as well as movements. These were not of the highest Parisian quality but were inexpensive and sound. The use of standard parts and the piecemeal nature of production together allowed a wide variety of carriage clocks to be made. Here we will concentrate on the types that may be purchased for around £1000 or less.

Figure 2 *A striking clock whose style and arabic numerals suggest a date early in this century. Shown here untouched though in working order, its price would be nearer £450 once overhauled and with the case cleaned and restored.* H *(without handle) 14 cm ($5\frac{1}{2}$ in). The Clock Shop. Price £250 (c US \$367)*

The majority of carriage clocks that are encountered are of what is called 'full size'. This is anything between $5\frac{1}{2}$ and 7 inches when the handle is up. A few 'giants' were made in the finer cases, and these measure 9 inches with the handle up. These were not common amongst French carriage clocks, and this size was more popular with English carriage clock makers since it could more readily house their bulkier movements. Miniature carriage clocks or *Mignonettes* were made in sizes ranging from $3\frac{1}{4}$ inches to $4\frac{1}{4}$ inches with the handle

Figure 3 *Corniche-type timepiece by the important maker Margaine, whose mark appears on the back plate. The clock is marked on the dial by E. White of Paris and London, also a clockmaker but in this instance the retailer. About 1880.* H *(without handle) 12.7 cm (5 in).* PATRIC CAPON. *Price £375 (c US $551)*

raised. These were usually timepieces only, but rare examples with complete strike work are known. Mentioned here are the standard sizes, but individual makers offered some intermediate sizes often containing a standard size of movement.

The range of cases is enormously wide, but one can enumerate a few of the standard types which are likely to be encountered on the market. The early carriage clocks, dating from before 1850, appear in simple one-piece cases (see *Figure 4*). These are usually more squat in shape than the later clocks, and have plain cases which are brazed together in contrast to the later multipiece cases in which many cast and pressed components are screwed together. The latter method superseded the former since it was less costly and allowed for more variation. The cheapest and most basic clock was called the *Obis*. In *Figure 7* a typical example is illustrated, absolutely plain, with a case of pressed brass and the hands friction-fitted with no pin securing them. While the majority of carriage clocks from side view reveal three vertical plates, in *Obis* models economy allowed only two, and this is a useful distinguishing factor as it makes the clock slimmer front to back. From 1880 until the 1930s very large numbers of these clocks were produced. They were available as timepieces with or without alarm but did not have elaborate strike-work. They were not made by the best makers and are scorned by most clock dealers today.

Figure 4 *A decorative example of a carriage clock with the early one-piece case, (notice that the corners at the top are brazed together). This is attractively engraved and it strikes and repeats on a bell, another early feature dating it to the 1840s.*
H *(without handle) 12.7 cm (5 in).* DEREK ROBERTS ANTIQUES. *Price £1400 (c US $2058)*

Superficially similar to the *Obis* but normally of good quality is the *Corniche* case (see *Figures 3 and 6*). The case is more substantial, slightly more elaborate and usually has a handle that is prevented from falling forward by stops. A *Corniche* case may house a more elaborate movement than an *Obis*. It is the most frequently found carriage clock of good quality today. Made from the 1870s, it has many variations.

The most expensive standard carriage clock case was called a *Gorge* (see *Figure 7*). Made from the 1860s it was used by the best makers, and housed movements of high quality. The cases were constructed with more care than cheaper clocks, and are of good quality, heavy gauge metal. *Gorge* cases remain the most desirable of the standard types of case, and can command a premium today. Oval cases of good quality were also made in various sizes and these can command prices similar to a comparable *Gorge*.

Although the aforementioned traditional styles with their lacquered or gilt brass cases remained popular throughout, by the end of the 19th century carriage clocks had also been adorned with every kind of decoration. The best of these contained good quality movements and were expensive in their own day. Some can command well over a thousand pounds today.

Buying a clock

Factors affecting the price of a carriage clock include the complexity of the movement. The cheapest clock is a timepiece – that is, a clock which does not strike. The presence of alarm-work makes no difference to the price. The value of a clock is enhanced by a strike mechanism and further if it repeats. Striking is on either a bell or, after the mid 19th century, a gong. These may normally be seen outside the back plate of the clock, – the gong is a blued steel coil of about two inches diameter. The most complex strike mechanisms which involve striking on two different bells or gongs, appear in the best quality cases and their prices are outside the scope of this article. These are called *Petite sonnerie* or *Grande sonnerie* and the especially rare *Minute repeater*.

The case style is another factor. There is some concordance between the standard of case and the standard of movement which should incline a buyer towards the better *corniche* and *gorge* cases and away from the *Obis*. A travelling box, originally provided with every clock, only enhances value if it is complete with original key and both are marked with the clock's own serial number. Keys are of standard sizes and lost ones are not difficult to replace.

Large quantities of ordinary carriage clocks were not signed by their makers. Clocks made by certain makers who did sign their work (usually with a mark on the backplate), are valued especially highly. The most prominent of such names are Jacot, Drocourt and Margaine. Not all the clocks by these makers were marked, however, and some have a mark concealed within the movement, perhaps because of a retailer's special requirement.

Perhaps the most important factor affecting price is condition, which is closely allied to quality. Many carriage clocks used a cylinder escapement (see *Figure 8 left*). When worn out these were often replaced with a more accurate new lever escapement. Although this improves the time-keeping it ruins the value of a clock as a collector's item. Original lever escapements are found on carriage clocks of good quality. These are characterised by good design and careful finishing and attention to detail; for example the brass platform is often silvered. Although it is more expensive, the repair of a worn lever escapement is normally possible and is greatly preferable to replacement in a good clock.

Figure 5 *Gorge-cased fine quality carriage clock by Jacot, one of the especially desirable makers. The elegant but simple case houses a movement with a strike and repeat.* STRIKE ONE. *Price about £1200 (c US $1764)*

Buying from a specialist dealer is advisable for a novice, since guarantees will be given about the condition of the clock, it will be cleaned, serviced and in working order. Much can be learned from such dealers and they are usually pleased to help enthusiastic amateurs. Carriage clocks do also appear in auctions regularly. To buy here is, of course, to turn one's back on the guarantees and advice that a specialist dealer can offer. For the brave and the confident, however, the apparent savings are enough to encourage a bid. It must be borne in mind that most clocks at auction will need a good overhaul and clean at least, and this can cost from £30 to over £100 depending on the complexity of the clock. Ask the advice of the auctioneer, especially if it is specifically a clocks auction – he will probably be prepared to differentiate those that are worthwhile for a private buyer from those that are destined for a long sojourn at the restorer's. Most of all, examine the clock closely. Ask for a key and wind it up. If it goes, however sluggishly, chances are that an overhaul will set it to rights. The more complex the strike work, the more expensive it will be to restore. Look carefully also at the dial. Some dealers regard a perfect dial as essential. Bear in mind that disfigurement may be expensive to restore, and it is difficult to find a good dial restorer, so be disinclined to purchase one that is in a poor state.

Figure 6 *Corniche carriage clock with strike and repeat (notice repeat button on top of case) by well renowned makers Aubert and Klaftenberger, Paris. On the right is the clock's original travelling box, bearing the corresponding serial number. About 1865.*
H *(without handle) 14 cm ($5\frac{1}{2}$ in).* PATRIC CAPON
Price £775 (c US $1139)

Figure 7 (below) *The 'Obis' clock is the humblest of carriage clocks. The case is made of thinly pressed metal so the clock is lighter than better quality examples. An example such as this could be found for less than £100 but is not the best choice for a first time buyer.*
SOTHEBY'S
Estimate £80–£150 (c US $117–220)

Brass cases often respond well to gently cleaning with soap and water. They may be relacquered or regilt, or left as they are depending on their state and the purchaser's taste and pocket. If they are to be restored, it is preferable to replace their original finish – that is gilding or lacquer as appropriate. Beware of shiny new-looking clocks at auction. They may be poorly restored but unsaleable by a dealer for some reason, or they may be reproductions. Be aware when buying a cheap clock – perhaps an *Obis* – that you may have to spend as much again on restoration. It is more sensible to buy the best you can afford, that needs the minimum attention.

Restoration and cleaning should be carried out by a recommended expert. The British Horological Institute can offer names of members who are restorers. Having bought a clock, bear in mind that it will not go for ever if unattended. Five years is the longest that oil will last so have it overhauled and cleaned at such intervals.

Figure 8, L to r, *Three platform escapements as they might be seen looking down through the top window of a carriage clock. A cylinder escapement used on obis and cheaper forms of corniche; a good quality lever escapement found on better clocks; a modern lever escapement frequently found as a replacement. Notice the substantial differences in design quality and finish.* Courtesy SOTHEBY'S

Figure 9 *Decorative carriage clock with strike and repeat in an engraved gilt-brass gorge case. Unusually for a gorge it does not bear a mark, but is nonetheless finished to a high standard. About 1860.* SOTHEBY'S Estimate *£700-£900 (c US $1029-1323)*

Prices

Although price indications are variable since all the factors mentioned must be taken into account, some sample prices for 'full-sized' clocks may be helpful. A *Corniche* timepiece of reasonable quality will cost about £200-£300, though by Jacot, Margaine or Drocourt a figure of £600 would be realistic. A *Corniche* with strike and repeat will cost £400-£600 or nearer £900 by a 'name'. *Gorge* clocks range from around £1000 for strike and repeat to £2000 and more for *Grande sonnerie* work. Miniature clocks command a premium. Auction prices are lower for the reasons mentioned above. Reproductions of mechanical carriage clocks are available and for comparison it is worth noting that these range in price from about £140 to over £600 for standard types. A clock from the heyday of carriage clocks must surely be the better purchase.

Bibliography

Charles Allix's book, *Carriage Clocks, their history and development* (Antique Collector's Club, 1974) is the authority on this subject.

SCOTTISH PEBBLE JEWELLERY

Deborah Scott

Scottish jewellery has a long history, rooted deep in Celtic and Viking traditions. These distant influences have pervaded Scottish jewellery throughout the ages, but in the 19th century the traditional forms became high fashion. This fashion was set off by the young Queen Victoria, whose enthusiasm for Scotland was expressed in her purchase of a castle at Balmoral in the 1840s. Increasingly, Scotland became the place to go for holidays and all things Scottish were popular.

Scottish pebbles had been used in 18th century jewellery, cut and polished and set in silver or gold in a number of traditional forms. Their rich and varied but earthy colours appealed greatly to the nature conscious Victorians, and pebble jewellery became popular for souvenirs and fashionable wear. A great deal of such jewellery was made, and as the century wore on this reflected a more general Victorian taste, and owed only its symbolic and traditional origins to Scotland. Indeed it is a moot point how much of this jewellery was made in Scotland. Some maintain that as much as 80 per cent of all 'Scottish' pebble jewellery we see today has never been near Scotland and had its origins, rather less romantically, in Birmingham. A few pieces do bear Birmingham hallmarks, and some say that the Birmingham pieces are mostly of this century. It seems, however, perfectly plausible that the 19th century Birmingham small workers, with their reputation for fashionable novelties, would not have been slow to profit from this fashion for agate-set jewellery. Whether one will ever be able to distinguish the 'real McCoy' from the Birmingham versions seems doubtful. It is tempting to suggest that all the high quality pieces are from Scotland, and the rest from Birmingham but there is no evidence to suggest that no good pieces were made in Birmingham.

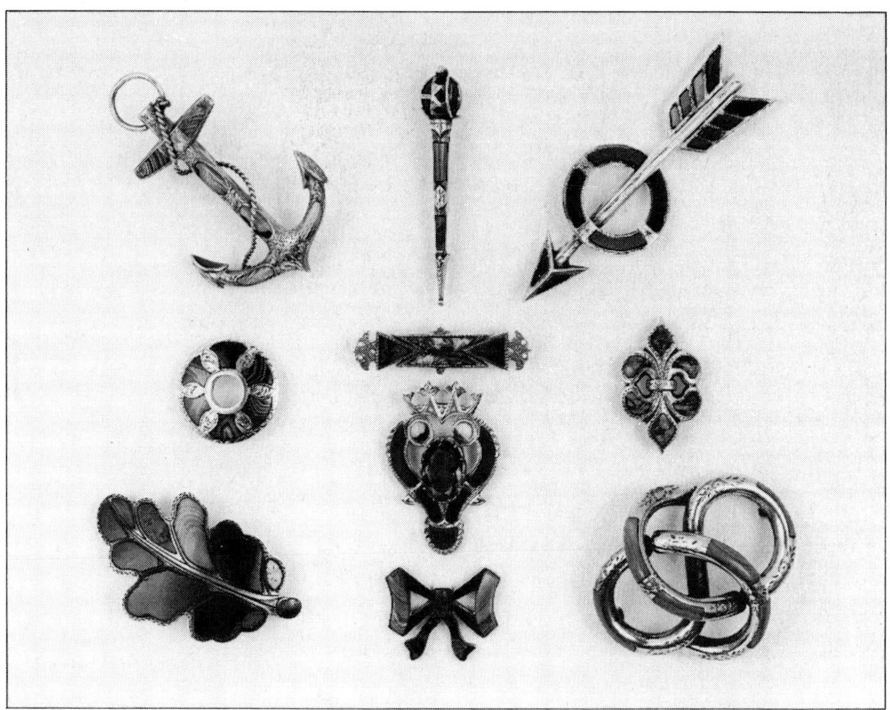

Figure 1
Top Row (left to right). *Silver anchor brooch set with grey agate £175 (cUS$294).* DIANA FOLEY. *Brooch in form of a sword and scabbard, hallmarked Birmingham 1924 and not well made. £45 (cUS$76)* M. MARKOV. *Arrow and hoop brooch set with agate £225 (cUS$378)* DIANA FOLEY.

Second Row *Small round silver brooch, a simple piece well executed. £125 (cUS$210)* DIANA FOLEY. *Bar brooch set with pink and grey granite. £68 (cUS$114)* M. MARKOV. *Brooch of traditional Scottish 'luckenbooth' form, crowned and set with agates and a cairngorm. £125 (cUS$210)* DIANA FOLEY. *Small silver brooch in form of a double fleur-de-lys, set with granite. £160 (cUS$269)* DIANA FOLEY.

Bottom Row *Oak leaf shaped brooch, silver set with agates. £145 (cUS$243)* M. MARKOV. *Bow brooch, with agate £148 (cUS$248)* M. MARKOV. *Silver and grey agate endless knot brooch. £298 (cUS$500)* BRIAN & LYNN HOLMES.

Early examples of this jewellery, from the 18th and first half of the 19th century were usually simple. Small brooches or lace-pins with a single stone supported by a plain silver claw setting were typical (see figure *2* (2). By 1850, craftsmen were becoming more adventurous and in the 1860s and 1870s all manner of jewellery was made from pebbles and precious metal. The Victorian taste for the bold and flamboyant was influential, and blended with the Scottish tradition for large plaid pins to give rise to the impressive brooches that were made. Most of these adopt traditional Scottish forms – the round, convex shield shape sometimes with a hemispherical stone in the centre (see *Figure 4 (2)* for this shape), annular (ring shaped) and penannular brooches (cleft ring), or those with designs derived from the 8th century Hunterston brooch. *Figure 4 (12)* is a peculiarly Scottish shape from these origins. Also copied from historic relics was the manner of engraving the silver mounts. In the more Scottish pieces, where the Victorian desire for pretty scrolls and flowers did not dominate, the silver was engraved in panels of contrasting patterns, and with a characteristic naive fervour *(Figure 4 (5), (9)*. Another traditional form is the Luckenbooth brooch. These silver heart-shaped brooches were historically sold from locked booths near Edinburgh Castle, and they too were set with agates in the 19th century (*Figure 1* centre). Celtic motifs especially endless knots, were recurrent themes *(Figure 4, (4, 16) & Figure 1*, bottom right).

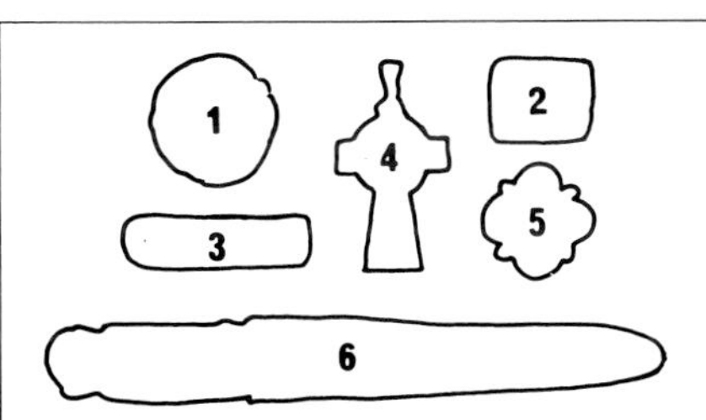

Figure 2
1) *Silver, grey agate and paste cairngorm pin. £95 (cUS$159)*
2) *Silver mounted moss agate pin, an early example of the simple type from about 1840. £38 (cUS$69)*
3) *Grey and pink granite bar brooch. £58 (cUS$97)*
4) *Celtic cross of unusual red granite, set in gold and with a river pearl centre, with locket back. £465 (cUS$781)*
5) *Brooch with grey banded agate and amethyst centre in silver. £75 (cUS$126)*
6) *Dress dirk, a rare and splendid piece with agate set handle topped with a large cairngorm. Mackay & Chisholm, Edinburgh 1881. £1800 (cUS$3024).*

All from JOSEPH BONNAR.

Other themes owed less to tradition and more to fashion. Queen Victoria being the head of the Order of the Garter, the buckled strap representing the garter became a popular motif. *Figure 4 (8, 15, 17)*. St. Andrew's Cross, a diagonal cross, is also a recurrent theme, as are anchors, dirks and thistles. Non-traditional forms, such as bracelets and earrings, also became popular.

The structure of this jewellery varies. The stones traditionally used are those that are found in Scotland – agates of many colours with marvellous natural striations, and other forms of chalcedony (quartz) including cornelian (rust red), bloodstone (green with red flecks), and jasper. These stones have a natural affinity for each other, the warmth of their earthy colours being enhanced by the contrast of texture offered by a silver setting. Amethysts and cairngorms (purple and yellow/brown transparent quartz) are also native Scottish stones and were included in some Scottish jewellery. They add a glamorous touch but because of their colour are not always successful additions aesthetically. Granite, both pink and grey, was also used though not mixed with agate. Granite-set jewellery is typical of the maker M. Rettie of Aberdeen, and some pieces do bear this name. The lapidary work seen in pebble-set jewellery is frequently of high quality. In the best pieces the stones are shaped and polished to lie perfectly flush within their setting. No rough edges may be felt. The result is a robust piece of jewellery combining the smoothness and colours of the stones with finely engraved silver or gold. Most pieces are silver-backed but some examples are backed with slate. In the latter cases, the silver is minimal, and may consist of some claws holding the stones in place, and a hinged pin *(Figure 4 (16)*. From their more primitive structure it is tempting to suggest that these are provincial craftsman's work, perhaps from Scotland.

Figure 3 *An example of the finest Scottish agate work from the 1860's showing many of its best characteristics: finely worked silver, perfectly fitted agates topped by an enormous cairngorm. The contents include a variety of small agate-set pieces. This casket is now the property of the National Museums of Scotland. Photo courtesy of* JOSEPH BONNAR.

As the fashion for pebble-jewellery reached its height, pebbles were taken from other sources to fulfil demand. Malachite, with its wonderful rich green colour was used, and it seems that other stones were imported from lapidaries in Germany.

This jewellery has had an enduring appeal, and has continued to be made during this century. Even specialist dealers fight shy of committing themselves on the matter of dating particular pieces. The consensus is that pieces made this century, including modern copies, are generally poor quality souvenirs, displaying none of the fine workmanship of the 19th century work.

Collectors should check condition carefully. A poorly fitting stone may be a replacement, and damaged stones should be avoided as restoration is extremely difficult. Gold settings are two or three times the price of silver set pieces, and the number and colour of the stones also enhances the price. Grey striated agate, like grey granite, is less popular and fetches lower prices than its more colourful counterparts. Certain shapes, for example garter brooches, knots and bows, are especially popular. While the finest gold-set pieces are now so much in demand as to command prices that would have been unthinkable only a few years ago, silver pieces still offer some scope to collectors (and are often aesthetically more pleasing too). Across the border in Scotland, prices tend to be lower than London.

Sources

Scotland is of course a good hunting ground for pebble jewellery. The fashion was so general, though, that much is to be found south of the border.

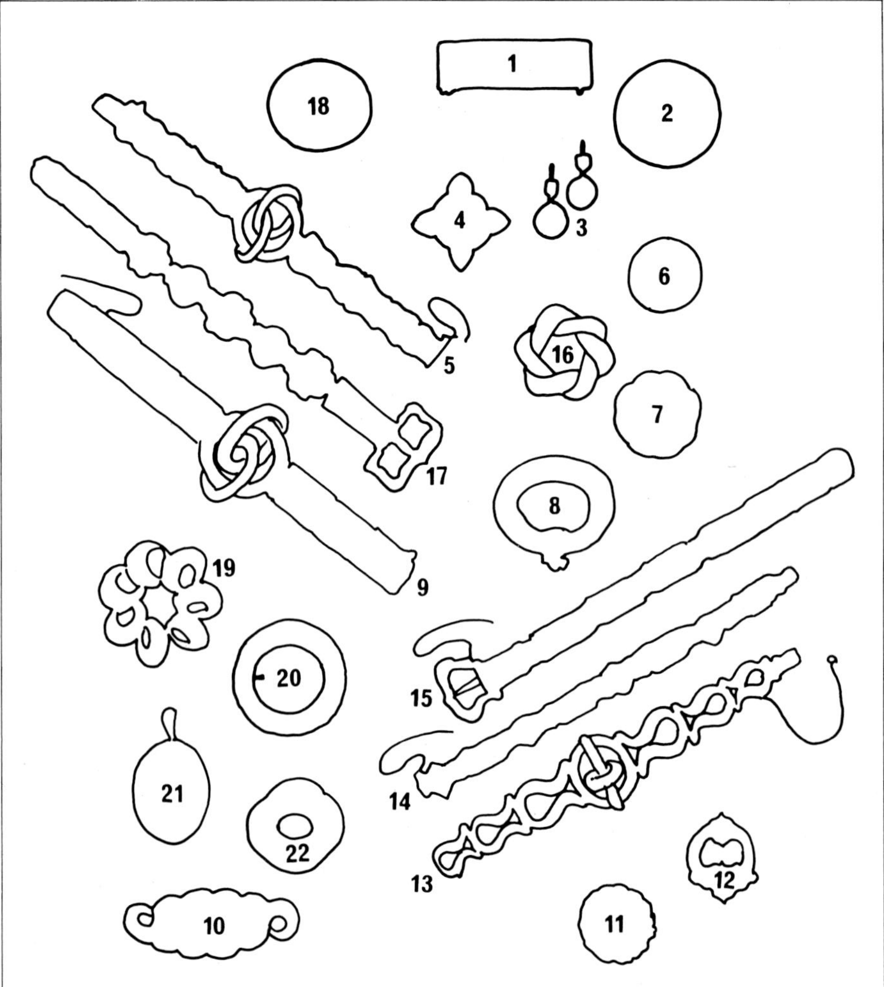

Figure 4

1) *Hinged gold bracelet with colourful agates closely fitted in entwining panels. A top quality piece in both design and execution. £1500 (cUS$2520)*

2) *Unusual brooch with hemispherical centre set with cabochon agates of many colours in intricately engraved gold. £750 (cUS$1260)*

3) *Pair of earrings of bloodstone and cornelian set in engraved gold. £388 (cUS$652)*

4) *Gold-set brooch of intertwined Celtic design. £430 (cUS$722)*

5) *Bracelet of malachite set in engraved silver. £495 (cUS$831)*

6) *Brooch of convex 'shield' shape with agates set in gold. £545 (cUS$915)*

7) *Brooch with cairngorm centre, surrounded with raised arcs of agate, set in gold. £555 (cUS$932.4)*

8) *Brooch of elaborate, garter form with agates of especially bright colours in gold. £635 (cUS$1066)*

9) *Bracelet with each agate panel bordered by different engraving in silver. £885 (cUS$1486)*

10) *Malachite brooch backed with silver and marked Bradford, Torquay, an example of how widespread this fashion became. £250 (cUS$420)*

11) *Gold brooch with bloodstone and cornelian surrounding an amethyst. £450 (cUS$756)*

12) *Gold brooch of a typical Scottish design derived from the Hunterston brooch, set with agates, amethyst and cairngorms. £580 (cUS$974).*

All from BRIAN & LYNN HOLMES.

13) *Grey agate and silver bracelet. £365 (cUS$613)*

14) *Bracelet with gold-set links of a form popular in Scots jewellery. £350 (cUS$588)*

15) *Bracelet of strap form, set in silver and slate backed. £185 + VAT (cUS$310)*

16) *Brooch of interwoven star form, slate backed with silver fitting. £180 (cUS$302)*

17) *Bracelet with quartered agates in clover leaf shapes, and silver strap setting. £325 (cUS$546).*

All from M. MARKOV

18) *Brooch with engraved silver setting, stylised St. Andrew's cross, and shaped agates to borders. £185 (cUS$310)*

19) *Brooch formed of overlapping silver hoops each set with malachite. £245 (cUS$411)*

20) *Annual brooch with contrasting agate sections set in silver. £220 (cUS$369)*

21) *Silver locket set with pink and grey Aberdeen granite. £185 (cUS$310)*

22) *Brooch of grey agate with silver. £98 (cUS$164).*

All from DIANA FOLEY.

PASTE JEWELLERY

Deborah Scott

Antique paste jewellery has a special appeal to collectors since it combines beauty and craftsmanship with more accessible prices than those commanded by precious stones. By the same token however, it is now so much in demand that fine pieces seldom come onto the market. While keeping their eyes open for fine 18th century and early 19th century examples, collectors should also consider later 19th century pieces.

Paste is glass, and it was applied to jewellery in France, England and Spain from about 1700 onwards. Eighteenth century paste was not the fake jewellery of its time. Its different qualities were flaunted with colours being used that could not possibly be imitating real stones. Another 18th century characteristic was the cutting of pastes to many different shapes to fit the mount exactly with the minimum metal showing, whereas it was not economic to cut precious stones this way (see 5 opposite). Silver was predominantly used for mounting 18th century paste, though towards the turn of the 19th century some jewellery was gold backed.

During the 19th century, standards set in the previous century declined and mechanical methods increasingly replaced individual craftsmanship. Paste became imitative, and styles followed the fashion for diamond jewellery. National differences, often discernible in the 18th century, are all but obscured in 19th century paste jewellery as techniques and fashions converged. Nineteenth century paste is frequently open-set, in imitation of the setting that became popular for brilliant cut diamonds. The cutting of shaped pastes was not seen in the 19th century as standard sizes and shapes of paste were more economic to produce.

The price of paste jewellery is affected by its date; although precise dating is not possible, 18th century and pre-1830 pieces are more desirable than Victorian and later examples. Condition is important too. Much paste was backed with foil and a closed setting. If dampness or air have penetrated the setting, the foil will have tarnished, spoiling the colour and lustre of the paste. Coloured pastes are more valuable than white paste, and much rarer. Blue, bright yellow and opaline are especially desirable colours. Wearable pieces command higher prices than things like buckles, unless the paste is especially fine.

Sources

Most antique jewellers will keep examples of paste jewellery whenever they can find it, and some may be found in antique markets.

December 1986

(1) *Victorian swallow brooch of spectacular size, open-set in silver with gold back. Across wings 13.5 cm (5¼ in). THE PURPLE SHOP £250 (c US $357)* **(2)** *Victorian aquamarine-coloured paste necklace. DAVID KER £295 (c US $422)* **(3)** *Brooch with flower 'en tremblant' and drops 'en pampille' – it has its original fitted box. Mid 19th century. LOUISE STROUD £400 (c US $572)* **(4)** *Necklace of fine quality backed with gold, about 1800. DAVID KER £950 (c US $1358)* **(5)** *Mauve paste sévigné in silver setting, about 1770. LOUISE STROUD £400. (c US $572)* **(6)** *Late Victorian swallow brooch open-set in silver. BRIAN & LYNN HOLMES £120 (c US $171)* **(7)** *Green and white earrings set in silver and gold backed. Early 19th century. DAVID KER £450 (c US $643)* **(8)** *Victorian green and white heart-shaped pendant or brooch, on silver. DAVID KER £170 (c US $243)* **(9)** *French fleur-de-lys brooch in closed silver setting, late 19th century. DIANA FOLEY £125 (c US $178)* **(10)** *Small red and white brooch or veil pin on silver, about 1800. LOUISE STROUD £58 (c US $83)* **(11)** *Blue and white paste earrings, probably of 1920s. DAVID KER £145 (c US $207)* **(12)** *Victorian star brooch. THE PURPLE SHOP £48 (c US $68)* **(13)** *Victorian flower shaped brooch, in silver. RICHARD DIGBY £60 (c US $86)* **(14)** *Early 18th century silver buckle converted to a brooch, possibly French. DIANA FOLEY £110 (c US $157)* **(15)** *Green and white tiara set in gilt metal, about 1820. DIANA FOLEY £125 (c US $178)* **(16)** *Edwardian bow brooch fluently modelled, on silver (with original box) DAVID KER £490 (c US $700)* **(17)** *Late 18th century ring with blue and white paste set on silver with blue enamel, gold backed with gold shank. DIANA FOLEY £195 (c US $279)* **(18)** *Early 20th century silver fly set with white, green and red paste DAVID KER £80 (c US $114)* **(19)** *Mauve and white paste parure in gilt metal comprising a necklace, brooch and earrings (not shown). About 1820-30. LOUISE STROUD £250 (c US $357)* **(20)** *Pendant of paste in the suffragette colours of purple and green, with pearls. Early 20th century. BRIAN & LYNN HOLMES £69 (c US $98)* **(21)** *Victorian star brooch with white paste in silver surrounding a real amethyst. THE PURPLE SHOP £78 (c US $111)* **(22)** *Foiled topaz-coloured paste surrounded by white pastes as a small brooch or veil pin. About 1830. LOUISE STROUD £35 (c US $50)* **(23)** *Pink foiled paste with pearls on gold, about 1820. LOUISE STROUD £50 (c US $71)* **(24)** *Edwardian leaf brooch with fitting for a hair pin. THE PURPLE SHOP £38 (c US $54)* **(25)** *Victorian green paste necklace set in gold. DAVID KER £550 (c US $786)* **(26)** *Victorian brooch featuring acrobatic monkeys encrusted with white paste. BRIAN & LYNN HOLMES £148 (c US $211)* **(27)** *French bracelet with white paste set in silver, of about 1920s. DIANA FOLEY £250 (c US $357)* **(28)** *Spanish earrings of about 1790, of silver. DAVID KER £180 (c US $257)* **(29)** *French pendant in the form of a 'Normandy' cross. 19th century. DIANA FOLEY £165 (c US $236)* **(30)** *Flower basket pendant, probably French, early 20th century. BRIAN & LYNN HOLMES £99 (c US $141)* **(31)** *Victorian bracelet of bows and flowers on silver. BRIAN & LYNN HOLMES £70 (c US $100)*

1
2
3
4
5
6
7
8
9
10
11
12
13
14
15
16
17
18
19
20
21
22
23
24
25
26
27
28
28
29
30
31

Top row, l to r: *Art Deco, enamel. £92 (c US$142)* MEROLA. *Reproduction of a 'Hunter' aeroplane with sapphire engine, early 1950s. The engine has a small sapphire at the top. £195 (c US$302)* TREVOR ALLEN. *Art Deco Egyptian revival bird and obelisk. £85 (c US$131)* JOHN JESSE & IRINA LASKI. *Hearts, Diamonds, clubs and spades, about 1940. £495 (c US$767)* N. BLOOM
Second row: *Heart shaped, enamel and diamond. £1150 (c US$1782)* ANNABEL JONES. *Mother-of-pearl, gold and sapphire, 1920s. £345 (c US$534)* HOLMES. *Amethyst, about 1910. £245 (c US$379)* RBR GROUP. *Cream and grey enamel, about 1920s. £92 (c US$142)* MEROLA. *Essex crystal hunters and dogs, late Victorian. £1100 (c US$1705)* MASSADA.
Third row: *Mother-of-pearl and turquoise kidney links. £395 (c US$612).* JOHNSON, WALKER & TOLHURST. *Classical figures in silver and gold. £720 (c US$1116)* PAUL LONGMIRE. *Platinum Cartier links set with sapphires, about 1930. £1250 (c US$1937)* HANCOCKS. *Tortoiseshell piqué, late Victorian. £120 (c US$186)* THE BUTTON QUEEN. *Enamel, about 1915. £69 (c US$106)* TREVOR ALLEN. *Art Nouveau leopard and foliage motif, gold and diamond. £546 (c US$846)* NICHOLAS HARRIS.
Bottom Row: *'The Duchess', a West solitaire, about 1885. One of a pair. £60 (c US$93)* THE BUTTON QUEEN. *Victorian ferns, gold and dendrite, £590 (c US$914)* ANNABEL JONES. *Enamel, late Victorian. £60 (c US$93); gold lockets [illegible] hair, late Victorian. £400 (c US$[illegible]); satirical scene showing Napoleon III, 1870s. £30 (c US$46)*

FASHIONABLE CUFF-LINKS

Vanessa Nicolson

Cuff-links are enjoying something of a comeback. From appealing to a rather specialised taste, many designs, especially those dating from the 1920s and 30s are attractive to a much younger market. They add a touch of glamour or humour to an otherwise plain shirt, saying more about the wearer than an ordinary button. And they need not be a male prerogative as they are not necessarily 'masculine' in design, and matching jewellery can be found.

During the 17th and 18th centuries a type of sleeve button was in use which can be considered the precursor of the cuff-link. Most of these were made of cotton like a toggle, although jewelled ones also existed. But cuff-links as we know them date from the mid 19th century, when the turned back cuff became popular.

The Victorians liked intricacy of design, as well as amusing ones with mechanical devices that enable them to swivel or open up. In 1873 a patent was taken out for 'West solitaires'. These are large and single rather than joined by a chain, so they hold the cuff close together. The one illustrated here is called the 'Duchess', based on a picture by Gainsborough. Other Victorian cuff-links in the illustration include a pair of enamel ones with a flower decoration, a pair of tortoiseshell piqué ones, and those that open up, in typical Victorian fashion, to reveal a tiny locket of fair hair.

Designs in cuff-links reflect styles appearing on other forms of jewellery. The Essex crystal hunting cuff-links can be matched with tie pins and brooches. The beauty of this one (illustrated) is that the two dogs and the two hunters are all slightly different, whereas at first glance they may seem the same. So are the two classical busts, looking more like two couples of Victorians in fancy dress.

Like earrings cuff-links can become separated, but it is worth buying a single one for a collection if it is particularly interesting. The one pictured here is a very unusual satirical scene depicting Napoleon III.

At the end of the 19th century women started using special buttons (for day wear) which could be removed and changed. Some of these have probably been mistaken for cuff-links, but there is no reason why they should not be so used.

Cuff-links from the 1920s and 30s are usually brightly coloured and geometric in Art Deco style, or elegantly subtle for evening wear. The latter often come as part of dress sets, combining materials such as silver, rose diamonds and mother-of-pearl. I have not illustrated the plain gold cuff-links that date from this period, as dealers confirm that when these are wanted they are usually bought new.

September 1986

TORTOISESHELL PIQUE

Deborah Scott

Figure 1 *Italian fan with guards and sticks of tortoiseshell piqué. The guards are inlaid with silver and engraved mother-of-pearl panels, while the sticks bear only silver* piqué point *designs. About 1720.* SOTHEBY'S. *Sold for £330 (c US$462).*

As an art form piqué has been largely unsung by comparison to its decorative peers such as enamelling and lacquering. Only one book has been devoted to it, and that as long ago as 1923, when the collector Herbert C. Dent committed his researches and collection to paper. Valuable as this is as a pictorial reference, in 60 years the market has changed and prevailing opinions about origins no longer coincide with those published by Dent.

Piqué is gold and/or silver inlaid into tortoiseshell (or sometimes ivory) forming patterns and decorative scenes. Mother-of-pearl may also be inlaid in the same way. When small rods of metal are inlaid vertically, giving an overall appearance of a pattern made up of dots, the term *piqué point* is used. Where flat strips of metal are inlaid horizontally for elaborate and extensive patterns, the technique is called *piqué posé*. Further terms include *foules point d'or* – the tiny dots of metal forming delicate lines of pattern; and hair-work, a type of *piqué posé* where the design is formed by fine silver strands.

No doubt the unusual properties of tortoiseshell are largely responsible for the enduring popularity and success of piqué work. True tortoiseshell comes from the shell of a marine turtle – the hawksbill turtle, native to Asian tropical waters. Its most important characteristic is its malleability. When gently heated, either by immersion in hot water or using smokeless charcoal, it softens and may be moulded or shaped. While soft, its edges may be joined and once cool these seams are invisible, except through the inconsistencies of figuring on the shell. In this softened state, points or strips of gold or silver can be inlaid into the surface. On cooling, the shell contracts, holding the metal tight without the need for further adhesive.

The origins of this method of decoration are obscure. One school of thought holds that it must have originated in France in the 17th century. Some say that perhaps André Boulle, who gave his name to a remarkable form of marquetry in brass and tortoiseshell (buhlwork), may have been responsible for piqué. Another school suggests that piqué originated in Naples in the late 17th century. This is the more recent theory, and allows that by the early 18th century, the art of piqué had been adopted by France and many other European countries. Whether the Huguenot craftsmen played their part in disseminating this skill through Europe after the Revocation of the Edict of Nantes in 1685 depends on the extent to which they had been practising piqué work before that time. Whatever the answer, no doubt European craftsmen of several countries were quick to try this attractive method of decoration, and produced the variety of 18th century piqué work that may be seen.

The attractive figuring of tortoiseshell, its strength and lightness meant that it was ideally suited to small decorative objects, and particularly to snuff boxes. The great majority of piqué that survives

Figure 2 Centre: *a fine example of late 19th century piqué, a cheroot case with gold, silver and engraved ivory inlay in chinoiserie design. L 15 cm (6 in). HALCYON DAYS. Price £510 (c US$714)*
Left and right: *two late 18th century boxes, the round one with gold and silver inlay and gold rims; the oval, despite its French inspired star design, is of the typically English, top-hinged form. M. EKSTEIN LTD HALCYON DAYS. Prices £260, £1150 (c US$364, $1610).*

from the 18th century is found on small boxes including snuff boxes, bonbonnières and jewel caskets, a selection of which is illustrated here. Problems of attribution to a country of origin flourish in this area, along with problems of dating. In considering each piece, attention must be given to several factors. For instance, the shape of the box: how does it compare to other boxes of known date or origin? French gold boxes can be of assistance here, with marked examples giving some guidance for comparison. English silver snuff boxes likewise. Details such as hinges, thumb-pieces and mounts all help with attribution.

The two French boxes in *Figure 4 (a & c)* shown here are actually marked with the charge and discharge marks for Paris. Their origin and date can thus be certain, but even if they were not marked their shape and the use of different colours of gold in their floral designs is reminiscent of Parisian gold boxes of the period.

Earlier French work is much more delicate and, as Julia Clarke of Sotheby's points out, almost entirely *piqué point,* with animals, figures and fables as decoration. Mother-of-pearl inlay with extensive silver *piqué posé* showing busy scenes suggests an Italian origin. This work varies from high quality, with the silver and mother-of-pearl itself engraved in great detail *(Figures 4e and f),* to coarser examples lacking engraving, possibly from provincial sources. Some fine *piqué point* decoration, with scrolls, diaper patterns and trailing lines of vinery also suggest an Italian origin *(Figure 4l).*

Recognition of English boxes is assisted by their shape. The flat oval with a projecting hinge is common amongst English silver snuff boxes of the 18th century, and an example in piqué is shown here *(Figure 4k).* The robust hair-work chinoiserie scene in silver on this box is also typically English of the early to mid 18th century. Oval boxes with a top-hinge, like that shown on the right in *Figure 2,* are another English style. Slender rectangular boxes are also known at this period, while later in the 18th century the neo-classical influence is found in pointed oval and round boxes with restrained, classical decoration after Adam. Round flat boxes, like those made in papier mâché, were in vogue in England and on the Continent from the late 18th to the early 19th centuries.

If generalisations may be hazarded, silver is more commonly found on English and German piqué boxes and gold more on French (a pale gold) and Italian (a redder gold). But since exceptions must be manifold, perhaps it is better to assess each piece individually according to the factors mentioned, always bearing in mind the extent to which fashions travelled, and indeed their perpetrators and executors.

After reaching its apogee in the 18th century, piqué would appear to have played itself out. The resulting decline in design quality was accompanied by a decline in popularity during the first part of the 19th century. Towards the middle of the century, however, there was a new impetus for piqué, as a fashion arose for jewellery of tortoiseshell thus decorated. The light weight of tortoiseshell and its malleability made it ideally suited to the bold earrings, brooches and other adornments of the period. Once embellished with piqué designs in gold, silver or coloured metal, an elegance and lightness were imparted that gave it great appeal. *Figure 5* shows some examples of the imaginative shapes which this material took on at this period.

Figure 3 *Some good examples of early 20th century tortoiseshell piqué with the fashionable neo-Adam style decoration. A pair of candlesticks mounted and inlaid with silver, hallmarked 1917; silver backed and mounted clock by William Comyns. The front of the case is inlaid with silver and abalone as a vase of flowers. 1907. H 17 cm (6¾ in). SUE AND ALAN THOMPSON. Prices £1350, £840 (c US$1890, $1176).*

In the 1860s jewellery was made by hand, at least in part, but before long the Birmingham jewellery industry was able to mass-produce it, using machines. This led to more formal patterns with simple elements repeated.

The renewed fashion for tortoiseshell piqué spread beyond jewellery to the Victorian equivalents of the earlier objects of vertu. Examples shown here are a spectacles case *(Figure 4j)* and a cheroot case *(Figure 2)* with exceptionally fine quality work.

Late in the 19th century another application for piqué on tortoiseshell became fashionable. This was its use for toilet sets – trays, brushes, boxes, pots and all the paraphernalia of the dressing table. These were made with the tortoiseshell mounted in silver and invariably inlaid with revived neo-classical designs in silver *(Figures 4 b, g & i).* This fashion seems to have gained momentum in Edwardian times, for many examples

a
b
c
d
e
f
g
h
i
j
k
l
m
n

Figure 5 *A collection of Victorian tortoiseshell piqué jewellery, showing the variety of imaginative forms to which this decorative technique was applied in the 1860s. Earrings £345-£385 (c US$483-539); butterfly brooch £145 (c US$203); buckle £158 (c US$221); bracelet £210 (c US$294); cross £79 (c US$110); heart £148 (c US$207).* BRIAN AND LYNN HOLMES.

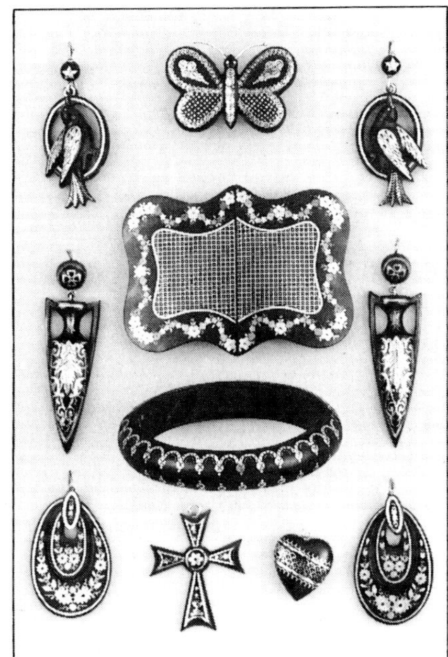

Figure 4 (opposite) *(a) French snuff box decorated with birds and a flower basket in two colours of gold, with silver mounts and engine turned decoration to the surface. Charge and discharge marks for Paris, 1765. £1950 (c US$2730) from* HALCYON DAYS.
(b) Box from a toilet set, the top decorated in silver piqué with applied silver border, 1880-1890, £260 (c US$364) from SUE AND ALAN THOMPSON.
(c) Oval French snuff box with floral decoration in three colours of gold, and gold mounts bearing charge and discharge marks for Paris 1756-62. £2300 (c US$3220) from HALCYON DAYS.
(d) Round box mounted in gold and decorated in elaborate piqué posé *and* point *with gardening trophies. Mid-18th century. Possibly Neapolitan. £1950 (c US$2730) from* HALCYON DAYS.
(e) Exceptional Neapolitan jewel casket with silver and mother-of-pearl decoration showing a game of billiards and other scenes. About 1740. W 15 cm (6 in) £6650 (c US$9310) from HALCYON DAYS.
(f) Snuff box of cartouche shape, with silver and mother-of-pearl decoration, about 1740, possibly Italian. £685 (c US$959) from HALCYON DAYS.
(g) and (i) Two Edwardian trinket boxes with tortoiseshell lids, decorated with classically inspired designs. £325 and £285 (c US$455, $399) from SUE AND ALAN THOMPSON.
(h) Shuttle with two colour gold decoration of birds and insects. Mid-18th century. £840 (c US$1176) from HALCYON DAYS.
(j) 19th century case for spectacles in boldly figured tortoiseshell with silver and mother-of-pearl inlaid. £250 (c US$350) from M. EKSTEIN LTD.
(k) English snuff box with 'hair-line' piqué in silver, about 1720. £660 (c US$924) from HALCYON DAYS.
(l) Neapolitan bonbonnière with exceptionally delicate piqué posé *and* point *in gold, with birds and vinery, about 1740. £2100 (c US$2940) from* HALCYON DAYS.
(m) Fine English snuff box decoration in gold with strapwork border and a central vignette of a fable, about 1730. Price in excess of £3000 (c US$4200) from S. J. PHILLIPS LTD.
(n) Late 19th-century pen with gold floral designs, and seal set in one end. £265 (c US$371) from SUE AND ALAN THOMPSON.

bear hallmarks of that period. Hallmarks were applied if a certain weight of silver was used in an article. Other decorative articles made in tortoiseshell piqué at this time include those shown in *Figure 3*, as well as frames, desk sets (for example, the pen shown in *Figure 4n*), knife boxes and many others. William Comyns was a silversmith whose name is connected with much of this type of work, in the late 19th and early 20th centuries.

Collecting

Collectors will find that fakes are not a problem in this field. Tortoiseshell coloured celluloid is not unheard of but its stuck-on decoration should give it away. So elaborate is valuable piqué work that the difficulties of faking it put it beyond what is worthwhile to unscrupulous craftsmen. Tortoiseshell is a brittle material, and must be treated with care, avoiding changes of temperature, and exposure to strong light. On early pieces there may be some minor restoration. This may be seen as a slightly different colour of metal, or perhaps some change to the surface of the tortoiseshell. The Edwardian examples have frequently been restored by polishing and attention to the surface, to which they respond rewardingly. These kinds of restoration, if well done, are acceptable to most collectors. With jewellery, collectors should check whether the metal inlaid is precious, and the condition of fragile extensions and details. A point for American buyers is that it is an offence to import tortioseshell that is under 100 years old into the United States. Be sure that invoices state clearly that pieces for export to America are at least this old.

Prices for tortoiseshell piqué reflect rarity with early, fine pieces commanding several thousands of pounds. Victorian jewellery and Edwardian boxes can command over £200 depending on interest and condition, as examples illustrated here demonstrate.

Bibliography

Vivienne Becker, *Antique and 20th Century Jewellery*, 1980.
Eric Delieb, *Silver Boxes*, 1968.
Herbert C. Dent, *Piqué: A Beautiful Minor Art*, 1923.
Clare Le Corbeiller, *European and American Snuff Boxes 1730-1830*, 1966.
G. Bernard Hughes, *English Snuff Boxes*, 1971.
Kenneth Snowman, *Eighteenth-Century Gold Boxes of Europe*, 1966.

Sources

Early tortoiseshell piqué is difficult to find, but major dealers in objects of vertu may have examples. They are included in sales of objects of vertu at the main salerooms. Later piqué may be found in antique markets.

November 1985

ENAMELLED CIGARETTE CASES

Erika Speel

For the last few decades cigarettes have been marketed in elegant, efficient packets. These lightweight, throw-away fliptop cardboard boxes have displaced the cigarette cases which were widely used in the past. Before modern manufacturers' packaging methods were introduced, it was customary to transfer the contents of freshly opened packets to airtight containers to prevent squashing of the cigarettes and loss of the tobacco's aroma. It was also more stylish to offer cigarettes to friends from an attractive box or case. Cigarette cases were designed as convenient, portable containers. They were slim and shaped to be worn on the person, in a gentleman's waistcoat or trouser pocket; box-shaped etuis were offered for the handbags of ladies who smoked. The cases had to open out flat in the manner of a book, had to shut easily with a good closure presenting a smooth exterior, and be constructed for durability.

A number of materials could be used for cigarette cases but the best ones were made of gold or silver. These metals were very suitable for enamelled decorations, which added charming, interesting, witty or stimulating pictures to the lids of such cases. From the practical point of view, the inlaid enamelwork made the articles feel more substantial while actually economising on the weight of precious metal. It also protected the most vulnerable portion of the case, the lid, from rubbing down by frequent handling and cleaning of the metal. This was particularly important for silver cases, as the surface of sterling and lower grades of silver tarnishes and darkens to the characteristic gun-metal grey with exposure to air, and although cleaning is not difficult, each time the surface is 'skinned' there is a slight loss of metal weight. The very fine layer of gilding which sufficed to protect the interiors of the cases from tarnish was not a suitable protection for the exterior. The enamelwork could cover a substantial part of the case, leaving a smooth and pleasant surface finish and giving opportunities for decoration with suitably scaled, detailed pictures produced with unfading pigments.

Enamelled cigarette cases were produced in workshops where in previous generations similar work had been applied to far costlier pieces such as snuff boxes, cigar cases, watch cases and jewellery. The major centres for the production of these cases were in England, Germany and Austria. From the 1880s onwards new outlets were being sought for the skills of traditionally trained craftsmen and artists and this period coincided with the growing social custom of cigarette smoking. Adapting traditional enamelling techniques to the decoration of cigarette cases therefore allowed a number of the workshops to continue in business. A number of changes had to be made to suit the new format and the predominantly silver bases, but essentially the methods of the past were perpetuated in the enamellers' workshops. The finely painted and patiently made enamelwork, finished with a brilliant gloss, contrasted with the plain, austere lines of the metal parts of the cases.

The appeal which the painted enamel pictures had for the original owners of these cases still attracts the present-day collector. The pictures can be enticing, humourous or nostalgic, giving insight into the taste and fashion of the period. These articles were made to serve a useful purpose, designed to function efficiently for a long time, and decorated to please the customers. To remain in fashion, topical subjects were added as the need arose. The enamel painters worked on designs which were ordered by retail stores of jewellers' shops for their stock, and private orders were undertaken in addition. A standard range of designs was offered by means of printed catalogues.

The changes in the subjects which were offered and developments in styles of execution can be clearly seen, but despite these outward variations, the craftsmen adhered to their traditions. What comes across most strongly is the fact, which decorative artists have known throughout the centuries, that when it comes to a private and personal article, what pleases and entertains men of action are representations of vivid hunting and sporting themes and pictures of beautiful women. More universally, the range of subjects for cigarette cases includes miniature copies of well known paintings *(Figure 2g)*, historically interesting figures, motifs of fashionable 'types' and popular hunting and racing themes. The repertoire also offered portrait pictures, studies of horses, dogs and cats, and floral and geometric designs, the latter being very popular on cases for ladies. Designs which had proved to be popular on enamelled boxes in the past were carried forward to the decoration of cigarette cases . These included motifs based on the pictures of Watteau and Boucher, showing the familiar rustic lovers, or *fêtes-champêtres* and woodland scenes.

It had long been a popular convention

to show allegorical or mythological scenes which could provide settings in which unclad girls were shown as nymphs or goddesses. These subjects were largely replaced after the 1900s by bolder pictures. The compositions then centred around a single, attractive girl, usually with flowing tresses, alluringly dressed, or seen at her toilet or posing nude. The backgrounds to these studies could be exotic fantasies, but many showed contemporary settings with finely painted details. The artists working in minature on enamel had always been expected to excel in the delicacy of treatment for all their work. This factor, together with the fine colours and finish of quality enamelwork, endowed the pictures with great visual appeal. The idealised treatment applied equally to the portrayal of subjects which were considered suitable only for display to friends gathered in the intimate atmosphere of the smoking room, and therefore often hidden on an inner 'secret' lid.

Pictures of the hunt and other equestrian themes never lost their appeal. As the 20th century progressed, a wider range of sports was represented. The motifs included yachting, golfing, tennis, cycling, football *(Figure 2d)*, motor-car racing and flying. Items specifically commissioned by clients include miniature copies of famous paintings, portraits, and promotional subjects such as the 'Girl with Benz' motif *(Figure 1c)*. Of particular historical interest are the cases decorated with battle scenes, Boer war soldiers, and souvenirs of actual events such as the Prince of Wales' Derby win shown on a box marked 1896 *(Figure 2h)*, and there are also many cases showing Regimental Colours, which were made for members of the Armed Services.

Although the metal cases were manufactured in quantity, to standardised shapes and sizes, the enamelled decorations were added individually to each piece in the specialist workshops. It was therefore possible for the customer to choose the decoration which suited his requirements and have this applied to a case of either gold or silver of suitable shape. Consequently, it is possible to find cases of different types with identical enamelled pictures, showing only minor variations of line and shading in the hand-made work. The versatility of the enamelled cigarette cases made them ideal presentation pieces. They were suitable for prize-giving at races, sporting tournaments, dog shows, club events and the celebration of individual achievements. The motif could commemorate a holiday or honeymoon, birthday or retirement. It is not unusual to find an engraved inscription in a case, which can reveal a little of the history of the article and may give its approximate date of manufacture. This can be useful as the marks to be found are not always helpful in this respect. For instance, a case with a picture of a strong young man carrying two pretty girls across a river has an inscription which shows that this was a present from a father to his son for his 21st birthday. Another evocative inscription is from a student to his teacher, the case in question showing in monochrome the picture of a bird soaring through the sky. For the 'man who has everything' it was considered appropriate to give a cigarette case decorated with little symbols of a racehorse, a ballerina, a hand of cards and a bottle of champagne – the ensemble

Figure 1 *(a) Modish enamel painting based on copper alloy metal, marked as Alpacca on the inside of the case. Probably German, 1920.*
(b) Subjects with Oriental motifs were fashionable at various periods. Austrian, probably 1910. Silver.
(c) One of a series of enamelled cigarette cases produced for promotional purposes for the firm of Benz. The background to the painted motif is of translucent enamel over an engine-turned silver ground, giving brilliance of tone. Austrian, about 1920. Silver.

a

b

c

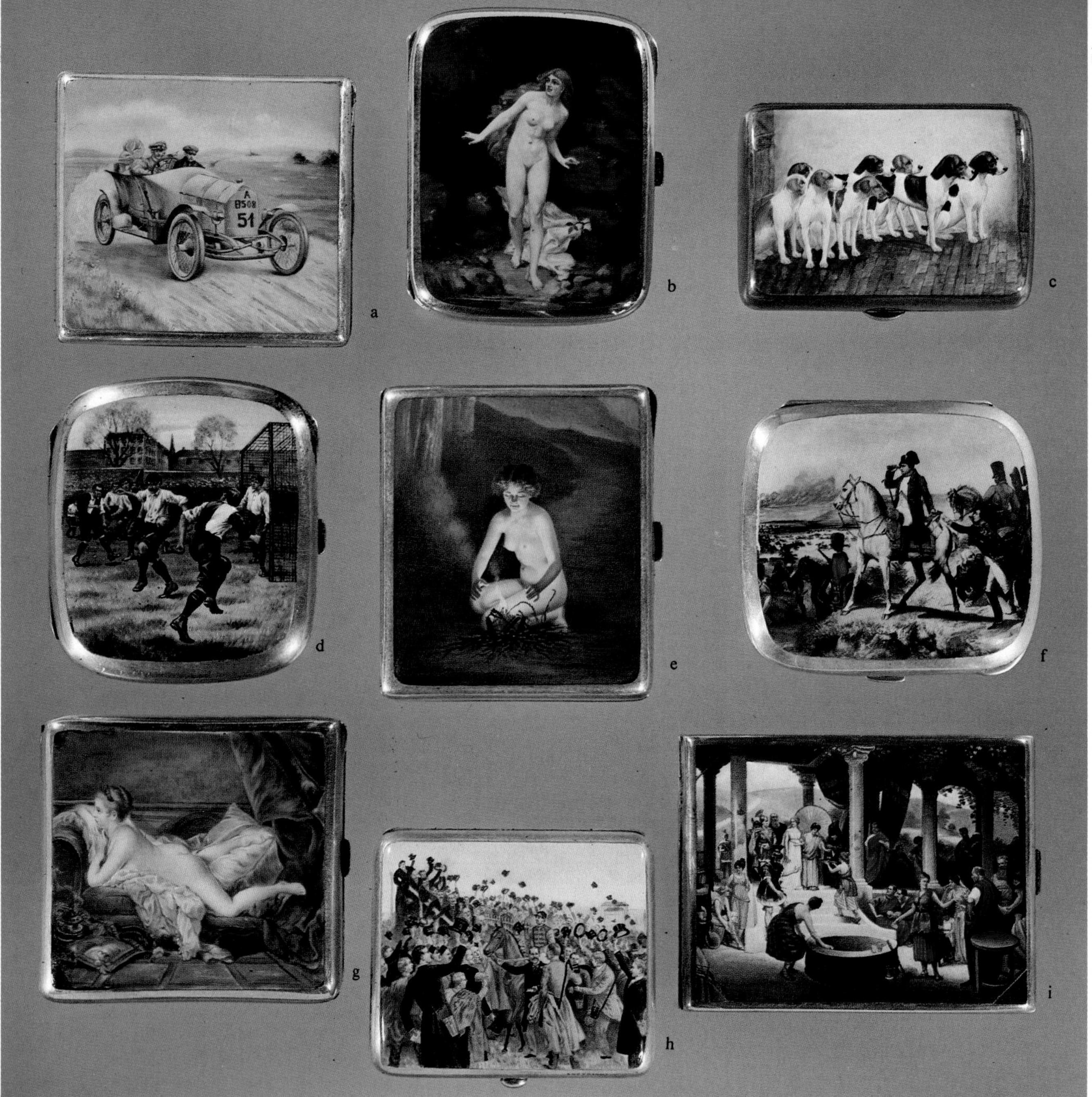

being known as 'The Road to Ruin'; such an example may have an inscription listing a number of friends *(Figure 3c)*.

For technical reasons, when enamelwork is added to a gold or silver base the purity of the metal has to be high. In England the silver cases had to conform to the sterling standard, but Continental cases were often a little lower, generally 900 or 800. Because therefore the intrinsic value of the metal was great, many of the enamelled cigarette cases were sold for scrap when they went out of fashion. The pieces surviving for collecting therefore represent only a small proportion of a large output. Gold examples are very rare indeed. Occasionally an enamelled case made of copper alloy can be found, decorated in the same way as the precious metals, but this combination of materials was inappropriate for the cigarette cases. The enamelled cigarette cases which are available for collection are, therefore, silver.

The method of applying painted enamelwork to the silver cigarette cases was to cut away a shallow recess in the top surface of the lid and to lay in and fire a grounding of enamel. This grounding could be an opaque colour, usually white, or transparent. For transparent backgrounds the silver surface was patterned by engine-turning to increase the lustre of the colours fired over the brightened metal. Once the enamel ground was laid in and fired smooth the artist painted the required picture with vitrifiable overglazes made from metallic oxides, which combined with the enamels during re-firing. These pigments offered a fairly full palette of colours and allowed fine control of the work. A great deal depended on the expertise with which the colours were applied, the number of stages in which the composition was completed and careful judgement at every firing. Finally, the picture was crowned with a very fine layer of clear enamel, giving it a protective and glossy surface. This also brought the enamelwork up to the level of the surrounding

Figure 2 (left) *(a) Interesting specialist subject, showing an early sports car with its passengers including a lady swathed in a protective headscarf. German, about 1910. 835 silver.*
(b) The vertical format chosen for many cigarette cases made them suitable for decoration with standing figures. A beautiful woodland nymph with flowing tresses was a favourite subject. German, about 1900-1910. 900 silver.
(c) Hounds, horses and other subjects related to hunting themes remained a popular choice for decoration of cigarette cases over several decades. This example is English and was made in 1893. Sterling silver.
(d) Lively scene showing a group of footballers, a theme originally chosen for the decoration of cases to be presented to members of winning teams and contemporary enthusiasts. The inscription shows that this case was presented in 1921. Austrian. 900 silver.
(e) Fine miniature painting, the enamelwork created with great finesse and expertise, the colours controlled to show the reflection of the fire in the skin tones of the figure and subtle tints in the background details. The effect of glowing embers in the fire have been produced by inlaying gold foil under red transparent enamel. German, about 1920. 900 silver.
(f) 'Historical' subject of Napoleon on his white charger, demonstrating how the enameller's materials can give sharp definition and a feeling of space on this reduced scale. Marked: ESMERALDA. *Probably Austrian. 900 silver.*
(g) One of the most charming enamelled cigarette cases, this finely painted miniature in enamel is a faithful copy of Boucher's famous painting of Mademoiselle Louise O'Murphy. German, 1920. 900 silver.
(h) This case is fascinating both for its historical interest, showing the scene of jubilation when Persimmon *won the classic Derby for King Edward VII when Prince of Wales, and as an example of an unusual crowd theme in this medium. English, 1896. Sterling silver.*
(i) A larger cigarette case of the former favoured from about 1920 onwards. Austrian. 800 silver.

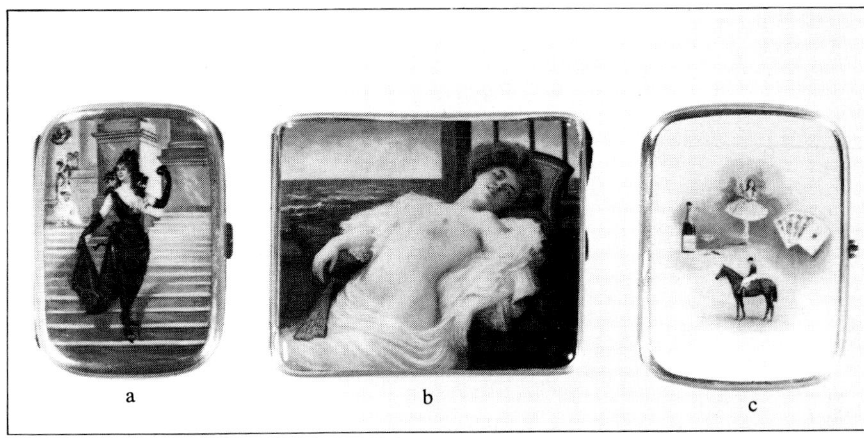

Figure 3 *(a) The 'lady at a masked ball' motif was used as here, with a detailed painted background, or in silhouette style showing the figure against a plain silver background. Import mark Chester, 1909. Sterling silver.*
(b) There are many variations of this pose of a reclining, semi-draped girl. Import mark Chester, 1910. Sterling silver.
(c) The trade catalogue of the period lists this decoration as 'The Road to Ruin' – it was a popular motif which remained in fashion for at least a decade. Birmingham, 1913. Sterling silver.

rim of metal. The various stages of work and separate firings could take ten or more operations. The high firing required temperatures in the range 750°-800° Centigrade (1382°-1472° Fahrenheit), when the metal glowed red and the enamels would begin to flow. Firing each time would take between one and three minutes, depending on the particular enamels and overglaze pigments employed.

To enable complex pictures to be laid in quickly, or when many versions of a particular design were required, it had been customary from the mid-18th century onwards to transfer outline designs by means of specially engraved dies. The whole picture was then carefully painted in with colours. With the exception of certain larger scale motifs and animal portraiture, outlines should be as delicate as possible for quality work. The careful gradation of colours and good skin tones are the results of fine craftsmanship; finely executed background details also show the hand of a master painter in this medium.

A method which was in use from the late 19th century was that of photographic transfer. With this technique the image could be overpainted in whole or in part with the overglaze pigments, or the picture could be left as a black and white or sepia and white monochrome. The method was successful with portrait subjects, but for detailed compositions there was a tendency for closely set outlines to appear thickened or blurred.

Collecting

The collector of enamelled cigarette cases still has a wide field to choose from. Prices range considerably according to subject matter and also, of course, condition. Items with stimulating and finely painted pictures in good condition reach £600 to £1000 (US$654-1090) or higher at major auctions. But interesting and good pieces can be acquired for considerably lower amounts and there are opportunities in the £100 to £200 (US$109-218) range for those on the look out for these articles. Although enamelled surfaces are durable, some scratching of the topmost layer of clear glaze is generally to be found on cases which have been in frequent use. Providing the scratches are not so deep as to go through the clear glaze into the painted work and the grounding, this seldom detracts from the appeal of the work. Small fragments may have chipped away from the corner areas of the background or, if repaired, the restoration may be visible on close inspection, but again in view of the age of the articles this should be acceptable, providing the overall effect is good. Deep cracks running through the glaze tend to catch the light and spoil the beauty of enamelwork, and unfortunately this cannot generally be masked. An exceptionally high gloss with a milky sheen should be carefully examined, as this may indicate a restoration which may turn out to be less durable than the original enamelwork.

Enamelled cigarette cases are offered from time to time by many of the antique shops specializing in silverware and smaller articles.

All enamelled cigarette cases shown are from GRAYS ANTIQUES, *London W1.*

May 1985

ORIENTAL CARPETS FOR THE HOME

Deborah Scott

The term 'Oriental carpet' embraces a wide field, geographically stretching from the Balkans to Peking, and including the work of nomadic tribes, settled villages and town workshops as well as the rare Islamic court carpets of the 16th and 17th centuries. Although earlier examples exist, the great majority of carpets seen on the market today date from the 19th and early 20th centuries. Those pre-1850 may be termed 'classical' rugs, but it is the later ones that offer the buyer of limited means the best choice. The terms 'rug' and 'carpet' are applied freely and are here regarded as interchangeable, although in the United States, the term 'carpet' is generally restricted to the wall-to-wall variety. Some dealers use the terms mat, rug, and carpet to give some (ascending) idea of size.

Unlike other antique dealers, carpet dealers can only display a small part of their stock at one time. The rest is, perforce, stacked in piles or rolled up. The dealer will, of course, be happy to show any of these pieces but will be happier still if he is given some idea of what a customer wants, especially in terms of size and cost. It is therefore particularly helpful if the customer sets some parameters, however loose, in advance of a visit.

First of all he must establish why he wants to buy a carpet. Is it for decorative purposes, or does it represent the first purchase of a potential collector, newly interested in the artistry and history of

Figure 1 *Daghestan prayer rug from the North Eastern Caucasus, about 1900. This example is in fair condition and its pile is evenly low. In better condition the price would be nearer £4000. 139 × 117 cm (4ft 7in × 3ft 10in)* COATS *£950 (c US $1463).*

oriental rugs and carpets? These two demands may be satisfied by a single piece, but the purpose has a bearing on the importance of other features such as quality, condition, size and colouring. While someone with a primary interest in a rug for furnishing will be especially concerned about size, colour and durability, a collector will be much more flexible on such matters, choosing perhaps to buy a small example of good quality and a certain age from a particular region.

A financial limit should be established before setting out. Unfortunately it is possible to spend a great deal on nothing at all in this business if one is careless, but careful research and diligent homework will go a long way towards achieving fair value for money. Given this proviso the old maxim of buying the best you can afford is well considered here. The question of investment inevitably arises, since there are dealers who will offer this as an encouragement to their customers. Reputable dealers are honest enough to reinforce the advice this book invariably gives – that the collector's primary

Figure 2 (below left) *Mahal rug from the area around the town of Arak (previously Sultanabad) in North West Iran. About 1910. 197 × 119 cm (6ft 6in × 3ft 11in).* VIGO CARPET GALLERY *£500 + VAT (c US $770).*

Figure 3 (below right) *Hamadan of the late 19th century, a little worn but with plenty of life left. Hamadan has been a major centre for carpet production in Iran, with numerous villages contributing their work. Turkish influence may be seen in some Hamadan rugs. 182 × 99 cm (6ft × 3ft 3in)* COATS *£450 (c US $693).*

Figure 4 *Two Baluch rugs. The substantial difference in price is due more to the quality than to the size. Both are of about the same date, 1910-20.*
Left, 213 × 106 cm (7ft × 3ft 6in),
Right 157 × 89 cm (5ft 2in × 2ft 11in)
VIGO CARPET GALLERY *£1600 & £480. Both + VAT (c US \$2464, \$739).*

reason for buying antiques must be because they give pleasure. Having said this, the better the condition and quality of a rug, the better it will hold its value.

Factors affecting the price of carpets are manifold. It is these factors taken in combination that affect the price for any single piece, but the most salient is condition. Although high standards of restoration are possible, the cost is high, and it is not advisable to buy a rug requiring any more than 10-15 per cent of its surface to be restored. This varies with quality, for with the more valuable pieces a high restoration cost can be still a small fraction of the value of the piece. The rarest, museum-quality rugs should not be restored but rather conserved to stabilise them. In the under-£1000 category, only the most minor restoration is really advisable, involving perhaps the securing of fringes and borders. Even wear on a rug, rendering the pile evenly 'low', as the jargon puts it, is more acceptable than patches of wear on an otherwise good carpet. The difference in price between a rug in good condition and one that is worn is substantial. Collectors with an academic interest can take advantage of this to buy worn examples of good quality work in order to learn about colouring and design. They must bear in mind however, that such pieces must be treated gently, perhaps hung (correctly supported) or placed in a quiet corner to avoid further wear and tear. *(Figures 1 and 8)*.

Someone who wants a rug to walk on will have different priorities. Sound condition is important if a rug is to receive much wear. Under £1000 this will mean looking at rugs from this century especially the Persian village rugs from the 1920s, such as Hamadans and also some late Turkoman and Baluch rugs. If a rug is to be placed where it will not suffer great wear, there are late 19th century rugs which may be in this price bracket because they are unevenly worn, but are by no means worn out. *(Figures 5 and 6)*.

There is another alternative for those who are not concerned with antiquity, but want a durable piece for this price. In Turkey currently, there is a revival of traditional methods of weaving and a return to the use of vegetable dyes. The results are bold and bright, and follow local traditional designs. They improve with use which is certainly an advantage from a practical point of view.

There are pitfalls awaiting the unwary and ill-advised purchaser of old rugs. It is difficult for the inexperienced eye to notice what it is *not* seeing. Sometimes a patch of wear on a rug has been cut out and the remainder stitched back together – a process called 'cutting and shutting'. Likewise, worn or unravelling borders may have been removed, and new borders bound further in, making the rug smaller than its original size. These practices are undesirable inasmuch as they adversely affect the value of any piece. If adequately reflected in the price, and if honestly declared, however, the choice is open to the customer. Recognising these changes requires experience of unaltered carpets. Look carefully at a rug to see if the design is balanced. Notice the binding on the edges of unaltered pieces. New binding may be a *bona fide* repair to an original edge, but it may also signify the removal of borders. Examine the surface of the rug carefully. In bald patches the warps and wefts may have been disguised by painting them.

Rules for the care of carpets are based on common sense. As with any other textile, direct sunlight will cause fading, and should be avoided. Carpets should be cleaned at least every three years. This is best done by a specialist who may be located via a reputable specialist dealer. On a more frequent basis, the removal of grit from the pile will help reduce wear. This is best achieved by turning face down onto paper or sheeting and tapping all over. Vacuuming is also helpful, preferably with a small hand-held machine and with the pile. Care should be taken to check for loose threads beforehand. If in any doubt, especially with fragile pieces, it is advisable to consult a specialist. Signs of wear, when edges become threadbare or fringes start to unravel, should be repaired as soon as possible. This is very much a case of 'a stitch in time'. Some of the books mentioned below give further advice on cleaning, care and simple repair.

To a first time buyer, the carpet market seems like an impenetrable jungle. From the shops with their noisesome come-ons such as 'closing-down' and 'slashed prices' to the elegantly displayed galleries of the specialists, from Sunday afternoon 'bankrupt stock' auctions to Sotheby's and Christie's, where should he turn? First of all he must do his homework to establish his taste and set the parameters mentioned above. Helpful books are listed below but these are no substitute for looking and touching. The Victoria and Albert Museum (London SW7) has a study collection which is open to the public by appointment. Advice on price is less easy to find.

Auction records are of limited use since they rarely give an idea of condition, which is so influential. In the beginning the best advice is to befriend a reputable dealer. This involves trust, but a good dealer will jealously guard his reputation, and will be keen to offer a fair price and will describe his goods honestly. There is a premium to be paid for his expertise, but in the early stages of buying, particularly for those with a collector's interest, this is money well spent. Such dealers will usually offer to exchange any

Figure 5 *Kazak, a Caucasian rug from the mid 19th century with bold geometric design typical of the area. It has minor repairs to the edges, some corrosive wear to dark brown areas, and is more worn (though quite usable) in the centre than on the borders. These factors are reflected in the price. 243 × 112 cm (8ft × 3ft 8in)* J. P. J. HOMER *£750 (c US $1155)*

Figure 6 *Yuruk, an Eastern Turkish/North West Persian tribal piece of the late 19th century. This piece is in a usable condition, with a lowish pile and new selvedges. 228 × 114 cm (7ft 6in × 3ft 9in) J. P. J. Homer £850 (c US $1309).*

purchase for the paid price at any time. If a considerable period of time (several years) has elapsed it may be advisable to seek a second opinion of the current resale value of the rug before taking up this offer of exchange. Foreign buyers may not find this offer beneficial if the vagaries of currency exchange rates have worked against them.

A reputable dealer will offer a formal invoice describing the carpet and its condition as accurately as possible. He will also be a source of advice and possibly service when cleaning or repair is required. No such service is offered by the auctions. The established auction houses which have specialist sales often have some carpets with estimates under £1000. A buyer must be experienced enough to establish the condition of the piece, spot any damage, and have some idea of value. Close examination in good light is essential, so ask to see any pieces that are inaccessibly displayed, or else avoid them completely. Some auction catalogues give an indication of the state of the pieces, but a buyer must satisfy himself. If he lacks the necessary experience, it is best to consult a dealer, who will charge a commission for his advice.

At all costs avoid hotel auctions, which often advertise themselves as selling bankrupt stock or as 'warehouse clearance'. These have an appalling reputation, and many an innocent bidder has been led on to pay far too much. Likewise beware of shops which claim to be 'closing down' or having a 'special liquidation sale' for 11 months a year. These sell mainly mass-produced modern rugs which are probably of little interest to readers.

April 1987

Figure 7 (above left) *Baluch rug of the late 19th century. The typically sombre colours are contrasted in this example with an unusual white border, a desirable feature. 172 × 122 cm (5ft 8in × 4ft) DAVID BLACK £950 (c US $1463).*

Figure 8 (above right) *An example of Turkoman weaving from about 1880, this is an* Engsi *or rug designed to cover the entrance of a tent. The design incorporates many motifs, but the central cross shape or* hatchli *is typical of an* Engsi. *147 × 104 cm (4ft 10in × 3ft 5in) ATLANTIC BAY CARPETS £1200 (c US $1848).*

Bibliography

Many books have been written on this subject. The following three are especially helpful to novices.

Carpet Magic by Jon Thompson (Barbican Art Gallery 1983)
World Rugs and Carpets edited by David Black (Country Life Books 1985).
Rugs and Carpets of the World edited by Ian Bennett (Country Life/Hamlyn 1978)

The quarterly magazine of carpets and textiles, *Hali*, publishes much information of interest to collectors including a selection of auction prices. (Hali Publications Ltd, London).

FREDERICK HURTEN RHEAD, POTTER

Bernard Bumpus

The Potteries have produced many remarkable families over the years and one of these, the Rheads, is the subject of an exhibition which has recently opened at the Geffrye Museum in London. Among ceramists who worked in England, Frederick Alfred Rhead and his daughter Charlotte are well known to collectors. Much less is heard in Britain about the members of the family who crossed the Atlantic to work. Of these, Frederick's eldest son Frederick Hürten Rhead, became one of America's greatest and most versatile potters. Today his designs are much sought after and fetch, by British standards at any rate, large sums.

Frederick Hürten Rhead was born in 1880 in Hanley and was named after his maternal grandfather, C. F. Hürten, the noted Copeland's flower painter. He was a sickly child and when young had to wear leg irons. However, he soon grew out of these and was able to take full advantage of the rigorous educational regime then in vogue. He left school at the age of 14 and was apprenticed to his father, the art director of the Brownfield Pottery, which had just been reorganised as a Guild. His education continued, meanwhile, at evening classes at the Wedgwood Institute in Burslem and at the Stoke, Hanley and Fenton Art Schools. The ewer (Figure 1), which carries his signature, may have been designed and painted by him while attending one of these schools.

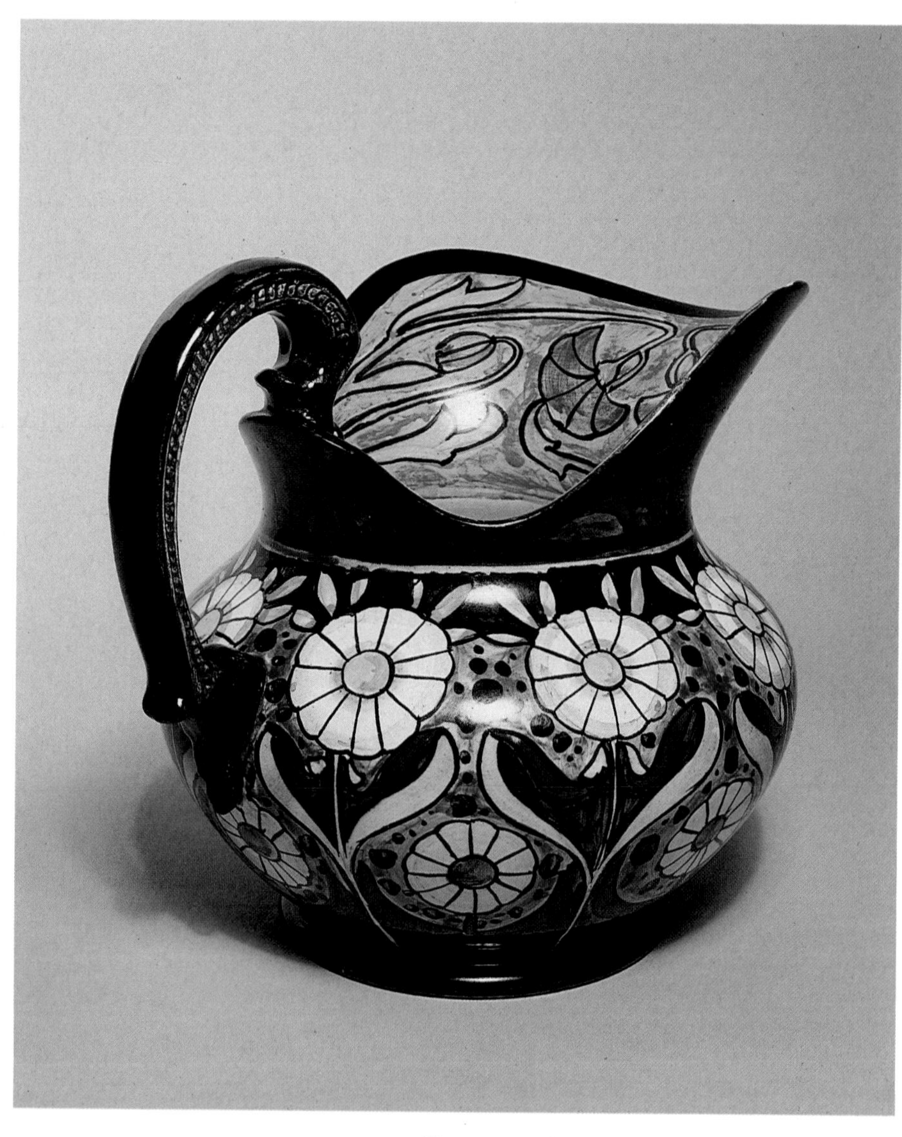

Figure 1
Ewer, about 1898. Signed on base 'F. H. Rhead Art Nouveau'. H23 cm (9¾ in). Probably decorated while at art school.

Brownfield's was at the time a leading pottery with a skilled and versatile workforce, so Frederick Hürten would have received a sound practical training. But the Guild arrangements proved to be less than satisfactory in practice and within a few years the operation was wound up. By that time, however, Frederick Alfred had become art director at Wileman & Co – later to be renamed Shelley Potteries. Frederick Hürten, with his brother Harry, went with their father to help him.

Frederick Hürten had meanwhile been appointed an instructor in design at the Longton Art School, thus carrying on the family tradition established by his grandfather who had been a pioneer of art education in the Potteries. His talents must have been apparent even then for in 1899 he was also made art director at Wardle & Co., Washington Works, Hanley.

As a young art director, Frederick Hürten continued to learn. 30 years later, writing in *The Potters Herald,* he described in some detail the methods used by a Wardle thrower, Tom Naylor, who worked at a wheel turned by his red-haired daughter. During a day he might make one hundred dozen jugs. Frederick's account is so fresh and vivid that he must have been deeply impressed.

Collectors will associate the name of Rhead with the type of decoration known as tube-lining – a form of embellishment like icing a cake in which liquid clay is piped onto the object to form a raised line. Frederick Hürten was as adept at tube-lining as other members of the family so it is no surprise to find that turn-of-the-century Wardle pieces are decorated in this way. The vase in Figure 2 is an example. The firm also made attractive pedestals and stands, sometimes tubed with stylised trees or flowers, which are undoubtedly Frederick Hürten's designs. *The Pottery Gazette* in December 1901, praised Wardle's flower pots and pedestals 'for a skill and taste in slip painting much in advance of previous efforts'.

But change was in the air for in June 1902 Frederick sailed for the United States. Towards the end of 1901 he had married and it may be that he felt the need for a move. At any rate the break with the Potteries was to be permanent. Immediately after arriving in the U.S. he was working, in association with W.P. Jervis, for the small Avon Faience Company at Tiltonville in Ohio. Jervis was another emigré from the Potteries; a

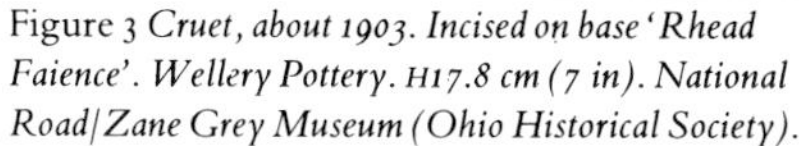
Figure 3 *Cruet, about 1903. Incised on base 'Rhead Faience'. Wellery Pottery. H17.8 cm (7 in). National Road/Zane Grey Museum (Ohio Historical Society).*

Figure 2
Vase, about 1901. Incised on based 'H. Rhead'. Wardle & Co. H15 cm (6 in). An example of tube-lining, for which other members of his family were famous.

Figure 4 *Vase with poppy decoration, about 1906. Roseville Pottery. H48.2 cm (19 in). One of the attractive sgraffito range, decorated in coloured slips. Zanesville Arts Centre.*

Figure 5 *Tiles, signed and dated 1911 University City. 25.4 cm (10 in). Exhibited at the New York Society of Ceramic Arts in 1911.*

Figure 6 (opposite) *Examples of Fiesta ware, 1935. In 1939 Rhead claimed that Fiesta was 'the most successful table ware line made in any factory anywhere . . .' By permission of* Goldenseal *West Virginia Department of Culture and History.*

few years older than Frederick's father, he must have known the family well so it was probably he who arranged the job at Tiltonville. Soon the pottery was using new glazes and designs, some of them tube-lined, and clearly Frederick's work. Moreover, several of the patterns were very similar to those used by Wileman's.

The Avon job was short lived and a few months later Frederick moved to Zanesville, also in Ohio, where he was engaged by the Weller Pottery. Weller was an altogether bigger concern and already had expatriates on its payroll. Frederick immediately set his stamp on the Weller productions by introducing new lines, one with the odd name of Jap Birdimal ware. This range, many pieces of which were again tube-lined, consisted for the most part of Japanese figures, Geisha girls and the like, and animals or birds often with stylised leaves or bubble-like objects which were at once decorative – and easy to tube. Jap Birdimal ware must have been produced in quantity for pieces are not too hard to find in the U.S., and some tube-lined pieces can also be found marked 'Rhead Faience', such as the cruet illustrated in Figure 3.

Frederick's urge to educate was not stilled by the move across the Atlantic and in February 1903, the influential journal *Keramic Studio* published the first of many of his designs, a plate decorated with a band of stylised orange poppies. The next year a number of articles on 'Brush Work' appeared, written jointly with Jervis, to be followed, a few years later, by an important series 'Pottery Class'.

By 1904 Frederick Hürten Rhead had moved again, this time to another Zanesville business, the Roseville Pottery, where he was appointed art director. Once more he put tube-lined wares on the market and also designed a striking sgraffito range, decorated in coloured slips. The poppy vase (Figure 4) is a typical example. Ten years later, in an article in his magazine *The Potter,* he described the problems involved in introducing this line with its new decorative techniques. Instead of trying to retrain the existing decorators, who were set in their ways and relatively expensive, he took on some female art students from the local High School. Using a step by step process, he trained these girls from scratch and, at the end of two months, ten of them were sufficiently skilled to carry out even the most complicated patterns. Frederick remained at Roseville until 1908 when his brother Harry succeeded him as art director.

After briefly renewing acquaintance with W. P. Jervis at the latter's Oyster Bay Pottery, he was invited to join the School of Ceramic Art at University City, St. Louis. This was part of the educational project set up by Edward G. Lewis for The American Women's League. Here he was to be associated with the French ceramist Taxile Doat, who had been induced to leave Sèvres temporarily, and the outstanding American ceramist Adelaide Alsop Robineau and her husband. He was also engaged to write a textbook, *Studio Pottery,* for use by the League's students. The link with Adelaide Robineau was long standing as Frederick Hürten continued to give advice and provide her with glaze formulae until her death in 1929. Less permanent was the American Women's League, however, which collapsed in 1911. The Robineaus soon left University City, followed by Frederick – though not before he had made some attractive pieces, such as the peacock tiles (Figure 5).

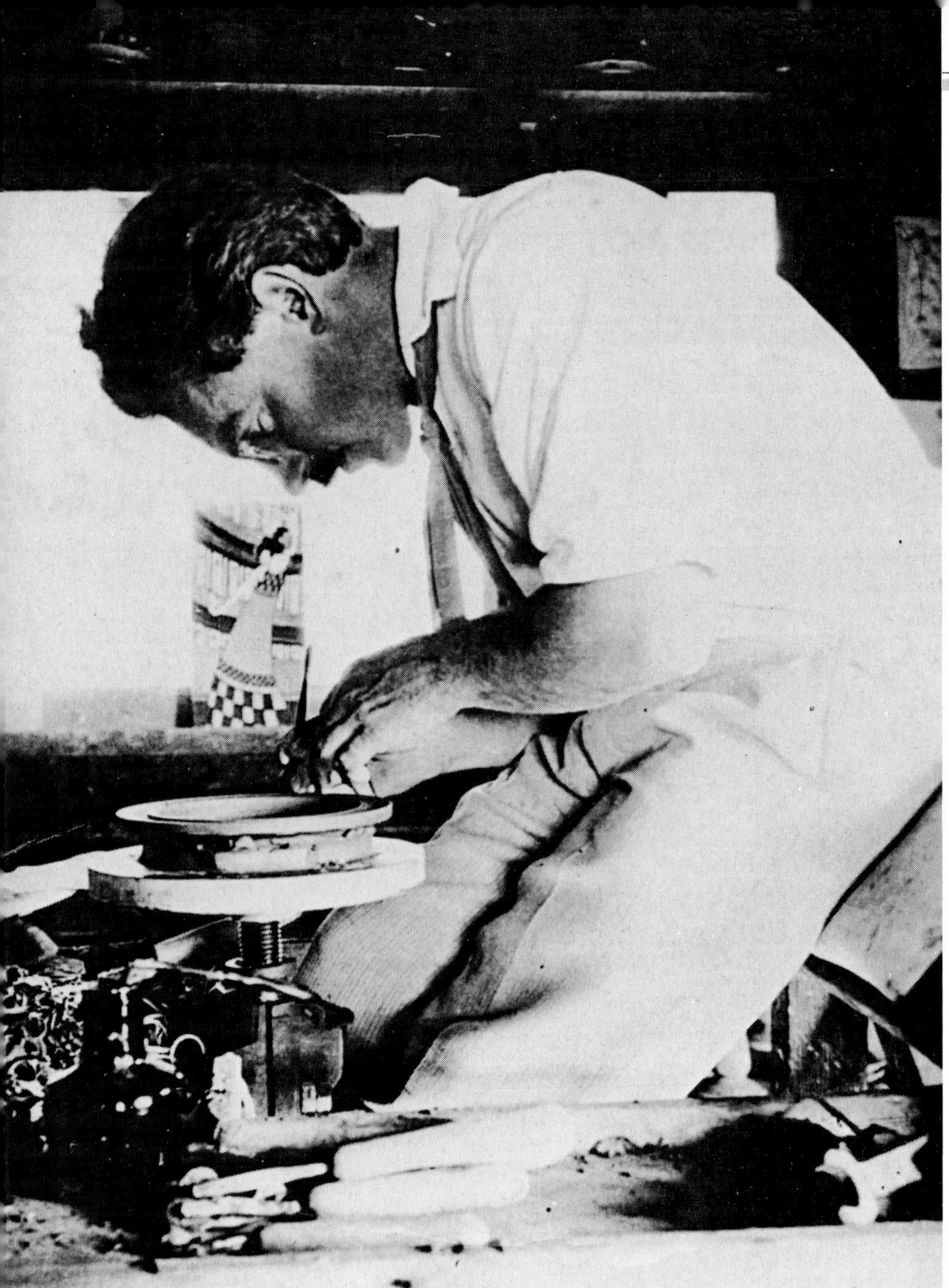

Figure 7 *Frederick Hürten Rhead at work in the Rhead Pottery, about 1916.*

Frederick then moved west – to California. First, in 1911, he took charge of a pottery that had been set up as part of the Arequipa Sanitorium to provide therapeutic employment for girls recovering from tuberculosis. Two years later he established his own pottery at Santa Barbara (Figures 7 and 9) and some most exciting pieces were made there. These wares received fulsome praise in a history of Santa Barbara, published in 1917. So fulsome, indeed, that Frederick may have had a hand in writing the section dealing with the Rhead pottery which proclaimed: 'In his factory . . . may be seen some of the most perfect specimens of art pottery ever produced . . .' Nevertheless, the venture declined, due mainly, no doubt, to the War and a general loss of interest in art pottery, although Frederick himself was not a good businessman. By August 1917 the doors of the Rhead pottery had closed for good.

Frederick then returned to Zanesville where he joined the American Encaustic Tiling Company as Research Director. This was an important post as American Encaustic was at the time the largest maker of tiles in the world. The General Manager of Minton, Hollins & Co referred to it after a visit in 1921 as 'more like a colossal machine than a tile factory'. Frederick did not confine himself to research, of course, though his main responsibility was connected with bathrooms and their fittings, but continued to design, as a sideline, many ornamental wares. The elephant is one such unusual piece (Figure 8). He had, in 1918, married his second wife, the American artist and sculptress Lois Whitcomb, and she too undertook design work for the company, including a series of tiles with signs of the zodiac which were illustrated in the April 1923 issue of *The Pottery and Glass Record.* The chief designer for the company was an old friend of the Rhead family, Léon Solon, a former art director of Minton's and the deviser, with John Wadsworth, of Minton's Secessionist ware.

In 1927, Frederick was offered a professorship at Ohio State University. He refused, though not it may be surmised without some soul searching, and instead accepted the appointment of art director for The Homer Laughlin China Company in Newell, West Virginia. This was a change indeed, for the company claimed the distinction of being the largest producer of tableware in the world. In future Frederick's talents and energies were to be mainly devoted to the design and production of useful wares.

His greatest achievement for Homer Laughlin was the devising of the Fiesta range, introduced in 1935 in a striking range of colours including a red, made with a Uranium glaze and mildly radio-active (Figure 6). The objective, Frederick stated, 'was to make a product that would be neither too extreme in style or too conservative to be out of place in modern surroundings'. He added: 'A satisfactory decorative job in ceramics often seems so simple in effect that it is difficult to realise that considerable research and developoment has to be done. To me, Fiesta appears so obvious that I forget about the preliminary work until I see the scores of unused drawings and models and the hundreds of various colours we have made.' By 1939 he was able to claim Fiesta as 'the most successful table ware line made in any factory anywhere . . .' Events seem to have proved him right and today Fiesta is widely collected, red dinner plates originally costing 10 cents fetching $10 or so (about £7). Fiestaware even currently forms the focus of an exhibition at the Cultural Centre at Charleston, West Virginia.

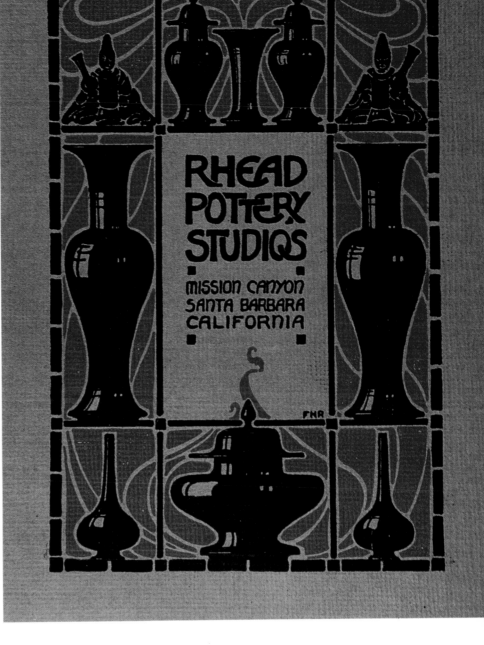

Frederick produced other successful lines for Homer Laughlin including some striking decorative designs for the New York World's Fair in 1939. He also continued his educational activities, running popular and well attended evening classes. However, a growth developed on his lip which, by 1940, was causing concern. In the summer of 1942 he was admitted to hospital in New York City but treatment proved to be ineffective and on 2 November he died. A tribute to him in the 1942 annual report of The United States Potters Association concluded with the following: 'Fred Rhead will be greatly missed by the industry and by his community. Generous of time and money, quick of perception and vigorous in expression, when he died the mold, the case and the block were broken; we shall not see his like again.'

There have been other American ceramists more skilled in individual aspects of their craft but as an allrounder – designer, decorator, modeller, craftsman, chemist and educator – he has surely never been surpassed.

April 1986

Figure 8 *Elephant, designed while Rhead was with the American Encaustic Tiling Co, about 1924. American Ceramic Society, Columbus.*

RHEAD POTTERY STUDIOS

MISSION CANYON
SANTA BARBARA
CALIFORNIA

FHR

Figure 9 *Trade card for the Rhead Pottery in Santa Barbara, California.*

ROYAL WORCESTER'S IMITATIONS

Anita Ellis

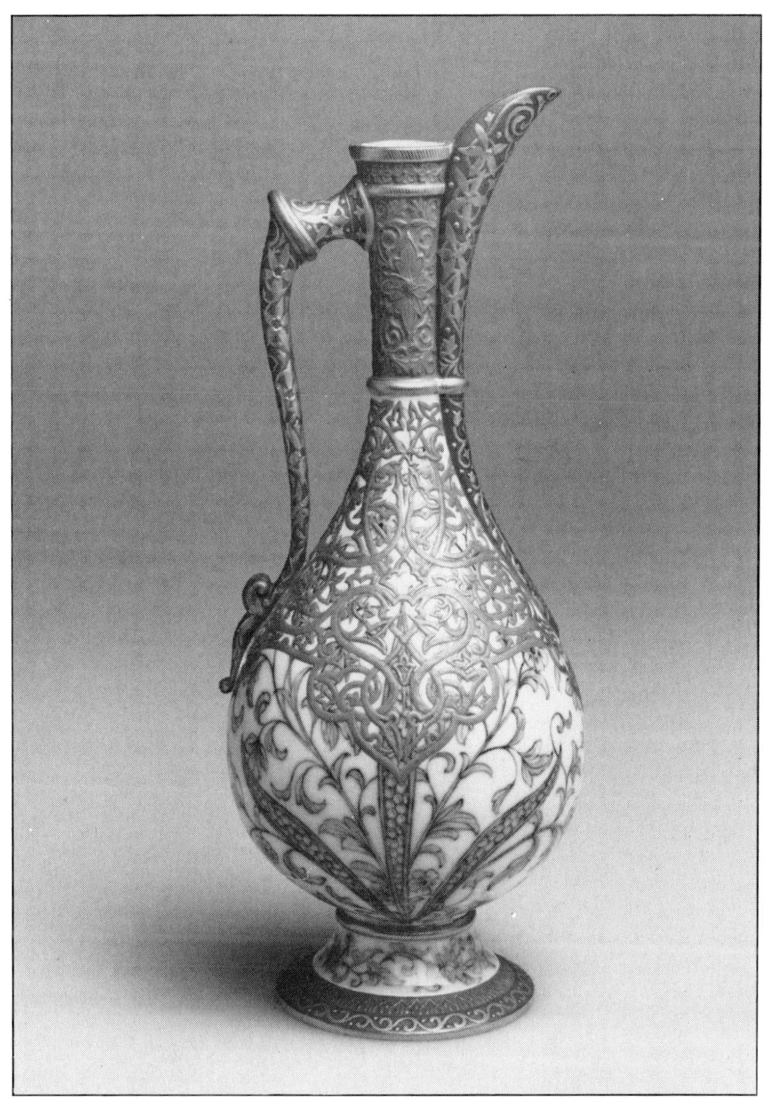

Figure 1 (opposite) *Vase, 1883. Gilded by Charles H. Deakins. 38.1 × 17.8 cm (15 × 7in). Copper ground inspired by the Near Eastern, or Persian idiom.*

Figure 2 (above) *Persian Cruche or Ewer, 1882, Decorated by 'RS'. 35.6 × 14.6 cm (14 × 5¾ in). The 'metal mounts' are made to look like oxidised silver with gilt decorations.*

In the last third of the 19th century the English ceramic industry produced objects made to imitate the appearance of all kinds of media other than porcelain. This striking phenomenon was decidedly contrary to 18th-century endeavours when the greatest desire was simply to produce, or at least imitate, porcelain itself. Little, if any notice has been paid to the 19th-century imitations in porcelain even though they can be quite spectacular. The materials represented are wide ranging and are a tribute to the state of the art at the time. There were replications of metals such as gold, silver, copper, bronze, and gilt bronze; of enamel techniques including Limoges, repoussé and champlevé, of lacquer ware, of Parian marble, of ivory, of horn; also of precious and semi-precious stones such as ruby, turquoise and coral. There seemed to be no media or technique that could not be replicated in porcelain.

One of the English porcelain works that produced some of the finest imitations in porcelain is the Worcester Royal Porcelain Company. A small survey of its products dating from the last third of the 19th century will give a glimpse of the quality of this striking phenomenon. Many of the designs for Worcester's metal imitations were taken from the Near and Far East. All things exotic were considered highly fashionable at the time. A vase *(Figure 1)* of 1883 is taken from the Near Eastern, or Persian idiom. The original invoice describes this vase as '. . .copper ground w. gold Persian design'. Unless one handles the vase, it is virtually impossible to determine that the 'copper' is, in fact, porcelain covered with a copper-coloured ground. Printed in purple overglaze on the bottom of the base are the words PATENT METALLIC. Worcester thought enough of its copper ground to proclaim exclusive rights to the metallic finish. The factory received many patents during this period for gilding, metal plating and glaze effects. Both the interior and the bottom of this vase lack the copper finish and are obviously porcelain. Also, the bottom is marked with Worcester's ceramic trademark, making it clear that imitation, not forgery, was the intent. The vase is signed on the bottom in gold with a conjoined C D for Charles H. Deakins (or Deakin), the decorator. Deakins worked at Worcester in the 19th century and is noted for his elaborate gold decorations, especially raised gilding. He is also noted for not having a nose and wearing a black patch over the space. His gilt decoration on the copper ground body is a beautiful expression of the arabesque.

While the entire object could be made to look like metal, as in the last example, Worcester could also create a piece to look as if it were partly metal. A Persian cruche, or ewer *(Figure 2)* of 1882 is described in the original invoice as '. . .u/g [underglaze] blue Persian design and mounted in metal'. The 'metal mounts' are imitations of oxidised silver with gilt decorations. There is no metal whatsoever attached to this piece. It is an all-porcelain form partly glazed with a metallic finish. The painted underglaze blue decoration beautifully exemplifies its Persian archetype, and the 'metal mounts' replicate Near Eastern metal work.

Ivory was a highly prized commodity familiar to

Figure 3 (above) *Tusk Ice Jug, 1886. Decorated by 'DP'. 22.9 × 16.5 cm (9 × $6\frac{5}{8}$ in). This jug not only imitates ivory, but the body is made to look like the end of a tusk carved to form a jug.*

Figure 4 (right) *Vase, 1880. Gift of Alfred Duane Pell, 1925. 17.8 × 14.6 cm (7 × $5\frac{3}{4}$ in). Imitation of the Chinese cloisonné enamel technique.*

England because of her colonisation of India and trade with the East. As early as 1862 Worcester exhibited a new type of porcelain, called Ivory Porcelain, at the International Exhibitions held in London. The soft creamy tones of the Ivory Porcelain, which was glazed Parian ware, made it a success with the public for years to come. A tusk ice jug *(Figure 3)* of 1886 not only imitates the substance of ivory, but the form of the tusk as well. The body is made to look like the end of a tusk carved to form a jug. The original invoice describes this piece as '. . .ivory w. encrusted gold'. There were many different ivory colours at Worcester. Stained ivory, as exemplified here, is comprised of two colours, a yellow base and brown shading. The 'encrusted gold' was applied over a raised pattern making it appear in relief. To get the gold decoration, actual gold was powdered and mixed with a medium to make it liquid. The medium burned away in the kiln firing leaving a matt gold finish that would be burnished to a shine. The tusk ice jug not only represents gold and ivory, the vertical portion of the handle imitates horn. The 'horn' and the 'ivory' combine with the gold decoration to form a jug of unique character.

Figure 5 (left) *Warrior Vase, 1877. Attributed to the modeller James Hadley. 33 × 34 cm (13 × 13½ in). Inspired by Japanese lacquer, the whole is a tour de force of Victorian ceramics.*

Figure 6 (above) *Vase, 1876. Decorated by James Callowhill. 40.6 × 22.2 cm (16 × 8¾ in). The effect achieved is of a rich Indian enamel on metal.*

Two large tusk vases, elaborately carved and pierced, were exhibited by Worcester at the 1873 Universal Exhibition in Vienna. At that time, a reviewer in the *Art Journal* commented: 'In these the imitation is so admirable that even on close inspection it is almost impossible to discover they are not remarkable specimens of dainty chiselling, for it is only by the touch detection is possible.'

A different ivory colour can be seen in a vase *(Figure 7)* of 1883. The original invoice describes this piece as '. . .pene'd [pencilled, or put on with a brush] ivory mod'd gold [raised gold] w. Persian design & jewells'. The ivory colour of this vase is a soft white with no shading. The form is exactly the same as the vase in Figure 1, only slightly smaller. The raised gold creates a sensuous arabesque design highlighted with 'jewells.' The ruby, turquoise and coral settings are all imitations of precious and semi-precious stones that were considered exotic and fashionable at the time. In the jewelling process, droplets of gold or enamel are applied to the surface.

The 'jewells' can be large and singular as in Figure 7, or they can be small and clustered as in a cabinet plate *(Figure 8)*. This pierced plate of 1886 is jewelled with hundreds of gold, white and turquoise droplets each placed by hand. The holes in this plate were hand cut one at a time when the clay was leather hard. This incredibly fine piercing, or reticulating, could take months of slow careful work. One slip of the knife could lead to two holes being cut into one, which would ruin the piece. The piercing is attributed to George Owen, the most skilled craftsman working in this technique. The marvellous landscape in the centre is attributed to Charles Bright, one of the finest gilders at Worcester.

Non-Western enamelling was also a source of inspiration at Worcester. The Orient had held great influence in Western design since the 17th century. By the 1870s and 80s the influence was unprecedented. One result was that the Chinese cloisonné technique was widely imitated. A vase *(Figure 4)* of 1880 looks just like Chinese enamelled metal with its colourful floral pattern on a yellow round. Each colour is within a gold outline that gives the impression of cloisons, or compartments formed by a network of metal bands that hold the enamel colours. Worcester also borrowed the look of Indian enamelled metals. Because of British rule over India, imports from that country were common to most English households by the 1860s. A vase *(Figure 6)* of 1876 is made of a green porcelain body. Dark green porcelain was an experimental ware first exhibited by Worcester at the Paris International Exhibition of 1878. The green body covered with a clear glaze suggests a rich green enamel, a colour commonly used in the Indian technique. The front depicts an Indian inspired cartouche surrounding a stellate floral design where every element is outlined in gold. The overall effect is a rich Indian enamel on metal. This vase is signed by James Callowhill, one of the finest painters ever to work at Worcester.

Prior to 1854, Japan had been closed to the West for

Figure 7 *Vase, 1883. 30.5 × 14.6 cm (12 × 5¾ in). The imitation of precious stones adds to the Persian inspired design.*

many decades. The West had lost all contact with the Japanese culture. In that year Commander Perry's expedition to the Far East succeeded in gaining admittance to Japan, and Japanese trade began to flow towards the West. By the 1870s, imitations of anything Japanese, including Japanese lacquer ware, were everywhere. Japanesque vessels were a particular favourite at Worcester. A 'Warrior Vase' *(Figure 5)* of 1877 exemplifies the finest replication of Japanese lacquer of the period. Worcester exhibited a vase like this in 1873 at the Universal Exhibition in Vienna. Although this vase is unsigned, the modeller was probably James Hadley, who did Worcester's modelling for most such exhibition pieces. Hadley is regarded as the finest ceramic modeller of the 19th century. The original invoice described this vessel as '1 Warrior Vase black & gold advanturine, bronze and gold figures.' The vase is composed entirely of porcelain. The 'black & gold advanturine', seen on the sides framing the vase, is taken from Japanese lacquer. Advanturine (avanturien, or aventurine) lacquer is generally composed of a black ground that is sprinkled with silver or gold dust. In Japan, artists applied this lacquer to wood, metal and to porcelain. An 1872 *Art Journal* article entitled 'The Art of Japan' states: '. . .the Japanese artist is aided by the rich colours which the various descriptions of lacquer placed at his command. . .The Avanturien, which resembles the Venetian glass of the same name, is a lacquer full of gold spangles. . .

Two years later another *Art Journal* article (vol. XIII) entitled 'On the Progress of Our Art-Industries: The Royal Porcelain Works, Worcester' states: '. . .his [R. W. Binns, director at Worcester] perfect imitation of the aventurine porcelain of the Japanese is his latest triumph. . .'

The 'Warrior Vase' imitates more than just lacquer. The figures in the composition display bronze and gold finishes, while their swords imitate the silvery steel for which Japanese blade weapons are famous. The facial treatment of the two warriors is exquisite, with each hair of their respective heads painted individually. 'Bronze' and gold are repeated in the elephant head handles and the various relief decorations. The one true aspect of porcelain in this vase is the background of the warrior composition. It is a painted, underglaze blue decoration of a sunrise. No doubt this is an allusion to 'The Rising Sun' of Japan.

The fashion for porcelain imitations of other media and techniques was sparked, in part, by the influx of exotic materials during the last third of the 19th century, and a growing middle class that willingly supported such vagaries in ceramics. It can also be suggested that once the formula for true porcelain had been discovered, and the kilns mastered during the Industrial Revolution, there was simply no other challenge left to the industry.

Figure 8 *Cabinet Plate, 1886.* DIAM *19.7 cm (7¾ in). The delicate piercing is attributed to George Owen; the gold landscape in the centre to Charles Bright.*

Bibliography

Henry Sandon, *Royal Worcester Porcelain*, 1973.
Llewellynn Jewitt, *Ceramic Art of Great Britain*, 1879, pp.143-154.

Illustrations: Cincinnati Art Museum, Ohio. Photos: Ron Forth.

June 1986

ENGLISH CERAMICS IN PARIS

Bernard Bumpus

The Musée des Arts Décoratifs in Paris opened its doors for the first time in 1877, a relative latecomer to the list of European museums, which, in the course of the 19th century, had been set up to link art and industry. Over the years the Museum made modest acquisitions of English ceramics and glass, by purchase or gift, but most of these pieces have remained in store and are invisible to the casual visitor. Recently I was fortunate enough to be able to see some of these pieces and to examine the Museum's records. The purchases, at least, must have been bought for good reasons and although the records reveal nothing, it is interesting to speculate about what these might have been.

Figure 1 *Doulton stoneware vase with all-over dot decoration by William Baron, H37 cm (14½ in). Made specially for the 1878 Paris Exhibition.*

Figure 2 (right) *Minton's vase in tinted Parian, H40 cm (15¾ in), decorated with putti and swags in* 'pâte-sur-pâte' *by Lawrence Birks. The vase has a crowned globe backstamp printed in gold and two paper labels indicating that it was part of the Minton display at the 1878 Paris Exhibition.*

The 19th century holdings include purchases made at the 1878 Paris Universal Exhibition, nineteen Doulton Lambeth pieces, a gift to the Museum by Sir Henry Doulton in 1882, some items acquired at the 1889 Paris Universal Exhibition and sundry other gifts. Early in this century some of the successful lustre wares made by Pilkington's Tile and Pottery Company were also added to the collection. These include a few of Walter Crane's designs.

This article describes the acquisitions made at the great Paris Universal Exhibition of 1878. The last exhibition held in Paris had been in 1867. This had been followed in 1870 by the disaster of the Franco-Prussian War, and, the next year, by the horror of the Commune. So this was a special event and everything seems to have been done to make sure that it was a success. It inspired George Augustus Sala's book *Paris Herself Again*, much press coverage, several special magazine supplements, and, when it was over, a number of official reports.

The ceramics acquired by the Museum included three pieces from Minton's, six pieces of Doulton's Lambeth stoneware and three items from the Worcester Royal Porcelain Company. Four pieces of glass were also bought from Thomas Webb of Stourbridge.

The Minton items were the most spectacular and certainly the most expensive. Inevitably, perhaps, they included a covered vase with *pâte-sur-pâte* decoration *(Figure 2)*, probably Minton's most prestigious line at the time. The decoration of putti and swags on this tinted and glazed Parian vase is by Lawrence Birks, and carries his monogram. Lawrence was the cousin of Alboin Birks and both were pupils of Louis Marc Solon. Solon had worked at the Royal Manufactory at Sèvres until the Franco-Prussian War when he fled to Stoke-on-Trent where Minton's lost no time in taking him on. Lawrence is sometimes regarded as being a less successful artist than Alboin but, if judged by this vase, he seems to lose nothing by comparison with his cousin. One wonders why the Museum did not buy a piece decorated by Solon himself for there were many examples of his work in the exhibition. Perhaps it was national pride – or perhaps the prices were just too high. The Lawrence Birks vase cost the museum 725FF. With the exchange rate at around 25FF, to the £, this would be equivalent to about £950 today. A Solon piece would have been much more expensive.

The vase has a crowned globe backstamp printed in gold. This is of great interest as the authoritative catalogue for the 'Minton 1798-1910 Exhibition', held at The Victoria & Albert Museum in 1976, states that the crown was only added to the globe early in the 1880s. It also has two applied paper labels, one inscribed *Minton's Paris Exhibition 1878 141* (the item number in the Minton record book) and *T. Goode & Co London Minton Paris Exhibition 1878*. Goode's, of South Audley Street in London, had bought the whole of the Minton exhibit before the exhibition opened. Unfortunately, though, this firm's records relating to the exhibition no longer exist and were probably destroyed during the war.

However, it was another Minton item, a faience vase over one metre high, which was the Museum's most expensive buy. Standing on a square plinth, it was painted with parrots and pheasants perched on the branches of trees alternating with fruiting stems bearing peaches and plums. This imposing piece has, unfortunately, been mislaid but the surviving Minton records fill in some of the gaps. The piece was made with Minton's red body, taken from Cocknage Hill, and was painted by Mussill. Mussill, an Austrian, was another 1870 refugee from Sèvres who had been taken on by Minton's. He would never accept a salary but insisted on being paid for each piece and for this job he got £20. The cost to the Museum was 3150FF, a sum described in the records as *prix fort*. The equivalent today would be around £4150.

The third Minton item, another piece of faience, cost a more modest 131.25FF, or about 5gns *(Figure 4)*. This is a ewer decorated with pomegranates modelled in relief. It carries the date mark for January 1878. The Minton records show that this 'Pomegranate Ewer', as it was named, number 2100, was specially made for the Paris Exhibition. Presumably this particular piece of faience was purchased because of Minton's reputation at the time as Europe's leading manufacturer of such wares.

The Museum also bought three Royal Worcester pieces which are illustrated in *Figure 6*. The pierced vase, which has an ivory porcelain body, may have been the work of George Owen, the leading exponent of this type of decoration. It was relatively expensive, costing 574FF, and was doubtless acquired as an example of the type of work for which Royal Worcester was celebrated. The other pieces reflect the interest in things Oriental that prevailed at the time. One observer in Paris noted that the Worcester exhibit 'consisted of an immense variety of ornaments and vases, chiefly of Japanese style of decoration'. Indeed, Japan and things Japanese featured prominently throughout the exhibition which even included a model Japanese farm with a full-scale farmhouse. The jug with a dragon handle and blue scale decoration had first been modelled in 1872 so was not a special production for the exhibition. Nor was the square bodied vase which has a streaky brown glaze, very much in the oriental manner. This piece, shape number 190, was another 1872 design. Similar pieces were produced by French potters at the time so it must be supposed that this vase, very much in the French taste, was purchased for the purpose of comparison.

The Doulton purchases are illustrated in *Figures 1 and 5*. The most striking is the tall vase with all-over dot decoration *(Figure 1)*. It was the work of William Baron,

Figure 3 *Cut glass decanter by Thomas Webb H19.4 cm (7½ in). A good example of the virtuosity of the Webb craftsmen and no doubt purchased in 1878 for that reason.*

Figure 4 *Minton's faience Pomegranate Ewer, H53 cm (21 in). Made specially for the 1878 Paris Exhibition.*

Figure 5 (top) *Group of typical Doulton stoneware items purchased at the Paris Universal Exhibition in 1878. The bowl 21 cm ($8\frac{1}{4}$ in) was the work of Eliza Simmance and William Baron. John Broad was responsible for the tazza. H10.5 cm ($4\frac{1}{4}$ in), and Elizabeth Atkins and Clara S. Barker for the tapering jug H21.5 cm ($8\frac{1}{2}$ in). Unidentified artists were responsible for the tankard H21.5 cm ($8\frac{1}{2}$ in) and the cylindrical vase H15 cm (6 in).*

Figure 6 *Group of three Royal Worcester pieces purchased at the Paris Exhibition in 1878. The pierced vase H28.5 cm ($11\frac{1}{4}$ in), of ivory porcelain, was perhaps the work of George Owen.* The Dragon Jug *H29.5 cm ($11\frac{3}{4}$ in) and the square vase H31.5 cm ($12\frac{1}{2}$ in) were both modelled in 1872. The Royal Worcester display at the Paris Exhibition included a large number of pieces 'in the Japanese taste'.*

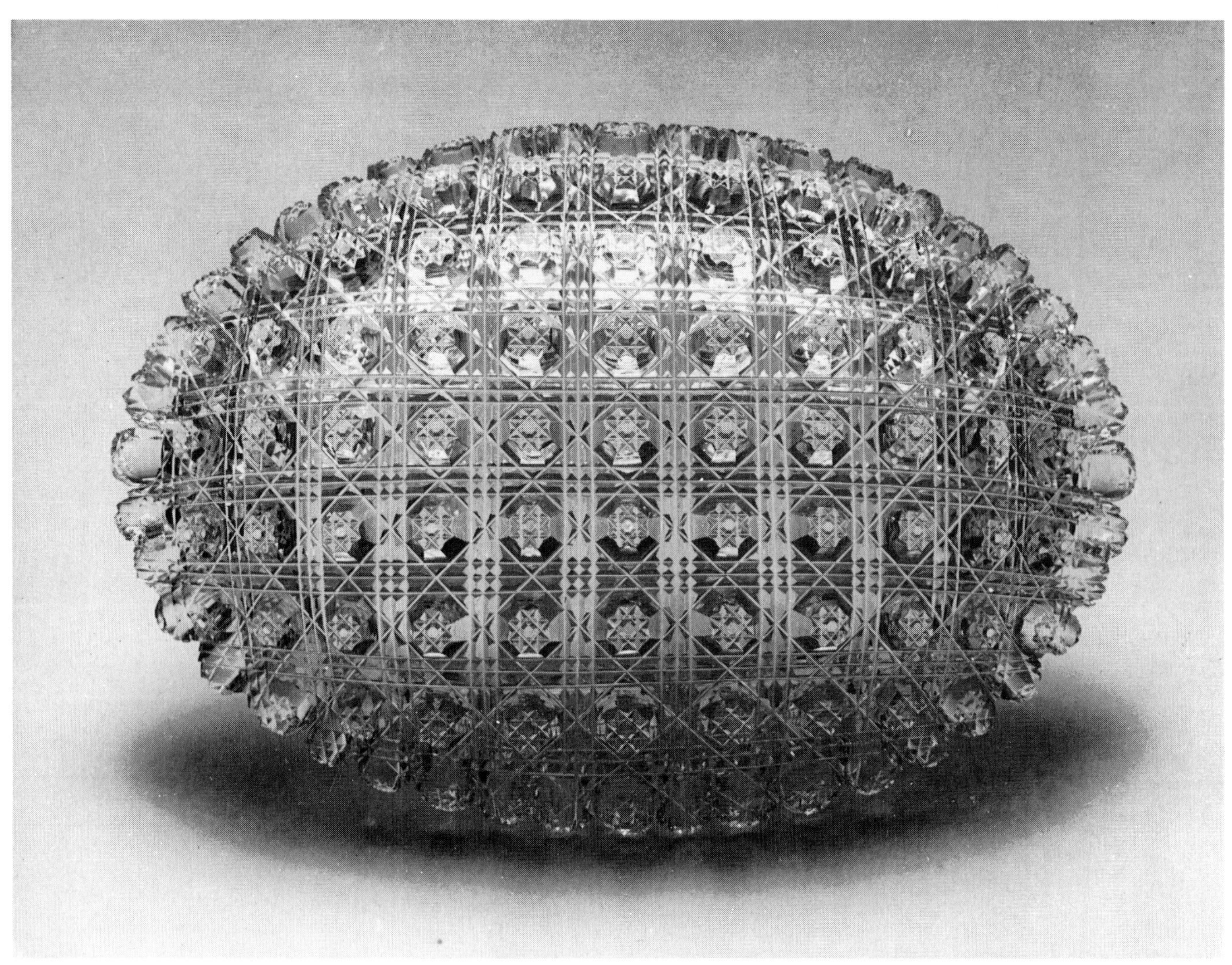

and an applied paper label still attached to the vase records that it was made specially for the exhibition. This piece, at least, has surfaced periodically and was last seen in 'L'Exposition des Expositions Universelles' which was held at the Musée des Arts Décoratifs in 1983.

Baron was also responsible, with Eliza Simmance, for the decoration of the bowl illustrated in *Figure* 5. The tazza was the work of John Broad while Elizabeth Atkins and Clara S. Barker jointly executed the tapering jug. The other two items, the tankard and the small cylindrical vase, are the work of unknown artists. All still have their original paper labels recording that they were earmarked for the Paris Exhibition.

These pieces are typical of the output of the Lambeth works at that time and were presumably purchased for that reason. However, of the artists responsible for these pieces, only Eliza Simmance and John Broad were regarded as being outstanding by John Sparkes, Director of the Lambeth School of Art, and mentor of them all. Miss Simmance was also the leading exponent of the Doulton version of the *pâte-sur-pâte* decoration. Making use of a number of coloured slips, this had been introduced specially for the Paris Exhibition. However, the decoration on the Museum's bowl does not feature this technique. Prices paid were accordingly fairly modest: the bowl, for instance, cost 52FF while the small cylindrical vase was obtained for only 13FF – about £16 in today's currency.

The Doulton exhibit as a whole was much praised. The American Commissioner, Blake, for instance, in a report to the United States House of Representatives, observed that: 'The possibilities of art in clay have found in Doulton, in our time, their greatest exemplifier. The objects so made not only have beauty of form and decoration, but they are remarkably strong and durable'. Most commentators also tended to single out the work of George Tinworth and Hannah Barlow, and it is perhaps surprising that the Museum's Doulton purchases did not include works by

Figure 7 *Cut glass tray by Thomas Webb L 30 cm (11⁴/₅ in). This piece was selected for inclusion in the exhibition* Glass from World Fairs: 1851-1904 *recently held at the Corning Museum of Glass in the United States.*

either of these artists, the more so as Tinworth had been responsible for the spectacular *Springs and Fountains of the Bible Fountain* in the Exhibition's Prince of Wales court. However, Sir Henry Doulton made some amends for these omissions by including works by each of these artists in his 1882 gift to the Museum.

A group of four pieces of glass from Thomas Webb, of Stourbridge, was also bought at the 1878 Exhibition. Unlike the ceramics, these are now on display in the glass section of the Museum. Webb's were generally regarded at the time as the leading European glassmakers and in many ways superior to the principal French firm, Baccarat. Commissioner Blake remarked that the firm 'had the finest display of flint and coloured wares, and deserved the grand prize they received. Their flint glass was the finest in the exhibition and was superior in brilliancy to the French, which still retains a trace of the bluish tint so noticeable in their glass in 1867'. The Artisans Report of The Society of Arts, however, was less enthusiastic. While agreeing that Baccarat was honestly beaten and that the Grand Prize awarded to Webb's was an acknowledgement of this fact, the writer observed that Webb's wonderful court 'did not carry him away a captive of its power'. There was, he complained, 'no creative power'. And he went on: 'Monotony was its taint. Cutting and engraving, engraving and cutting, were the beginning, middle and end of the artist's idea'.

The glass purchases made by the Museum seem to have been intended to reflect pieces both simple and elaborate. The carafe *(Figure 8)* provides an example of the brilliancy of the plain glass to which the American Commissioner drew attention. On the other hand, the glass tumbler in the same illustration has a wonderful iridescent finish – another Webb speciality. The cut glass tray *(Figure 7)* and decanter *(Figure 3)* are good examples of the virtuosity displayed by the Webb craftsmen. The tray is an unusual piece for which the Museum paid 100FF. It was recently selected for inclusion in the 'Glass from World Fairs: 1851-1904' exhibition, held at the Corning Museum of Glass in the United States from April to October 1986.

Despite their reputation, Webb's did not find the Exhibition profitable, nor did the Parisians appreciate the quality of their wares which were much more expensive than the local products. Anticipating a good trade, Webb had established a depot in Paris before the opening of the Exhibition. But according to a report in the July 1878 issue of *The Pottery and Glass Trades Journal,* practically no business was done. Perhaps that is why the Museum was able to acquire the iridescent glass tumbler for 2.60FF – a mere £3.50 even at current prices.

A few more pieces of glass were bought from Webb's and also from Powell's at the Paris Exhibition in 1889 and are now displayed in the Museum's glass room.

Acknowledgement

My grateful thanks for their help is due to Mme. Evelyne Possémé and M. Jean-Luc Olivié, of the Musée des Arts Décoratifs; Louise Irvine, Director of Historical Promotions, Royal Doulton; Joan Jones, Curator, Minton Museum and Harry Frost, Curator, Dyson Perrins Museum, Worcester.

May 1987

Figure 8 *Carafe and tumbler by Thomas Webb of Stourbridge. Both were purchased at the 1878 Paris Exhibition. The carafe H33.5 cm (13¼ in) overall was probably acquired as an example of Webb's brilliantly clear flint glass while the tumbler H14.6 cm (5¾ in) has an iridescent sheen. Webb's won the Grand Prize at the Exhibition, their flint glass being regarded as superior to that of the leading French company, Baccarat.*

All the objects illustrated are in the Musée des Arts Décoratifs.

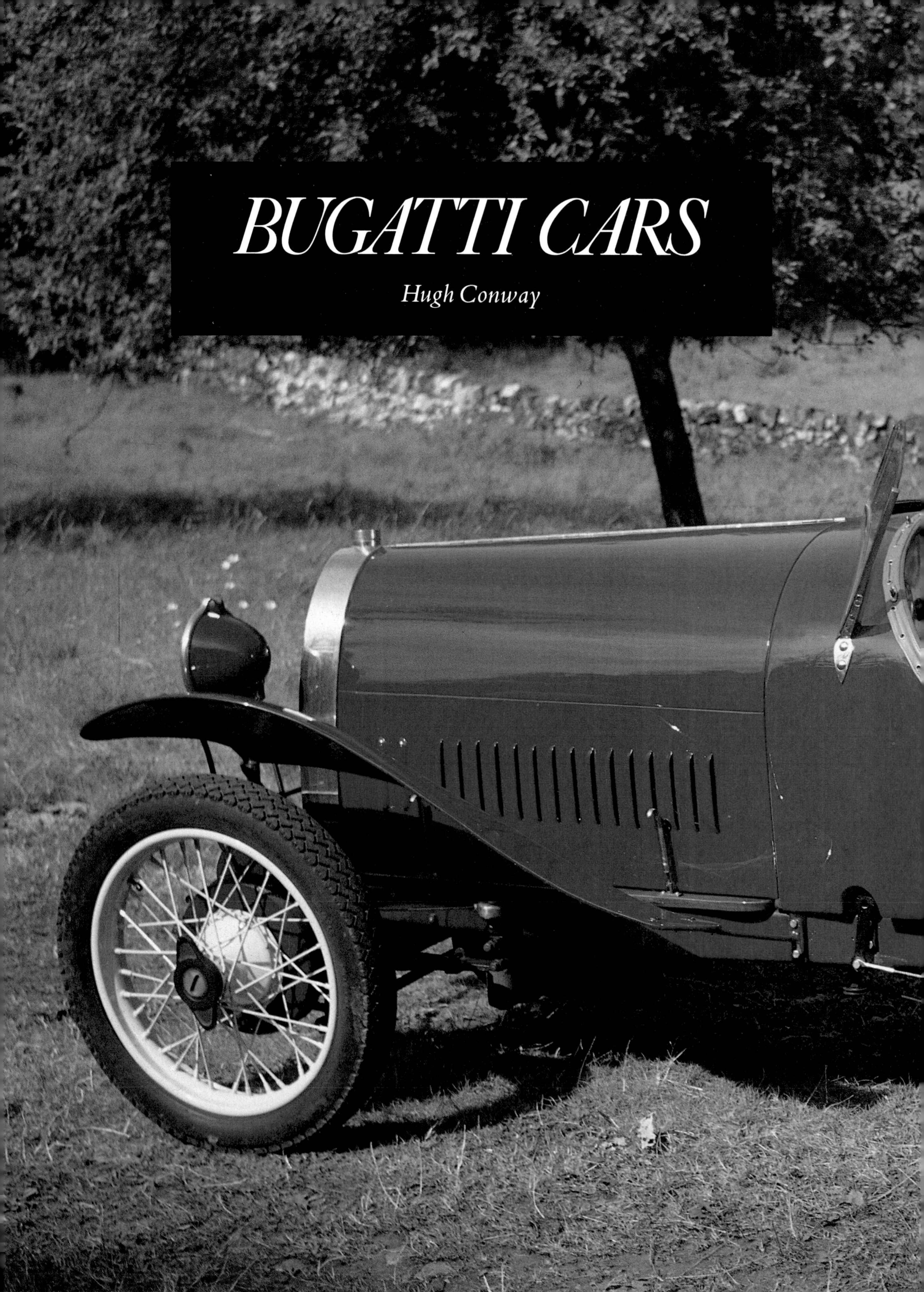
BUGATTI CARS
Hugh Conway

To the collector of antique or vintage automobiles the two names or marques which stand out beyond all others are Bugatti and Ferrari – beyond even Rolls-Royce or Mercedes. Ferrari is not yet indeed an antique, since as a make of car it dates from a mere 1940, and since Ferrari himself is still in active control of the factory. But in terms of collectors' interest Ferrari and Bugatti are evenly matched, the early 1950 or 1960 Ferraris and Bugattis from the late 1920s and 1930s.

Both cars have histories based on racing on the one hand and on the other splendid, often beautiful coachwork – Ferrari by the best bodybuilders in Italy, and Bugatti mainly from his own factory in Alsace. Thus the interest shown today may have been encouraged by the publicity that racing gave the marque in contrast to the more sedate image, for example, of Rolls-Royce. Racing certainly helped the reputation, at one time, of Mercedes and Bentley before it was absorbed by Rolls-Royce; other names of fine cars have disappeared from all but a few memories – Hispano Suiza, Isotta Fraschini, Minerva . . .

It remains for history to show the true significance of Ferrari, but the position of Bugatti is not in doubt. The reasons can be considered and conclusions drawn. The primary reason must lie in the personality of Ettore Bugatti himself and how he created his company and factory. But it must be acknowledged that the family around him are probably of equal importance in establishing his reputation. His father, Carlo was a remarkable designer and builder of art-deco furniture and an equally talented silversmith. His younger brother Rembrandt was a talented animal sculptor whose works are today fetching almost as much as the cars at auctions! Indeed he had the distinction of being awarded the Legion of Honour in France when in his twenties – sadly he took his own life in 1915, depressed by the war and the invasion of Antwerp, where he did most of his work in the Zoological Gardens. And finally Ettore's son Jean by the year 1930 was to have an important effect on the factory output with many fine coachwork designs which did much to contribute to today's interest in Bugatti cars.

The story of how young Ettore came to be a car designer and manufacturer is a remarkable one. In 1899, having dabbled in motor-cycle and tricycle racing in North Italy at the age of 18, he soon realised that the new art of motorcar manufacture was something for him, and managed with the tolerance and support of his father and two family friends, the Counts Guilinelli, to produce a complete four cylinder car which ran well, and created a great deal of interest when exhibited in Milan in 1901. By any standards this was a remarkable 'tour de force', although history has seen such precocious brilliance before and since (Stanley Hiller's helicopter?).

A distinguished visitor from German Alsace to the Exhibition was struck by the car and took a licence to make it, with the young Bugatti being taken on as Designer – his father had to sign the contract as the son was under age! Thus the De Dietrich Company in Niederbronn began to make his cars, in an over-competitive market, which they gave up in 1904; then Bugatti continued as a consulting designer for Mathis in

Figure 1 (previous page) *Bugatti's early 4 cylinder models were notable for their simplified bodywork, Bugatti expecting the weather protection to be worn by the passengers.*

Figure 2 (above) *Ettore Bugatti and his talented son Jean at a race meeting in France in 1936.*

Strasbourg, then the famous Cologne firm of Deutz, until, tired of working for others, he managed to find a backer to allow him to open a factory under his own name at a small town in Alsace, near Strasbourg, called Molsheim, which started production in 1910.

Even before he set up this factory he had managed to find a few customers for his cars who were struck by his personality and evidently forgave the many faults of these early cars – perhaps few of the contemporary vehicles were much better – and he was able to publish some of their adulatory letters. In the four years of the factory before an invading Germany army closed it down in August 1914 he produced some 400 small 1.4 litre cars, well made and with good performance, but very expensive; again he attracted a specialised clientele drawn to this unusual type of vehicle, not to be compared with the large, heavy cars typical of the period, nor indeed the early attempts by others to produce 'cycle' cars of poor construction.

The combination of Italian nationality, designing for a large successful industry, a circle of wealthy friends and acquaintances competing in the Prince Henri or Herkomer Trials of Bavaria, imperfect German and French, his attractiveness, and above all a strong personality created around him what can best be described as a mystique which was to remain with him until his death – and must be the foundation of the continued interest in him today.

Remaining in France during the war, offering his services to the French Government to design a number of aero engines, one of which was taken up by the US Government for local manufacture, clearly helped to maintain his prestige. When war ended, he got his factory back undamaged, and soon was making and selling his little car to a hungry market. Licenses were sold to Italy, Germany and to Crossley Brothers in Britain, and although not many cars were made by these licensees, the resulting income was helpful, and allowed him to resume racing seriously. He competed in the French Grand Prix at Strasbourg in 1922 and thereafter for many years. He was now able to build larger cars, the 1922 racing machine being an 8-cylinder 2 litre and as time went on larger models were seen.

With racing as a means of publicising achievement, he appealed to customers who wanted a car 'with some fizz in it', as Henry Royce declared when he sought a car during the War. Certainly the Bugatti of the 1920s had performance, very fine road manners, a feature rarely seen in other cars of that period; it had its faults, the brakes were poor, and often you would oil up a spark plug! But the owners loved their cars – Lady Cholmondeley wrote that hers was a little jewel, Lord Carnarvon was most satisfied, and Sir Robert Bird, MP for Solihull extolled the virtues of his on House of Commons notepaper – all these testimonials being used by Bugatti!

After 1926 when Bugatti won the World Championship with his Type 35, his factory was busy enough to allow him to produce larger touring cars, and excellent 3 litre, a fine 5 litre, both eight cylindered, and then finally the incredible 'Royale' of no less than 12.7 litres, the largest car ever put on the market – 78 HP by the old RAC formula. Although intended for kings, no king ever owned one, although King Alfonso intended to buy one, but was exiled from Spain before he could take delivery.

Figure 3 *Customers demanded stylish 4-seat bodies but the weather protection, even in this 1925 model was minimal.*

4343 AZ

igure 4 (opposite) *In 1928 Bugatti put the acing 35B engine in a touring chassis, the ody being rightly labelled '3½ seater' by the actory, this produced the first Grand Sports car apable of 100 mph, known as the Type 43.*

Figure 5 + 5a *Seeking more power Bugatti added a supercharger in 1927 to produce the famous Type 35B; the appearance of the polished 'square-cut' engine continues to delight the eye.*

BUGATTI
B.249

Rumour of King Carol of Romania or Zog of Albania were merely rumours, but a French clothing manufacturer, a German doctor, and a food manufacturer from Britain eventually received theirs! Unfortunately the early 1930s were a time of financial crisis, and the other three cars Bugatti made of this type were unsold, until finally passing on cheaply after the 1939 War.

The Molsheim factory survived the depression by being given good contracts by French railways for high speed railcars, of original design by Ettore himself, full of novel features and using up production of the Royale engines not wanted for motor car production. Of unusually fine appearance these successful railcars seem indeed to be worthy progenitors of the modern French TGV, being eventually withdrawn after the recent war.

While Bugatti continued to produce a few racing cars in the 1930s he could not compete with the Government sponsored Italian Alfa Romeos, nor German Auto Unions and Mercedes and the money thus spent might have been put to better use – but for Bugatti not to produce racing cars was unthinkable! While Ettore spent much of his time on railcar design, his son Jean ran the factory and produced the last successful Bugatti the 3.3 litre eight cylinder Type 57 – perhaps the best of the 1936-39 sporting saloon cars competing with the Rolls-Bentley, Delage, Delahayes of the period.

Jean himself had a fine sense of line, and was responsible in particular for some very good coachwork made by the

Figure 6 *Bugatti's extravagant Royale car had the largest engine ever used in a production motor car; the first of the six built, only 3 being sold pre-war, went to Mr A. Esders of Paris, who did not drive at night and wanted no headlamps. This beautiful body was designed by Jean Bugatti and made at the Molsheim factory.*

Figure 7 *A later development of the racing car known as the Type 55 was fitted with a fine roadster body designed by Jean Bugatti – to some the most beautiful sports car ever produced.*

body shop at Molsheim. He is credited with the shape of the body on a remarkable roadster body on one of the Royale chassis, and in particular the two-seater sports body on the Type 55, which is really a racing model converted for road use – to many an eye the most beautiful sports car ever produced. Under his direction several standard bodies of fine line were produced for the Type 57, including an experimental car with 'gull-wing' doors, anticipating by several years the 'Gull-wing' Mercedes coupé of the 1960s.

The total production of all Bugatti cars from 1910 to 1939 when production ceased was about 7800, of which some 2000 remain; all are interesting and today fun to drive – some indeed exciting! Even the worst type, in poor condition seems able to fetch over £20 000 at a sale, a good 35B or 51 racing car at least £150 000, a 55 anything up to half a million pounds, and a Royale changed hands a few months ago for $8 million! To some of us, this is a pity, because we are not likely to see a £250 000 car very often on the road, and Bugattis were meant to be used and enjoyed – but those of us who bought a Bugatti for £200 30 years ago can hardly complain!

One interesting conclusion can be drawn from the rise in value of the cars – that there are enough of each desirable model; were a type unique it would not be so attractive – a collector prefers to have one of a few remaining, and to ensure that his is of unquestioned authenticity, with a continuous history, and better than the other similar ones. To this end the wealthy collector will spend large sums in one of a few restoration shops which can be found to put the cars into a state far better than they ever were when they left the factory!

But the rise in value has also seen an increase in the market for spurious cars, of questionable origin, or put together from parts and claiming false factory serial numbers. In spite of 'caveating the emptors' it seems surprising how gullible many a buyer becomes when attracted by a fine looking Bugatti, believing what he is told, or maybe not caring! It certainly makes work for a few conscious experts anxious that the car and its history should not be debased – too many cars were 'the personal car of Madame Bugatti', one even being displayed at a recent show in Paris bearing a sign that it was the former car of Mrs Jean Bugatti, Jean having never married!

But no doubt an antique market is what it becomes, and perhaps a Bugatti as an example of 20th Century artefacts is as important in its own way, as a Turner or a Constable. And if you get a chance to look at one closely, open the bonnet or hood to see the technical aesthetics of the engine!

Figure 8 *By mid-1930 the production Bugatti was the model 57, this 'Atalante' coupé being ordered by Lady Cholmondeley, and seen here at Houghton Hall photographed by Lord Cholmondeley.*

August 1987

BUYING A DINING TABLE

Deborah Scott

Figure 1 *Good solid Victorian mahogany table extended by two original leaves. This one pulls out to insert leaves while slightly later examples had a winding mechanism. The comparative slenderness of the legs also suggests an early Victorian date. About 1850. 178 × 112 cm (70 × 44 in). HILL RISE ANTIQUES. Price £1280 (c US$1792)*

There are those who regard a dining table as no more than a convenient means of keeping their dinner off the floor. Others see it as a most important and potentially expensive outlay, second only to the purchase of their house or flat. It is for the second group that this article is written. Those who can afford several thousands of pounds will be offered a goodly choice of period tables that can extend to seat all their friends and relations at once. But here we are aiming to encourage those who cannot take out a second mortgage for this purpose so, with one exception, the tables shown here all cost less than £1500 – some much less.

The history of dining tables is well documented elsewhere (see *The Shorter Dictionary of English Furniture* by Ralph Edwards), so here only the briefest outline will be given. Dining tables have evolved over the past three centuries in response to the changing circumstances and demands of those eating off them. From early days when people ate at long narrow 'refectory' tables in draughty halls, there came the development during the 17th century of the gate-leg table. This allowed a smaller group to eat more sociably at a round or oval table in a room specially for dining. The swinging gate-legs of these tables allowed them to be stored and moved much more readily than the heavy refectory tables. Early in the 18th century as mahogany began to replace oak for the best furniture, oval or round tables were made of this wood. These worked on much the same principle as the gate-leg, except that the legs were of cabriole form, and without the lower stretchers. This gave them a lighter, more elegant appearance. Most such tables had four legs, but the largest ones might have six or even eight legs to add stability. Where large numbers were to be seated around a table, a pair of square-ended drop-leaf tables could be placed end to end. A more elegant way of extending a square ended drop-leaf table developed about the middle of the 18th century. This was the addition of a pair of D-end (semi-circular) tables which could be removed and used as pier tables when not required for dining.

The problem with all these tables was the excessive number of awkwardly placed legs with which diners had to wrestle when seated. The solution came towards the end of the 18th century in the form of the pedestal. Dining tables were supported on one or more pedestals, with leaves inserted to extend the length. This style of dining table has remained popular up to the present day. During the 19th century the style of the pedestal evolved to conform with Regency, William IV and early Victorian tastes, but in this century it is the original late 18th century version that has been most widely reproduced.

The Victorians favoured substantial tables made of mahogany or oak with a heavily turned and sometimes carved leg at each corner. The legs of early examples, dating from about 1850, are elegant compared to the bulbous, ornately carved neo-Elizabethan legs that followed late in the century. These tables may either pull out to allow leaves to be inserted, or have a winding mechanism to crank the two ends apart. Some ingenious mechanisms for enlarging tables were developed in the 19th century, including patented methods for expanding circular tables. Original versions of these can fetch tens of thousands of pounds today.

Choosing a table

The first decision a buyer must make is whether he wishes to seat more than six people at his table. The number of people that can be accommodated is one of the major factors controlling the price of antique dining tables. There is a disproportionate leap in value between tables that can seat four to six people, and those that can seat eight or more. A useful rule to remember when assessing a table is that the average diner needs a width of 24 inches at the table edge to be comfortable. Slender guests and forfeiting the side plates can make an eight-seater out of a generous six, but remember that guests may expand over the period that you own this table so try to afford a large table if at all possible.

Having said that, in a small flat or house, a four to six seater may be ideal. The choice is wide. There are the 19th century single pedestal small dining or 'breakfast' tables, which may be oval, round of square. Shown here *(Figures 2, 3 and 4)* are some examples, ranging from an elegant early 19th century table for £1350 to a heavier looking one for less than £500. Amongst pedestal breakfast tables, those with platforms *(Figures 3 and 4)* on which the trunk of the pedestal sits and from which the legs or feet descend, tend to be less expensive than those with the lighter looking pedestal shown in *Figure 2*.

Shown in *Figure 5* is an attractive small

Figure 2 (left) *Elegant mahogany breakfast table on a centre pedestal with four feet. A table this size can seat six people. About 1810. 145 × 96 cm (57 × 38 in). DAVID & SARAH PULLEN. Price £1350 (c US$1890)*

Figure 3 (top right) *William IV breakfast table with an attractively figured top resting on a sturdy platform pedestal. The flaps are extended to give a square top, making this a versatile table for a small flat. About 1835-40. W 104 cm (41 in). BINSTED ANTIQUES. Price £975 (c US$1365)*

Figure 4 (bottom right) *Round mid-Victorian tilt-top table supported by an octagonal pillar on a triangular platform. This is mahogany veneered onto a pine base – the veneer joins may just be seen on the top. About 1860. Diam 117 cm (46 in). BINSTED ANTIQUES. Price £450 (c US$630)*

Figure 5 (above) *Georgian mahogany oval drop leaf table, suitable to seat four or six. Its decoratively carved frieze is an attractive detail. About 1760. 124 × 106 cm (49 × 42 in). DAVID & SARAH PULLEN. Price £595 (c US$833)*

Figure 6 (below) *Georgian mahogany drop leaf table large enough to seat eight or ten people. An example of a type of table widely ignored in this country and thus offered at low prices. About 1780. 167 × 127 cm (66 × 50 in). DAVID & SARAH PULLEN. Price £585 (c US$819)*

mahogany drop-leaf oval table of the mid 18th century that would seat four to six people. There are also oak gate-leg tables of this size. These may be bought for as little as £300-£400 at auction, but expert advice is important as all kinds of marriages between tops and legs are common, and there are many reproductions.

Mahogany drop-leaf tables deserve particular attention as they are currently undervalued and widely ignored. A table like that shown in *Figure 5*, dating from the late Georgian period and able to seat six comfortably, may be bought for less than £300. A larger example that can seat eight to ten people, *(see Figure 6)*, must represent excellent value at under £600. One of the criticisms levelled at these tables is their instability. This especially afflicts those with slender tapering legs, while the more robust pad-footed or square legged examples suffer less. Those large drop-leaf tables that have six or eight legs are firmer and thus more desirable though even they rarely make more than £500 to £600. Drop-leaf tables were also made in oak, emulating the mahogany styles. These are approximately half the price of mahogany, and thus a good buy for anyone who does not insist on mahogany *(see Figure 11)*.

Although drop-leaf tables may be found inexpensively as there is little demand for them currently, there are some points that should be checked before snapping up such a 'bargain' table. Stability has already been mentioned, and one of the factors

Figure 7 (below) *Oak gate leg table dating from the late 17th or early 18th century. These tables are prone to all kinds of repairs and marriages between top and legs, and are currently out of favour. W 117 cm (46 in).* PHILLIPS. *Sold for £360 (c US$500)*

affecting this is the state of the leaf hinges and, particularly, the knuckle joints. These are the joints on which the legs swing out. Although the centre pin may be replaced without too much difficulty, if the joint itself is badly damaged or broken, it can cost around £40 to repair. Another problem is warped leaves. However difficult it is in a crowded shop, do be sure to extend the table fully so that the structure can be checked and the warped leaf discovered. This is not a curable problem, and will seriously affect the stability of the table.

The leaves of drop-leaf tables may be round, rounded or square. Some dealers particularly scorn the latter, describing them as D-end tables that have lost their D-ends. they see them as merely a good source of mahogany for making replacement leaves for the desirable pedestal table. Indeed the desirability and high price of long tables, both pedestal and Victorian has led to much 'improvement' and many additions being made to tables. Given the forces of supply and demand, and the fact that a dining table is regarded by many buyers as primarily functional furniture, this is understand-

Figure 8 (above) *Georgian mahogany drop leaf table of a type most commonly broken up for the wood. The slender tapering legs make this less stable than the square legged or pad footed variety, but still functional. This table could easily seat six, and eight at a slight squeeze. About 1830. 152 × 99 cm (60 × 39 in).* HILL RISE ANTIQUES. *Price £280 (c US$392)*

Figure 9 (below) *Reproduction of the classic Georgian pedestal dining table. There is a great demand for this type of dining table, and it extends to the 20th century reproductions. An original example from about 1820 of about 9 × 4 ft might cost £5000–£7000. 183 × 91 cm (72 × 36 in).* BINSTED ANTIQUES. *Price £725 (c US$1015)*

Figure 10 (above) *18th century oak refectory table capable of seating six comfortably. This is an attractive example of an early style of table particularly suitable for a country cottage. 145 × 74 cm (57 × 29 in).* MOLLIE EVANS. *Price £900 (c US$1260)*

Figure 11 (below) *Oak drop leaf table. This is the country or provincial version of the mahogany drop leaf. It probably dates from the early part of the 19th century. 157 × 106 cm (62 × 42 in).* ANNA YANDELL. *Price £290 (c US$406)*

able. After all if a dealer can hardly sell a drop leaf table for £300, while the wood from it can perhaps convert a 6 ft table for £1000 into a 10 ft table readily saleable at £2000, one must see his point. Although from a functional point of view a table with additions and changes may be quite acceptable at a price, an antique collector should be sure to find out what has been done to any table he wishes to buy before parting with a large sum of money. Ask the dealer, who should, if they are 'bona fide' additions he has made himself, be ready to point them out and, of course, examine the table closely. Pay attention to the surface – genuine leaves may often be a different colour as they have had less exposure than the structural parts of the table. Check the edges of the leaves – do they match? Look underneath – how does the wood compare, and is the metal fitment for the edge clips a recent addition? Many antique collectors may find the humble

mahogany drop-leaf, despite its shortcomings, a much more attractive proposition than the amended versions of grander, bigger tables.

The finest large tables are well beyond the cash limit set for this article. A beautiful D-end table of about 1790, over 9 foot long might cost £4000 to £5000, and a Regency two pedestal table of the same size from £5000-£7000 or more. Victorian tables of great size with a leg at each corner (similar in style to *Figure 1*) may be found for much less than earlier large tables, and come within the £1500 limit. A Victorian oak example, 10 foot in length, sold recently for £1300 and a Victorian walnut example that could seat 16 people sold for £1500.

Auction rooms that deal in antique furniture are bound to sell dining tables frequently – certainly in London several come up for sale every week. Larger furniture dealers usually have a selection of tables, and even the local general antique shop may squeeze one in occasionally. Finding the right example at the right price may take a little time, but there is plenty of choice in the price range, so there is no need to feel compelled to buy the first piece one sees.

Two words of warning – check the height of your dining chairs and make sure they, plus your knees, will fit under the lowest part of any frieze under the table top. Secondly, dining tables tend to be dwarfed in the wide open spaces of the sale room or showroom. Do not overestimate the size of table that will comfortably fit into your dining room – always measure both the room and the table and allow enough space for chairs plus people around the table.

April 1986

Figure 12 *Although well outside the price limit of this article, this is a classic example of a mahogany D-end dining table of about 1790. Notice that between the D-ends is a drop leaf centre table, fully extended. 292 × 106 cm (115 × 42 in). HALLIDAYS. Price £4000-£5000 (c US$5600-7000)*

FIRE GRATES

Deborah Scott

Figure 1 *George II grate with brass fret and pedestal legs showing the squareness of design that contrasts with the curves of later grates. The value of this grate is enhanced not only by its antiquity but also by its small size. W 53 cm (21 in). NIGEL BARTLETT £1800 (c US$2574).*

At a meeting in 1863 an architect remarked that, 'An Englishman's love for his fire-place is so deeply rooted that, even supposing it could be shewn that a close stove possessed greater advantages, I am sure he would most reluctantly relinquish all the comfortable associations with which it is connected.' Now that central heating has rendered the open fire redundant in many homes, this English love of the fire place is alone responsible for its continued survival. Indeed, in recent years with the advent of gas-fired imitations of coal and log fires which may be fitted to any grate, there has been a resurgence of demand for traditional fire grates from both town and country homes.

In early times logs were supported by metal firedogs or andirons which sat at either side of the hearth. During the reign of Queen Anne, coal began to be more generally available as fuel. The successful burning of coal in the fire place required some sort of a container to hold it together in a readily combustible mass. Thus the fire basket evolved, at first supported by the firedogs, then later fused with them and a heavy metal fireback as a unit, the dog grate or stove grate. Coal was not, however, immediately universally popular. Although efficient in terms of heating, it was dirty and in open fire places often caused intolerable smoke. The reduction of smoke became a major pre-occupation, and inspired many changes in fire place and grate design throughout the 18th and 19th centuries.

During the 18th century the dog grate developed to become decorative as well as utilitarian. The vestigial firedogs became mere ornamental legs at either end of an ornate pierced fret or apron, above which sat a narrow, compact fire basket, now raised well above the hearth *(Figure 3a)*. These grates followed contemporary fashions, with gothic, rococo and chinoiserie motifs finding expression on the frets, supports, finials and sometimes even the bars of the grate. The neo-classicism of the 1760s, championed by the Adam family had its effect on fire grates, substituting simplicity and repetition for ornate fantasy. The dog grates of the late 18th century attained an elegance in decoration and proportion that makes them highly desirable to this day. Grates were made of iron with polished steel or brass for the most visible parts. Robert Adam, however, favoured the expensive silver-coloured alloy called Paktong, imported from China. This did not tarnish or rust, was easy to engrave and had a lustrous sheen.

Another type of grate which lent itself well to neo-classical decoration was the

Figure 2 (opposite top) *Late 18th century polished steel fire grate embellished with engraved decoration over a pierced fret. The elegance of its proportions is typical of its period, but its straight front is in contrast to the more usual serpentine outline. About 1770-1780. W 105 cm (41½ in).*

Figure 3a *Steel fire grate with finely engraved and pierced fret which sweeps across the front in a serpentine curve echoed by the fire bars above. This example dates from about 1780-90, but compare it in line and detail to the late Victorian copy, also in steel, shown in Figure 3b. W 89 cm (35 in). T. CROWTHER £3500 (c US$5005).*

Figure 3b (inset) *Late Victorian version of a late 18th century fire grate, in steel. Notice the narrower width and straight front, only curving forward at the ends. The back and the fire bars have been replaced. W 61 cm (24 in). THE FIRE PLACE £315 (c US$450).*

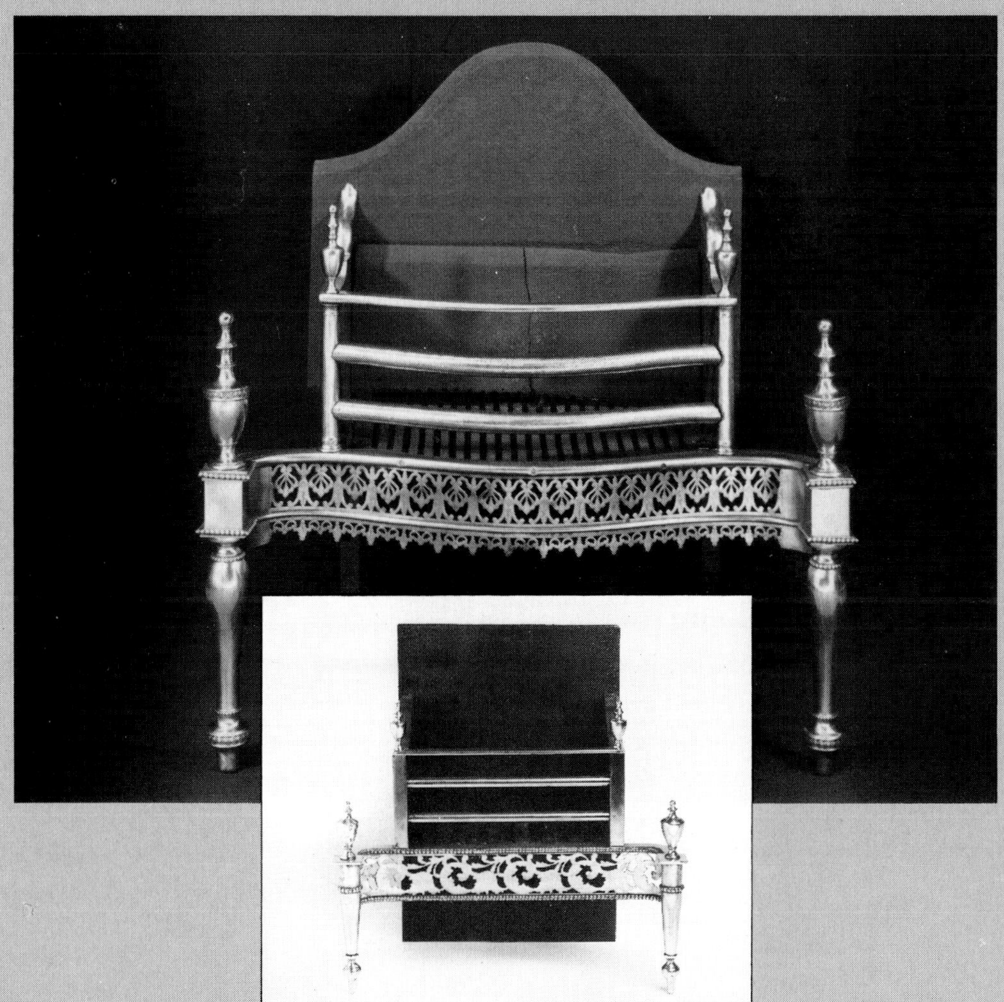

hob grate. Probably in use before the middle of the 18th century in secondary rooms of country houses, these grates were built in to the fire place (*Figure 5*). As their name suggests, they are characterised by having a hob on either side where a kettle could be kept warm. These hobs are formed by the flat surfaces of two hollow pillars, between which the fire is supported by a grid and fire bars. In the second half of the 18th century, the cast iron plates, of which such grates are constructed, bore moulded designs in classical taste. One of the leading manufacturers of these grates was the Scottish foundry of Carron, and this name is frequently encountered on grates. John Adam, a member of the famous family of designers was a partner in the Carron Company, and the Adam influence is seen in the delicate elegance of so much cast ironwork of the period.

This type of hob grate was pleasing in appearance and could be made in small sizes for use in bedrooms and studies for example. Its tendency to smoke, however, caused a decline in popularity early in the 19th century. The problem of smoke had already led in the 18th century to a narrowing of the fire place, and more particularly of the throat of the chimney. The idea of this was to concentrate the draught, thus sucking the recalcitrant smoke away up the chimney. This, however, meant that the fire consumed large quantities of coal. One answer to this conundrum came in the form of the register grate which filled the entire fire place, and had an adjustable iron plate at the base of the flue to regulate up-draught. Such grates, also known as enclosed or framed grates, became popular in the second half of the 18th century. Often made of polished steel, the frame itself bore most of the decoration, which might be engraved or applied, while a decorative pierced fret below the grate might echo the same theme. In such grates the sides of the fire basket also offered hobs, but that these were always used as such seems unlikely since the decorative knobs would get in the way (*Figure 6*).

The 19th century fire place was frequently filled by a cast iron register grate, with cast decoration sometimes further embellished with steel or brass ornaments. Early in the century these maintained the square form of the opening, the firebars spanning between perpendicular supports. During the Victorian period the firebasket was lowered, the surround became increasingly elaborate with moulded or tiled decoration. The flue was minimised and was often concealed by a hood above the fire. In some cases the fire opening itself became arch-shaped within the square plate, with a flap to the flue close above the basket. In all these register grates, considerable advantage in heating was enjoyed not only from the control of the draught, but also from the heat radiated by the whole iron facia.

Free-standing dog grates were also made in the Victorian period, though it would appear that registers were more common, especially in town dwellings. Like so much in this period, these dog grates were derived from earlier styles, although the command of proportion and attention to detail they show do not compare to those of a century before. Because of the smaller fire places of the Victorian period, they tend to be narrower than their Georgian prototypes, though often taller, and with more depth front to back. Metals used include polished steel, brass and occasionally German silver – an alloy which, like Paktong, has an attractive warm hue and does not rust.

Figure 4 *Fine example of an early 19th century framed grate with lavish decoration in cast iron. Notice the high fire basket, hobs on either side and chimney closed but for a vent which controls the up-draught. About 1820. W 99 cm (39 in). LASSCo £550 (c US$786).*

Buying a Fire Grate

From an architectural point of view, some attention should be paid to the period and style of room in which a grate is to be placed. While all sorts of building work can be undertaken to modify the shape and size of the fire place, the process will be both cheaper and more appropriate if the original type of grate is replaced. Innumerable town houses built in Victorian and Edwardian periods were equipped throughout with register grates. Since these were made to standard sizes, it is not difficult to find replacements. Those lucky enough to have a Georgian fire place may choose from free-standing dog grates, framed grates or hob grates. Perhaps most elegant of these, especially when combined with an appropriate period surround, is the polished steel framed grate. A fender which matches the fret would be highly desirable with such a grate though one would be lucky to encounter such a thing.

Another factor to bear in mind is the cost of fitting. Any of these grates apart from the free-standing examples will require a builder to fit them. While this is not a difficult job and any competent builder should be able to do it, it is arduous and time consuming and therefore may cost as much as £200-£300. Fitted grates have to be packed with rubble, not just for stability but also to distribute the heat which might otherwise burn through the metal. Builders' work may also be required to adjust the chimney, especially in the case of hob

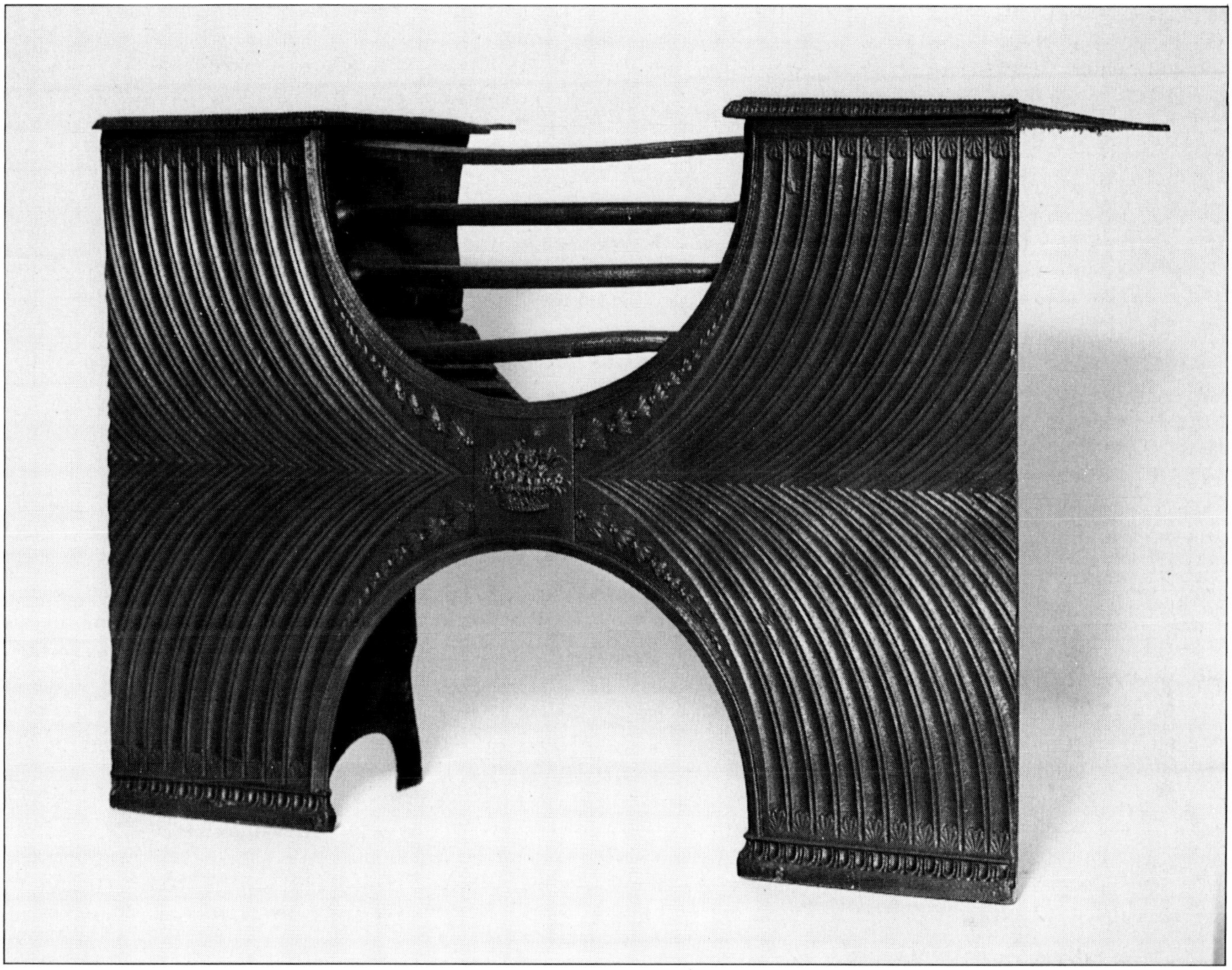

Figure 5 *Late 18th century hob grate typically constructed of cast iron plates, the front bearing decoration while the two tops form the hobs. The wrought iron fire bars are curved and tapered towards the ends in the period manner. This one lacks a back plate. W 93 cm (36 in). WALCOT RECLAMATION £430 (c US$615).*

grates with their bad reputation for smoking. It must also be remembered that once fitted only the bravest is going to dare to take such a fire grate away with him when he moves house. Those likely to move house might prefer to consider a free-standing, hence portable, fire grate.

Prices are affected by various factors. Eighteenth century grates are not common, and command high prices – usually well over £2000 – whatever the type. Amongst these, special features like exceptional decoration or design, or Paktong (very rare) add further to the price. Brass is also desirable, indeed so much so that a Victorian copy in brass of a Georgian dog grate can command as much as the original in steel. This may be as much for pragmatic reasons as aesthetic, for those who live in especially damp areas where rust is particularly likely to be a problem with iron and steel. Various treatments may be used to prevent rust including furniture polish which gives a wax coating, vaseline or lacquer.

The condition and especially the authenticity of a grate will be of importance to those interested in antiques. Generations of fires will have taken a toll of the fire-bearing parts of a grate and so it is likely that these may have been replaced. Less acceptable is some of the complete restructuring that is seen, with replacements not conforming to the style

Figure 6 *Polished steel framed grate of the late 18th century, decorated with applied paterae and engraving. Amongst the most elegant of fire grates, these also represent a successful attempt to reduce the problem of smoke. W 94 cm (37 in). NIGEL BARTLETT £2500 (c US$3575).*

Figure 7 *The Victorian register grate that until recently everyone was only too happy to dispose of. Now once more finding favour, the aesthetic appeal of the tiles is all important, though they are usually dominated by an unattractive brown colour. Notice the low, hooded fire basket. About 1870.* W *96 cm (37¾ in).*
Walcot Reclamation £276 (c US$394).

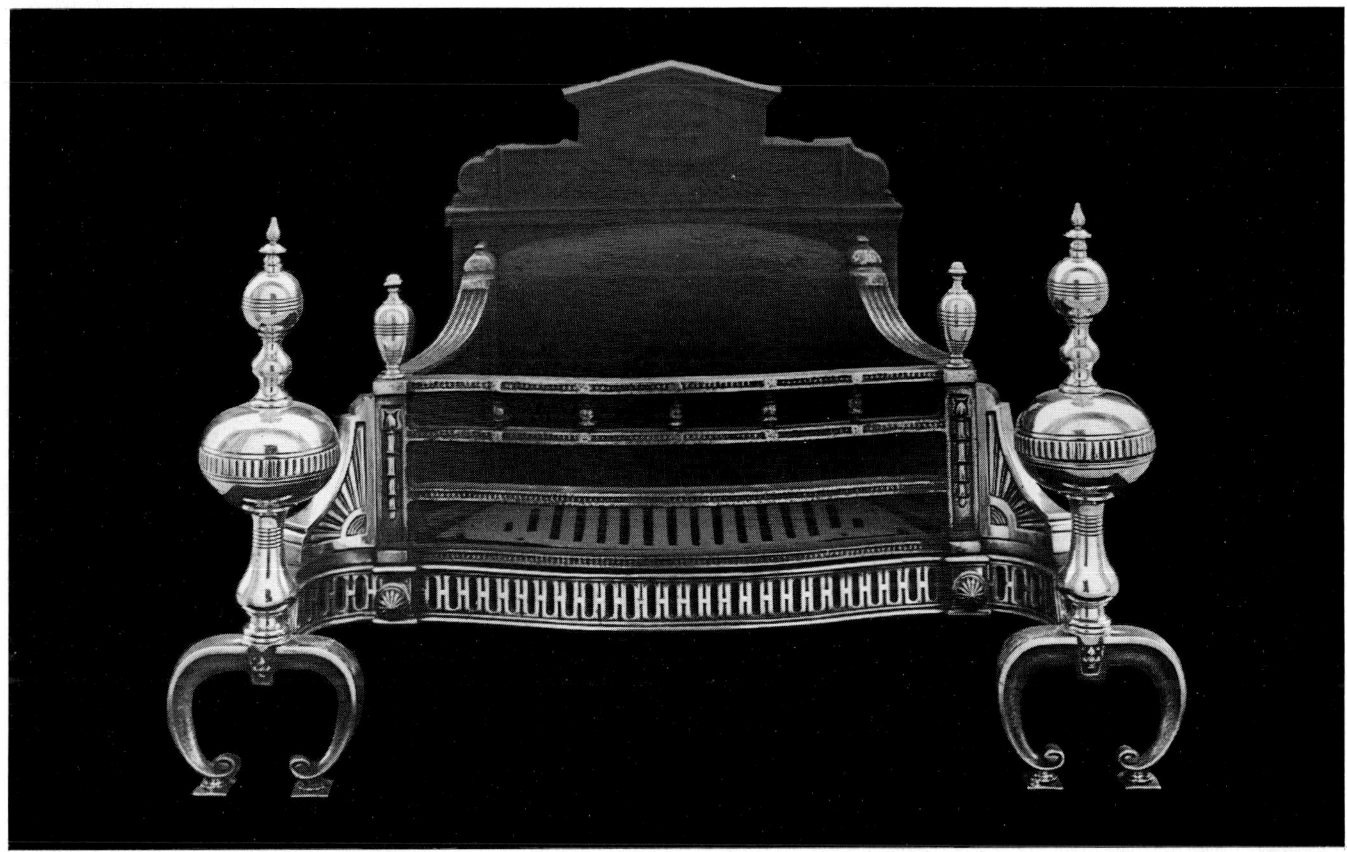

of the original. The examination of authentic examples will allow recognition of those that are not; observe the construction of a Georgian dog grate, for example: the use of rivets rather than small screws, hand-threaded screw fittings, the top rim of the fire basket in one piece not three, the sides of the fire basket separate from the top rim, the tapering shape of the fire bars, the curving supports to the back legs and the manner of their attachment. This is not to say that only entirely original grates are worth looking at, only that an antique collector should know all he can about the condition and approximate age of his intended purchase, accepting the inevitable consequences of age and use.

Prices of fire grates start at around £60 for a tiny cast iron hob grate. Larger hob grates can cost £200-£400. Victorian cast iron register grates vary in price according to their aesthetic merits, age and condition, with many available between £150 and £400. Victorian dog grates range widely. The finest quality imitations of Georgian designs in brass or other fine metal cost well over £1000, while less spectacular steel dog grates of smaller size may be found for £300-£400. Good Georgian framed grates or registers, and fine 18th century dog grates can cost several thousands of pounds.

Some dealers sell fire grates primarily as useful furnishings and their main concern is the refurbishing of their stock to a practical (and saleable) standard. More rewarding for someone with an interest in antiques and authenticity will be dealing with certain specialists who have an academic as well as a commercial interest in their stock. Fitted grates, especially Victorian registers, are to be found in abundance at architectural emporia.

Selected Bibliography

The Fashionable Fire Place 1660-1840 by Christopher Gilbert and Anthony Wells-Cole. Leeds City Art Galleries, 1985.

Decorative Wrought Ironwork in Great Britain by Raymond Lister. David & Charles, 1970.

January 1987

Figure 8 *Victorian brass fire grate. Although its elements are derived from earlier designs, it is not a reproduction – rather a successful example of Victorian eclecticism. W 93 cm (36 in).* NIGEL BARTLETT *£1200 (c US$1716).*

LIBERTY'S FURNITURE

Vivienne Woolf

The curious fact which differentiated Liberty's from other shops is that whereas all the others promoted the names and reputations of each of their designers, Liberty's insisted on their complete anonymity. Thus the early history of Liberty's Furniture Department is vague. It is impossible to identify most of the designers whose work came to be recognisable in the last years of the previous and early years of this century as being in the 'Liberty Style'. The house style was the work of many, only some of whom can be identified. The main sources of information about Liberty's cabinet work are the Arts and Crafts Exhibition Society's catalogues as Liberty's exhibited their work in these Exhibitions and a short-lived house magazine called the *Liberty Lamp,* in which members of staff recorded their memories. It seems likely now that most of the designs for Liberty furniture were produced in the Liberty Studio, but that the pieces of furniture were made in the small workshops of Soho by independent craftsmen, who duly affixed Liberty labels to their work.

Liberty's was founded by Arthur Lasenby Liberty and opened on the morning of 15 May 1875 at 118A Regent Street. Its original name was East India House and it sold nothing but silks from the East. In 1883 the firm moved to larger premises down the road. Everything was trundled down from East India House in handcarts by the staff. Carpets and furnishings were sold at the new shop, named Chesham House and it was from here that the furnishing and decorating studio was inaugurated in 1883 in Newman Street, under Mr Leonard Wyburd. Liberty's began to make their own furniture and interior woodwork in a nearby cabinet factory.

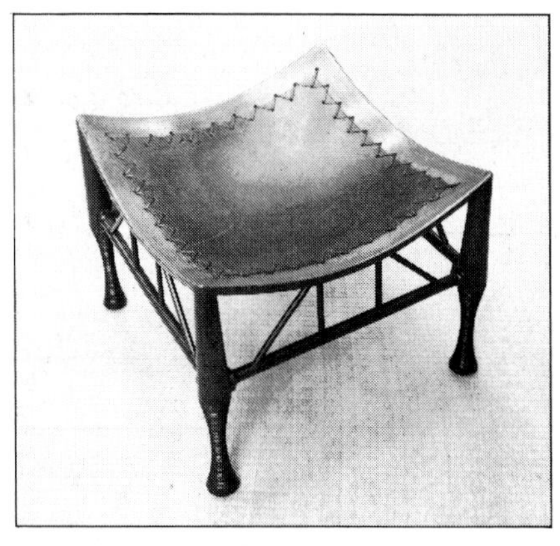

Figure 1 *'Thebes Stool'. Mahogany with turned decoration on the legs, and leather seat. Made for Liberty and Co. and registered with the Patent Office, 1884. Victoria and Albert Museum.*

Figure 2 (opposite) *Combination wardrobe in oak and ash with panelled doors and cupboards. The tiled washstand having a turned gallery with stylised brackets and moulded cornice. Label in drawer: 'Liberty and Co., Ltd London W'. Probably designed by Leonard Wyburd and Liberty Studio, about 1900. Liberty's.*

At this time the Art industries of the Far East has begun to extend their influence to the West. At the International Exhibition of 1862, the arts and crafts of Japan proved to be one of the most compelling attractions. The firm Farmer and Rogers for whom Arthur Liberty then worked, bought up most of the Japanese exhibits to form the nucleus of their oriental warehouse. When Liberty started his own shop he determined to change the whole look of fashion and interior design. He would not pander to mid-Victorian taste, created by the Industrial Revolution, but would apply Eastern motifs, with which his past experience had made him so familiar, to Western industries. Those who controlled machines would be shown how to use them in such a way as to obtain artistic results.

Items began to be made specifically for Liberty's in the East and these were supplemented by those made in London workshops. There was a tremendous effort to produce 'Japanese furniture' of bamboo, combined with floor matting and lacquered or inlaid panels. There were also 'Arab' sideboards, wardrobes and writing tables made in the style known as 'Moorish Moresque'. Indian, Chinese and Egyptian influences were

Figure 3 (below) *Oak Centre Table on tapered ring turned supports with geometric shaped frieze in the Moorish taste. Probably made by Liberty and Co. about 1880. Liberty's.*

Figure 4 (right) *Arm chair designed by George Walton and made for Liberty's by William Birch of High Wycombe. Walnut inlaid with mother-of-pearl. Victoria and Albert Museum.*

strong too. One of Liberty's earliest and most popular furniture designs was the so-called 'Thebes stool'. Based loosely on an Egyptian model, it consisted of three curved legs set into a curved seat, itself made from a single block of wood. It was first made in 1884 and Liberty's went on making it in oak and mahogany until about 1902. The same name was used for a four-legged low stool slung with a thonged leather seat *(Figure 1)*.

Liberty's contribution to the Japanese craze of the late 19th and early 20th centuries and its effect on decorative design was fundamental. The Japanese-style bamboo furniture was made in the Soho workshop of a Frenchman, Monsieur Fortier, whose best and almost sole client was Liberty. He was known to speak hilarious English and was a great favourite with the staff. He first appeared in a trade directory in 1876, describing himself as a Basket Maker, but he soon assumed the title Caneworker and moved first to Carnaby Street then to 55 Dean Street, where he remained during the 1880s.

Another cabinet maker associated with Liberty's in the beginning was a Scotsman called James Thallon. He owned a cabinet factory, and by arrangement with Liberty's made furniture in their name and acted as their representative. Liberty became his main customer and in about 1887 took over his workshops, James Thallon becoming an employee of the firm. From 1887 until the closing of the Cabinet Workshop in 1940 there was a remarkable continuity of personnel despite various changes of premises. The first foreman under James Thallon was George Wolfe. His pride of craftsmanship was such that when a contract was finished he wrote on the walls 'This work was fixed by George Wolfe of Liberty and Co.', and the date. In 1912 the Cabinet Works moved to Highgate where it came under the supervision of Albert Pannell.

At the end of the 19th Century, Liberty and Co. was the shop which

Figure 5 *'Athelston' oak wardrobe with stylised pierced supports, the panelled door having a decorative landscape panel in various stained woods. By Liberty and Co., Art and Crafts Movement. Liberty's.*

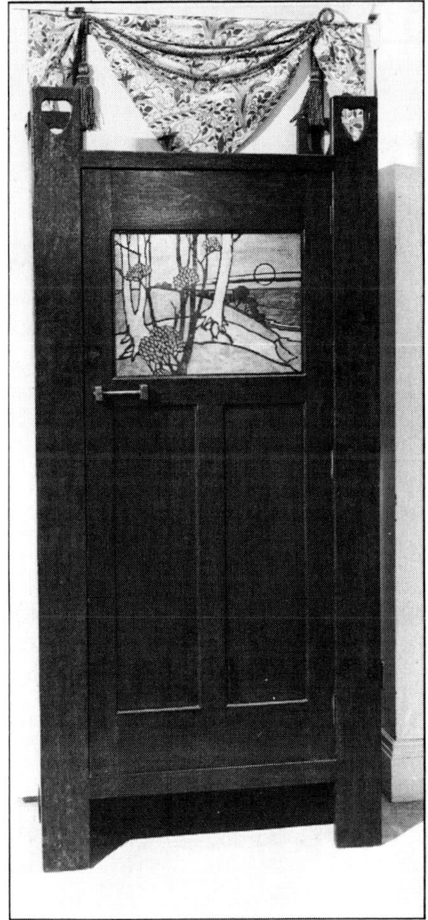

brought an original contribution to the Arts and Crafts Movement in England. This Movement was the inspiration of social change and it created an atmosphere where personal ideas could be encouraged. So closely were Liberty's wares identified with this progressive movement, that what became known as 'Art Nouveau' in France and Britain has always been known in Italy as 'Stile Liberty'.

The combination wardrobe and washstand *(Figure 2)* which is labelled 'Liberty and Co. Ltd., London' was made at this time and was probably designed by Leonard Wyburd. He created designs not only of Eastern inspiration, but also within the style of the New Aesthetic Movement. He had made a particular study of Arab design. A great feature of his style was the use of Moorish wooden arches with fretwork tracery across doorways and corridors. It was a joke at Liberty's that 'Mr Wyburd could draw them (Moorish wooden arches) blindfold'. The mahogany cabinet *(Figure 8)* depicts this Moorish style and was probably designed and made in Liberty's workshops. The oak centre-table is in similar style *(Figure 3)*.

George Walton was a Scottish architect who designed furniture for Liberty's. He opened a business in London in 1897 and was in business for more than 20 years. There is a good deal of his furniture about. His elegant pieces were a welcome relief from Wyburd's massive designs. The armchair *(Figure 4)* was designed by Walton and made for Liberty's by William Birch of High Wycombe. This firm made a number of pieces of furniture for Liberty's, mostly in 'natural English Walnut'. E. G. Punnett was one of their employees. He joined the firm in 1901 and made chairs and some cabinet furniture for Liberty's. His designs include elegant drawing room pieces and others in a curious original style, which is a combination of Art Nouveau and supposedly rural English forms. These designs, reflected in Saxon titles such as 'Ethelbert' and 'Athelston' were part of a serious attempt to provide an alternative to Art Nouveau, which in this country was thought to have reached unreasonable extremes after 1900. The oak wardrobe *(see Figure 5)* is described as 'Athelston' style. The oak stick stand *(Figure 6)* is also typical of the stylised form produced by Liberty's in 1900.

J. S. Henry was another firm who designed for Liberty's and made a speciality of decorated furniture in the Art Nouveau Style. From 1880, when he started business, John Sollie Henry had concentrated on the new and unusual. In *The Cabinet Maker* of October 1895, some of his furniture is described as being 'most fanciful' in shape.

Figure 6 *Oak stick stand on stylised capped supports with pierced vertical lath in stylised form. Label 'Liberty London'. Arts and Crafts Movement. Liberty's.*

C. F. A. Voysey was another of the distinguished independent designers who either worked directly for Liberty or influenced the design studio. Two of the most characteristic features of his furniture were hearts punched out of the ends and long strap hinges.

Other designers who designed for Liberty's were Harry Napper and Mackay Hugh Baillie Scott (1865-1945). The latter was an architect who wrote that furniture . . . 'should appear to grow out of the requirements of a room' . . . Much of his furniture was characterised by highly decorated fruit and flower inlays. Baillie Scott designed much of his

Figure 7 *Chair sold by Liberty, about 1904-1906. Appears in Liberty Catalogues: 'Inexpensive Furniture' about 1905. Victoria and Albert Museum.*

furniture for the cabinet maker John White. By 1901, White issued a catalogue of furniture made to Baillie Scott's designs at his Pyghtle Works, which numbered at least 120 pieces. This furniture was sold through Liberty's and also through White's showrooms in Bond Street.

Jessie M. King (1873-1949) was a Scottish designer and illustrator. She was best known for her work in book design and illustration, but she also worked for Liberty's.

By the beginning of this century, Arthur Liberty began to react strongly against the excesses of the Art Nouveau Style he had so helped to foster. Albeit that the production of the pieces of furniture in the early days remains something of a mystery, Liberty's were always renowned for the quality and original design of their furniture. However, as mentioned in the *Liberty Lamp* of July 1927, 'a revulsion of feeling took place, and the demand came for period work such as Tudor, William and Mary, and the Brothers Adam . . .'

Another reason for the changing styles of Liberty's furniture came about with the revival of interest in ancient Celtic. Morris, Faulkner and Co made a cabinet in 1861 of inlay work with Celtic inspired initials on the lid, and Celtic designs with the interlac motif began to appear in magazines and pattern books. Liberty's launched ranges of so-called 'Cymric' silver and 'Tudric' pewter which were the last important results of the neo-Celtic tendency: a fusion of Art Nouveau and Celtic.

Archibald Knox (1864-1933) was closely identified with Liberty's as a designer at this time. By 1900 he was their main designer and the inspiration behind their Celtic Revival, encouraged also by Liberty's Welsh Managing Director, John Llewellyn. Most of the designs were now for machine production. In 1904, Knox both taught and designed for Liberty's, producing designs for silver, pewter, carpets, textiles, jewellery and pottery.

At the turn of the century, the furniture stocked and sold by Liberty's was not confined to their own production. The firm imported the work of many distinguished Continental designers, for example, and this aspect of Liberty's work has continued throughout the history of the firm.

The most important works undertaken by The Cabinet Works and The Design Studio in the 20th century were major schemes of interior decoration. The dictum of 'Art for Art's Sake', prevalent at the turn of the century, was replaced by the feeling that houses, as 'machines for living', should be considered as a whole. Between 1895 and 1914 complete decorative schemes were made and installed by Liberty craftsmen in France, Germany, Switzerland, Hungary, Italy and South Africa. In 1914 at the outbreak of the First World War, Liberty's had on their books a large order for the Archduke Ferdinand of Austria as well as the King of Serbia and a contract for the Czar in St. Petersburg was proposed too. Probably the largest single job was the exterior and interior woodwork in the Tudor style for their Regent Street premises and these stand today as a testimony to the skills of their designers and craftsmen.

Acknowledgements

I would like to thank Mr K. R. Wootten, Head of the Antiques Department at Liberty's, for his valuable assistance and also Ken Jackson and Philip Spruyt de Bay of the Victoria and Albert Museum Photographic Studio for taking the photographs.

Bibliography

Liberty's: A Biography of a Shop by Alison Adburgham.

Liberty's 1875-1975. Catalogue of the exhibition held at the Victoria and Albert Museum to mark Liberty's centenary.

Arts and Crafts in Britain and America by Isabelle Anscombe and Charlotte Gere.

British Furniture 1880-1915 by Pauline Agius.

The Liberty Style. All colour paperback. Introduction by Victor Arwas.

Fortunes Made in Business, 1900 Part 5: Life Struggles of Successful People: Liberty: The Maker of the House Beautiful.

'The Growth of an Influence' *The Art Journal*, February 1900.

'A Note on the Decoration of the Day' by Charles Hiatt. *The Studio, 111, 1897*.

Journal of The Society of Arts, March 23, 1900. Article on furniture by A. L. Liberty.

Figure 8 *Mahogany cabinet fitted with bookshelves and leaded glazed cupboard. The winged shelves and cresting rail with spindle turned in the Moorish Manner. Probably designed and made in Liberty's workshop. Liberty's.*

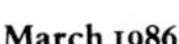

HOLLAND & SONS, CABINET MAKERS

Vivienne Woolf

On reading The Day Books, or business records of Holland and Sons, one is struck not only by the meticulously detailed recording of the work of one of the most esteemed Victorian Cabinet-making firms, but also by the fascinating insight these books give into Nineteenth Century life. From Queen Victoria herself – at Balmoral, Buckingham Palace, Windsor Castle and Osborne – to the humblest servant's room, from constructing the stands at Edward VII's coronation in 1902 or arranging Princess Sophia's funeral in 1846 to supplying '2 doz. Leather Buttons at 2/-' for a home in Oxford Square, London, Hollands' work was prolific and various. There was hardly a British institution that Holland and Sons were not involved with. They made furniture for the Palace of Westminster, the Reform and Athenaeum Clubs (among others), the British Museum, the Royal Academy, All Souls, Oxford and even the shop-fittings for John Lewis, the Oxford Street shop in the early twentieth century.

Hollands also showed at exhibitions, including London 1862, Vienna 1873, Paris 1867 and 1872, where they displayed among others, furniture designed by Bruce Talbert, whom they are said to be the first London firm to have employed. *Figure 2* shows an oak, fruitwood and marquetry breakfront cabinet made by Holland to Talbert's design. It was exhibited in the Paris Exhibition of 1867 and is regarded as one of Holland's most important works. In one of the contemporary *Art Journal Catalogues,*

Figure 1 *Satinwood armchair c. 1858. Courtesy of Victoria and Albert Museum.*

Figure 2 *Oak, fruitwood and marquetry breakfront side cabinet designed by Bruce Talbert. Inscriptions on its super-structure read: 'May good digestion wait on appetite': 'Health on both, Mirth becomes a feast' and 'We have all great cause to give great thanks'. Courtesy Christie's.*

the cabinet is described as follows:- 'Messrs. Holland and Sons exhibit, among other works (all their contributions being for Gothic furnishing), a DRESSOIR for a dining-hall: it is of oak, inlaid and relieved by gilding, the centre of the canopy being surmounted by a goblet with a carved subject in bas-relief, and mottoes from 'Pericles': the arched panels below the canopy are filled with solid inlays representing fish, fruit, game etc. The metal work is entirely of hand-wrought brass. The artist who has supplied the designs is Mr B J Talbert. It will suffice to say of this admirable production of Art – manufacture, that it fully sustains the renown of an establishment that has long been everywhere, famous'. This cabinet was sold for the highest price paid to date for an item of Victorian furniture (£81 000) at Christie's on 22 January 1986 and is now in private hands. The oak writing table *(Figure 6)* was also made to Bruce Talbert's design.

Sir Charles Barry is another designer whose work Holland and Sons executed. The table illustrated *(Figure 3)* is made to Barry's design and is very similar to one made by the firm to his design for the Reform Club in 1840. Other designers employed by Holland were G. E. Street, Gottfried Semper and J. K. Collings. The cabinet illustrated *(Figure 4)* was designed by Semper and shown at the Paris Exhibition of 1855. In the Day Book for March 1865 an oak bookcase with inlaid decoration, glass doors and brass mounts is described. This was made to a design by G. E. Street and found its way, eventually, to the Handley-Read Collection (G. E. Street's second wife, by the way, was the daughter of William Holland, son of the firm's founder). Hollands were continually interested in design, but said about it: 'the principal impediments to the progress of the manufacture of elegant cabinet makers' work in this country are caused by a great want of designers, draughtsmen and modellers: in fact of all the directors of art. The very few who can assist, demand and are paid with such excessive rates, that their services are dispensed with, except on important occasions'.

Of some of Hollands' exhibits at The Vienna Exhibition of 1873, the following was said at the time:- 'Holland and Sons have filled their bookcase, a wonderful mixture of gothic ornament and leather scrollwork with books: this at the same time shows everyone how unsuitable the great lavishness of gold on an object, through whose windows we see delicately gold ornamented book spines looks' and 'Holland and Sons show a round table with costly inlaid work already seen eleven years ago in London. The bookcase already mentioned is one piece unsuited to the dignity of English furniture exhibition. A salon cupboard and a table with metal arrangement and inlaid pieces of wood brightly coloured, partly damaged by fire in style of Louis XVI were praised by the French.' (In fact Hollands made a good deal of Louis XVI inspired furniture.)

Hollands' exhibition pieces contrasted quite strongly with their everyday products and, indeed, their records show an enormous variety of woods – such as Rosewood, Birchwood, Ebony, Walnutwood, Satinwood, Tulipwood – and styles of furniture used, according to the client's demand. In one of their catalogues, they boast, for example, of work done in the 'Italian Style' best fitted to a Hall or Dining Room, or 'the Moresque style in much request for the Smoking Room where comfort is looked for' and so on. *Figure 1* illustrates one of their less lavish satinwood armchairs and *Figure 5* a chest of drawers forming part of a suite of bedroom furniture made to Pugin's design for The Duke of Marlborough in Hungarian Ash. This last mentioned is a wood Hollands are often identified with now as they seemed to use more of it than any other cabinet maker of the time. One of their interesting commissions was recorded in the Day Book for the year 1868 and was for a Mr Thornton of Knowle Cottage, Sidmouth, Devon. They made some beautiful marquetry furniture for him, much of it stamped. The satinwood drawing-room cabinet with ivory and ormolu decoration *(Figure 7)* is an example. That Hollands worked for Mr Thornton is now well documented (see *Victorian Furniture* by Symons and Whineray) particularly as the bulk of this furniture came up for sale at Sotheby's about

Figure 3 *Maple table designed by Charles Barry. Courtesy of Haslam and Whiteway.*

ten years ago – having by then come into the hands of Mr Thornton's grand-daughter.

The firm of Holland and Sons first appeared in the London directories in about 1815 under the name of Taprell and Holland 'Cabinetmakers etc' at 25 Great Pultenay Street. Little is known about Taprell and William Holland, the other partner, is thought to have been connected with the architect, Henry Holland. The firm changed its name to Holland and Sons in 1843 and in 1846 to William Holland and Sons. The Great Pultenay Street address was dropped in 1826 and, after various changes of address, the firm took over what were to become their best known premises, 23 Mount Street, in 1852. This address was originally shared by a firm called Thos. Dowbiggin and Sons. They were already occupying it when Hollands moved in. Dowbiggin's name crops up from time to time in connection with Holland, such as the juxtaposition of their names, 'Dowbiggin and Holland' on a lithographed plan of the Duke of Wellington's lying-in-state. The relationship between the firms is not entirely certain but it seems probable that Hollands took Dowbiggins over. At any rate, Hollands were very much the senior partner.

Hollands were appointed Royal cabinet makers early in Victoria's reign. The Day Book 1850–51 gives some fascinating insights into the furnishing of Osborne, for example. Their work here is well documented, too. (See, for example, 'Holland and Sons and the Furniture of Osborne House' by Edward Joy, *Antiques* Vol XCIX No. 4, April 1971). Henry Whittaker was concerned with Hollands in the design for furniture at Osborne, although his precise contribution there is unclear. The Day Book of 1862 gives details of furniture made and maintained for Windsor Castle.

The following extracts from the Day Books give some insight into the variety and extent of Hollands' commitments outside of their work for Queen Victoria and others already mentioned.

August 8, 1826, for the Horticultural Society:

'A sett of Mah. Dining Tables 4′ 9″ wide, 2 round corner

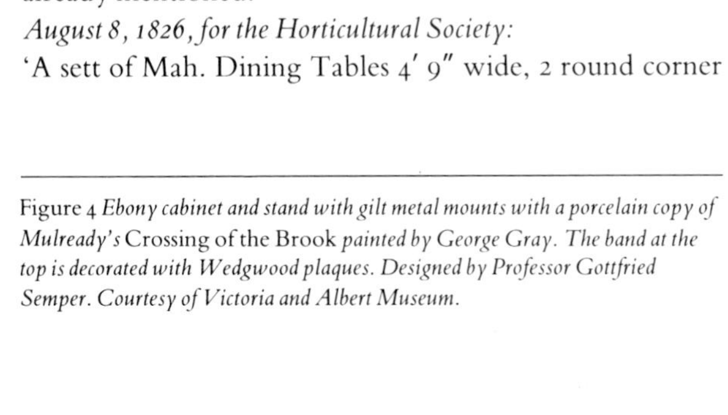

Figure 4 *Ebony cabinet and stand with gilt metal mounts with a porcelain copy of Mulready's* Crossing of the Brook *painted by George Gray. The band at the top is decorated with Wedgwood plaques. Designed by Professor Gottfried Semper. Courtesy of Victoria and Albert Museum.*

Figure 5 *Hungarian Ash chest of drawers part of a suite of bedroom furniture made to Pugin's design for the Duke of Marlborough, bearing the Duke's Gothic 'M' sign on its handles. Courtesy of Jeremy Cooper.*

Figure 6 (opposite top) *Oak writing table designed by Bruce Talbert. Courtesy of Michael Wisehall.*

Figure 7 (opposite below) *Satinwood Drawing Room Cabinet made for Mr R N Thornton, Knowle Cottage, Sidmouth in 1868. Courtesy of Victoria and Albert Museum.*

ends and 3 movable flaps, 4 turned carved legs to each on good brass castors wt. sliding frames, moulded edges to top good Spanish wood . . . £29.'

In 1835 there is a long list of 'Repairs and Jobbing' at the United Services Club.

December 31, 1839 for the House of Commons:
'8 long seat cushions stuffed with the best hair and covered in green morocco leather . . . £118-9-2'.

During the 1830s and 1840s Holland supplied a considerable amount of the internal woodwork for the Houses of Parliament. They also (together with other firms such as Gillows and John Webb) supplied much of the furniture. A large number of pieces of furniture stamped by them survives there.

In 1843, '8 Spanish mahogany single chairs and 8 Spanish mahogany portfolio stands, highly polished', were provided for the British Museum.

By 1850, Hollands' clients included most of the nobility, such as Earl de Grey, Lord Foley, Lord Cholmondeley, the Barings. In 1849 they arranged the funeral of a Colonel La Touche, for whom they had done much work the previous year. The work included 'A very elegant and highly enriched cabinet for end of room with richly chased ormolu mounts . . . with panels of Black marble raised florentine flowers and fruit of precious stones marble and ivory of the choicest description . . . £39-18.' and '2 Pier Tables between windows richly gilt and carved to correspond with console . . . £15.'

It is worth mentioning an example of the work they did in their capacity as 'Funeral Directors'. This was for the funeral of a Mr William Cameron in 1872 and included: 'A stout lead coffin complete . . . £6-15, a Hearse and four to Highgate . . . £3-10, Feathers and Velvets for the Hearse and velvets for horses . . . £2-2, 4 coachmen's cloaks . . . 4/-, A stout oak case made of 1½ inch stuff with a chamfered plinth round the bottom and edge of lid chamfered made in the best manner and French polished, 8 solid brass crescent handles with octagon loops and back plates, grills and highly burnished . . . £13.'

In 1851 they did some work for Lord Palmerston and made some furniture including 'a set of Mahogany Library Steps french polished . . . £3-18' for the Governor of The Bank of England.

Thomas Baring's house was furnished from top to bottom by Hollands in 1872 down to bedroom furniture

for spare servant's, upper housemaid's, butler's and housekeeper's rooms, and even a pestle and mortar and marble pastry slab for the kitchen!

In the same year, a great deal of work was done for the Athenaeum Club (see 'Holland and Sons, and the Furnishing of the Athenaeum' by Simon Jervis, *Furniture History* Vol VI, 1970 pp. 43-61). In 1892, Hollands did some work for the Army and Navy Club, Pall Mall. The most interesting entry against this club was in the Day Book 1902-3; Edward VII's Coronation. It included 'Decorating The Stand erected for Coronation Procession on Pall Mall Front and St James's Square Front' and covering the various tiers of seats with braided and fringed red and blue cloth hung with garlands of flowers and bearing The Royal Coat of Arms.

In June 1902, against the Cavalry Club, the entry includes: 'Erecting Stand for Coronation Procession and draping same as per drawing including cash paid fees, plan

Figure 8 *Satinwood Dining Table stamped Holland & Sons and bearing a brass retailer's plate inscribed. 'S & H Jewell, 29, 30 & 31, Little Queen Street, Holborn, WC'. Courtesy Sothebys.*

Figure 9 *Oak architect's desk c. 1862, containing wash basin inside it. Courtesy of Haslam and Whiteway.*

and copies prepared by Architect for Westminster City Council. Waiting on the Council Surveyor, obtaining his consent and getting Licence (sic) for same and signing duplicate . . . Per Estimate £279' and 'Fitting up Shields with Armour to Design . . . £45-2: Man's time going to Aldershot for Cavalry Swords, packing ditto in cases and bringing to London, including travelling expenses . . . £1-15: The wreaths and Festoons to design . . . £30-5.'

Hollands were also chosen to supply a 'State Throne Chair' costing £238-10 for the opening of Parliament by Edward VII in 1901.

In about 1890, William Morris & Co bought the Ebury Street cabinet-making workshops of Messrs Holland. By now these workshops must have become almost indistinguishable in their methods from other cabinet makers, producing quantities of furniture and even using machine-carving. (It is interesting to note that William Morris started stamping their furniture after this date). The Mount Street premises remained and Hollands continued trading from them until 1968 when the company went into liquidation.

In the first decade or so of this century the Day Books show that much carpentry, plumbing, polishing, stripping etc was done by Hollands but hardly any cabinet-making. For example, they did some carpentry at the Oxford and Cambridge University Club in 1913 and in January 1922, they adjusted and rehung curtains and repaired the lock on a basement door for A A Milne!

In 1944 Hollands did some building work for the Royal Academy's 'Back to Work Exhibition' and in 1945, they were very involved repairing Air Raid Damage.

The last entry in the Day Books is on May 4, 1947. It concerns renewing wall tiles in a school. However, what Holland and Sons are particularly remembered for is the great variety and skill of their craftsmen and the scope of their work. Their surviving pieces – some still in the environments for which they were made – stand not only as evidence of this, but also as reminders of a bygone age.

Acknowledgements

I would like to thank Robert Howell. Many dealers were helpful to me, but I would particularly like to thank Michael Whiteway and Martin Levy. Photographs Ken Jackson and Philip Spruyt de Bay.

Bibliography

Holland and Sons Day Books in the National Design Archives of the Victoria and Albert Museum.

Victorian and Edwardian Decorative Art. The Handley-Read Collection Exhibition Catalogue by Simon Jervis, 1972.

British Furniture, 1880-1915 by Pauline Agius, 1978.

World Furniture, An Illustrated History, Ed. by Helena Hayward, 1965.

The Houses of Parliament, Catalogued by M. H. Port, 1976.

Nineteenth Century English Furniture by Elizabeth Aslin, 1962.

Illustrated History of Furniture by Frederick Litchfield, 1892.

June 1987

NOEL G TERRY'S FURNITURE

Peter Brown

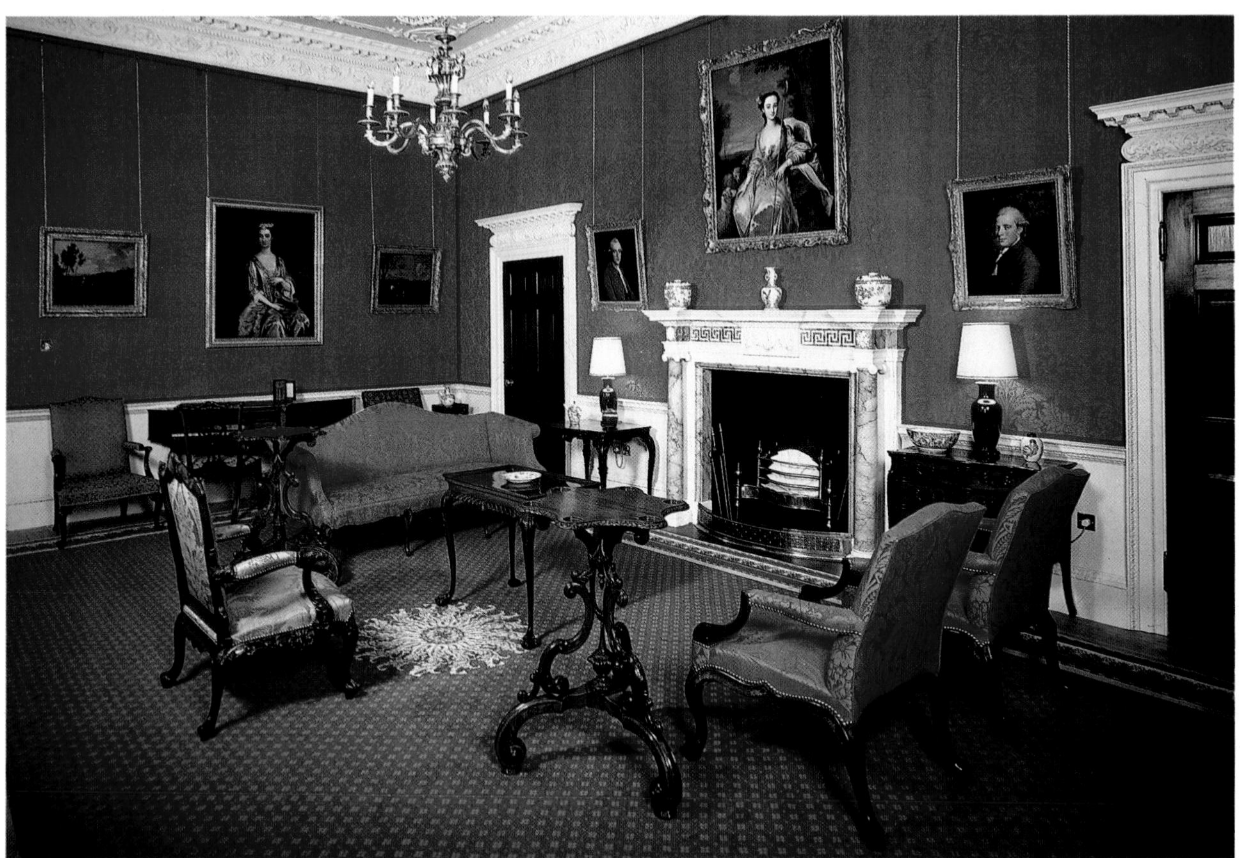

The gift of a unique collection of furniture and clocks to the York Civic Trust, who were at that time seeking to acquire and thereafter restore what was unquestionably the finest Georgian townhouse in York, was bound to create interest. When the collection was made up of outstanding English pieces mainly of the mid Georgian period and intended for an interior completed in 1762 then the prospect became very exciting.

The restoration of Fairfax House, York, England, was carried out by the York Civic Trust in 1982/84. The property was purchased from the York City Council whose decision to sell was undoubtedly influenced by the availability of this collection for permanent display in the house. By bringing together house and furniture the York Civic Trust, under the inspired Chairmanship of Dr John Shannon, have created a whole which is far greater than the sum of the parts. The result is what many describe as the finest townhouse of its type in England.

Noel G. Terry, whose great grandfather founded the Terry confectionary business, was born in York in 1889. With Queen Victoria still on the throne of an England

Figure 1 *The Saloon hung in red damask, provides a setting for some outstanding Georgian furniture. The centre chair is upholstered in contemporary Blue Damask. The two teatables have 6 wells in the top for tea bowls and are illustrated in the* Dictionary of English Furniture *(1st edition).*

Figure 2 (above) *One of a pair of mahogany armchairs in the Saloon, attributed to John Gordon. They stand on cabriole legs and are carved with a foliage and fish scale pattern. Originally part of a 24 piece set at Ditton Park in Surrey.*

Figure 3 (below) *Noel G. Terry and his wife Katherine with their four children. The picture was taken in 1933 at the height of his collecting activities.*

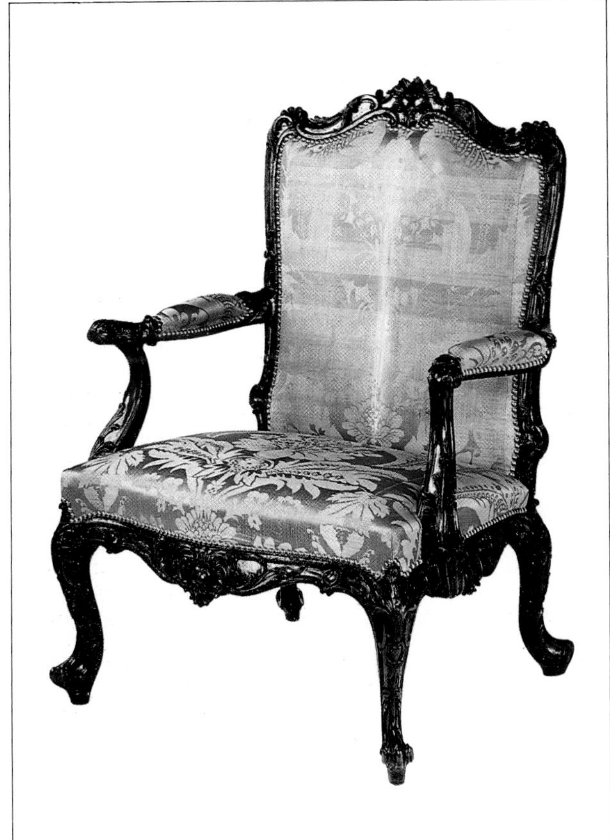

conscious of its greatness and the guardianship of its Empire, it was a confident, self-assured environment for the early life of a young man, educated at Marlborough and destined to govern a large family business.

His leanings were to politics and economics tempered by a passion for music, especially Wagner. It was a constant source of disappointment to his eldest son, Peter, who was continually deprived of listening to the popular music of Joe Loss and Harry Roy on the radio, in favour of the more esoteric *Tristan & Isolde*.

Figure 1a (above) *Mahogany armchair in the Saloon, about 1760-65, that bears a close resemblance to one of Chippendale's designs for a 'French Chair' in the Rococo style, plate XVIII. Formerly part of the F. Howard Read Collection and one of Noel Terry's later purchases in 1975.*

Noel Terry's education at Marlborough stopped at 16 when he went to work for the Midland Bank in Middlesbrough and it was not until 1911, at the age of 22, that he joined the family business in York. Commissioned in the West Yorkshire Regiment at the outbreak of war, and later wounded, in 1916 he married Katherine Leatham, youngest daughter of Henry Earnest Leatham, an important York industrialist with interests in flour mills and other Yorkshire firms and the creator of an impressive collection of porcelain and jade.

This link with an established collector probably had the greatest effect on a young man keen to make his own mark in the world. Noel Terry enjoyed telling the story of

Figure 4 *The original fireplace in the Library is surrounded by bureau bookcases, 2 George II single chairs with carved interlaced splats, needlepoint seats and cabriole legs, a sofa table edged in coromandel-wood, and wing chairs upholstered in twill.*

his first purchase, a piece of porcelain which could possibly, in his eyes, be of the Ming dynasty! The dutiful father-in-law spent some time inspecting and weighing up the piece before pronouncing – 'Very nice m'boy – but hardly a collector's piece!'

An important lesson, and obviously well learnt when viewing the consistent quality of subsequent acquisitions. His collecting started in earnest in 1918 with the purchase of a bureau bookcase for the grand sum of £44, and he acquired his first important painting five years later, a still life by R. Steenwyck (1655), for about the same amount.

By this time Noel Terry had risen in the firm to joint Managing Director, a post that he held with his half uncle, Sir Francis Terry. Desiring a suitable residence, he approached Walter Brierley, the noted York architect (and sometimes described as 'the Lutyens of the North') and asked him to design a new house in York. The site chosen was on the Tadcaster Road, overlooking the Knavesmire. Not selected, I may add, for its proximity to the racecourse, a sport that he had no time for, but because the common land was protected from being built upon. Some protective restrictive covenants were also thoughtfully imposed on the land on either side of the proposed house. The result was the creation of 'Goddards', completed in 1927. It was the last house which Brierley designed and in it he brought together many of the lessons he had learnt over the years so that it is neither Jacobean, nor Georgian, Queen Anne or Venacular, but a fusion of all these styles. In the autumn of that year the family moved in and by 1929, following the birth of his third son, Richard, Noel Terry set about furnishing the house.

His tastes were very particular and surprisingly consistent, with a dislike of gilding and anything too ornate, coupled with a demand for excellent quality. This

was soon understood by the three firms of dealers he placed his trust in, and who were able to keep him in touch with current developments. Gradually, over the years, he began creating his own personal sample collection and in it he brought together individual masterpieces, both major and minor, rather than attempting to assemble the balanced furnishings of a period home.

His local dealer was Charles Thornton, with premises at The Adam House in Petergate, York. Over the years they developed a close personal relationship and the Thorntons regularly visited 'Goddards' on social as well as business occasions. He supplied some superb pieces of 18th century furniture in the 20 years leading up to 1948 and items such as the spinet and the two teatables in the Saloon *(Figure 1)* and the bureau bookcase in the Library *(Figure 4)* passed through his hands. Noel Terry made a practice of never querying the asking price, reasoning that dealers would only add the amount deducted onto the next purchase.

The other firm to whom Noel Terry went for most of his pieces was Mallett of London. I suspect that the relationship developed because a director of Mallett, at that time, was also the director of a machinery firm which made chocolate processing plant and the bond of common interests developed into one of mutual trust. Whatever the reason, there was a positive frenzy of acquisitions in the years leading up to the Second World War with Mallett supplying 70% of all items. Some superb examples were bought during this time and they include the William and Mary Bureau Cabinet *(Figure 9)* purchased for £790 in 1935, and the artist's table in the Library *(Figure 6)*. In an effort to preserve his collection at home, Noel Terry instigated a bonus scheme for his staff whereby they earned ten shillings a month extra if nothing was broken or damaged during that period. No mention has been made, however, whether the children received extra pocket money for refraining from Battledore or indoor Cricket!

During the war, far greater matters captured his attention and in 1944 he was awarded an MBE for his services as Controller of the Royal Observer Corps in York. The death in 1943 of his second son, Kenneth, a pilot in the Royal Air Force, had a devastating effect on the family and friends.

One of the fascinating features of many of the pieces in the Terry collection is the abundance of secret drawers. It was a poignant occasion when we discovered some secret slides in a tallboy which contained old school reports and letters about Kenneth, together with pencilled messages passed between pilot and navigator during flights. One alarming message read 'Will torpedo explode if we do a belly flop?'

With the ending of hostilities the collecting resumed unabated with Charles Thornton and Mallett vying for Noel Terry's custom. Between them, during the ten short years to 1954, they supplied 52 pieces of furniture and clocks including some of the most important examples. Noel Terry, by this time had decided on the period that he preferred and the items purchased dated, almost without exception, from the mid 18th century. What is surprising is that although his library contains numerous definitive reference books on English furniture, including Edward's *Dictionary of English Furniture*, Macquoid's *History of English Furniture* and Symond's *English Furniture*, he did not possess any copies of Chippendale's *Director*.

Some outstanding pieces acquired in this period were a pair of chairs by John Gordon *(Figure 2)* bought from Mallett for £900, a Bombé Chest *(Figure 7)* and the

Figure 5 *One of a pair of Mahogany Torcheres, about 1760. These stands were intended to support candlesticks. Formerly in the possession of Earl Howe, Bucks and in the Leidersdorf Collection, before Noel Terry's acquisition in 1974.*

THOMAS 4TH VISCT FAUCONBERG.

kneehole table *(Figure 6)* in the Library. Charles Thornton supplied the bureau bookcase *(Figure 4)* and the Tompion longcase clock (also *Figure 6*).

During the 1950s there was a distinct lull in collecting. It was a time when the children were moving away to seek their own path in life and it was no doubt a time for reflection. A serious illness in 1960 and subsequent operations to his eyes and stomach caused considerable anxiety and for the remaining 20 years of his life he felt that he was living on borrowed time. In fact they proved to be the richest and most rewarding years of his life. A passionate lover of the city of his birth, he was one of the four Founders, in 1946, of the York Civic Trust which he served as Honorary Treasurer for 25 years. The last ten years of his life showed an ever increasing commitment to the preservation and enhancement of the city and it was this that led to his determination that the collection should remain as an entity for the benefit of the City of York. He therefore set about establishing a Charitable Trust to preserve and endow it. Having recovered his health to some extent, he began collecting again in 1963 with a purchase from Hotspurs of a secretaire cabinet and continued to buy one or two pieces a year right up to 1978. Each item was exceptional, again concentrated around the mid-18th century and turned what was an outstanding collection into what Christie's have described as the finest private collection of its kind formed in England in the last 50 years. *Figure 8* illustrates just two of these pieces and they are fitting testament to the work of the artisan craftsman which Noel Terry revered.

He had in his lifetime often expressed the wish that the collection should remain in Goddards and open to the public but he was wise enough not to tie the hands of his Trustees too tightly and he left the decision to them with the proviso that whatever happened, the collection should stay as an entity in York.

A Tudor style house with a collection of predominantly mid-Georgian mahogany was an unhappy blend. The smallness of the rooms, distance from the centre of York

Figure 6 (opposite) *Part of the Library with a kneehole table in the pier, decorated in the Gothic taste and similar to a design in Chippendale's* Director. *The longcase clock is by Thomas Tompion, about 1680 and attends an artist's table with its top rising on a rachet and supported by cluster column legs.*

Figure 7 (above left) *George III mahogany bombé commode of Chippendale's* Director *design. The top edge is decorated with gadrooning and the splayed legs terminate in scroll toes. This piece supports a bracket clock by Tompion & Banger and is attended by two single chairs with waived top rails, and vase shaped splats.*

Figure 8 (above right) *Mahogany secretaire attributed to William Vile with an elaborate cut-work superstructure and a fall front writing compartment. Semi secret drawers are concealed in the friezes and it stands on richly carved legs flanked by C-scroll brackets. The side chair is one of four walnut George I chairs with spoon shaped backs veneered in burr walnut and drop-in seats covered in contemporary needlepoint.*

and the nature of access were just three of the factors which influenced the Trustees to decide against leaving the collection where it was, and when the York Civic Trust broached the idea of restoring Fairfax House as a permanent home for the collection, the best possible solution became apparent. The City Council, who had originally declined to sell the house to the York Civic Trust changed its mind in the light of the Trustees' offer and Dr John Shannon had effectively performed a minor miracle in York.

For the future, the Trust has the constant dilemma of maintaining the separate identities of the house and the collection.

A 20th century English gentleman's collection of furniture does not necessarily coincide with the tastes of an 18th century Viscount and from documents found in the Wombwell collection the picture that begins to emerge is of Fairfax furnishings, too rich for Noel Terry's taste. This is a dichotomy which will confront us in future.

Whilst the collection provides the great bulk of the furnishings there are many gaps which need to be filled. The paintings, for example, are not of the same quality as the furniture and we hope to encourage loans and gifts of items which will not detract from the integrity of the collection, but complement it. Over the next few years we will be hoping to lay the Dining Room table properly, preferably with some 'Liverpool' china which we know the Viscount possessed and glass and silver of the period. In the bedrooms we will be looking to lay the dressing tables up, finish the beds with some steps and provide some washing sets for the two rooms. In the Saloon and Library, the piers cry out for a pair of glasses.

As visitors return to the house during the years, to show friends, or just to see what developments have taken place they will, I hope, observe some appropriate refinements.

Figure 9 (opposite left) *William & Mary walnut bureau cabinet. The panelled doors enclose pigeon holes and small drawers and the fall front reveals a fitted interior. The columns, capitals and base to top and bottom section conceal secret drawers within.*

Figure 10 (opposite right) *Dressing commode, formerly in the possession of the Dukes of Manchester at Kimbolton Castle and bearing a close resemblance to a design by Chippendale. The pivoting mirror above is flanked by narrow cupboards that may have been intended for wigs and the drawer below is elaborately fitted out for dressing.*

Figure 11 (opposite below) *Walnut Stool, about 1720, with elaborate ringed cabriole legs that stand on ball and claw feet. The needlework on the seat, illustrating a garden scene, has been considerably repaired at some time, but still retains many of its original features.*

Figure 12 (above) *Mahogany centre table, about 1755-60, with richly carved cabriole legs and bowed frieze. Formerly part of the Leidersdorf Collection, acquired by Noel Terry in 1974.*

Photographs: Jim Kershaw.

Note

Generous sponsorship by Christie's has enabled the York Civic Trust to produce a 150 page colour catalogue of the furniture and clocks in the Noel Terry Collection. Copies may be obtained from Fairfax House, Castlegate, York YO1 1RN.

June 1986

WORKING WOMEN IN THE 18TH CENTURY

Ian Caldwell

Recently I was reading the will of James Moore, a cabinet-maker to King George I, who died in 1726, when a passage in it caught my attention: 'To James Moore [his son] my materials of trade namely Woods and Tools at the election of my wife Elizabeth if she follows the Trade to pay him one hundred pounds and she keeps the materials.' (Public Records Office, probate 11/627, folio 10.)

I found the idea that Mr Moore considered that Mrs Moore might take up her husband's tools after his death and follow the trade of cabinet-making most intriguing.

James Moore had a partner, John Gumley, and I was further intrigued when I learned that, with him, it was not his wife but his mother who continued to run the business after the death of her son. Unfortunately the furniture supplied by 'Mrs Elizabeth Gumley & Co.' cabinet makers for St. James's Palace and Kensington did not meet with the approval of the Comptroller of the Great Wardrobe in 1729. He recommended that the bill that they submitted should not be paid in full, and shortly afterwards they were dismissed from royal service. (Treasury Letter Book, vol XVIII, p.420.) This may not reflect so badly on the competance of Mrs Elizabeth Gumley as it appears but more on the mood of the Comptroller as at the same time he wrote to the Master of the Great Wardrobe that 'Richard Roberts, joiner and chair-maker [should] be no longer employed in the King's service,' and he had been working for the King for over ten years.

Figure 1 *Two of the twelve mahogany chairs 'with hollow seats' supplied by Catherine Naish in 1766, flanking a walnut side table attributed to James Moore, formerly at Kensington Palace. Reproduced by gracious permission of Her Majesty the Queen.*

Pursuing this theme I found that a number of women were admitted to the freedom of the Upholders Company during the 18th century, as the records show. (Guildhall Library MS 7142/1.) This is a typical entry: 'Jane Lancester daughter of Benjamin Lancester late citizen and Upholder of London was this fourth day of May 1748 by patrimony admitted into the freedom of this company and bound to perform all the orders made for the work of the same. [signed] Jane Lancester.'

Katherine Harris was admitted on the 2nd February 1708, Catherine Wood on 5 May 1725, Elizabeth Chapman on 10th October 1747, Susan Abell on 4 March 1748 and Frances Broughton on 8 June 1749. These women were all the daughters of deceased members of the company and were admitted by 'patrimony'. Perhaps this was because they had been dependent on their fathers, probably helping them in the workshop, and after the death of their father they had no option but to try to continue the business to earn their daily bread.

I noticed that in one section of the record book of the company the clerk struck a line through certain entries among the men and wrote the word 'dead' in the margin. Jane Lancester also had a line struck through her name but 'married' is written in the margin. She presumably no longer needed to work to earn a living.

At the same time that Thomas Chippendale was at work, that most renowned of cabinet-makers, there was a woman, described as a joiner in the Lord Chamberlain's accounts, who achieved what the great Chippendale had failed – royal patronage. Her name was Catherine Naish and she provided furniture for the royal palaces early in George III's reign. The Great Wardrobe Accounts show that she charged £205 for a large 'four post mahogany State Bedstead with carved head-board bearing a scroll supporting a crown.' (See R. Edwards and M. Jourdain, *Georgian Cabinet-Makers,* Country Life, 1955, p.102.) She also provided split wicker cradles for the King's children (and the King proved very fertile) for which she charged 'as usual' at the rate of £13.2s. Twelve mahogany chairs 'with hollow seats', now in Buckingham Palace, were made by Catherine Naish in 1766.

Two of these chairs can be seen in *Figure 1* flanking a walnut side table which stands on carved, hoof feet. This table was probably made by James Moore, the royal cabinet-maker mentioned earlier. It has been suggested by Clifford Smith, in his book on Buckingham Palace (1931) that this table was made for Queen Anne for Kensington Palace, though he did not provide any documentary evidence. The royal cabinet-maker to Queen Anne was Gerreit Jensen and this table is quite unlike any of his known work. In the Great Wardrobe Accounts the firm of Gumley and Moore supplied 'a large Walnuttree fframe for a marble table' in 1724-25, to Kensington Palace. The following year they supplied 'a wallnuttree frame for a very large Marble Slab.' The table in the photograph is in the style of Moore's later work, such as the chairs made for Stowe and Beningbrough Hall. There are four of these tables, in all, from Kensington Palace. In 1727-28 Elizabeth Gumley and William Turing, the new royal cabinet-makers following the

Figure 2 *Trade card of Ann Buck, 18th-century new and antique furniture dealer. The head is Queen Anne's. Courtesy Geoffrey Wills.*

Figure 3 *Top of one of a pair of side tables, about 1780. The decoration of the tops are painted on a pink ground, including medallions, depicting female figures, attributed to Angelica Kauffmann. Victoria and Albert Museum.*

deaths of both James Moore in 1726 and John Gumley in 1728, supplied 'two very large walnuttree frames for marble slabs.' Perhaps these were made to the design of the two earlier tables and would account for all four. The tables are large, measuring 77¼ in long and 31 in deep. (Public Records Office LC5/47, pp.100, 107, 129.)

There were women furniture dealers also working at that time as the trade card of Ann Buck shows. (See J. E. Hodgkin, *Rariora,* 3 vols, c.1900, p.62). She was the widow of Henry Buck who died in about 1750, and she bought and sold all sorts of household furniture, new and old. The head on the card is not hers but Queen Anne's *(Figure 2).*

Angelica Kaufmann's name is often used to describe a particular style of painted decoration on antique furniture, particularly of delicately painted figures on medallions in Neo-classical style. She was a Swiss artist, born in 1741, who travelled and painted in Italy before coming to England in 1766. Here she became one of the founder members of the Royal Academy and a good friend of Sir Joshua Reynolds. She was employed by the Adam brothers and painted ceilings and murals in many of their houses and almost certainly the decorations on some of their splendid commodes and console tables. She was also employed by the Royal Academy, along with others, to decorate St. Paul's Cathedral, in 1773.

Figure 3 illustrates a painted table top dating from about 1780 which is attributed to Angelica Kauffmann. It is the top of one of a pair of side tables acquired by the Victoria and Albert Museum in 1871 (Mus. No. 349 & A 1871). In the Edwards Catalogue (vol IV, 1931) is the record that one of the tables 'bears the word ANGELICA on one of the painted ovals'. The technique of painting on copper has the great disadvantage that the metal expands and contracts under changes of temperature which causes the paint to flake off. These tables were much restored after the Second World War and the word Angelica is now lost.

You will, no doubt, have heard of George Hepplewhite. But you never would have done so had it not been for his wife, Alice. Not a single piece of George Hepplewhite's furniture is known, not a bill, not a letter. Without Alice he would have faded into obscurity. After his death in 1786 Alice carried on the business at Redcross Street, Cripplegate, trading as A. Hepplewhite and Co., Cabinet-Makers.

The name of Hepplewhite became widely known after Alice published a book of furniture designs in 1788, *The Cabinet-Maker and Upholsterer's Guide,* two years after the death of her husband. But it is *his* name which has found its way into furniture history.

Why should it be George Hepplewhite that became famous and not Alice? Why has everyone assumed that the designs were his and not hers? Examine the title page of the book and you will see that it clearly says 'from drawings by A. Hepplewhite and Co. Cabinet-Makers.' *(Figure 5.)* There is absolutely no mention of George anywhere. If the drawings had been his would not his good wife have given him a mention?

The book was such a success that it ran to three editions, with minor alterations in the second edition, but the third edition of 1794 contained substantial alterations, including some entirely new

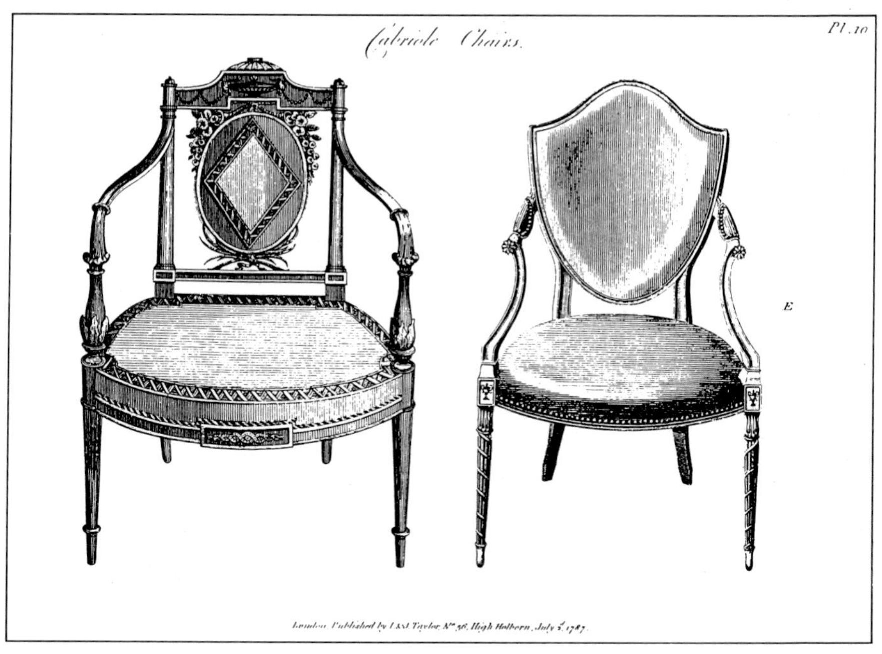

Figure 4 *Alice Hepplewhite's 'Chairs with Stuffed Backs', the one on the left 'executed with good effect for His Royal Highness the Prince of Wales.'*

designs for chairs which George could not possibly have done from the grave. These alterations were probably provoked by Sheraton's criticism of the earlier designs in his Drawing Book, published in 1791, where he wrote: 'if we compare some of the designs, particularly the chairs, with the newest taste, we shall find that the work has already caught the decline, and perhaps, in a little time, will suddenly die in the disorder.' (See T. Sheraton, *The Cabinet Maker and Upholsterer's Drawing Book*, 1791, p.10.)

Alice Hepplewhite, like Catherine Naish, may have been making furniture for the Royal family (Figure 4). In the third edition of her book, under 'chairs with stuffed backs', she writes: 'The designs E F plate 10 are of the newest fashion; the arms to F, though much higher than usual have been executed with good effect for his Royal Highness the Prince of Wales.' This is one of the chair designs not found in earlier editions.

At that time the Prince was building and furnishing the Brighton Pavilion and deeply involved with Mrs Fitzherbert, a woman twice widowed and a Catholic to boot. While it is true that no bills have been found in the Royal Accounts from either Alice or George Hepplewhite this could be due to the fact that the Prince was engaged in wild expenditure and, by 1794, had run up debts approaching two thirds of a million pounds.

Many of the designs in Alice's book are of feminine and delicate furniture giving support to the idea that they are by her rather than her husband. Whatever the truth Sheraton has been proved wrong when he said that the designs for chairs were going to 'die in the disorder' as any catalogue of reproduction furniture will tell.

So, surprisingly, there were women joiners, cabinet-makers, interior decorators, upholders and furniture designers in the 18th century, long before women's liberation was dreamed of. As the seasons come and go in cycles, so do attitudes and fashions. Hair and hem lines have a habit of growing and shrinking with the generations just as society accepts or rejects the idea of women working.

October 1985

THE
CABINET-MAKER
AND
UPHOLSTERER's GUIDE;
OR,
REPOSITORY OF DESIGNS
FOR EVERY ARTICLE OF
HOUSEHOLD FURNITURE,
IN THE NEWEST AND MOST APPROVED TASTE:
DISPLAYING
A GREAT VARIETY OF PATTERNS FOR

Chairs	Tea Caddies	Hanging Shelves
Stools	Tea Trays	Fire Screens
Sofas	Card Tables	Beds
Confidante	Pier Tables	Field Beds
Ducheſſe	Pembroke Tables	Sweep Tops for Ditto
Side Boards	Tambour Tables	Bed Pillars
Pedeſtals and Vaſes	Dreſſing Glaſſes	Candle Stands
Cellerets	Dreſſing Tables and Drawers	Lamps
Knife-Caſes	Commodes	Pier Glaſſes
Deſk and Book-Caſes	Rudd's Table	Terms for Buſts
Secretary and Book-Caſes	Bidets	Cornices for Library
Library Caſes	Night Tables	Caſes, Wardrobes, &c. at large
Library Tables	Baſon Stands	Ornamented Tops for Pier Tables, Pembroke Tables, Commodes, &c. &c.
Reading Deſks	Wardrobes	
Cheſts of Drawers	Pot Cupboards	
Urn Stands	Brackets	

In the PLAINEST and moſt ENRICHED STYLES; with a SCALE to each, and an EXPLANATION in LETTER PRESS.
ALSO
THE PLAN OF A ROOM,
SHEWING THE PROPER DISTRIBUTION OF THE FURNITURE.
The Whole exhibiting near THREE HUNDRED different DESIGNS, engraved on ONE HUNDRED and TWENTY-EIGHT PLATES:
FROM DRAWINGS
By A. HEPPLEWHITE and Co. CABINET-MAKERS.

THE THIRD EDITION, IMPROVED.

LONDON:
Publiſhed by I. and J. TAYLOR, at the ARCHITECTURAL LIBRARY, No. 56, HOLBORN, oppoſite GREAT TURN-STILE.
MDCCXCIV.

Figure 5 *Title page of Alice Hepplewhite's book, with no mention of her husband, and containing new designs done 8 years after George Hepplewhite's death.*

ROYAL CARTES DE VISITE

David Lee

Figure 1 *The Prince of Wales by Camille Silvy, 1859-61.*

Whether contained in ornately bound albums or lying loose in packs, cartes de visite are a frequent sight in auction rooms, antique shops and flea markets. They were introduced in Britain towards the end of the 1850s and remained popular with photographers and customers alike until after the First World War. The immense number that were produced has contributed to their being neglected as historically important or precious pictures meriting close study. If we choose to look at them at all it is because some peculiarity of fashion captures our interest or inspires nostalgia.

Cartes are, nevertheless, widely collected and contain much valuable information. Although many of the rarer examples portray Victorian royalty and celebrities an overwhelming majority depict sober looking citizens attired in their Sunday best, standing or sitting stiffly amidst an assortment of vaguely classical accessories such as pillars, balustrades and vases.

On account of the carte's commonness it is easy to underestimate their radical significance when they first appeared. Promotion of this style of picture was crucial not only in the wider availability of portraits but also in the distribution of landscape views and the first photographic news illustrations. But cartes are important principally because they depict those whose appearance would not have been recorded without photography. The carte introduced unknown places and peoples to a new audience which, formerly, had little access to pictures of any kind and which could not otherwise have afforded to own a copy of their own portrait.

Given the significance of such a development it is extraordinary that the story of their introduction in Britain has never been accurately established. Indeed, it has frequently been clouded by misinformation. Like most 19th century fashions the carte de visite was first promoted in France. After photography was publicly announced in 1839 commercial exploitation of the medium was slow. Realising that progress lay in mass production and cheapness Alphonse-Eugene Disdéri (1819-89) lodged a patent request on 27 November 1854.

His innovation consisted of a method whereby a full-plate negative could be subdivided into ten small compartments, thus increasing by ten times the number of photographs resulting from each plate. By utilising this advance Disdéri claimed that 'all the time and expense necessary to obtain one print is divided by ten, which reduces to very little the price of these ten prints'. Oddly, he never exercised his financial rights as the patent holder, an altruism he must have lived to regret since, following a conviction for fraud, he died a pauper in Paris and had his funeral costs met from public funds.

Disdéri's invention was to revolutionise the production of photographs, as it supplied the means by which cartes de visite were made, and yet it took five years for the new small format (about $3\frac{1}{2} \times 2$ in) to catch on. Even Disdéri appears only to have used the process intermittently until 1859.

Initial stimulus to the proliferation of carte sales in France was given by the private visit of Napoleon III to Disdéri's studio on the evening of Monday 9 May 1859. The Emperor was due to leave Paris the next day to head French troops in the war with Austria over the latter's occupation of Italian states. The frequently repeated and colourful tale recounting how Napoleon halted a column of 100,000 war-bound troops in the Boulevard des Italiens while he dashed into Disdéri's atelier to have his picture taken has, unfortunately, no foundation in fact. The Emperor left Paris ten days after his army and travelled by train to the campaign zone.

The real visit to Disdéri by the Emperor is recorded by the Paris correspondent of *The Times*: 'His Majesty, accompanied by the Empress, visited this afternoon the rooms of a well-known photographist on the Italian Boulevards – I suppose to have their portraits taken. They arrived without any escort, or even outrider, and were

Figure 2 *Emperor Napoleon III by Disdéri, 1859.*

received with acclamation by the groups on the boulevards, as it was the hour when everyone was abroad, and the weather was magnificent'.

A later communiqué confided that on his departure for the front Napoleon had left Empress Eugènie 'his orders and instructions to guide her, and his photograph, newly taken, to console her.' In order to exploit the favourable publicity encouraged by Napoleon's patronage, Disdéri lost no time in marketing his fortunate scoop in carte de visite format (*Figure 2*). Thousands of copies were sold quickly in the upsurge of patriotism generated by the war.

But the urgent desire for cartes de visite amongst Parisians did not stop with purchasing their leader's portrait. As had previously occurred in Britain when Queen Victoria gave official approval to the stereoscope by buying a viewer after witnessing its demonstration at Crystal Palace, Napoleon's visit to Disdéri was interpreted as a conspicuous endorsement of the latest photographic novelty. In emulation of their Emperor Parisians flocked to studios to sit for portraits in carte size.

Two months after this much publicised event an English magazine recorded that 'the placing of portraits on visiting cards appears to be more commonly practiced in Paris than here'. From this observation it is apparent that photographic visiting cards were not new in Britian. However, a distinction must be established between the photographic visiting card and the carte de visite photograph. The function of the former was implicit in its name, while the latter was simply a portrait photograph whose name was a convenient description of its small size, but not of its function.

Using photographs on visiting cards had first been proposed by Louis Dodero, who stated in 1851 that in his opinion it was only a matter of time before photographs were put on visiting cards, as they had already featured in far less likely places. In 1854, two other Frenchmen suggested the same development, stating that until this date visiting cards had only included the name and address of the bearer. They proposed not simply the inclusion of a straightforward portrait but of a variety of poses descriptive of the circumstances under which the card was left. Thus: 'at ceremonial occasions the visitor was to be photographed wearing gloves, the head bowed as in greeting etc as social etiquette requires; in inclement weather he was to be shown with an umbrella under his arm; when taking leave a portrait was furnished in travelling costume.'

These proposals were not adopted immediately. In fact, not until 1858 in England were photographers advertising the sale of pictorial visiting cards. These featured a tiny oval portrait on the face of the card in a similar style to one advertised by Herbert Watkins in *The Illustrated News of the World (Figures 3 & 4)*. Watkins was supported in his promotion by Marion and Company, a French paper manufacturers which had opened a London branch in 1857. In 1884 Frank Bishop, a director of Marion, claimed with some justification that 'we ourselves were the publishers who introduced the carte de visite into England'.

It has often been stated with regard to cartes de visite that they were never used as visiting cards, as this would have been in questionable taste. Yet newspaper references in 1859 plainly testify to the fact that before the fashion for cartes de visite – of the type we know so well today – became established, there was indeed a brief phase in which tiny medallion photographs were used to adorn calling cards.

J. Werge, an English photographer, wrote that in 1858 he was making visiting cards at two guineas per hundred

paper. (Samples are forwarded free.)

MARION'S PHOTOGRAPHIC VISITING CARDS.—Substitution of a Photographic Portrait for the old system of Printing. The Photograph by Herbert Watkins.

MARION'S WEDDING CARDS.—Miniature Photographic Portraits of the "Happy Pair," photographed by Herbert Watkins, are mounted in two elaborately-ornamented escutcheons, surrounded with orange flower blossoms and love knots stamped in silver, and the card forms a graceful and appropriate souvenir of the blissful event peculiarly adapted for preservation.

MARION'S PHOTOGRAPHIC NOTE-PAPER and WAFERS.—Miniature Photographic Portraits are applied on the paper instead of stamping, and also used as wafers.

PAPETERIE MARION, 152, Regent street, W.

(Catalogues sent post free.)

Figures 3 & 4 *Advertisements in 'The Illustrated News of the World,' October 1858.*

Figure 5 *Her Majesty Queen Victoria by Mayall, 1860.*

Figure 6 *The Queen and Prince Consort by Mayall, 1860.*

Figure 7 *H.R.H. the Prince Consort by Mayall, 1860.*

Figure 8 *H.R.H. the Prince of Wales by Mayall, 1860.*

The pictures of the Royal Family that promoted the carte style.

in the same style as Watkins's. He further observed: 'I believe I was the first to introduce that style of portrait, but there was not much demand for it, and the more popular and better paying style which soon followed crowded it out altogether ... Everybody wanted cartes de visite, but only a few wanted and used the photographically illustrated "visiting card".'

Subsequent to the carte's immense popularity during the years 1860 to 1864, a period referred to as 'cartomania', there occurred a rash of claims – like Werge's – alleging first use of photographic visiting cards. For example, Sir David Brewster expressed a widely held opinion when he attributed its introduction to Ferrier of Nice in 1857. This view is supported by references in the autobiography of Princess Louisa of Tuscany, published in 1911. She refers to the Duke of Palma having gummed his photographic portrait onto a visiting card and that Ferrier, alert to its commercial applications, promoted this innovatory use.

Other Britons besides Werge also staked their claims as inventors. Hugh Welch Diamond, a doctor who subsequently became famous for pictures of the insane, presented an equestrian portrait in visiting card size to the Queen in 1852. A commercial photographer, T. Bullock of Macclesfield, also asserted that he too was placing portraits on the backs of visiting cards as early as 1857.

Without disputing the merits of individual claimants the prime stimulus to the sudden growth of carte de visite portraits was undoubtedly Disdéri's. The conspicuous patronage of the Emperor transformed what was until that time a minor photographic application into a major novelty industry.

Following the advertisement of Disdéri's tiny format by Napoleon III the general demand for cartes in Paris was instantaneous. Inside four months 'this ingenious photographic application' had become 'all the rage'. A year later, in June, 1860, a Parisian correspondent to an English magazine reported that 'the vogue enjoyed here by card portraits in general really passes belief. Several of our artists do nothing else, and their ateliers are besieged by the crowd.'

The arrival of the popular form of the carte de visite in England was slightly delayed. But the success it had achieved in Paris, then regarded as the trendsetter of European taste, guaranteed its ultimate adoption in Britain. One year after Disdéri had photographed the Emperor in widely publicised circumstances, John Jabez Mayall (1810-1901), a prestigious photographer in London's Regent Street, obtained permission to take card pictures of Queen Victoria and the Royal Family with a view to placing them on open sale. They were marketed eight weeks after the session, in July 1860, and were available individually or in sets *(Figures 5-8)*. This event was momentous not only for its promotion of the carte style but because it was the first occasion that such consent to profit commercially from sales of their pictures had been given by royalty. Mayall's good fortune was received with envy by other photographers and continued to be mentioned many years after. On the evidence of surviving examples sales were enormous. Considering the Queen's subsequent shrewdness in using the distribution of her portrait for inspiring loyalty, it is likely that the spur given to French patriotism by Disdéri's royal pictures was a motivating factor in Mayall being granted permission to visit Buckingham Palace.

The history of the popular portait photograph in Britain begins with Mayall's royal pictures. But the forceful impetus they gave to the promotion of card pictures was not alone responsible for encouraging British

Figure 9 *Disraeli by H. Lenthall, about 1850.*

Figure 10 *Portrait of a Gentleman by Alphonse-Eugene Disdéri (1819-89).*

interest in the carte format.

In mid-summer 1859 Camille Silvy had left France to set up a portrait studio in Porchester Terrace, West London. He was soon to become literally and metaphorically 'the great aristocrat of the profession'. His pedigree (he was a count), consummate technical skill in photography, knowledge of the latest Parisian fashions, and his conservative aesthetic already evident in his earliest cartes, were instrumental in establishing the popularity of the new genre, at least among the so-called 'upper ten thousand' of British society.

From the evidence of his surviving business records (preserved in London's National Portrait Gallery), Silvy had already nurtured a healthy demand for small portraits by the close of 1859, well in advance of Mayall's royal photographic appointment in May, 1860. Since there are apparently no surviving British full-length portrait cartes de visite which can be dated, as firmly as Silvy's, to before 1860 it was almost certainly the Frenchman who was responsible for popularising the style in England *(Figures 1, 11, 14, 15)*. He would have witnessed the carte's burgeoning popularity in France, prompted by the success of Disdéri's royal pictures, just before his emigration to London.

Manufacturers and picture wholesalers, originally set up to capitalise on the fashion for stereoscopic cards, immediately recognised the potential of the new fashion. Advertising of equipment specifically designed for producing card pictures began in the autumn of 1860 in the wake of Mayall's royal scoop, and continued unabated for a decade. Trade proceeded so briskly that by December, 1860 the London Review could report the arrival of a major craze: 'We all know what firm root photography has taken in its outward and visible manifestations; how our fashionable thoroughfares are succumbing to its influence, whole quarters apparently changing to crystal palaces, as far as their roofs are concerned, and picture galleries as regards their private doors. Royalty, statesmen, philosophers and actresses are to be seen à la carte in every shop window.'

By the beginning of the next year, 1861, numbers of photographers and their assistants employed in Britain had swelled, from 51 in 1851, to 2,954. Within one year of the popular introduction of the carte de visite into Britain the character of High Streets throughout the land would be changed by a phenomenon referred to as 'The New Picture Galleries', whereby nearly every shop, including those without primary interest in photography, exhibited pictures of celebrities and newsworthy figures in their windows. It was subsequently estimated that 105 million cartes de visite were sold in 1862 alone.

Although most cartes today are much later in date, it is these earliest and much rarer cartes, by Mayall, Disdéri, Silvy and their contemporaries, which are among the most prized by today's collectors.

March 1987

Figure 11 *The Prince Consort by Camille Silvy, 1859-61.*

The image of the cartes de visite is approximately 5.1 × 8.9 cm (2 × 3½ in); when mounted 5.7 × 10.2 cm (2¼ × 4 in).

Figure 12 *The Prince Consort by John Jabez Mayall (1810-1901), 1860.*

Figure 13 *Charles Dickens by Herbert Watkins, about 1860.*

Figure 14 *Portrait of a man by Camille Silvy, 1859-61.*

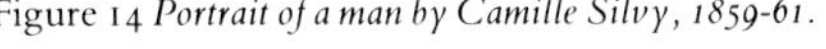

Figure 15 *Portrait of a lady by Camille Silvy, 1859-61.*

A W CUTLER REDISCOVERED

Denis Thomas

Now that market barrows and charity shops, as well as jumble sales and auction rooms, are being scoured by collectors looking for good examples of early photography, it is encouraging to come across such a splendidly gifted professional as Alfred William Cutler. He has come to light only recently since a descendant combing through the attics of the family home (Rose Hill House, in Worcester) discovered several albums of his work, along with glass plate negatives and several hundred prints. He rescued them and handed them to his son, Nick Darton, a young schoolmaster, to catalogue.

This was to result in the first exhibition of Cutler's work, at the Gardner Art Centre, University of Sussex, in May 1984. Cutler would have been highly gratified to find himself the object of such attention. Not that he lacked professional recognition in his lifetime – he made a comfortable living by selling his pictures to the illustrated magazines. But it would have vindicated his choice of vocation, in a family which regarded him as a bit of a rapscallion. The Cutlers were typical mid-Victorians of their class: strongly religious, intent on missionary service and good works. Alfred, sadly lacking in this respect, took himself off to New York when he was in his twenties, intending to make his living by writing.

This may not have been as fanciful an ambition as it seems. His grandmother was Maria Hack, a sister of Bernard Barton, the Quaker poet of Woodbridge, and achieved some celebrity as the authoress of high-minded books for young people. His mother, Julia, had also written half a dozen books for children. Alfred, on arriving in New York, intended to carry on the family's literary tradition.

He soon found that he had almost no talent for spinning the sort of tales that appealed to editors. He found a job as a stenographer, dashing off articles and essays in his spare time. He was a methodical fellow, as his journals and ledgers – rescued from the family attic – show. Looking through them with Nick Darton at his home in Lewes, Sussex, I noted a few examples. A piece on 'Dangers in English Railway Carriages' was smartly returned by *Travel Magazine*. Another, on 'Seeing London from a Bus Top', was returned by no less than twelve different journals. A third, on 'How a Bicycle Was Made to Run on Water', was accepted by *Scientific American*; but there is a note in Cutler's tidy hand saying that the magazine cut it to only 200 words, so it earned him a mere $4.

However, by this time (the early 1900s) he had bought himself a camera in the hope that if he took pictures to go with his articles, they would stand a better chance of being accepted. There is no evidence that they did. But all at once he began making his mark, not as a writer but as a photographer.

He gave up his office job and began to travel, using his home back in Worcester as his base. His first commission seems to have been from a steamship company, who paid his passage and expenses to Cuba in return for twenty photographs. Other journeys funded in this way, or by commissions, took him to Spain, Portugal, Egypt, Sicily, Austria, Hungary. His account books show that foreign travel was not too expensive 80 years ago: a second class rail ticket from London to Paris cost him £2.17.0. He could get a hotel on the Continent for 25 shillings and an interpreter for the day for little more than half a crown. The biggest fee recorded in his accounts book is £500, for a set of pictures delivered to *Harper's Magazine*.

Disappointingly, there are no details in his letters or records of the equipment he used or of the technical methods by which he achieved such excellent results. Since a quantity of dry-plate negatives have survived, along with some early Eastman roll-film, his career can be seen to have spanned the old epoch – the Golden Age so movingly celebrated in the Victoria & Albert Museum's superb exhibition in summer 1984 – and the beginning of the new. It is apparent, however, that he did his own processing, except when he occasionally shipped a packet of plates direct to the journal concerned.

His professional visiting card was significantly worded. It said: 'Mr A. W. Cutler, Photographer of Human Interest Scenes in Great Britain and Foreign Countries'. The term 'human interest' pinpoints a distinctive aspect of his work. Scenes showing the life of the streets and markets brought out the best of his talent. Rarely, in such subjects, does one feel that the people in them were aware of the camera's eye – which indicates a mixture of patience and tact in the photographer, along with an instinct for exactly the right moment to open the shutter.

Cutler's scenes of East Side New York,

Figure 1
One of the sights of London – flower girls in Regent Street. 26 July 1908.

Figure 2
Selling cucumbers at two a penny and vegetable marrows (in small white tin) at four a penny in Petticoat Lane, London. 26 July 1908.

Figure 3
Bargain Hunting. Lower East Side, New York. 1909.

Figure 4
Ox girl of Oporto, Portugal. 1911.

Figure 5
Hat and braces merchants. (Hats at one shilling, suspenders at tuppence halfpenny or five cents.) Lower East Side, New York. 15 August 1909.

among the newly-arrived immigrants, reveal him as one of the best of the early photo-journalists. Nothing is contrived, posed or rearranged. The participants are individuals, not types; their evident poverty is dignified by decency and hope.

His London street-scenes have the same feeling of unsentimental humanity. A group of flower-sellers prepare their baskets in a setting that could serve for the opening scene of Shaw's *Pygmalion*; a puff of fumes from the new-fangled motor car announces the impending demise of the horse-drawn omnibus clattering down Regent Street *(Figure 1)*. In Petticoat Lane two young girls, one of them a gypsy, sell cucumbers at two a penny *(Figure 2)*. In Covent garden, an elderly woman stands all day minding the whips of coachmen, her eyes expressing unimagined sorrows.

Much other fine work of Cutler's has been lost. It exists only as sheets snipped from the magazines he worked for, notably *The Sphere*, pasted into scrap-books. Nick Darton says there is little chance that original prints of these have survived. However, he is hopeful of one day unearthing more Cutler originals in New York, in the archives of the famous – and durable – journals which were glad to buy his work.

As a photographer, Cutler deserves to take his place among the pioneers of his time. Collectors who have had the chance to see and buy his work have begun to spread the word. For those who have not, Nick Darton is preparing further exhibitions, each work enlarged to frameable size, printed from the original negative or, in some cases, from a copy negative taken from an immaculate original print.

Cutler would surely have done more to preserve his work, had he not met a sudden and dramatic end in 1922, when he fell to his death from a hotel window in Italy. The circumstances are vague. He was said to be demented by fever at the time; but the affair remains a bit of a mystery. So, too, does Cutler's private life. More or less cast off by his family, he never married or made a permanent home. However, his address book, containing an impressive number of women's names, married and unmarried, suggests that he was by no means alone in the world – a world that excited his curiosity, and made him, in the end, an artist.

August 1985

THE GIBSON GIRLS

John S. Grioni

Perhaps even the more elderly readers of this book cannot remember the Gibson Girls who epitomised the American ideal of femininity at the beginning of our century. This predecessor of the pin-up and model was immensely popular and dominated anglo-saxon fashion for at least 20 years.

Charming, beautiful and shapely, with their perfect complexions, healthy bodies and patrician gestures, these young women were perhaps a touch haughty, but constantly serene. Their crowning glory was their abundant hair, held in place by little combs or grips, which framed their un-made up, natural features.

Outdoors

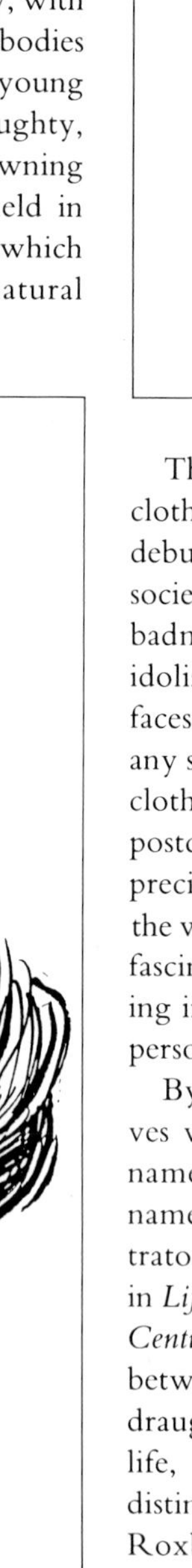

Fair-haired

They dressed with exquisite taste, in clothes which were the dream of every debutante. They went to the races, into society, to the theatre; played croquet, badminton and golf. They were so idolized by the middle class that their faces were reproduced everywhere, on any surface available: scarves, tiles, table-cloths, sheets, screens, albums, fans, and postcards for collectors (which are now precious items). They even appeared on the wallpaper for 'a bachelor's room' their fascinating faces quite capable of producing insomnia. Youth in bloom was then personified by The Gibson Girls.

By now you will have asked yourselves why on earth they were given this name? Charles Dana Gibson, their namesake, was the great American illustrator who launched this particular look in *Life, Scribner's Magazine, Harpers, The Century* and *Colliers,* making it in vogue between 1890 and 1910. A very able draughtsman, humourist and observer of life, Charles Dana Gibson was both a distinguished and elegant man. Born in Roxbury, Massachusetts in 1867, he revealed his artistic talent from an early age, passing from cut-outs to illustrating and to painting and portraiture later on. The family moved to Flushing, Long

Daring

Island, and the boy frequented the Art Students League in New York, one of the best art schools in America. The teachers at the time included Thomas Eakins, Kenyon Cox and William Merritt Chase, and C. D. Gibson remained there for a very active two years. Thence he decided to follow the great American tradition of illustration, perfecting his art with perseverance, choosing pen and ink as his particular medium. Edwin Abbey, Howard Pyle, Felix Darley, Arthur Frost and Albert Sterner were among the best known magazine and newspaper illustrators of that period, together with Kemble, Smedley and Reinhart. Frederic Remington, the future painter of the West, was also a pupil of the Art Students League who had just begun to be noticed.

Expanding his knowledge, Gibson was able to educate himself through the best graphic artists of the time. He was familiar with the drawings of Daniel Vierge and Adolf Menzel; the English artists such as Cruikshank, John Leech, Charles Keene and the Pre-Raphaelites; and, later, Phil May, who had developed his method of expressing an idea with very few lines. But he particularly admired George du Maurier, whose figures possessed all the charm of the British upper-class lady, which Gibson soon adapted into an American prototype. Every young girl now tried to look as much like his drawings as nature would permit.

Indoors

Meanwhile he opened a studio in New York. His flexible technique and confident touch approached the style so typical of his mature years, just during the age that the new photo-mechanical process was freeing the artist-illustrator from the long bond with the engraver. 'Photogravure' was able to reproduce the image without intermediaries in the original style of the drawing, hence capturing its initial spirit and vivacity.

With his 'Gibson Girls' this talented artist, in harmony with his time, created an American myth which had millions of followers and in which he was the first to believe in absolutely, until the First World War dissolved the dream.

At the end of the four long years of conflict the world had changed. Gibson continued to draw; he illustrated many books including *The Prisoner of Zenda* by Anthony Hope and *Soldiers of Fortune* by Richard Harding Davis. He also became editor of *Life,* the humourous weekly magazine that had acquired his first drawing for $4 in 1886, and was a member of the National Academy of Design from 1932. Then, in his last years, he retired to paint in the peace of his home at Penobscot Bay until 1944, when on the 23 of December he died, in New York city, and his beauties entered the realm of memory.

Adapted and translated by Vanessa Nicolson.

May 1987

JOHN CONSTABLE'S MEZZOTINTS

Hilary Chapman

John Constable must be the best loved and best known of all 19th century landscape artists. His paintings of the English countryside, without grandeur or spectacle but with simple poetic beauty, express an almost religious feeling for the harmony of the natural world. He communicates to us the unchanging aspects of the rural scene for, although the horses and carts may have disappeared, we still share his feeling for the skies, trees and cool, moist atmosphere of the English landscape. We can understand the complimentary sarcasm that lay behind the remark made by the painter Fuseli to his servant: 'John, bring me my umbrella – I'm going to see Mr Constable's picture.'

The underlying principles in his depiction of the landscape was an understanding not only of the mood and 'light' of nature, but of the 'Chiaroscuro' of nature; that is, the interrelationship of light and tone. He realised the possibilities of print-making in exploring this phenomenon of the effects of light and tone in the landscape and had already had some drawings of his engraved in mezzotint before 1824. Mezzotint is a method of engraving which produces tonal values. The surface of the plate is roughened to retain the ink and the areas to remain light are scraped away. A velvety finish to the print with many graduations between light and dark is possible.

In 1829 he was introduced to the engraver David Lucas. Lucas was only 27 at the time but Constable was greatly struck by the sensitive and inspired technique of the young mezzotint engraver. He suggested two trial prints to explore the possibilities for a larger project that he had in mind. The results pleased him greatly and by 1830, Constable and Lucas were deeply involved in producing plates for the series of mezzotints known as 'English Landscape Scenery'.

The project proved a unique collaboration, the two men working very closely at each stage. Constable would submit a wash sketch which would be engraved onto the plate by Lucas. A proof would be pulled from the plate to be closely scrutinised by Constable who would adjust the balance of the tones or alter the composition. The plate was reworked, another proof submitted to the artist and so on, over innumerable pulls until Constable was finally satisfied with the results. (Examples of these 'progress proofs' can be seen at the Fitzwilliam Museum, Cambridge, England.)

Many plates were prepared and considerable discussion took place between Constable and Lucas to decide which of these plates would make up the series and what form it would take. It was eventually decided to issue it in five parts containing four prints each. The first part was ready and advertised in June 1830 but, due to continual problems and difficulties, the next four parts took two years to complete with the fifth part not advertised until April 1832. By early 1832, Constable was selling a few complete sets entitled, 'Various Subjects of Landscape Characteristics of English Scenery', with 20 prints, a frontispiece, vignette, introduction page and list of engravings. The printsellers of the time considered the project a risky one and their involvement with the series was minimal. By all accounts, their opinion was correct as Constable himself spoke of the project as being financially a 'dead loss'. However, a second edition was published in 1833 in conjunction with the publisher, Colnaghi, with some variation in the prints included and a changed introduction. Constable's interest in the series continued in spite of numerous difficulties, and up until 1835 he worked on a possible appendix of eight new subjects together with Lucas. These were not published in his lifetime, but in a letter to Lucas just before his death in 1837 he instructs him: ' – don't forget the Appendix's'.

Some of these proposed subjects were included by Lucas when in 1846, he published the 'New Series of Engravings of English Landscape' containing a further 14 plates, some of which were prepared solely by himself. Unfortunately for Lucas, this also was a commercial failure. The decay of mezzotint as a

Figure 1 Yarmouth, Norfolk. *Mezzotint by David Lucas. Bohn edition of the set (without publication line under the title) issued in 1855. 19.1 × 25.4 ($7\frac{1}{2}$ × 10in).*

Figure 2 *A Dell, Helmingham Park Suffolk. From the series of mezzotint engravings by David Lucas after John Constable known as 'English Landscape Scenery'. 17.8 × 21.6 (7 × $8\frac{1}{2}$in).*

reproductive art had accelerated by this time due mainly to the introduction of photographic processes which faithfully transcribed the qualities of painting, and Lucas's fortunes had considerable declined even before this venture failed. All in all, Constable's appreciation had brought Lucas no substantial success and a disappointed life ended miserably in the Fulham workhouse in 1881.

Figure 3 River Stour, Suffolk. *Mezzotint by David Lucas. 1st state with no cowman on the bridge. 17.8 × 24.1 (7 × 9½in) The British Museum.*

Although not a commercial success at the time, there was no lack of contemporary appreciation of the excellence of these prints. Collecting these prints can be interesting and rewarding, as nowadays we can recognise not only their technical brilliance, but acknowledge them as perhaps the greatest example in printmaking history of the collaboration between artist and engraver. Few complete sets now come on to the market although the William Weston Gallery of London give the following prices: if the set is in its original parts it would be now worth about £5000. If the set had been dismantled from its original paper wrappers and bound it would be worth £4000. This is assuming it is a first issue (1832-33). If it was the 1855 reprint it would be worth about £500. However, individual prints occur quite frequently in Print Galleries or at auction and are not expensive. A complete list of the published titles, together with those intended for the Appendix and the plates published by Lucas for the New Series of Engravings of English Landscape, can be found in *The Published Mezzotints of Lucas after Constable* by Andrew Shirley (Oxford, 1930).

It should be noted that, when collecting these prints, each of the plates in the series exists in several 'states', a 'state' being the same design with a variation in detail. Each time the prints were published some minor alteration would occur. Usually this was simply using a different type of lettering in the title or making the relevant alteration to the wording of the publication line. (In the case of the late edition published by Bohn in 1855, the publication line was removed altogether, see *Figure 1*.) A few prints occur in early 'states' where changes have been made to the composition. For example in the first state of 'River Stour, Suffolk' (*Figure 3*) there is no cowman on the bridge; he appears only in later states. A complete list of the varying states for each print can also be found in Andrew Shirley's book, although they are more accurately documented in O. H. Barnard *A Revised List of States – Lucas-Constable*.

These beautiful mezzotints are a constant source of delight and bring an understanding of the outstanding qualities of Constable's artistry. His intentions in producing the series are outlined in its introduction and were '. . . to display the phenomena of the Chiaroscuro of Nature, to mark some of its endless beauties, to point out its vast influence upon the landscape, and to show its use and power as a medium of expression.' How well he achieved his aim was due in part to the care and interpretive skill of David Lucas, perhaps the last of the great traditional mezzotint engravers.

March 1987

COLLECTING FOUNTAIN PENS

Deborah Scott

Along with wristwatches, leather luggage and cigarette cases, fountain pens are among those useful artefacts of the twentieth century that are now attracting the attention of collectors. Although the history of the fountain pen stretches way back to pre-Christian times, the first that was commercially successful was patented by the American Louis Waterman in 1884.

The main requirements for a fountain pen are that it should carry as much ink as possible which it should deliver only on cue, not all over the owner's pockets, that it be easy to fill and of a convenient size and shape. Between the end of the 19th century and the introduction of the Biro in 1945, great inventiveness was shown on both sides of the Atlantic as companies such as Waterman, Parker, Sheaffer, De La Rue (Onoto) and Mabie Todd vied

Figure 1 *An advertisement from the London Magazine of about 1912 for Onoto pens from Thomas De La Rue of London. Onoto advertisements are endearingly ingenuous, ranging from 'I am it in pens. 10/6 makes me your lifelong slave' to 'As British as the Pillar Box' on a wartime advert. Courtesy of Philip Poole.*

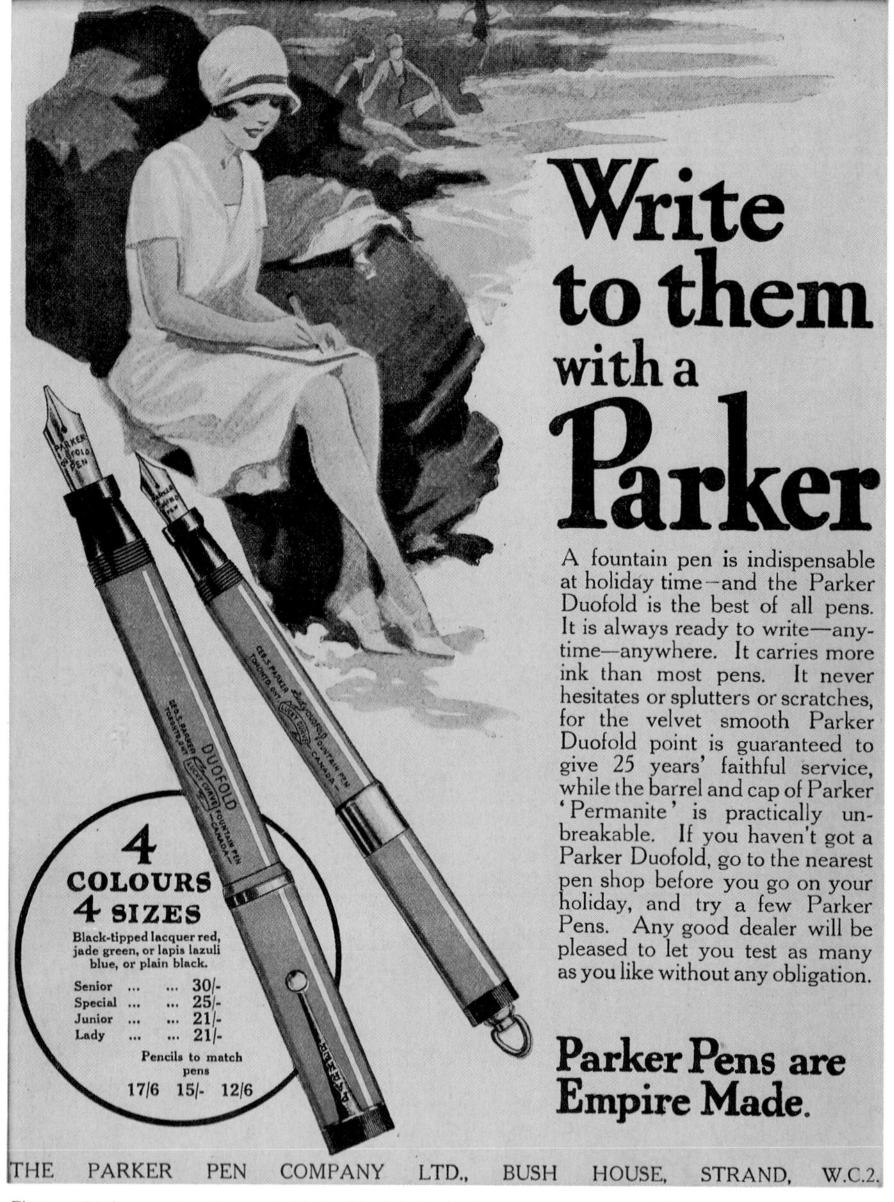

Figure 2 *Mid-1920s advertisement for Parker Duofold 'Lucky Curve' pens. Courtesy of Philip Poole.*

Figure 3 *Clockwise from top: (1) Red Parker Duofold of the late 1920s/early 1930s.* HIS NIBS *£155 (c US$248)*
(2) Conway Stewart pen of the 1920s, the orange ripple effect extending beneath the nib to the feed, as shown. PENFRIEND *£85 (c US$136)*
(3) Valentine, an English company taken over by Parker in 1941, this example with a particularly attractive cracked ice effect. About 1931. PHYLLIS GORLICK KING *£25 (c US$40)*
(4) Mentmore (makers of Platignum) Supreme, an English pen, 1940s. JOHN DILLAMORE *£25 (c US$40)*
(5) Parker Televisor, a pen with visible ink level. 1930s. PHYLLIS GORLICK KING *£25 (c US$40)*
(6) Silver filigree pen of about 1910, eye-drop filling. PENFRIEND *£95 (c US$152)*
(7) Waterman's Ideal silver filigree pen, early 20th century. MANSFIELD *£175 (c US$280)*
(8) Parker Vacumatic with translucent 'Television' barrel so that ink level may be viewed. The Blue Diamond emblem on the clip means that the pen is guaranteed 'for life'. About 1940. PHYLLIS GORLICK KING *£85 (c US$136)*
(9) Conway Stewart pen of about 1935 with black and silver cracked ice pattern. MANSFIELD *£95 (c US$152)*
(10) Waterman's small lever-filling pen, about 1933. MANSFIELD *£75 (c US$120)*
(11) Wahl-Eversharp pen in Art Deco style with grey pearl and flashes of pink. 1930s. JOHN DILLAMORE *£25 (c US$40)*
(12) Waterman's lever-filling pen. 1950s. PHYLLIS GORLICK KING *£32 (c US$51)*
(13) Swan self-filler (lever) by Mabie Todd & Co, made in England. 1930s. JOHN DILLAMORE *£25 (c US$40)*
(14) Wyvern, one of the medium priced range of English pens from the 1930s. JOHN DILLAMORE *£25 (c US$40)*
(15) The Acorn, a small 'pocket fountain pen' which advertised itself as leakproof, and was made by JP & Co. Complete with original box and instructions. HIS NIBS *£16 (c US$25)*
(16) Early Swan by Mabie Todd & Bard, New York, with decorative metalwork including a chain for a lady to wear the pen. About 1900. HIS NIBS *£65 (c US$104)*
(17) Dark brown lever-filling Swan, about 1935. MANSFIELD *£65 (c US$104)*
(18) Japanese jumbo fountain pen, a novelty pen from the 1940s with painted lacquer-effect. PENFRIEND *£65 (c US$104)*
(19) Waterman's lady's pen of about 1935. MANSFIELD *£55 (c US$88)*
(20) Swan gold-plated lady's pen with lever fill and suspension ring on cap, in original box. About 1920s. PENFRIEND *£88 (c US$140)*
(21) Onoto pen of typical long, slender form, with extending plunger filler mechanism. Late 1920s. PENFRIEND *£110 (c US$176)*
(22) Brown marbled Waterman's lever-fill Ideal of 1930s. MANSFIELD *£95 (c US$152)*
(23) Green mottled lever-fill Sheaffer lady's pen with ring on cap, about 1920. PENFRIEND *£98 (c US$156)*
(24) Green Sheaffer Lifetime, 1920s. HIS NIBS *£90 (c US$144)*
(25) Sheaffer with over-the-top or military clip, and showing the white dot which was Sheaffer's trade mark. About 1940. MANSFIELD *£85 (c US$136)*
(26) Conway Stewart with lever-filler, the flat top typical of the pre-war period. About 1938. MANSFIELD *£45 (c US$72)*
(27) Conway Stewart with pointed, post-war style cap. About 1945. MANSFIELD *£45 (c US$72)*
(28) Conway Stewart with attractive green chevron-patterned body. 1940s. JOHN DILLAMORE *£25 (c US$40)*
(29) The Abbey, a pre-war English pen from the lower end of the market, with a 'Goldine' nib. With original box and leaflet. HIS NIBS *£15 (c US$24)*
(30) Blue Swan with pointed cap and leverless filling – the top of the barrel twists to allow filling. 1939. MANSFIELD *£85 (c US$136)*
(31) Conway Stewart Dinkie, a tiny pen from the early 1930s in bright rainbow colours. PENFRIEND *£58 (c US$92)*
(32) Parker 'Lucky Curve' Duofold lady's pen, in Mandarin Yellow, about 1928. HIS NIBS *£150 (c US$240)*
(33) Parker Duofold in Mandarin Yellow, early 1930s. HIS NIBS *£120 (c US$192)*

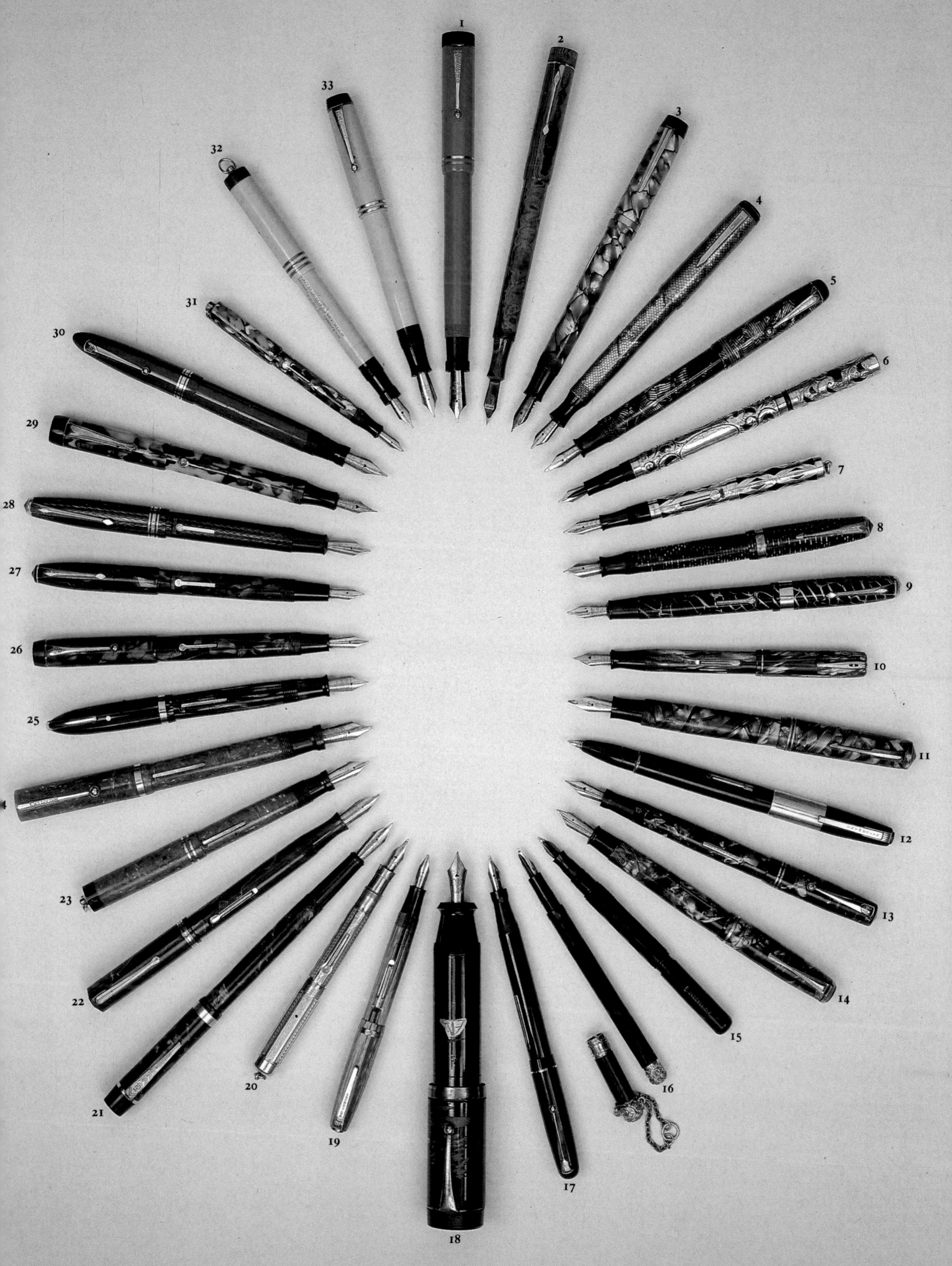
1
2
3
4
5
6
7
8
9
10
11
12
13
14
15
16
17
18
19
20
21
22
23
25
26
27
28
29
30
31
32
33

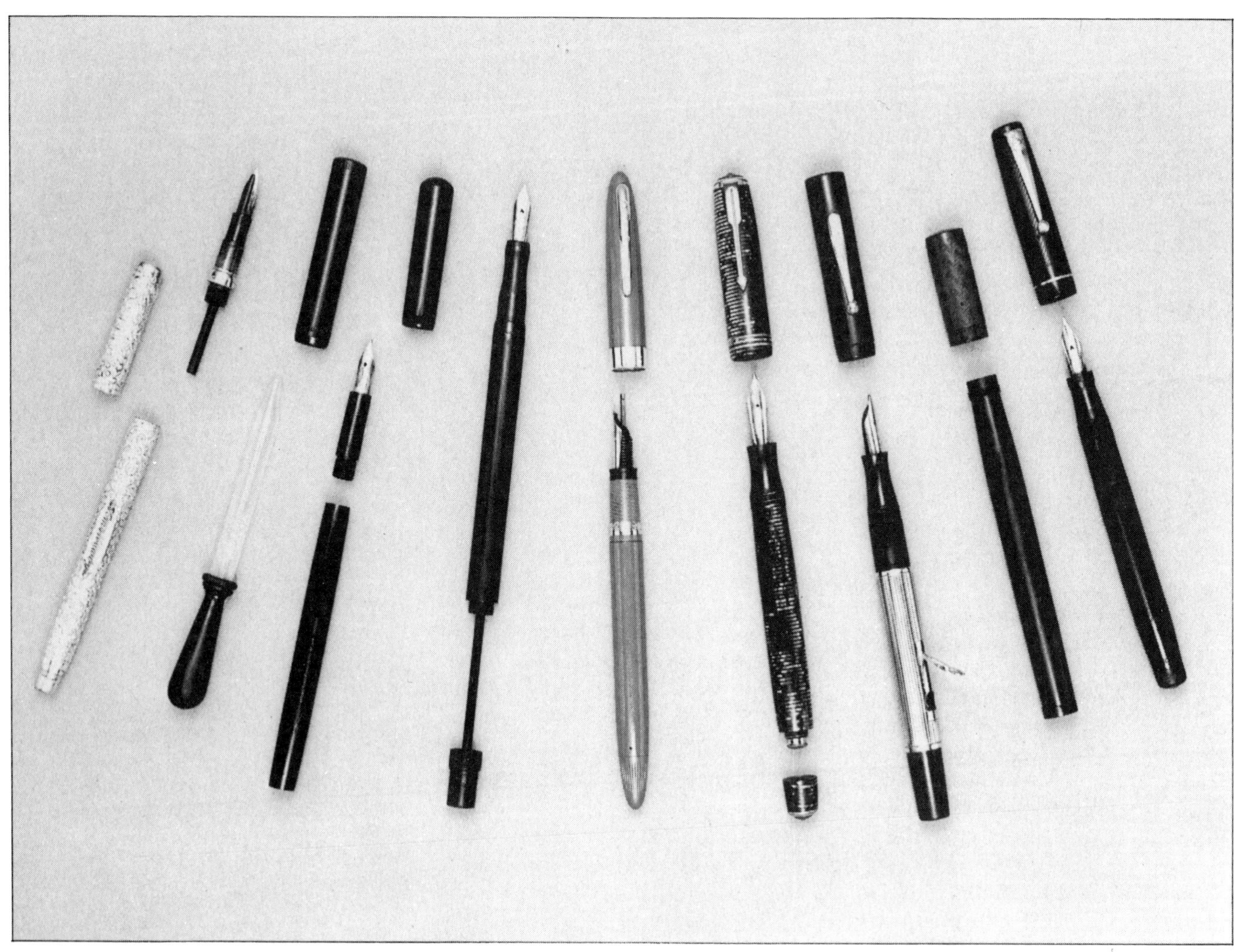

Figure 4 *A group of fountain pens illustrating a variety of filling systems. From left, (1) Mabie Todd & Bard ornate gold plated Swan pen of about 1900 complete with eye-dropper (right) which is used to fill the barrel.* PENFRIEND *£135 (c US$216)*
(2) Blackbird by Mabie Todd & Co New York, inscribed 'Made in U.S.A. during War'. This pen would also require an eye dropper to fill the barrel. JOHN DILLAMORE *£30 (c US$48)*
(3) Onoto pen with plunger filling system: the pen fills as the plunger is pushed in. About 1913. HIS NIBS *£20 (c US$32)*
(4) Sheaffer Snorkel, introduced in 1952 and reputed to be the most complicated pen ever marketed. Its snorkel is extended by unscrewing the top of the barrel, the pen may then be filled without the nib touching the ink supply. MANSFIELD *£80 (c US$128)*
(5) Parker Vacumatic which fills when repeated depression of the button on the end of the barrel creates a vacuum within the barrel and draws the ink in. JOHN DILLAMORE *£50 (c US$80)*
(6) Waterman's Ideal with gold barrel and lever filling, the lever shown here open. Waterman's introduced lever filling in 1913. About 1925. MANSFIELD *£150 (c US$240)*
(7) Waterman's retractor pen of about 1900, the nib is retracted within the barrel for safety when not in use. Filling requires an eye-dropper. PENFRIEND *£85 (c US$136)*
(8) Swan leverless pen introduced in 1933. Filling takes place when the end of the barrel is twisted gently one way (which depresses the rubber sac inside) then the other, allowing ink to fill the sac. MANSFIELD *£70 (c US$112).*

with each other to produce the best fountain pen. A large number of pens from this exciting period are finding their way into antique markets and shops, as people begin to re-discover the pleasures of handwriting in these word-processed days.

Shown on these pages are a selection of pens that can be found on the market today. The market in fountain pens bears the hallmarks of a new area of collecting. There is little consensus on pricing, and collectors relate instances of identical pens being picked up for a few pence in a jumble sale while costing £80 at a specialist (albeit cleaned, serviced and guaranteed). Despite this, one can still identify some factors that affect value, whatever the asking price. These include primarily quality. A fine period pen by one of the famous names – for example a Parker Duofold, Sheaffer Lifetime, Waterman's Patrician, De La Rue Onoto or Mabie Todd's Swan – is an object created in an atmosphere of intense competition when lifetime guarantees were commonly offered and design was all important. The advertisements that promoted these pens in their day proudly emphasised their quality, durability and stylishness. The potential market for fountain pens was enormous, and included even schoolchildren. Aware of this, pen manufacturers made a wide range of medium quality pens, that were inexpensive and thus accessible. There was a large number of manufacturers in this field; in Great Britain Conway Stewart, Burnham, Mentmore (which made Platignum pens) and Wyvern.

The second major factor affecting value is condition. While a little furniture polish can do wonders for the exterior of a plastic pen, interiors pose more problems. These pens, which may be as much as 80 years old, are surely beyond the terms of their lifetime guarantee. Specialist restorers exist who may be able to repair damaged or perished parts depending on whether they have the necessary replacements. Nibs that are bent can sometimes be straightened out but replacement is usually a specialist's job and again depends on the availability of an appropriate spare.

People buy pens for various reasons and these have a bearing on what they regard as acceptable condition. Those who want a pen specifically to use will be concerned to find one that suits their hand and is in full working order. Those who wish to make a collection of historical interest can afford to be less fastidious about the suitability of a nib for themselves and overall condition, though wise collectors will buy the best examples they can find. Collectors may choose a theme: perhaps pens made by a particular manufacturer, or they may choose the most beautiful and colourful of the 1920s and 1930s pens. A more academic approach might be to collect pens representing the various pen mechanisms that evolved over the years. *Figure 4* shows a few examples from the many different methods for filling pens, from eye-dropper to snorkel. It is important to appreciate that some of these pens, with filling systems now unfamiliar to us, must be handled with care. For example, fiercely twisting the end of a pen that is designed to be pulled and pushed as a plunger may well fracture the brittle early plastic of which it is made.

While many of these pens bear their trade name and maker's mark impressed on the barrel, dating is more difficult. Old advertisements in dated magazines and papers are helpful, but in the absence of these, stylistic details are the only clues. To give only the most general of guidelines, pens from the beginning of the century are usually black (vulcanite or Bakelite), sometimes with silver or gold. They are slender, and in the earliest the ink is placed in the barrel with an eye-dropper. Some self-fillers appeared from 1908 when Sheaffer patented the lever fill, while Parker introduced the button fill in 1916. *Figure 3 (6, 7, 16)* and *Figure 4 (1, 3)*. By the 1920s, coloured plastics were making possible a range of more daring pens and in the following two decades many decorative effects were created. Pens became fatter – partly a practical measure so that they could hold more ink – and were typically square ended as in *Figure 3 (1, 24, 26 and others)*. These are now once more fashionable and thus in demand. By the 1940s a more streamlined, pointed shape was coming back into fashion as in *Figure 3 (25, 27, 28, 30)*. The famous Parker 51 was completed in 1939 and so named to celebrate the company's 51st anniversary in 1888. Thereafter in the 1940s and 1950s many other pens copied its covered nib style, though to this day the Parker 51 has a loyal cult following.

Information about fountain pens is not easy to come by, but a book has been published in America which is a great help in dating the major American makes: Waterman, Sheaffer, Parker and Wahl-Eversharp. It is called Collectible Fountain Pens by Glen Bowen. There is also the Writing Equipment Society in Sheffield, England, which publishes a regular journal for its members which often contains articles on fountain pens.

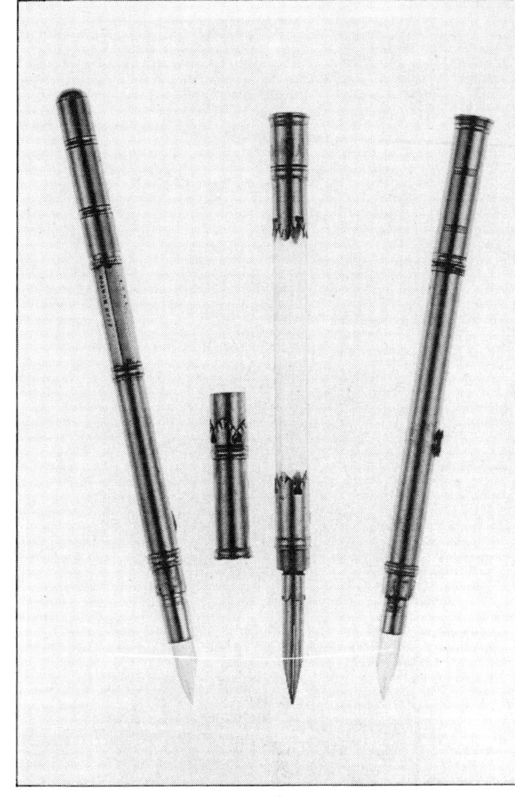

Figure 5 *Three very rare examples of early fountain pens. Left, silver pen patented by John Joseph Parker (no relation) in 1832, with early self-filling mechanism. Centre, George III pen of about 1780 with glass barrel and silver acanthus leaf mounting. One end has a silver mounted cork stopper while the nib may be covered by a screw cap. Right, silver Penographic fountain pen, a patented design by W. Robson of London, hallmarked 1820. This and the Parker pen (left) have nibs of horn. Private Collection.*

With thanks to Gerald Sattin.

June 1987

WRISTWATCHES

Deborah Scott

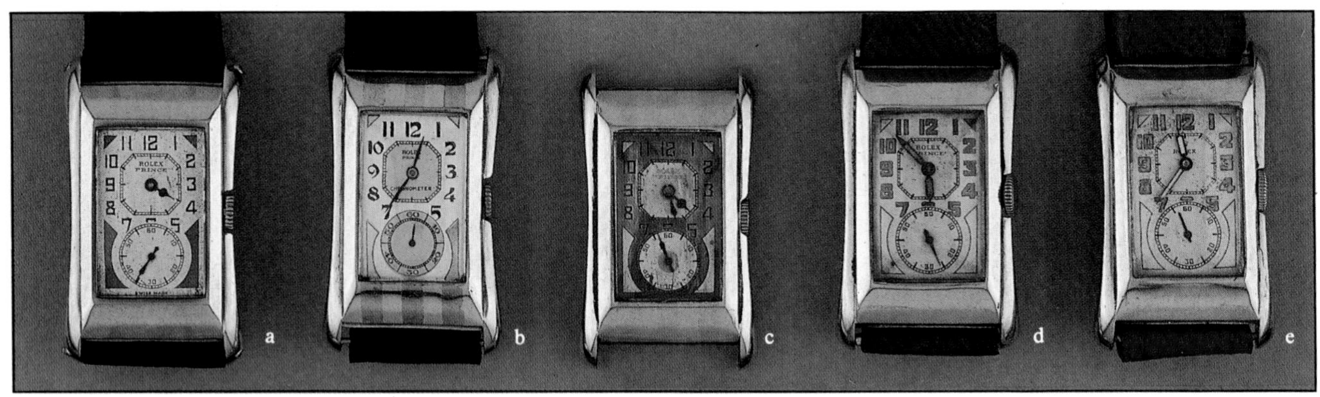

Figure 1. *A group of Rolex* Princes. *Notice the characteristic waisted shape of the rectangular case. All date from around 1930. a) 9-carat gold case, L 4.3 cm (1¾ in), £1650 (c US$1980); b) and c) two with the most desirable striped gold cases – 9-carat and 18-carat respectively, £2860, £3740 (c US$3432, $4488); d) and e) two examples with contrasting 9-carat gold cases of curved shape, £1870, £2090 (c US$2244, $2508).* SOTHEBY'S

In the last five years a new category has begun to appear in sales of clocks and watches held by the major auctioneers. This comprises wristwatches, the market for which continues to strengthen. More and more English dealers, hitherto interested only in pocket watches, are including wrist-watches amongst their stock. This is in response to an insatiable demand from foreign customers, especially Americans, Italians and Japanese. Several examples, gleaned both from dealers and from the salerooms, are illustrated on these pages and represent a cross section of today's market.

Before examining the market for wristwatches, it may be helpful to put them into their historical context. Hardly antique by pocket watch standards, wristwatches belong to this century. They do, however, have antecedents. There are tales of watches worn on the wrist as far back as the 18th century, and heavily ornate, bejewelled bracelets incorporating a watch exist which were made for grand ladies of the 19th century. It was not until technology allowed and lifestyles demanded that wristwatches became widely available. While early examples from the Edwardian period may be found, the great majority of wristwatches available on the market today were made after 1920. By the end of the 1920s, wristwatches had eclipsed pocket watches, and thereafter became increasingly elaborate and diverse. Examples from the 1930s exemplify this blossoming of the wristwatch, enjoying a fine marriage between imaginative design and technology. These qualities keep 1930s watches amongst those most sought after today.

The modern market for old wrist-watches appears to be dichotomous. On the one hand there are the watches of the 1920s, 1930s and 1940s, the appeal of which lies mainly in the stylistic contrast to modern watches. On the other there are watches which could be classed as second-hand. Modern looking watches, often of types still in production, by good makers have a second-hand value high enough to make them a viable prospect for auctioneers. For example, a gold Rolex Oyster which would retail new for over £5000 (c US$6000) could find a second-hand value at auction of perhaps £2000-£3000 (c US$2400-$3600). The price of second-hand gold watches is underwritten by the value of the gold they contain.

Another area of the wristwatch market which should be mentioned consists of jewelled ladies' watches. A marquesite example is shown here *(Figure 4h)*, typical of many on the market today. These delicate watches are usually classed as jewellery, since factors controlling their price have more in common with jewellery than with other watches. Since they are thus a separate market they have only a token representative here.

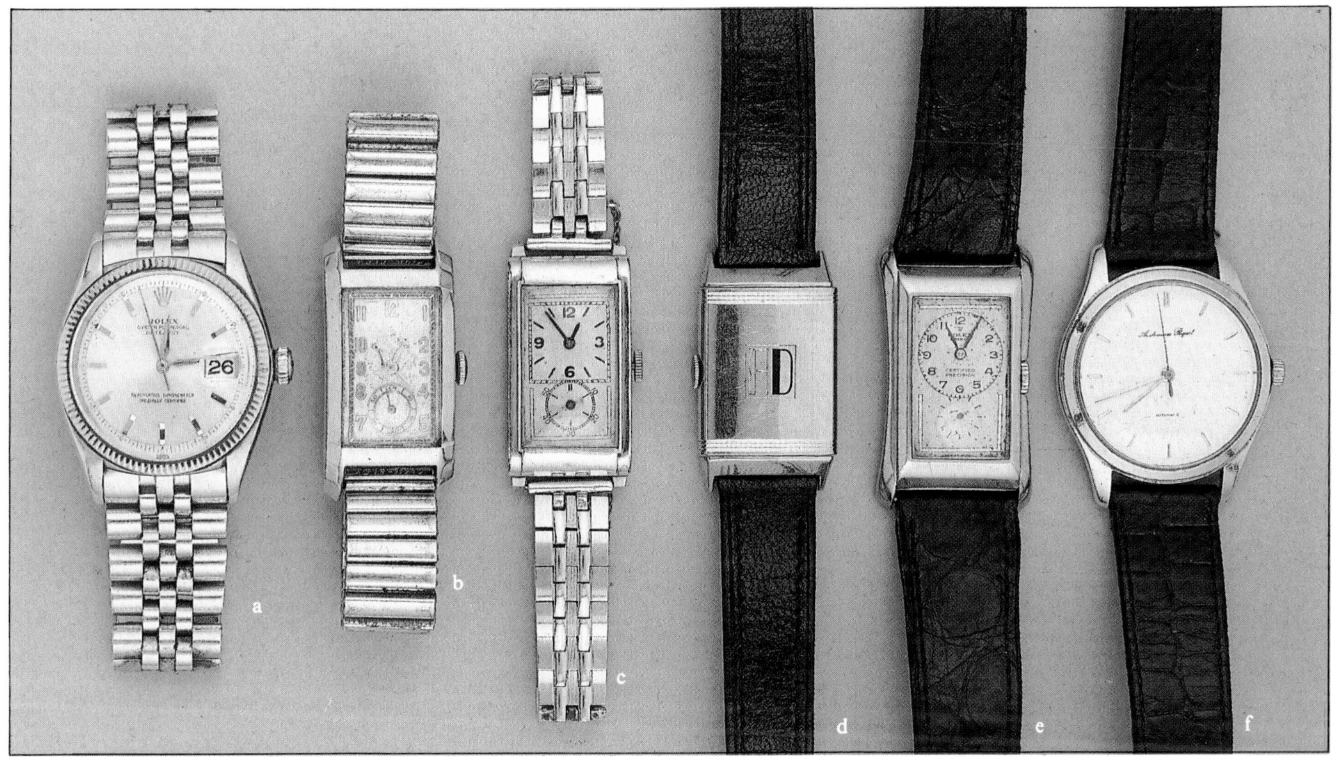

Figure 2 *a) Gold Rolex* Oyster Perpetual Datejust *watch,* DIAM *3.6 cm (1½ in). £1500 (c US$1800); b) Gold Rolex rectangular watch, the dial or curved shape, £800 (c US$960); c) Gold Rolex rectangular watch, £1350 (c US$1620); d) steel cased watch by Le Coultre with sliding* reverso *case, £400 (c US$480); e) Rolex* Prince *in gold of two colours, £1500 (c US$1800); f) gold self-winding watch by Audemars Piguet, a distinguished maker, £400 (c US$480).* PHILLIPS

So what are the chief factors affecting the price of wristwatches? Most important of all is the maker. A well known and respected name such as Rolex, Patek Philippe, Cartier or Audemars Piguet commands a much higher price than a similar watch by a less illustrious maker. The most obvious instance of price being affected by a name is provided by Rolex, so much so that any watch bearing it is immediately increased in value. As to whether such respect is soundly based, dealers agree that the Rolex mechanism is of better quality and more reliable than any others, though from that point of view there is little to choose amongst the best names. The value of old Rolex watches is further enhanced by modern Rolex advertising which promotes its top quality, stylish image.

Another factor that has a major effect on prices in this market is fashion. At present the rectangular watches of the 1930s are enjoying great popularity. The current advertisements for a major New York fashion house show all their models wearing these watches. There is a hierarchy of desirability amongst rectangular watches. Most desirable, indeed almost a byword in watch dealing circles, is the Rolex *Prince,* examples of which are shown here *(Figure 1).* Even amongst Rolex *Princes* there is distinction. At the top of the scale are 'stripey' watches, with cases featuring longitudinal stripes in gold of contrasting colours. Whether a case is of 18- or 9-carat gold is important to its value, while at the other end of the scale are those with cases of silver or steel *(Figure 6b).* Rectangular watches which are of curved section, fitted to the wrist, are also currently in vogue. Round watches of the same period contrast in value to the rectangular and square examples. The original maker's box is a desirable addition to a Rolex or other fine watch.

Additional features or complications add to the value of a watch. For example a dial showing the phases of the moon is a valuable feature, as are perpetual calendar functions, automatic winding, and other refinements that are found when watches become elevated to chronometer status. The ultimate in such features must be the minute repeater. On such a watch the touch of a lever will cause the repeater train to strike the hours, quarters and minutes past the hour. When a fine watch such as this is so rare that an example can fetch well over £10 000 (c US$12 000), it seems a pity that its electronically chirruping descendants are commonplace today.

Novelties are also sought after. The *reverso* watch, made by Jaeger-Le Coultre has an ingenious case that allows the watch to be reversed, so that the face is turned inwards and protected – ideal for sportsmen *(Figure 2d).* Another amusing type which is bought more by collectors than by those wanting a watch for practical purposes is the digital type

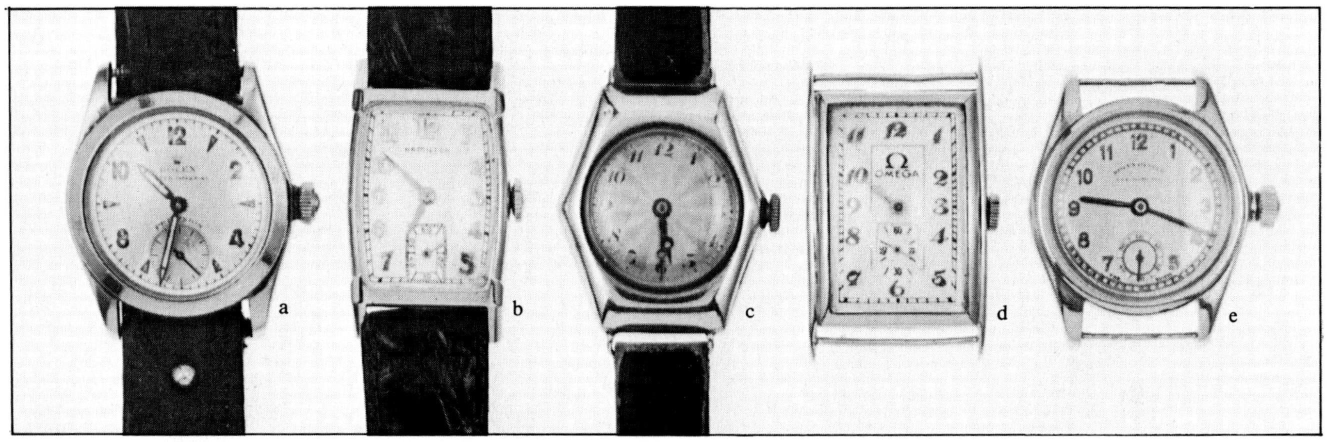

Figure 3 (above) *A group of less expensive watches from Phillips Monday (Pink Room) sale. a)* Rolex Oyster Imperial *with steel case, probably 1960s, £120 (c US$144);*
b) Hamilton (an American make) gilt metal watch, 1940s, £280 (c US$336);
c) Rolex hexagonal gold watch, 1950s, £120 (c US$144);
d) rectangular gold watch by Omega, 1950s, £100 (c US$120);
e) circular gold Rolex Oyster, *1960s, £310 (c US$372).* PHILLIPS

Figure 4 (left) *A selection of watches from Grays Antique Market. a) 9-carat gold Rolex octagonal watch of 1930s, £1100 (c US$1320);*
b) Rolex Prince with two coloured gold case, dated 1933, £2400 (c US$2880);
c) stylish 18-carat gold 1930s watch of curved shape, especially fashionable today, £1100 (c US$1320);
d) 1930s version of a digital watch, with gold plated case, £120 (c US$144);
e) attractive, rectangular 1930s watch with curved gold-filled case, by Gruen, £140 (c US$168);
f) round watch with fine quality case of 18-carat gold, retailed by Mappin, 1925, £300 (c US$360);
g) rectangular watch with 9-carat gold case, not marked, 1930s, £150 (c US$180);
h) marquesite ladies' watch, an elegant example of a type frequently found in the market, £120 (c US$144). CERBERUS *(first three);* STAND 301 *(others)*

Figure 5 (left) *A group of collectors' pieces.*
a) Asymmetric watch made by Patek Philippe in the 1960s, £6500 + VAT (c US$7800);
b) white gold Patek Philippe perpetual calendar watch, which automatically takes into account the length of each month and leap years; it also shows the phases of the moon, 1950s, £18 000 + VAT (c US$21 600);
c) Rolex Oyster *with bubble-back;* Oysters *were made with screw-fittings as waterproof watches; this one is of 18-carat gold, late 1930-early 1940s, £1600 + VAT (c US$1920);*
d) Cartier Tank Watch *from 1920s, a classic Cartier design still fashionable today; £3000 + VAT (c US$3600).* GRIMALDI

Figure 6 (above) *Some 1930s watches: a) Rolex 18-carat gold 'bull-back' watch, £1500 (c US$1800); b) Rolex* Prince, *the classic watch but with a silver case, £1300 (c US$1560); c) Rolex* Oyster, *octagonal thus more desirable than the cushion (squarish)* Oysters, *£1000 (c US$1200); d) Rolex 9-carat gold man's watch small enough to be worn by a woman, £530 (c US$636); e) gentleman's evening watch by Cartier, diamonds on white gold, £2000 (c US$2400).* THE PRUSKIN GALLERY

(Figure 4d) where the hours and minutes are individually displayed.

Women's watches, excluding ornate, decorative examples, do not compare in price to men's watches. The majority are too small to be currently fashionable, and women are more inclined to wear the smaller examples of men's watches, some of which, from the 1930s and 40s, are highly elegant *(Figure 6d)*.

An impecunious collector, who cannot afford the makes and models currently in fashion may take some hints from the above. He may find it worthwhile to seek out watches by little known makers, made in styles similar to those of the great houses. American firms like Hamilton and Gruen are examples whose watches are not yet highly priced *(Figures 3b and 4e)*. Round watches and ladies' watches, even by good makers, also offer some inexpensive buys.

Obviously, it is important that a watch is in working order, and is likely to continue that way. The salerooms do not, on the whole, give any guarantees at all about condition. They may point out a watch that has a serious fault, one that may be particularly difficult to remedy, but on the whole they sell 'as found'. Dealers, on the other hand, especially those who value their customers, usually offer a period of guarantee. This is worthwhile, for it is not always easy to have old watches mended, and some repairers may not be able to find parts. The British Horological Institute can advise on watch repairers amongst its members.

With certain makes of watch selling for thousands of pounds, there is bound to be some malpractice and fakes are not unknown. Rolex movements may be taken from poor cases and put into stripey gold ones to boost their value. Movements may be swapped around in other pieces, though ill-fitting or badly made cases can give such matches away. At worst, quartz movements are put into old cases. Collectors should familiarise themselves with the insides of watches, noticing hallmarks and serial numbers to forearm themselves against such skulduggery. They would be well advised, in the meanwhile, to buy from a reputable dealer.

Little has been written on this subject in English as yet. Collectors are referred to an Italian book recently published, which contains an English translation of the text. 'Ore d'Oro' by Giampiero Negretti and Franco Nencini gives helpful information about the makers and their watches and has many illustrations.

Sources

More and more auctioneers are including wristwatches in their clock sales and some good examples may be seen. Phillips also sell less expensive watches in their Monday 'Pink Room' sales. Most antique markets have several dealers selling watches – it is best to seek out those who specialise.

June 1985

PLASTIC ANTIQUES

Vanessa Nicolson

The term plastic has come to be associated with all that is cheap, disposable, mass produced. In fact, plastics from the 1920s to 50s have become highly collectable and are increasingly to be found with the dealers of Kensington and Knightsbridge rather than in markets and jumble sales. Plastics are becoming 'high art'. There is a Bakelite Museum, a plastics gallery at the Science Museum, and plastic objects are an occasional feature of the Art Deco sales in the most prestigious salerooms.

A great deal of the appeal is certainly nostalgic; these everyday objects perfectly embody our idea of domestic life in the recent past. Boxes for tobacco, studs, powder, napkin rings, inkwells – the type of commodity used in the home has changed so much that these ordinary things have acquired great curiosity value. On top of this, plastics are often bright and colourful, and lend themselves to interesting and whimsical designs.

The scarcest 'plastic antiques' are those manufactured by the early experimentors in semi-synthetic plastics. The great 19th century inventors were the Birmingham born Alexander Parkes (creator of 'Parkesine'), the Hyatt Brothers in the United States (who patented 'Celluloid' in 1870) and Charles Goodyear (inventor of 'Vulcanite' in 1838).

Parkesine was introduced to a largely indifferent public at the Great International Exhibition in London in 1862 in the section featuring 'Animal and Vegetable Substances used in Manufacture'. Parkesine products are extremely rare, and most of the surviving examples are to be found at the Plastics Institute in London, with a few examples in the Bakelite Museum. Parkes produced toys, jewellery, inkstands, writing cases and thousands of knife handles, but his company flourished only for a decade or so in the 1850s and 60s.

The semi-synthetic plastics were mainly employed to imitate natural materials. As well as looking expensive they were immensely practical. In 1896 *The House and Home Practical Guide* wrote: 'In cutlery handles, celluloid is preferable to ivory; it does not crack or discolour and is not affected by hot water.'

The hard rubber known as Vulcanite or ebonite was discovered by Charles Goodyear in 1838. It has a similar appearance to jet and its hard, black quality appealed to Victorian taste. Fountain pens and decorative boxes were made in Vulcanite but now it is usually only jewellery that can still be found in this material.

The great revolution brought about by these three materials was that they could look expensive (ivory, horn, amber and tortoiseshell were also imitated) but remained affordable. It was only much later that plastics were accepted for actually looking cheap, particularly in kitchenware. After the First World War the kitchen was no longer simply a utilitarian place, separated from family life, but a central focus. Plastic was more hygienic than wood, and more colourful.

The big name in the history of plastics was Bakelite. Originally used in the electrical, radio and car industries, it is a strong material that has survived well. The quality of Bakelite goods that can still be found range from the more expensive wirelesses and television sets of the 1930s, to the ubiquitous ashtrays, bowls and boxes. The man who started it all, Leo Baekeland, was a Belgian-born chemist, who in 1907 patented the first purely synthetic plastic, named Bakelite. The unfortunate chemist James Swinburne had reached the same conclusions as Baekeland but arrived at the patent office a day too late. Swinburne's company was in fact taken over by his rival in 1927, the year Bakelite Ltd was registered in Great Britain.

In the mid-1920s the new 'Beatl' picnic and table ware was introduced which shared the hardness and heat resistance of Bakelite but allowed the introduction of a wider colour range. In England it was marketed under the trade name 'Beetleware', 'Linga longa' and is most commonly known as 'Bandalasta' *(Figure 1)*. Urea formaldehyde, Bandalasta's technical name, was able to combine bright colours to achieve an effect of marble or alabasta. Matching sets of bowls, plates and beakers were made, as well as dressing table sets, table lamps and the popular palette-shaped cups and saucers.

Bandalasta achieved a great success at the Wembley exhibition of 1925. Large displays appeared in Harrods and in 1929 (the year production began in the US) the Beetle shop was opened in Regent Street to crowds of curious customers. However, the production of Bandalasta only lasted a few years and hence these objects are quite rare and expensive.

The growth of the plastic industry

Figure 1 (top right)
Bandalasta cup and palette-shaped saucer, bowl (DIAM 20.3 cm; 8 in) and teapot, 1927-32. Part of a larger set. JOHN JESSE. Price about £25-£150 per item.

Figure 2 (bottom right)
a) Cigarette case with hand decoration in marbled celluloid, 1930s. Similar boxes without the decoration can be found for as little as £4. H 8 cm (3 in). JOHN JESSE. Price £75.
b) Bourjois perfume box, 1930s. The door opens to reveal a miniature 'Soir de Paris' bottle. H 5 cm (3¾ in). ALFIE'S ANTIQUE MARKET (Stylo). Price £22.

B

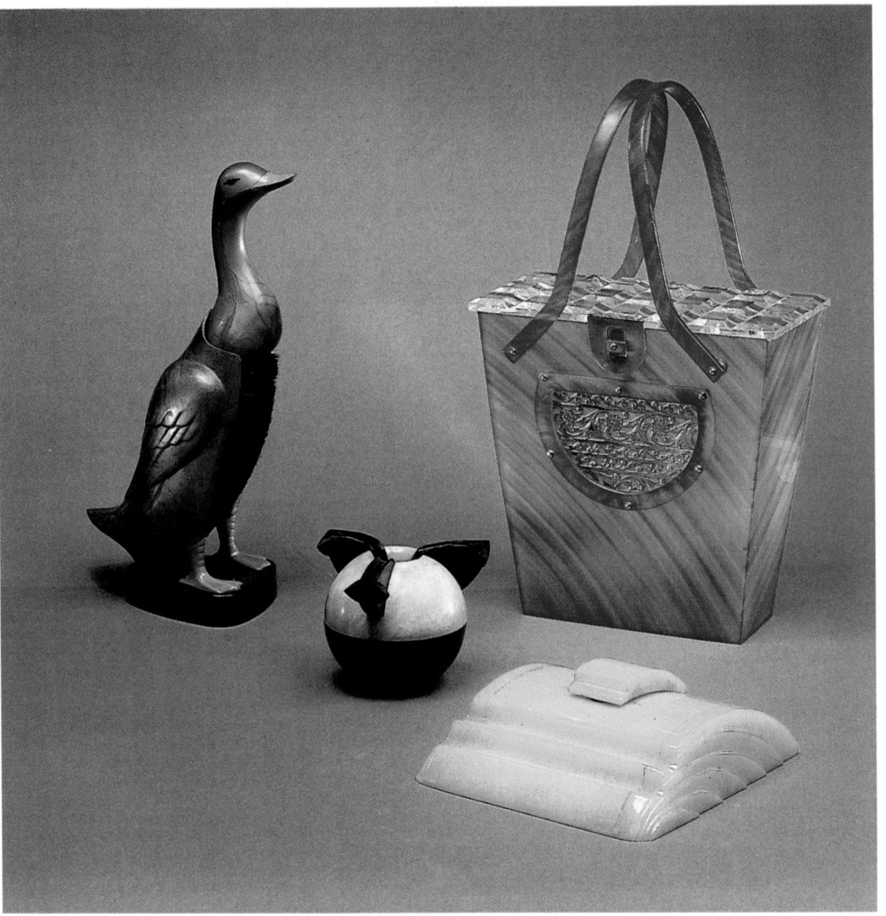

Figure 3 (above) *Bakelite viewmaster with seven reels of scenic views, early 1950s.* CAMDEN STABLES *(Stall 41).Price £15.*

Figure 4 (Left to right) *Clothes brush concealed as a duck, 1950s.* CAMDEN STABLES, *£9. Ashtray, manufactured by Roxon, about 1935.* JOHN JESSE, *£120. 1940s handbag with metal clasp.* MARILYN MELLINS, *£120.*
Foreground: *Carvacraft inkwell (the lid slides across), 1948-50.* ANTIQUARIUS *(David Rayner), £23.*

really took off in the 1930s. The material could be easily moulded and was well suited to the streamlined shapes and designs fashionable at the time. It was also light, durable, practical. Manufacturers began to exploit the 'fun' aspect of plastics, its bright colours and shapes. Companies concentrated on presenting their products in attractive, and not necessarily functional packaging. The boxes containing the Bourjois perfume bottles are an example of inventive design: a blue door with two pairs of tiny shoes outside it opens to reveal the 'Soir de Paris' perfume bottle *(Figure 2b)*. The packaging becomes more important than the product it contains.

Another popular design was the clothes brush concealed as a duck *(Figure 4)*. The really sophisticated models stand over a wood container carved in the form of an egg. Animal designs were very much in demand. A lot of them can be found in kitchenware – Penguin salt and pepper pots, rabbit, duck and dog napkin rings, egg cups in the form of chickens – the list is endless. Many of these can still be picked up very cheaply.

Decorative boxes were used for product packaging, and later they could be adapted as jewellery or cigarette boxes. Small boxes that had been sold with perfume or powder could be used to contain pins and cufflinks. Eventually handbags themselves, the ultimate containers, were produced in the late 1940s *(Figure 4)*. Although hard and inflexible in shape, the plastic handbag was light in weight and appearance. Plastic clothing also appeared at this time – the plastic raincoats and aprons, and later, shoes.

Collecting

Victorian celluloid objects are rare but can occasionally be found in markets, whereas the 'marbled' celluloid items produced in the 1920s and 30s are more common. Marbled celluloid could be made to look just like mother of pearl. Particularly desirable are the compact boxes or cigarette holders with decorative clasps, often in the shape of elegant hands *(Figure 2a)* which fetch much higher prices (£70-£100) than the plain ones. Celluloid can also be inlaid with other metals, so that monogrammed cigarette cases and such like were attractive presents in the 1930s.

A popular design for the vast number of cigarette boxes produced in the 1930s was the plain box with the imitation ivory lid, decorated with animal or mythological themes *(Figure 5b)*. These are highly collectable items and can be picked up from £1 (if slightly damaged) on a market stall, to £40 for a particularly unusual or ornate design in good condition. Thirty years earlier similar

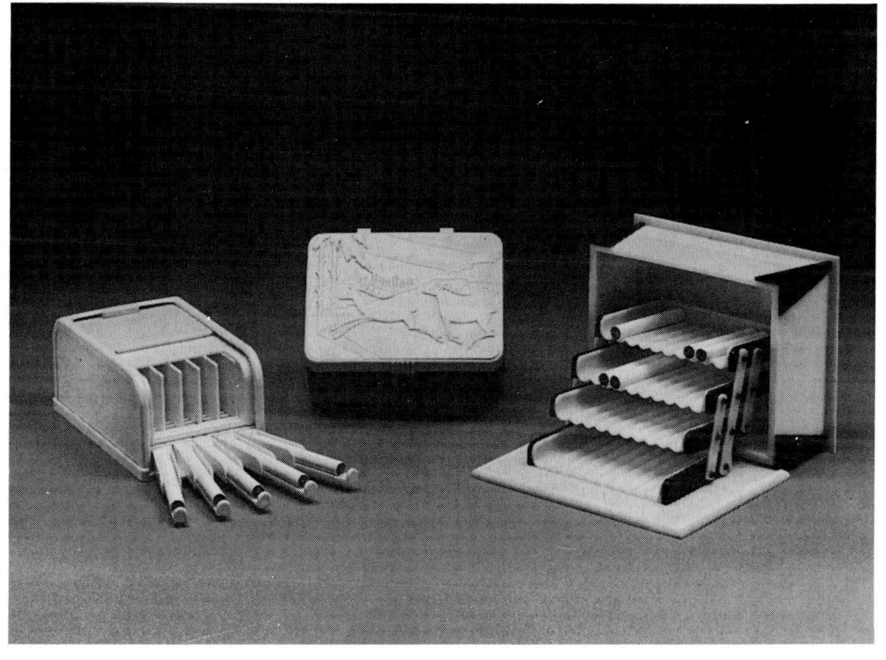

Figure 5 *a) 1950s cigarette dispenser. Five fingers come out when the top is rolled back.* CAMDEN PASSAGE. *Price £10.*
b) Cigarette box with running deer decoration on lid, mid 1930s. Prices vary from £1 (like this one which is slightly damaged and from a market stall) to £40 for unusual designs. CAMDEN STABLES
c) 1930s cigarette box which opens into compartments. COBRA AND BELLAMY. *Price £50.*

designs on the back of mirrors and brushes were being produced in Parkesine but are now virtually unobtainable.

The most unlikely objects seem to have been made in Bakelite: hot water bottles, children's rattles and yo-yos, candlesticks, jewellery, even coffins. People are still throwing out the common items like bowls and boxes, and these can be found in profusion on many market stalls. The more unusual objects are more expensive and a gem such as the Bakelite viewfinder made in the USA in 1933 with a vintage piece of film of New York can be picked up for £18. (A similar one is illustrated in *Figure 3*.) Without the film it was £3. Bakelite was also combined with other materials, such as the table on tubular steel legs, picked up by one collector for £2 in a boot sale a few years ago and now probably worth about £50. Bakelite came in a limited colour range, and unfortunately the colour dulls with age. The most common is the familiar mottled brown, the green and black shades are rarer and thus more expensive.

Dealers, however, have reported a dramatic drop in interest in Bakelite over last year. This may be due to the manufacture of cheap, modern imitations. Also the great Bakelite enthusiasts, the Italians and Japanese, seem to have had their fill and are no longer buying. Although dealers are not stocking so much because of this trend, the prices have not fallen and they are confident that interest will soon pick up again.

Melamine dinnerware, which was popular in the 1950s, is colourful, unbreakable, and still cheap. But although it does not chip, the cups and plates can look old from stains and scratches. A set of five bright yellow cups, saucers and plates in good condition recently sold at a market for £8.

Plastic kitchenware is perhaps not as collectable as the deskware produced at this time. The amber-toned desk sets made by John Dickinson & Co Ltd, named 'Carvacraft' are very collectable *(Figure 4)*. A complete set is hard to find, but individual pieces such as the ink-blotters or pen holders fetch about £14–£25. Although the streamlined shapes give the objects a 1930s feel, they were in fact manufactured between 1948–51.

Generally, collectors of plastics should go for unusual designs and, as Sylvia Katz points out in *Classic Plastics,* a mark of some kind, be it a patent or design number, a trademark or name, can help you identify the history of its manufacture. If an object is particularly rare but chipped or scratched it is still worth buying, but common objects such as Bakelite boxes and ashtrays are not, if in bad condition. It is worth persevering in a junk shop, jumble sale or bootsale to find one object that is attractive in design, condition and rarity.

Bibliography

Classic Plastics by Sylvia Katz, 1984, Thames and Hudson.
Art Plastic by Andrea di Noto, 1984, Cross River Press Ltd.

May 1986

The Policeman
H.G.HINE.

JAMES CATNACH & 19TH CENTURY BROADSHEETS

Helen Wodzicka

An entertaining way to gain insight into the popular taste of the last century is to look at its popular literature. Fortunately what was amusing or interesting then is fun today for a collector or a more casual student alike.

Chapbooks were small cheap books sold by chapmen or pedlars from the Middle Ages until the 19th century. The pedlars sold these books, trinkets, needles, laces and so on and broadsheets. The latter were printed on one side of coarse paper only and intended for pasting-up on ale-house or kitchen walls. They were an important link between isolated villages and farms with the outside world. The 19th century broadsheets printed by James Catnach and others in the Seven Dials area of London provide us with a direct link to the popular thinking of that time.

The chapbooks were usually very good value as some consisted of 7000 words or so with pictures too. Not bad for a penny! They were read by everyone who could read and admired by those who could not. Mostly the stories were traditional tales like Robin Hood or Robinson Crusoe. The tradition remained vigorous and later manifested itself in the subjects of the broadsheets.

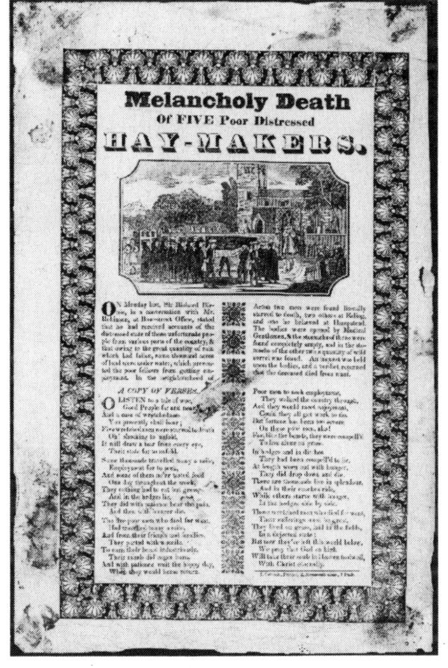

Melancholy Death
Of FIVE Poor Distressed
HAY-MAKERS.

Figure 1 (opposite) *A ballad seller or a patterer. From H. Mayhew,* London Labour and the London Poor.

Figure 2 *Melancholy death of haymakers. A typical small size broadsheet. The block would have been used many times for different stories. This one shows rather an attractive border of printers flowers, even if they are somewhat battered.*

All popular favourites were available on broadsheets. Ballads, patriotic songs and verse, election propaganda, historic events, news of the royal family, satires on the government were all important but not as important as the 'penny dreadfuls', the accounts of crime. Details of the most lurid 'dreadful, horrid murder most foul', the condemned man's arrest and trial, his dying confession or his last letter to his mother or sweetheart all sold well. Often the same letter was used for many different murders.

As important as the broadsheets themselves were the sellers. The earlier term 'chapman' was replaced by 'patterer' *(Figure 1)*. They were very colourful men, often the worse for gin, who lived a wandering existence on a precarious

The Mary-le-bonne TRAGEDY;

REVENGE

MURDER

Figure 3 *The Mary le bonne Tragedy. Catnach would follow up this account of the events leading up to the murder with one covering the trial, then the last confession or letter to the murderer's mother and then the description of the execution until every last bit of public interest was exploited.*

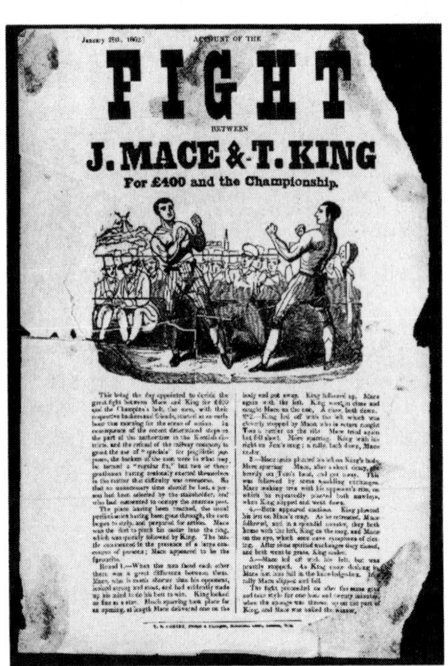
January 25th, 1862.

ACCOUNT OF THE

FIGHT

BETWEEN

J. MACE & T. KING

For £400 and the Championship.

Figure 4 *Fight account for 1862. An example of Fortey's work in a very similar style to Catnach.*

Figure 5 (opposite) *The affectionate daughter. A very large spectacular broadsheet showing Catnach's treatment of a traditional subject.*

income. The patterers declaimed the ballads, sang the songs or announced details of the murders. Some were nationally famous and were a mixture of beggar, pedlar and street-orator.

Broadsheets were sold at one penny or less. Songsheets were often advertised as three yards long but this usually refers to three columns of matter rather than the overall length. They too sold for one penny. Battledores, which were folded cardboard sheets with printed alphabet characters used to teach children to read, sold at a half penny. The authors were called Grub Street writers. Equally obscure are the many printers and journeymen who worked in this fairly lucrative business. Buyers were equally uncritical of the type, layout or quality of the illustrations. All the printer had to know was his market.

James Catnach was one printer who knew this market thoroughly. Usually called 'Jemmy Catnach' he was described as a 'plodding, ignorant, dirty, successful individual' and quite a lot is known about his career. He was born at Alnwick, Northumberland in 1792, the son of a Scottish printer. His father, John Catnach, was rather a good printer but not successful. After his bankruptcy and death Jemmy found himself, at the age of 21, in charge of his mother and sisters. He got going with one of his father's old wooden presses and a collection of odd type and woodcuts to produce chapbooks and broadsheets.

His home and printing shop were at Monmouth Court, Seven Dials in London. He never married and lived there until he retired even going so far as to hire a room there to live in once more until just before his death. His old press was fixed to the ceiling by steadying beams and would raise the ceiling several inches every time the bar was pulled home. It rocked the four-poster bed above 'like a cradle'.

Seven Dials was a notoriously tough district but Catnach was tough enough himself to glory in it. His printing was awful. The pages are crowded, the lines crooked or cut off short. If he was short of a letter he would substitute the nearest in shape. The woodcuts were bashed and battered and often used without the slightest relevance to the text. He pirated good ideas like Sherwood, Neely and Jones 'Tom and Jerry' series of 1821 *(Figure 6)*. He brought his version out the following year signed JAS. C–N–H.

He never let go of a money spinner if he could help it. He made a great deal of money from a murderer called Weare. After Weare was hanged he published a broad sheet called 'We are alive again' with so little space between the We and the are that it read 'Weare alive again'. This was a catchpenny or a cock. The patterers were often supplied with cocks or accounts of fictitious murders or events when there was a dearth of real excitement. The term comes from 'cook' as in 'cook up a story' or it may come from the 'Cock Lane Ghost' which was itself a famous cheat. The patterers would 'Crow the cock' to sell them.

He often wrote the dying confession or account of an execution some days before the event took place to be first with the news. He was caught out by reprieves several times. Naturally he received most of his money in copper. He had to boil it with chemicals to make it look new because people believed that fevers were caught from dirty money and nobody

THE AFFECTIONATE DAUGHTER

Giving an Account of Antony Molina, a rich and powerful Gentleman, who, for some treasonable offence against the State, was sentenced to be Starved to Death in a dismal, horrible Dungeon—shewing how his Life was most wonderfully preserved by the Milk from his Daughter's Breast.

See, Filial Piety, and Love exprest,
The Father nourish'd by the Daughter's breast;
Sentenc'd to Starve to Death, in Chains he lay,
But she sustain'd him Twelve Months and a Day.

The Emperor wondering much he was not dead
Found out at last the way that he was fed;
Amaz'd the tender sight he did behold,
And pardon'd him, and made her rich with Gold

THE following exhibits such a surprising and beautiful instance of piety, love, and affection in a child, as cannot be paralleled in the history of the world; it is worthy of being recorded in letters of gold, and ought to be had in every family, to impress upon the minds of their children the heroic example of this matchless daughter, whose memory will be held in honour and esteem to the latest posterity, and of whom may be said, in the language of Scripture,—"*Many daughters have done virtuously, but thou excellest them all.*"

Antony Molina, a rich, and powerful gentleman, was detected, among many others, (during a period of civil commotion) of plotting against the State, and exciting the King's subjects to rise up in rebellion against him; for which most unlawful and atrocious crime he was brought to trial, and, in proportion to the magnitude of his offence so was his sentence,—he was ordered to be chained to the wall of a dark, and loathsome dungeon, and there *Starved to Death*: and it was further declared, that any person discovered conveying to him any kind of food, should immediately suffer death.

He had several daughters, all of whom were genteelly married, except the youngest, Julia, who was married to a man in humble circumstances, for which he had quite disowned her, and had refused to see her for some years. This worthy daughter hearing of her father's cruel sentence, went unto each of her sisters, and asked if they did not intend to use their utmost exertions to procure a mitigation of his horrible doom. They all answered the same thing, namely, that their father had been engaged in a most unnatural conspiracy against the State, and that the wrath of Government was so strong against him, that if they interfered in his behalf, its vengeance would ruin them and their innocent families. Julia was almost distracted at their unfeeling disregard of an aged parent, and told them that although he had rebelled against his King, yet he had always acted the part of an affectionate, kind father to them in particular, and how cruelly they acted towards him; but, added she, "although he disowned me, and barr'd his door against me, yet he nourished my youth, and I will not forsake him in his old age; with the help of GOD, I myself will succour him, or perish in the attempt." Providence favoured her pious resolution: She gained admission to the royal presence, and falling upon her knees, pleaded to be admitted to her father's dungeon in such forcible and pathetic language, that her request was granted upon the terms that she should be searched every time she visited him, lest she might convey nourishment

Upon the tenth day of her father's confinement she was admitted into his dungeon, where she beheld her venerable parent, bound in chains, and stretched upon the damp stony floor. In agony unutterable she threw herself beside him and embraced him. He opened his languid eyes, and tried to speak, but his parched lips would not let him. Julia had lost an infant but a few days before, and her milk was burdensome to her, and as if inspired by Heaven, she bared her bosom, and moistened his mouth. It revived him a little, and she continued it all the time she was suffered to remain with him. For twelvemonths did this matchless daughter daily visit, and feed from her own breast her aged father, who began to recover his health, to the utter astonishment of the keeper, who was ignorant of the cause. At length he determined to watch the interviews between him and his daughter, which he did, and beheld such an affecting sight, such an instance of pious affection, as was probably never witnessed before. When the King was made acquainted with it, it softened his wrath so much that he instantly granted the aged Molina a pardon, re-instated him in his former possessions, and settled a thousand a year upon his virtuous and affectionate Daughter.

THERE was a wealthy gentleman
Who did most wickedly
With many more conspire against
The King's high majesty.
For which he was in prison cast
And bound with irons strong,
And there he was condemn'd to fast
Until his life was gone.
This cruel sentence was pronounc'd
That till his dying day,
He should not have one bit of food
His hunger to allay.
And that if any one should dare
To assist him night or day,
A solemn oath the Monarch sware,
To take their lives away
Within this dismal, horrid place,
And chained to the wall,
Fast down his aged, wrinkled face,
The scalding tears did fall.
Most grievously he languished,
And bitterly did cry,
For want of bread, one bit of bread,
I famish, starve, and die.
O that I had one crust to eat,
My hunger to control;
How precious is one grain of whea
Unto a hungry soul!
Had I this dungeon heap'd with gold,
I freely would it give,
All for a little loaf of bread,
That I might eat and ve.
Though it were mouldy, black, r brown
Or trodden in the mire,
It would be pleasing to my taste,
And sweet to my desire.
One drop of water let me have,
To cool my parched tongue;
O were I laid within the grave,
My sufferings would be done.
He many friends and daughters had,
The richest in the town,
Yet none durst come to succour him,
Dreading the Monarch's frown.
All but the youngest, and to her
He did behave unkind,
Because that she had married
Contrary to his mind.
The youngest to her sisters went,
All ladies, high and great,
And there did bitterly lament,
Their father's cruel fate.
O sisters dear, contrive some way,
His life for to preserve;
He in a dungeon pines away,
Condemned there to starve.
Alas! his wealthy daughters said,
We can do him no good;
You know 'tis death to any one,
Who dares to take him food.
The King's displeasure is so great
That we should ruin'd be,
Therefore we think it is as good,
That he should die as we.
His youngest daughter's heart did ache,
Most bitter did she cry;
Shall we our father dear forsake,
In his extremity.
Although he spurn'd me from his d
Because a poor man's wife,
Yet would I freely shed my blood,
To save my father's life.

Unto the Palace then she hies,
And falling on her knees,
With wringing hands, and bitter cries
These words pronounced she:—
"My helpless father, sovereign Liege,
Offending of your grace,
Is judg'd unto a pining death,
Within a dismal place.
Which I confess he has deserv'd
Yet mighty Prince," said she,
"Vouchsafe in gracious sort to grant,
One simple boon to me.
It chanced so I match'd myself,
Against my father's mind,
Whereby I did procure his wrath,
As fortune had assign'd.

And seeing now the time is come,
He must resign his breath,
Vouchsafe that I may speak to him
Before the hour of death.
And reconcile myself to him,
His blessing to obtain,
That when he dies, I may not then
Beneath his curse remain."

The Monarch granted her request,
Conditionally that she,
Each day unto her father went,
Should strictly searched be.
Meat or drink she could not bring,
To help him there distress'd,
But every day she nourish'd him
With Milk from her own Breast.
Thus by her Milk he was preserv'd,
A twelvemonth and a day,
And grew both fat and fair to see,
Yet none could tell which way.
The Monarch musing much thereat,
At length did understand
How he was fed—and yet the Law
Not broke at any hand.
And much admired at the same,
And her great virtues shown,
He pardon'd him—and honour'd her
With great preferments known.
Her father ever after that,
Did love her as his life;
And blest the day that she was made
A virtuous, loving wife.

Printed & Sold by
J. Catnach, 2, Monmouth-court
7 Dials.——Price Twopence.
......Travellers supplied......

The Death, Last Will, and
FUNERAL OF "BLACK BILLY":
ALSO, THE TEARS OF LONDON FOR THE
DEATH OF TOM AND JERRY.
JAS. CATNACH,
Ninth Edition.
PRICE TWOPENCE.
The Charlie's Rejoicing at the Death of Tom and Jerry.
FLOORED!!
THE
Charlie's Holiday.
GRAND CHORUS OF CHARLIES.
Solemn Funeral Procession of Tom and Jerry.
ADELPHI THEATRE
TOM JERRY
The Tears of London; or, the
DEATH
OF
Tom and Jerry.
Funeral Procession of Poor "BLACK BILLY."
POOR BLACK BILLY
BEGGARS OPERA

Figure 6 *Death of Tom and Jerry. Catnach's pirated characters are finished off.*

would change it. It is said that he got so much bad money that he had his back kitchen floor paved with dud coins embedded in plaster of paris.

His thirst for sensation earned him reprimands from magistrates and a prison sentence. He over-reached himself when he printed a libel about a local butcher saying that human bodies finished up in the sausages! The butcher got mobbed and beaten up as a result and Catnach got 6 months.

Soon he was back in business and selling $\frac{1}{4}$ million of his broadsheets and that in the face of stiff competition. When the need arose he could carve out a woodcut or write his own verse. He managed 15 verses of doggerel on 'Waterloo' for example.

Our cavalry advanced with true and valiant hearts
Our infantry and artillery did nobly play their parts
While the small arms did rattle and the great guns did roar
And many a valiant soldier bold lay bleeding in his gore.

This is a fair example of his style. The divorce of Queen Caroline, the death in child bed of Princess Charlotte and the life of Queen Victoria provided him with an endless source of royal subjects for his broadsheets. Prince Albert was a gift to the cartoonist and broadsheet writer alike.

Prince Albert's the man
Who will do what he can
That he'll please her will quickly be seen
He is now on his passage
With a cargo of sausage
As a dowry for our young Queen

Or, his most profitable rhyme reflecting the unpopularity of foreigners began

Here I am in rags
From the land of all dirt
To marry England's Queen
And my name is Prince Albert.

That was one of the politer verses!

After his death the business was carried on by WS Fortey *(Figure 8)* until 1883 when the premises were pulled down to make room for Charing Cross Road to be built joining New Oxford Street to Leicester Square.

The broadsheet never achieved quite the same popularity in the United States as it did in England but nevertheless they were widely read. They were imported and also printed there in large quantities. The subjects are identical to the English ones with the additional interest of some purely American activities such as the 'Indian Captivity'. Collectors interested in the American Civil War will find many moving reminders of popular feeling.

Figure 7 (opposite) *Murder by Thomas Riley on the body of his wife. Catnach leaves out nothing of the gruesome details. Note that none of these are dated so that Catnach could publish them at any time he wished.*

Most Dreadful and Barbarous

MURDER

BY THOMAS RILEY ON THE BODY OF HIS WIFE.

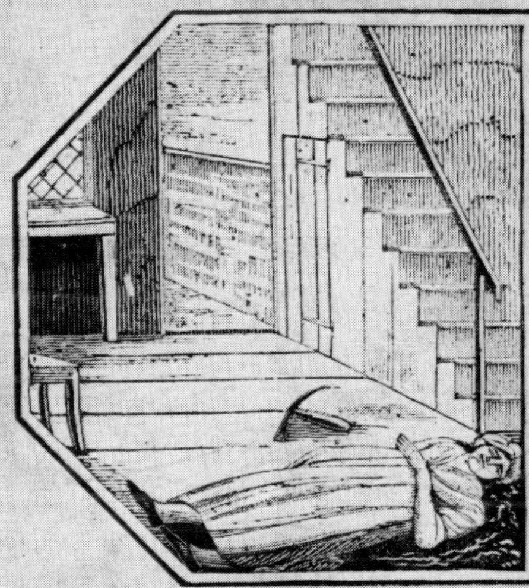

A Dreadful murder was committed at an early hour on Friday morning, by a husband on his wife. It appears that the murderer, an Irishman, named Thomas Riley, is a shoemaker, living at No. 5, Compton-street, St. John-street. He was in the constant unfortunate habit of drinking ardent spirits, and of quarrelling with his wife, who was also much addicted to the same vice; and such was the frequency of their broils, that their neighbours, who considered them for the last fourteen years, during which he had occupied the house as a housekeeper, an absolute nusiance, never attempted to interfere between them. Mrs. Elizabeth Gibson, who resides in the lower part of Riley's house, states, that about two o'clock on Friday morning she heard Riley, in a threatening voice scolding his wife, and say to her, using an abusive epithet, "What have you done with that gold ring?" She cannot say what reply the unfortunate deceased made; but more than this she did not hear occur between them. About twenty minutes before six o'clock, Riley knocked at the room door of Mrs. Bailey, another lodger in the house, and said, "Oh! Mrs. Bailey, Mrs. Bailey, my wife is dead!" Mrs. Bailey immediately hurried down stairs, & found Mrs. Riley covered with blood, and much disfigured. Riley was quite indifferent about the matter, and went out to get some refreshment. She was convinced the deceased had been murdered, and she followed Riley, & gave him in custody. The deceased was quite dead when her husband gave the alarm, and a more shocking sight than her body presented cannot be conceived. Her eyes were dreadfully swollen and completely blackened. On the right side of her head there was a deep triangular wound, and on the left there was an oblong wound extending nearly three inches transversely on the scalp. Several of her ribs were broken. The left breast over the region of the heart appeared as if it had been completely beaten in, exhibiting quite a hollow. The right shoulder was violently dislocated, and the arm, from the apex of the shoulder downwards, was black and mutilated. The body exhibited shocking marks of violence, almost covered with bruises. The bed on which the deceased lay was completely saturated with her blood, and the apartment appeared in the greatest confusion.

West, the policeman, deposed, that Friday morning, about six o'clock, the last witness met him in Compton-street, very much alarmed, and told him that Mr. Riley had murdered his wife, and was making his escape with a bag. Witness, who knew Riley saw him going in haste along the street with a bag upon his shoulder, and he pursued him and he stopped him in Aylesbury-street. He asked the prisoner whether he did not live in Compton-street? He replied, "I do." Witness inquired what had become of his wife? The prisoner answered, in a very agitated manner, "at home," and was so exceedingly flurried that he lost all power, and was scarcely able to walk. On taking him to the station house he searched his bag, and found some new leather and a silk handkerchief soaked with blood; and, on further examination, his clothes were found to be stained all over with blood. (The handkerchief was produced.)

Mr. Whitmore, the parish surgeon being sworn, deposed, that Friday morning, between seven and eight o'clock, he was called upon by the parish officers of Clerkenwell to examine the body of the deceased. He found an extensive tumefaction over the head and both eyes, and a corresponding discolouration in various parts of the body. On making an incision on the scalp he found it seperated from the cranium, and a quantity of extravasated blood was between them. There was a total disorganisation of the parts from external violence, and a taiangular wound on the superior part of the right hemisphere; also, a wound on the posterior part of the scalp. On opening the head, he found that the cranium was not fractured although exceedingly thin. There were some adhesions indicating old disease. The brain itself was healthy. On raising the sternum he found that five ribs were broken on the right side, and the ends pressing on the lungs below. The lining membrane was not torn through by the broken ribs. On examining the left cavity, he found nine ribs fractured. There was some fluid blood in the cavity, and evidences of long-standing disease. There was a fracture above the left ancle joint—the right scapula was broken into very many pieces. It struck witness that this must have been done by some communicating instrument of large size, and not by a poker, or any thing of the kind—they found his shoe covered with blood and human hair. On examining the prisoner, he found blood all over his garments and hands. He had a cut upon his left hand, and the deceased had similar cuts upon her hands.

The Jury returned a Verdict of Wilful Murder against Thomas Riley.

OH listen to a tale of woe which I shall now unfold,
When you the horrid deed do know 'twill make your blood run cold,
At Compton-street in Clerkenwell this wretched couple dwelt,
With drinking much and quarrelling, were deeply stain'd with guilt.

Last Friday morn at two o'clock some discord did ensue
When she was basely Murdered most terrible to view, (gore
Upon the bed extended all covered with
And quantities of human blood was lying on the floor.

The neighbours in amazement beheld the horrid sight
So horrible a spectacle did fill them with affright
The police apprehended him, and search'd him as he stood,
And there they found a handkerchief all soaked with blood.

Nine of her ribs were fractured, and horrid to declare, (and human hair,
The husband's shoes were covered with blood
To Newgate Gaol he is consign'd where he must wait to hear, (the forfeit dear.
The dreadful sentence of his crimes, and pay

J. Catnach, Printer, 2, Monmouth-court, 7 Dials.

TRIAL
And EXECUTION
At the Old Bailey of Seven Seamen for Murder and Piracy on Board the Flowery Land

THE EXECUTION.

Copy of Verses.

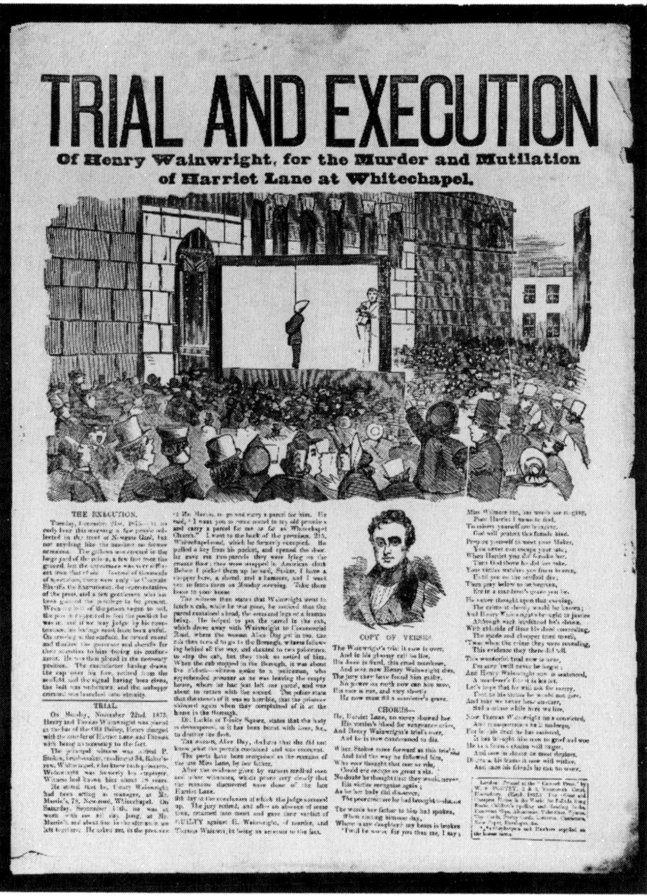
TRIAL AND EXECUTION
Of Henry Wainwright, for the Murder and Mutilation of Harriet Lane at Whitechapel.

THE EXECUTION.

TRIAL.

COPY OF VERSES.

CHORUS.

Figures 8 a and b *A typical Catnach trial and execution broadsheet. The block has been used again many times as in the version by W. S. Fortey. After his death Catnach's business passed to James Paul and then to W. S. Fortey in the 1850's. During the 1870's he changed his imprint, calling himself 'steam printer'.*

Chap books and broadsheets have survived because of the quantity printed and not because they were deliberately kept. There are many collections in Great Britain and the United States and many local museums have interesting collections. It isn't possible to be very fussy about the condition of something meant to be handled quite so much as a chap book or broadsheet but, with that in mind, it is possible to buy examples of the work of Catnach and his rivals for a reasonable price.

It is not easy to direct anyone to the best sources in order to obtain these broadsheets because they can turn up in the most unlikely places. They have been used for wallpaper in the past and many may well be hidden under layers of old wall paper to be discovered some day! Antiquarian book and print sellers are an obvious choice but it would be better to consult a specialist dealer. Prices vary enormously from one dealer to another and according to condition and rarity. Anything from £10 to several hundreds can be expected. Prices for Catnach have not changed very much in the last few years while prices for 18th century chapbooks and broadsheets have shot up. Naturally there is not an enormous market for Catnach so there are not many dealers either.

Note

All illustrations from St. Bride Printing Library, London. By appointment only.

Bibliography

The History of the Catnach Press by Charles Hindley, 1887. (Reprinted by the Singing Tree Press, Detroit 1969.)

The Story of Street Literature by Robert Collinson, 1973.

Chapbook bibliography by Victor Neuberg, 1964.

The History of Street Literature by Leslie Shepard 1973.

Murders and Moralities. English catch penny prints 1800-1860 by Thomas Gretton, British Museum, 1980.

July 1987

JEWISH CEREMONIAL ART

Miriam Kramer

The art connected with the Jewish religion reflects one of its principles: that it is primarily a home-based faith. The majority of objects, therefore, were made to be used by families in the home and not in the synagogue. This applied to items made for families at each level of society, from the poorest to the wealthiest.

Another point to remember is that Jews have lived in virtually every country, and that the artistic styles for their ceremonial pieces would reflect the styles of their host country. The three main areas now collected are eastern Europe, western Europe and North Africa. A knowledge of the art history of these areas, particularly of decorative arts, is useful in considering the styles of Judaica.

One consideration for artists when producing works for Jewish consumption is the prohibition in the Ten Commandments of making graven images. This has been taken literally to exclude portraying human beings, and frequently animals (although there are some exceptions, notably the lion, to the latter). The decorative emphasis, therefore, is on abstract designs and calligraphy.

Central to Judaism is the weekly observance of the Sabbath. The Jewish day begins at sunset the night before, and the Sabbath is therefore ushered in on Friday evening with the lighting of candles. Blessings are said over bread and wine, and the family sits down together to a special meal.

Figure 1 *A Polish early 19th century brass sabbath lamp, with typical six branch design. H66 cm (26 in). SOTHEBY'S NEW YORK. Sold for $3000.*

Every family, therefore, would have at least one Sabbath lamp. They were fuelled by oil and were of a similar design throughout Europe. They hung from a hook on the ceiling above the table, and had six or eight spouts; these were normally in a star design. The most frequent metals used were brass or bronze; silver was also used, particularly in Germany and Holland during the 17th and 18th centuries. The Dutch examples tend to be less ornate than their German counterparts.

From the beginning of the 19th century candlesticks began to overtake oil-burning lamps in popularity. Poland was particularly known for producing candelabra (of four or more branches) and candlesticks, with Warsaw one of the main centres *(Figure 1)*. This continued until the outbreak of the Second World War.

It is important to note that there would never be a solitary light to usher in the Sabbath; the domestic use of a single candle or wick is restricted to the annual commemoration of the death of a loved one. For Sabbath and festival use, at least two lights are lit, and the number frequently has a symbolic meaning. The number most in use for the last 150 years or so is two, which is a reminder of the two versions in the Bible, in Exodus and Deuteronomy, which exhort the Jews to 'remember' and 'observe' the Sabbath.

Just as the Sabbath is ushered in by a special domestic ceremony, so Jews take leave of it: it is marked after sundown on Saturdays by a short service called Havdalah (literally 'separation'). In this ceremony there is a multi-taper candle which is lit and extinguished in a few drops of wine spilt onto a special plate. Then a spicebox, filled with aromatics, is passed around the family. The idea is that it makes parting with the Sabbath a bit sweeter to smell the heady combination of spices. It is in the form of spiceboxes, or besamim boxes, that artists over the centuries have allowed their imaginations to run riot.

The main European shape for them is the tower *(Figure 2)*. There are variations on this theme, but for the most part there is a base, then a stand surmounted with a square box for the spices, a 'steeple' on top of that, an orb and finally a pendant. Frequently bells hang from the box. The earliest examples of this form, which originated in northern Europe, date from the mid-16th century, but as the shape worked its way south and east it became more and more ornate. By the time it reached parts of Italy and Hungary the box was heavily covered in fine filigree work.

In eastern Europe the tower shape was occasionally used but other forms were

Figure 2 *A silver filigree spicebox in the popular tower shape, complete with bells, orb and pendant. This example was made in Moscow in 1862.* H *32.5 cm (13 in).* I J MAZURE & CO LTD *£8000.*

Figure 3 *A silver spicebox made in Frankfurt-am-Main by P J Hochstadt about 1820. The interior is divided into four compartments.* L *7 cm (2¾ in).*
SOTHEBY'S NEW YORK. *Sold for $1900.*

more popular. In Poland, for example, fruit shapes were in vogue until the turret overtook them in the late 19th century, and flowers were the favourite Russian shape until the inevitable arrival of the tower. Popularity of these shapes, however, did not stop metalworkers from using others, and there are examples of fish, locomotives (particularly from eastern Europe), eggs and pomegranates (very popular in the Turkish market) available for the collector.

One other shape is worth mentioning. It is the plain, rectangular box, perched on four spindly or orb-shaped legs, which was popular in Germany in the 18th and 19th centuries *(Figure 3)*. These are attractive for their restraint and simplicity.

Just as the Jewish week is punctuated by the Sabbath, so the Jewish year is highlighted with various festivals, holidays and holy days. One of the major festivals is Passover, which lasts for eight days each spring. (Because the Jewish calendar is lunar the date for these festivals varies each year.) Each year on the first night of Passover Jews all over the world hold a service in their homes called a Seder. This is the Hebrew word for 'order', and the ceremonies follow a prescribed form telling the story of the exodus from Egypt. (It is worth noting that most scholars accept that the Last Supper of Jesus was a Seder, which explains why Easter and Passover virtually always coincide.)

Figure 5 *A brass menorah with a star of David finial. It was probably made in North Africa in the 18th/19th centuries.* H *31.3 cm (12½ in).*
CHRISTIE'S AMSTERDAM. *Estimate £1200-1800.*

Figure 4 *A 19th century polychrome ceramic Seder plate made in Germany for the English market. The central picture is of a Seder (note the Sabbath lamp hanging above the table), and on the rim the names of the various components of the Passover ceremony are written in Hebrew and English. Additional decorations are of Egyptian scenes to recall that Passover commemorates the Exodus from Egypt.* DIAM *27 cm (10¾ in).*
THE ANTIQUE CONNOISSUER PLC *£390.*

A number of particular foods must be on the table accessible for use during the Seder and it is customary to have them in the middle of the table on a particular plate, called a Seder plate *(Figure 4)*. This can be made of porcelain or metal, and is frequently decorated with calligraphy or, in later years, scenes depicting the Passover story.

The most important part of the meal, and of the week-long Passover festival, is the special non-leavened bread called matzo. It is eaten to remember the haste with which the Jews left Egypt after being slaves, when they had no time to prepare or to allow their bread to rise properly before the journey. During the Seder three pieces of matzo are required and over the centuries three-tiered matzo holders were made. The more sophisticated varieties incorporate the possibility of bowls containing the individual symbolic foods required for the Seder to be placed on top.

The Seder follows a prescribed liturgy contained in a haggadah *(Figure 6)*.

קדש

פֿר אלי זאכן זאלשט דוא
קידוש מאכן ·

דירה קידוש

ורחץ

גיט צו פֿר געסן · דיא
הענד צו װעשין

לאבֿרה לאש מאנוש אי ט
דירה ברכה ·

כרפס

איסט מין עסיק טונק ·
איט מיין שינק מיג
ציזוג · װילשטו װאל טון
דיין נשאה · אאך בורא
פרי האדמה ·

פואמרס דיל אפיו אי
אנפנירה איניל וינגארי די
דירה בורא פרי האדמה ·

יחץ

דיא איבערשטי מצה פֿון
אנגדר טײלט די העלפֿ'
צו אפֿיקומן אונטר דיא
זאן ביהאלט ·

פרטירה לה מצה מורה די
אינמידיו אי מיטירה לה
מידיה פון לוס מנטילס

מגיד

דש מאי אל וזץ פֿון
בעקין נעם · אול זאג
באש איט הוליר טטיש ·

דירה לה הגדה

רחצה

טון װעש דיא הענד · אול
אאך נטילת ידים בהענד

אי לאבֿרה לאש מאנוש אי
דירה ע לנטילת ידים.

הלל

דיא סיר זאלשטו אוף
אמכן · אול זאגן שפוך
פֿמר אלי זאלין ·

דירה הלל

מוציא מצה

אויך דיא אײבערשט
אליא צו · מאכן ניט פֿר
געט · אוג איט איין
שטיק פֿון די זאג אליות
אגה אול עט :

דירה המוציא איכלה די
אינכית' אי נו קומה ·
פארטירה די לה מידיה די אל
מידיו אי קומרה עודו מנסד
אי דירה על אכילת מצה :

מרור

אין חרוסת ואטיך טונגי
איין כזית מזגנוג :

אנפיניר' די לה ליגומ
איניל וינאגרי אי דירה על
אכילת מרור :

כורך

נעם איין שטיק פֿון דיא
דריטי אגה · אול עט
איט ביטר קרויט איא
ביטטו יליא :

פואמרס די סודם אי די לם
מגם אי אינפינירה איניל
חרוסת אי דירה זכר למקדש:

שלחן ערוך

ריכֿט אן דיין טיש אל
עטאיט ערין' װערט
דיר הש"י פֿיל גוטש
בשערין :

אורדינארן לה מסה :

צפון

נאך דז דוא האשט
גינעסן װנדר זארגן עט
איין שטיק פֿון דען
אפֿיקומן דער דא איז
פֿר בהרגין :

אי קומראן קאדה אונו
קואנטו אונה אזייטונה :

ברך

אלס דוא האשט גינעסן
אפֿיקומן · זאלשטו
בענטשן איט װײן :

דירה ברכת המזון :

נרצה

אול זײא ידי הגדה
פֿולענדן · בגלות זא
װערט מוגט גאם אסיא
זענדין :

יהי לנצי בי' ערנת

Figure 6 *A page of a Haggadah printed in Amsterdam in 1781 illustrating the various parts of the Passover service. The book contains instructions in Yiddish and Ladino.* BLOOMSBURY BOOK AUCTIONS. *Sold for £1800.*

Figure 7 *A fine silver and copper inlaid brass hanging menorah made in Baghdad about 1800. The hand motif is particularly popular in the Islamic middle east, and the Muslim crescent can be seen at the top. H 21.2 cm (8½ in).* CHRISTIE'S AMSTERDAM. *Estimate f 5000-7000.*

In addition to prayers, the story of the exodus from Egypt is told and the whole evening ends with songs; dinner is served in the middle. The haggadah gives calligraphers and artists the opportunity to embellish the words and is frequently very decorative.

Another particular object for Passover is Elijah's cup. It is a rule that hospitality should be extended to all those who may not have a Seder to attend. One person whose presence is hoped for each year is the prophet Elijah because his arrival heralds the coming of the Messiah. During a particular moment of the Seder the front door is opened in anticipation of Elijah's appearance. The Seder table, in addition to the Seder plate, matzo stand and place settings for the whole family, also has a special wine glass for Elijah. In some families this is an ordinary glass filled with wine which no-one touches, but over the years particular silver cups were made with Passover inscriptions for Elijah's use.

Another Jewish holiday, which is in fact relatively minor but which has acquired status due to its proximity to Christmas, is Chanukkah. This commemorates the rededication of the Temple in the second century BC by a band of Jewish zealots (the Maccabees). There was only enough sanctified oil to allow the candelabra in the Temple to burn for one day but due to God's miraculous intervention it burned for eight. The Jews mark this by lighting candles in a special candelabra, called a menorah, at home: one candle is lit the first night, two the second, and so on until the eighth *(Figure 5)*. Each menorah has, in fact, nine branches: one is a servant light used to kindle all the others.

The earliest extant examples tend to be from the late middle ages, but they are rare. The 17th century provides most of the early pieces, and that was also the time when one of the standard designs evolved. It is of a row of eight spouts in front of a backplate. The servant light is usually mounted on the backplate which is elaborately embossed and chased. The most frequent motif is a pair of lions, representing the lion of Judah, flanking a crown or a star of David.

These menorahs were made of brass or silver and were very popular, particularly in Poland. It is interesting to note that there are American and British copies made at the end of the 19th century and the beginning of the 20th: they were usually commissioned by immigrant Polish families who either had to leave their family heirlooms behind or wanted additional ones to present to their children.

As is frequently the case with Jewish works of art, the styles and materials follow closely the customs of the countries in which they were made. Eighteenth century Italian menorahs, for example, were usually of silver and were decorated with Baroque, Rococo or Neo-classical motifs. In the near East, the human hand, very important as an Islamic symbol, was frequently used as decoration for menorahs made in Iran, Iraq or Syria *(Figure 7)*. In Germany the candelabra style was preferred, decorated in a treetrunk and branch motif.

There are many more objects and works of art connected with Judaism which are used in a more communal context.

April 1987

INDEX

Illustrations are indicated by *italics*